Opera's Orbit

Exploring the dynamic yet problematic context of musical drama in
Rome, this study probes opera's relationship to modernity during
the late seventeenth and early eighteenth century. Opera instigated a
range of discourses, most notably among Rome's Academy of Arcadians, whose apprehension towards opera refracted larger aesthetic
and cultural debates, and socio-political tensions. Tcharos presents
a unique perspective, engaging opera as a historical force that established a sphere of influence across several genres and matrices of culture. The juxtaposition of opera against the prominent forms of the
oratorio, serenata, and cantata illustrates opera's constitutive role in a
trans-genre cultural matrix, where the dialogical connections between
musico-dramatic forms vividly capture the historicism, nostalgia, contradiction, and cultural reform that opera inspired. By illuminating
other genres as reactionary sites of music and drama, *Opera's Orbit*
boldly reconstructs opera's eighteenth-century critical turn.

STEFANIE TCHAROS is Associate Professor of Musicology at the University of California, Santa Barbara, where she specializes in early
modern Italian opera and related dramatic vocal music, issues of aesthetics, cultural history, and genre theory. She has published articles
and reviews in the *Journal of Musicology, Cambridge Opera Journal,* and
Music and Letters, and was a contributor to *The Cambridge History of
Eighteenth-Century Music* (2009).

Opera's Orbit

Musical Drama and the Influence of Opera in Arcadian Rome

STEFANIE TCHAROS

CAMBRIDGE
UNIVERSITY PRESS

CAMBRIDGE UNIVERSITY PRESS
Cambridge, New York, Melbourne, Madrid, Cape Town, Singapore,
São Paulo, Delhi, Dubai, Tokyo, Mexico City

Cambridge University Press
The Edinburgh Building, Cambridge CB2 8RU, UK

Published in the United States of America by Cambridge University Press, New York

www.cambridge.org
Information on this title: www.cambridge.org/9780521116657

First published 2011

Printed in the United Kingdom at the University Press, Cambridge

A catalogue record for this publication is available from the British Library

ISBN 978-0-521-11665-7 Hardback

For my parents, George and Emily

Contents

Illustrations

Figures

Music examples

Acknowledgments

As much as the creation of a book is a solitary act, it is also a shared venture, with a network of professional and personal contacts, academic and research institutions, which all help to usher initial ideas into final form. I have thoroughly enjoyed and deeply appreciated this collaborative aspect of the process.

This research in its initial phase was carried out during my time at Princeton University and was supported by the Committee for Italian Studies Fellowship and the Dean's Fund for Scholarly Travel. Since joining the faculty at UC Santa Barbara, I have received research support from an Academic Senate Faculty Research Grant and a Faculty Career Development Award. I am grateful to Lee Rothfarb who, as chair, assured generous research funds for my hire, and to David Marshall, Dean of the Humanities and Fine Arts, who provided additional funds during later stages of the project. I am also very appreciative of the publication subvention I received from the American Musicological Society, through the support of the Margarita Hanson Endowment Fund.

The opportunity to discuss and argue about material relevant to the manuscript was facilitated by my involvement with a number of academic organizations. The American Musicological Society and the Society for Seventeenth-Century Music gave me a forum in which to present my ideas publicly. I am also grateful for opportunities to present my work at conferences and symposia sponsored by the California Interdisciplinary Consortium of Italian Studies, the UCSB Early Modern Center, and the UCSB Center for the Interdisciplinary Study of Music (CISM). As a director and board member of this last organization, I have benefited from the discussions, presentations, camaraderie, and spirit that emerged from this group.

Many individuals have helped me complete this project by offering helpful counsel, sharing knowledge, or inadvertently inspiring ideas generated in the book. I would like to thank Margaret Murata for her exchanges with me, and for insights and suggestions, and, especially, Arnaldo Morelli, whose inspiring research provided important foundations for my own interpretive departures. I have special gratitude for generous suggestions offered by Georgia Cowart, Thomas Griffin, Robert Kendrick, and Lowell

Lindgren, who read early drafts and sharpened my thoughts and writing with their acumen. I also want to thank Daniel Albright, Michael Beckerman, Susan Boynton, Daniel Chua, Michal Grover-Friedlander, Mary Hunter, John Nadas, Massimo Ossi, and Neal Zaslaw for their chance conversations, meetings, or presentations that offered helpful information and innovative angles of thought. I am tremendously appreciative of the enthusiastic support I have received from my departmental colleagues and my current chair, Paul Berkowitz, and special mention must go to my dear colleagues in musicology – Derek Katz, David Paul, and William Prizer – whose warm collegiality and intelligent input provided great stability while I was finishing this project. I have been enriched by a vibrant campus of colleagues who provided a larger network for conversations and shared ideas. I would like to thank Elizabeth Cook whose questions about opera instigated unintended exploration, and I have special gratitude for generous and lively exchanges I have shared with Jon Cruz, whose curiosity and wealth of knowledge challenged me to conceive my project in truly novel ways. My students at UC Santa Barbara have been instrumental in allowing me to work out ideas in the ultimate workshop – the graduate seminar. The groups who filled my seventeenth- and eighteenth-century opera courses and the core of people who traveled along with me as we interrogated the genre helped to enrich my work with their discussions.

While doing research in Rome, I was provided kind assistance by the staff of the many institutions I frequented, in particular those at the Biblioteca Angelica, Archivio di Stato, Biblioteca Casanatense, Accademia Nazionale dei Lincei e Corsiniana, Biblioteca Nazionale Centrale Vittorio Emanuele II, Conservatorio di Musica Santa Cecilia, and Biblioteca Apostolica Vaticana, with special thanks to the staff of the manuscript reading room. In my home institution, I want to thank the wonderful staff at the UC Santa Barbara Arts and Music Library, with particular mention of gratitude to the music librarian, Eunice Schroeder, and the art librarian, Susan Moon, who provided valuable assistance in securing the book's cover image.

My student Katie Baillargeon served as an invaluable research assistant throughout many phases of the process. I am very grateful for the generous assistance provided by my colleague Alejandro Planchart, who carefully reviewed my music examples. I am especially appreciative of the copious assistance with translations I received from Giovanni Zanovello, whose guidance with the Italian materials was indispensable. My sincere thanks go to Vicki Cooper at Cambridge University Press, who supported the project from its early stages to completion, and to her staff, especially my editors, Dan Dunlavey and Rebecca Jones, for efficient and generous assistance.

Finally, there have been many friends and family members who have cheered me on, propped me up, provided emotional sustenance, shelter, and all kinds of small favors while I worked away on writing this book. I have deep fondness for the friends I have made in Italy who have witnessed this project over the years during my frequent visits there. I want to thank the Carlassare, Jacoboni, and Zanovello families for their kind support and assistance. Special thanks go to Irene Jacoboni and her husband, Salvatore, for their hospitality and dear friendship, and I have particular gratitude for Luisa Mattucci, who offered me not just a place to live during my many stays in Rome, but a community of Roman friends and compatriots who made each visit there special. To my extended family of friends and relatives, who often may not have understood all the particulars of writing a monograph, but applauded all my accomplishments none the less, I thank you for your fond and enthusiastic support. Last, but surely not least, I thank my immediate family of siblings and parents for their understanding, motivation, and unfailing love throughout what can be a very long and arduous experience. Above all, I acknowledge the backbone of support and patience maintained by those most immediate in my life. I offer my gratitude and deepest affection to Matt, a wonderfully intelligent and meticulous reader, and loving critic, who rode with me along the many paths of this project; and to our son, Jacob, whose birth was entwined with the completion of this book, but who somehow managed to make it to the finish line sooner.

Abbreviations

D-Mbs	Munich, Bayerische Staatsbibliothek
F-Pc	Paris, Conservatoire, in Bibliothèque Nationale de France
GB-Ckc	Cambridge, King's College, Rowe Music Library
GB-Lbl	London, British Library
GB-Ob	Oxford, Bodleian Library
I-MAc	Mantua, Biblioteca Comunale
I-MOe	Modena, Biblioteca Estense e Universitaria
I-Nc	Naples, Conservatorio di Musica San Pietro a Majella, Biblioteca
I-Ra	Rome, Biblioteca Angelica
I-Rac	Rome, Archivio Storico Capitolino
I-Ras	Rome, Archivio di Stato, Biblioteca
I-Rc	Rome, Biblioteca Casanatense, sezione Musica
I-Rli	Rome, Accademia Nazionale dei Lincei e Corsiniana, Biblioteca
I-Rn	Rome, Biblioteca Nazionale Centrale Vittorio Emanuele II
I-Rsc	Rome, Conservatorio di Musica Santa Cecilia
I-Rvat	Rome, Biblioteca Apostolica Vaticana
S-Sk	Stockholm, Kungliga Biblioteket: Sveriges Nationalbibliotek
US-MT	Morristown (NJ), National Historical Park Museum

Note to the reader

I have provided Italian texts only when the original source is not published, or in the instance that I have worked with the text closely and produced my own translation. For archival and manuscript texts, I have left orthography as in the original, except for minor modifications of punctuation or for clarity. All musical examples have been drawn from manuscript sources. Original aspects have been retained except for bar lines, which have been regularized.

Introduction: opera's orbit

In a book that explores the theoretical possibilities and manifestations of music and drama, it seems appropriate to begin by setting stages. It is also important to underline the plurality of stages that are relevant to this study, since the multiplicity of genres, contexts, and circles of agents involved are central to this book's conceptual premise. Opera and its numerous iterations, forms that ranged from the dramatic to the semi-dramatic, thrived in a world in which the multimedia potential of theater was both powerful and attractive. It is to the cultural presence, the historical legacy, the diversity, elusiveness, and controversy of the musico-dramatic stage that this book turns.

I begin by setting the first stage: Rome. In the late seventeenth and early eighteenth century this was a locale characterized by the splendor and grandeur of late baroque theater, from the architecture, art, and design that shaped the city, to the rituals of pomp and hierarchy enacted by papal sovereigns throughout the church's calendar year, to the social and political stages erected in public squares and within private walls of Roman *palazzi*, where local and foreign residents performed a range of ceremonies that embodied the practices of early modern sociability among the noble classes.

There are, nevertheless, some particulars to be considered and some choices I have made in conceptualizing the stages that form the objects of study for this book. The second stage is occupied by opera. The opera stage I refer to is not an actual stage of a particular theater or a context in which a given composer's works were performed. Rather, it is a metaphorical and symbolic stage for opera in Rome, a highly problematic space when we consider the history of opera in this locale. My book, in fact, arises from a fundamental contradiction in music and drama of late seventeenth- and early eighteenth-century Rome. This period enjoyed remarkable artistic vitality in the midst of critical and moral surveillance. Secular theater – but most importantly, opera – was a pleasure that regulators threatened to prohibit from time to time. Entertainment sometimes occupied sites of papal jurisdiction, subject to regulation and licensing. And yet, in spite of institutional dicta, evasions of authority persisted, some with apparent impunity. Rome's nobility, foreign dignitaries, and cardinal patrons

1

continued to attract and enlist poets, dramatists, stage designers, composers, and musicians of the highest repute, from both Rome and afar. Historians who study the reception of opera in this locale and period know well the contradictory truisms that were often played out. Despite the conventional wisdom that conservative papacies withheld the performance of opera and other types of theater, opera continued to survive, perhaps even thrive, in an atmosphere of containment and regulation.[1] In short, Rome was host to major and significant creativity in many artistic spheres, and especially in opera, even during a climate of occasional repression and restriction.

In this setting of contradiction and ambiguity opera was often a focus of concern and controversy. Even if the discourse and debate were not entirely new, opera towards the latter decades of the seventeenth century began to strike an apprehensive chord. Tensions surrounding opera were prominent in the papal edicts of religious conservatives. But beyond the papacy, intellectuals also took issue with opera's impact, registering their concerns with opera's abandonment of cultural inheritances linked to historical notions of poetic and literary aesthetics, and thus raising fundamental questions of the relationship between music and the other expressive arts. These contradictions underline the complexities of opera production in Rome, and reveal that an account of where, when, and who enacted bans or offered sanction for opera is not enough for interrogating that complexity. My focus is to treat the simultaneous censure of and desire for opera as a critical symbolic and symptomatic feature of this context, and more so of this historical moment. This is not a tension that can be adequately grasped simply by focusing on opera as a collection of discrete formal texts. Rather, to understand opera's relations within shifting cultural arenas requires treating opera as a larger phenomenon. The stage upon which I consider opera is therefore not just one of performance and production, and certainly not of a single stage, or even a stage that belonged to opera alone. *Opera's Orbit* explores the importance of opera as a multidimensional site, a site where opera served as a conduit for the interplay of a number of musico-dramatic forms.

As noted, we must recognize that opera became an object of attraction, interest, concern, even condemnation, within a number of influential Roman circles, with its influence felt across several different genres; opera is at the root of a division of aesthetic and political sensibilities that extended to agents and contexts operating with and yet beyond the papal sphere. Chief among them, and a central concern of this book, is opera's treatment by Rome's Academy of Arcadians. Therefore, a third stage for this book is Arcadia, and more specifically, Arcadian Rome as both a real and symbolic location that encompassed a series of figures, a range of debates, sets of discursive practices, and a collective mentality that were significant for and resonant with the assessment and redirection of history and culture in general, and of opera more specifically.

Scholars of opera and music have long recognized the importance of the Arcadians' criticisms of opera, and yet several of these scholars admit that these criticisms were generally inconsequential to the actual practice of opera.[2] In this case, the aspirations of the Arcadians and their critical proscriptions for opera are more telling than their influence over the practice of opera. The concerns of the Arcadians and the polemics they issued should be given some context, for theirs was not a debate held in isolation. In many ways, this circle of Roman literati echoed contemporary French aesthetic debates. The French criticisms of Italy's declining cultural standards were aimed, in large part, at a perceived downturn in Italian literature, a development in which opera was thought to have played a major role. Certain Arcadian members simultaneously adopted, transmuted, or rejected this foreign criticism. Yet, dating back to at least the mid-part of the seventeenth century, we can identify a growing concern over the direction of Italian artistic and literary practices. These practices were what critics identified as the products of *secentismo* or, more specifically, *marinismo* – the literary style characteristic of Giambattista Marino (1569–1625), marked by extravagant imagery and wordplay. This style came to be associated with artifice, triviality, and decadence in literature, but more importantly, by the end of the seventeenth century it was also seen as an indicator of culture's moral decline and its departure from the elevated models of past practice, of the truths and simplicities embodied in classical models of poetry, drama, and other arts.

In the literature on Arcadia, much has been made of the society's *neoclassical* stance. I agree with those who admit that a definition of Arcadia in neoclassical terms is, at best, problematic.[3] We might see the Academy of Arcadians as a whole, and their rise and development throughout the eighteenth century, as a reflection of and association with neoclassical movements and aesthetics, but when did that association find its roots? Can we call the first Arcadians – the original founders who birthed the academy – "neoclassicists" in the sense that this term would come to have in the mid-eighteenth century? I will leave these questions for other historians of literature, art, and the period in general; my own interest is to adapt "neoclassical" as one of several tendencies at work in Arcadian Rome around the turn from the seventeenth into the eighteenth century. We might better regard the Arcadians both as potential neoclassicists and as practitioners of a latent form of humanism repackaged within the newer terms of early modernity and the emergent strands of Enlightenment thought. As others have argued with more specificity than is argued here, the Arcadians are best understood within the emerging republic of letters whose origins date to the late seventeenth century. Groups like the Arcadians, its members, and even dissidents from within its ranks, as well as its detractors, believed on some level that a cultural institution might perfect the arts and sciences, correct past abuses, and thereby halt moral decline. In his recent study on Arcadia, Vernon Hyde Minor grounds the academy within this phenomenon – as an impulse to launch a new sense of taste, of *buon gusto*. He regards the Arcadians as more than an intellectual society of the era – rather as a vector for a new cultural stance embodied by reform movements of the first half of the eighteenth century.[4]

My own interest has been to approach Arcadia as a critical cultural nexus through which we might interrogate the broader application of "reform" aimed at opera and musico-dramatic culture. Within this faction of the Italian intelligentsia we are offered an opportunity to observe the most important tensions and reflections on opera at a critical historical turning point. In more specific terms, several Arcadian leaders and critics of the early movement regarded the theatrical practices of their day as falling short of the celebrated dramatic models of the ancients. They implicated opera as the central culprit in the abandonment of truth and verisimilitude in modern drama, above all imputing aesthetic erosion to opera's multimedia dimensions, especially to the element of music.[5] By 1700 the attack on music had become familiar. Music's ascendancy – a development that could be seen emerging much earlier in the seventeenth century – was evidenced by a musical semantic that had the power to reduce or even contradict the signifying role of words, and likewise to transform the dramaturgical role that composers (and singers) increasingly played in the signification of meaning. Most Arcadians equivocated when confronted with the subject of opera and its musical settings, perhaps an admission of opera's musical allure and a recognition of the impossibility of exorcising the genre outright. What seemed more rarely acknowledged or openly confronted was the blending of operatic forms with other distinct artistic forms of expression. Opera's problem was not predominantly that it challenged the primacy of word over music, but that the combinatorial power of word *merged* with music unleashed a new, modern mode for expression where the multiple and stratified "authoring" intrinsic to its creation complicated and thus made less stable (even if more evocative) the articulation of "text." This complexity of authorship adopted by opera entwined discrete strands of expressive practices and their cultural meanings. Ultimately, it would be difficult, if not impossible, to govern such strand-assemblages under any conditions of presumed equality.

The new sets of choices prompted by operatic production further intensified as competing expressive modalities responded to the changing contexts of performance. And these choices agitated against a culture in search of simplification, of pursuing more stable definitions and fixed enclosures. As several instances in this book will attest, the reform of opera rarely encompassed a conception of radical change, but rather turned towards the recuperation of something lost, and so was an act of retrieval, a way to draw clearer boundaries and hierarchies in the face of instability and ambiguity. Opera works for us as a critical lens for complicating reform since opera powerfully juxtaposed those elements of modern departure against a culture entrenched in stasis, retrospection, and nostalgia. Musical drama, as perceived through the polemics of the Arcadians, was at odds with the multifold practices of combining music, poetry, and semi-dramatic narratives. This very contradiction within the musical culture of Arcadian Rome is a central conundrum that arises throughout this book.

Opera's orbit – the effect of that pull opera exerted as locus both of artistic expression and of cultural reform – reflected and intensified Rome's instability in these decades. This instability had been instigated by shifting cultural and social ideologies, by reconfigurations of political authority, through crisis within the church and over the rise of secular culture, and by new economies and social classes.[6] If opera did not actualize any of these changes, at very least it had the powers to magnify them on stage, in performance, and through the effects of reception on its listeners and spectators. For the purposes of my analysis, opera thus helps to reflect the larger stage of Arcadian Rome where musical drama serves to highlight the complicated boundaries between what was private and public, sacred and secular, new class and old aristocracy, local and foreign – elements all struggling to find purchase and all up for negotiation during this momentous historical transition. The numerous stages through which I explore musical drama in Arcadian Rome are a refraction of this larger worldview.

Rome during the transition from the late seventeenth into the early eighteenth century remains a locale for which opera, music, and culture are understudied. In part, this is due to peculiar conditions of the locale – the on-again, off-again production of theater in this period and the need to account for *both* public and private opera cultures make evaluation of Roman opera difficult. Historical documentation and music manuscripts are often fragmented, scant, or missing altogether. The difficulties posed by opera's lacunae during this period are what forced me to reassess the local conditions, and to move beyond the confines of opera in order to examine a wider range of musical drama. What seemed to be missing from the scholarship was a deeper, analytical treatment of opera's relations, influence, and reception within the so-called "non-operatic" confines of vocal music in Rome. In fact, what has been sorely ignored in a context as particular and unique as Rome is an examination of how opera was frequently projected beyond itself and on to other musico-dramatic genres.[7] Opera's more expansive power of diffusion has been underestimated. In modern scholarship, the concept of diffusion is largely understood to indicate the spread and establishment of mid-century Venetian-style public opera in other cities within and beyond the Italian peninsula.[8] Less attention has been paid to how such diffusion affected parallel vocal-dramatic music making in various contexts.

Critical for the scope of this study was thus to recognize that as a historical force, opera established a sphere of influence the reach of which extended to genres whose histories never intended them to have deep association with opera; nevertheless, they were inevitably drawn into opera's orbit because that sphere corresponded with the aesthetic directions, cultural aspirations, and socio-political dimensions of this period. This, I believe, was opera's impact, and I choose to illustrate this through a greater range of musical drama. I have selected a specific constellation of genres based on their importance not merely as genres but also as cultural forms – for how they shaped individual performances and events in the Roman context, but mainly for the ways in which they mirrored opera culture and polemics during this period. I focus on the oratorio, the serenata, and the cantata not because these three genres were the only forms of vocal music marked by opera in the period. Far from it. This book does not aim to undertake a more comprehensive study of period-based musico-dramatic forms with the kind of detail, rigor, and interdisciplinary perspective that a larger study of urban musical practice in Rome deserves. Rather, I have chosen the three genres that are central to this study because arguably their institutionalization as seasonal ritual, political propaganda, or intellectual entertainment makes them ideal cases for further investigation. These genres form the other musico-dramatic stages considered in this book and they will become crucial for reading opera outside opera and across several matrices of music and culture.

It is important to recognize that the cantata, oratorio, and serenata each had its own singular tradition and history distinct from opera in Rome in the seventeenth century. In several cases, we could imagine the flourishing and perpetuation of each of these genres *without* opera. But genres do not choose history; they respond to it. Opera's influence was real and it intensified as the century came to a close, throwing each of the aforementioned genre trajectories into flux, even if their contact, interaction, and response to opera was more situational than programmatically intentional. Neither oratorio, cantata, nor serenata was a simple extension of opera, even if we might identify works from each genre that lean heavily towards operatic modeling. True, the socio-political predicaments and cultural parameters in Rome cast several of these non-operatic genres into what appear to be seasonal substitutions for opera. The well-known fluidity between public and private, sacred and secular, staged and non-staged, and thus opera and non-opera, makes any kind of scholarly categorization of the musico-dramatic genre continuum nearly impossible. My inquiry is not directed towards formal definitions of genre difference or similarity. Though such fundamental comparisons have their initial use, the situation of genre relationships in this locale is much more complicated. What I strive to reveal for the genres treated in this book are the dialogical connections as determined through genre collisions, and what they reveal about opera's orbit, and about the cultural tensions surrounding opera. But with each genre, I also consider how contact and interaction work in the opposite direction, noting how each genre influenced – in ways both real and perceived – opera's continued historical trajectory.

My approach to viewing opera across a select genre spectrum requires the concept of appropriation.[9] The appropriation of opera is evident in each of the three genres I consider, though it is not restricted to the employment of opera's formal traits and conventions but extends to the configurations of taste in dramatic music and to the intense rhetoric of aesthetic politics that opera inspired. We must therefore recognize how appropriation accentuates plural uses and diverse readings. In the selected examples this book explores, I relate how specific contexts, authors, and patrons found opera "useful" in diverse ways – as a form to model, as a source of aesthetic innovation, or even as a counterexample. What we learn in each instance is how opera pulled upon and was pulled within a culture of diverse musico-dramatic expression. Opera in this context appears as a phenomenon to be measured and equally as a measure of other genre rituals. When considered from these angles, opera no longer appears a simple predetermined and reified form. When we consider multi-genre relations, opera is more easily discernible and knowable in its complex relationships to the larger musico-dramatic field, in its ties to local realities, and as a site that hosted ensuing discrepancies and tensions that marked opera's career towards the century's end.

My aim is therefore to resituate opera within this broader landscape of genre relations in ways that place greater emphasis on something we might call an *operatic field*. How does the orbit of opera (a phenomenon) produce a pull (its effect) across a specific constellation of vocal genres? How does opera come to be displaced to, and perhaps remapped on and even within, these other genre sites? In what ways do opera's echoes resonate uniquely or differently beyond the actual boundaries of opera? These questions are crucial as they focus attention on how opera may have created conditions of cultural gravity to affect surrounding genres. Through difference and distance, the oratorio, serenata, and cantata uniquely reverberate opera. Each accentuates opera's musical, aesthetic, cultural, and social dimensions, and allows for critical assessment through rereading and recontextualizing opera's influence in diverse and contrasting arenas. It also allows us to reveal a deeper relationship of opera to other genres, not only one of mutual exchange, but also of contestation – in which some of opera's most critical elements and cultural implications are boldly registered. Using this trans-genre analysis, I aim to create a unique perspective on the history of opera culture by examining it from external vantage points rather than solely relying on opera as an explanation in and of itself. In doing so, I seek to broaden the conventional boundaries of musical drama to encompass these genres, and I argue that it is only by illuminating other genres as reactionary sites of music and drama that we can reconstruct a more complete understanding and retrospective of opera as embedded relationally in this historical context.

The approach this book embraces is meant to restore attention not just to a larger spectrum of music culture, but to one that operated within a specific historical period, and where a circumscribed locale works as a source for uncovering the broader cultural assumptions and ideological orderings of that era. Historical evidence, above all, has elicited the questions and issues I discuss, and as I will demonstrate in the chapters that follow, genre in this period (within and beyond musical culture) was an important epistemological and cultural construct. Genre's canonic use, as well as its manipulation and potential for sprawl, resonated deeply in a place and time where musical genres appeared distinct yet were caught in paradoxical juxtapositions of rigidity and pliability. In such cases, genres were deeply consonant with other socio-political conditions and incongruities, for the very period under study was wrought by pressures that mark culture and politics in moments of consolidation and entrenchment on the one hand, and unraveling crisis on the other.

Historical contexts are rarely conducive to the kinds of enclosure that a single-genre approach may require. Individual genre-centered scholarship has an immense history with deep and inherited epistemologies that have come to coincide with our modern understanding of genre. For musicology, such an approach has been unquestionably central to its pedagogy, if not its more traditional and general research methods. In many respects, there are good reasons to treat genre this way. Focus directed on a single genre undoubtedly sharpens our understanding of how to group and organize the multiplicity of characteristics and musico-stylistic conventions evident in specific modes of musical practices that belong to a historical era. My own research has been greatly informed by individual studies of opera, the oratorio, the serenata, and the cantata. I thus draw upon this rich and important scholarship in the field, but I do not replicate all of its specific procedures. As useful as such approaches can be, the singularity of focus, and the order and convenience they provide, should be treated carefully. Genres point to what is consistent, repeated, and definitive. Along with utility comes a tendency to emphasize abstract schematic relations whose essential and permanent qualities become ideal forms at the expense of recalling a genre's historical and social embeddedness – those aspects of a genre least amenable to isolation.[10]

Rather, it seems that history often embraces a wide range of constitutive practices where emergent *multiple* forms of music and their social conventions take shape. In the case of late seventeenth- and early eighteenth-century Rome, I discovered that a major drawback of reading individual musico-dramatic works as bound to a single category, effectively isolating a genre, was to miss that genre's expanded dimensional resonance with and among other genres. In most opera studies, the relationship between other genres and opera is ignored; in studies of non-operatic vocal music, opera's influence is more typically reduced to formalist comparisons, or to brief and generalized statements of cultural reciprocity. This genre-isolating tendency has also been the dominant mode of study in many of the musico-dramatic forms of the period. As a consequence, genre – regardless of its centrality to musical culture – is embraced but has not been adequately problematized.[11] My analysis demonstrates that there is seldom a hard and fast boundary between one genre and another, and yet, as categorical entities, all genres imply a sense of and a need for enclosure, even if the maintenance of that enclosure remains difficult in practice. My shift towards understanding genre relationships does not supplant the analytical importance of a genre's autonomy, but it does ask that we recognize and identify important things to be learned by placing emphasis on a genre's intertextual potential. This approach moves the analytic focus away from the confines of the single-genre study to a framework that restores the processes by which trans-genre developments unfold aesthetically and culturally. In essence, I explore how assumptions of the period can be brought into visibility not merely in terms of the meaning of the distinctiveness of a genre, but in and through the cultural forces and processes that bring genres into their vibrant interrelationships. Inasmuch as genres enter into particular relations, certain historical junctures can also condition this phenomenon. From this vantage point I consider how genres not only constitute a cultural form that makes music conventions visible, but also point to conditions of inclusion or exclusion contingent on the historical landscape in which they are formed and applied.

In attending, then, to the historical views and perspectives, I walk a fine line when interrogating the terms of genre. Genre distinctions are certainly central to period practitioners, whose writings and definitions of genre exemplify how normative categories are on their lips and central to their aesthetic conceptions. These same genre distinctions also become intellectual carryovers that will later emerge in the evolution of our own scholarly lexicon, where the boundaries between individual genres are carefully distinguished and less often complicated. This very condition and development is something this study hopes to unravel. As I work towards the recognition of genres as constitutive formations within a larger contextual field, my concern is to draw out the modes in which musico-dramatic genres intersect *and* are intersected by a host of cultural influences. With one foot firmly anchored in the canonical forms that take hold in the period, I strive to resituate genre as a component that derives meaning and value from a larger arena of aesthetic options that are also profoundly scripted by social and historical contexts. What I argue is that even with a categorical construct like genre, certain choices are made, leaving a number of uncertainties that lie beyond those choices, what Mikhail Bakhtin called *surplus* – "after all the rules are applied and all the generalizations have been exhausted."[12] In this study I probe the encounter between the pre-given patterns of a genre and the messier and less given outcomes of how individual works and events associated with that genre behave and, at times, misbehave, and what that behavior might reveal.

My treatment of genre is insistently, indeed necessarily, heterochronic. No one work, event, or performance is governed by a single "present" only, no matter how pervasive the weight of that present may be. The very categorization of a work as representative of a particular genre entails constraint by the past on the present. Thus, genre helps to show how the molding of musical culture occurs over different measures of time, over a continuous span as well as in the moment of creation or performance. Each genre study in this book is treated, therefore, synchronically and diachronically.[13] In their synchronic moment, I examine specific musical works belonging to a known genre and consider the convergence of their narrative process with the sites and spaces of their performance, the agents involved, aspects of ritual, and reception within the context that conditioned that moment. The synchronic allows us to capture genres as products of temporary and shifting delimitations, even if genres also reflect past experiences. In their diachronic dimension, I demonstrate that a genre is at once riddled with traces of its own past while at the same time replete with reference to other works – their repetition and transformation – with which the genre in question has come to be associated. Genres are thus heavily time-laden and may be understood as being, in some sense, crystallizations of their past, but a past that is largely shaped and constrained by immediate and present experience.

My research makes selective use of the ideas of a number of twentieth-century genre theorists who have problematized genre in ways relevant to this study. More so, perhaps, than others, I regard Mikhail Bakhtin's treatment of genre useful for understanding the fundamentally dynamic nature of genre interaction.[14] Drawing on the legacy of Russian formalism and its critique, Bakhtin's sociological lens reveals the importance of moving beyond structural conventions, shifting instead to viewing genres as sites of discourses, infused with references, quotations, and influences that recall a genre's historical and social formation. Bakhtin viewed genres as receptacles of a culture's thought processes and ways of being: "throughout the centuries of their life [genres] accumulate forms of seeing and interpreting particular aspects of the world."[15] He argued for seeking out the mutual interactions of genres within a single unified period, for the manner in which "they can mutually delimit and mutually complement each other, while yet preserving their own generic natures."[16] While the idea of genre facilitates certain principles of autonomy, as in "generic natures," Bakhtin also recognized the potential impact of some genres having significant sway over others, what many formalists regarded as a dominant genre phenomenon – when one genre amidst all others colors and transforms other genres that surround it. Genre theorists had long established the precedent that genre dominance was a strong force driving hybridization, the process by which genres undergo modification and combine with one another, producing variant forms and even entirely new genres.[17] The process of hybridization and long-term genre evolution is not unimportant. However, for the purpose of this study, I focus on the consequences of genre overlap and interaction, and how relations are shaped by the major forces that mark a distinct period and locale.

My dynamic treatment of genre has led me to place opera at the center of a nexus of social relations that influenced the musical dramatic genres I discuss. While the relations considered here are not comprehensive, my approach reveals the motivations of select social agents as they interacted with opera, whether directly or indirectly and from the domain of other musical dramatic forms. Thus, the social milieu characterized for each genre discussion is not mere background, but serves to highlight relationships I believe are informative about opera's role and influence. The individuals highlighted in these discussions cannot be treated as embodiments of an epoch; rather, these figures should be viewed as products of their world, personalities who themselves created or were shaped by a series of discourses that reveal how experience was appropriated and structured. These discourses – in the forms of historical and polemical writings – are to be read for their overall ideologies, as well as their rhetorical mechanisms and strategies. They are evidence of the crucial social currents that surround a musical culture, enacted through negotiations between artist, patron, institution, critic, and audience. I therefore listen for the voices represented by these perspectives as they murmured, sometimes loudly, within the context of academies, in institutions of sacred devotion and education, through written tracts, through the conjuring of genre definitions and comparisons, and through the performance and practice of music. All of these interactions, I argue, affected the simultaneous maintenance and resetting of genre boundaries, with opera often at the center of this network of cultural brokerage.

Ultimately, in this book I seek to create a conceptual hub where I attempt to mediate a number of domains. One of these domains reconsiders the historical and cultural ramifications of opera, the legacy and problems that opera carried from its origins through the first hundred years of its early modern development. Opera's resurgence as public theater, its enduring value as entertainment in the face of scorn by moral and aesthetic gatekeepers, and its larger role within the culture of Arcadian Rome, all inform this investigation, especially when considering the juxtaposition of opera against other important musico-dramatic forms. For this reason, my study interrogates the domain of genre, but genre that acquires significance through intertextual relevance, as genres contain complexities beyond their categorical form and reveal ways of seeing a particular world. Genre thus reveals how music may serve a moment in time, a series of agents, and a number of institutions in historically specific ways, often to adjudicate myriad cultural tensions. Genre also functions as a host for the mediation of stylistic traits and category assignments with the kind of social and cultural "surplus" that is intrinsic to a specific locale. With this in mind, genre offers a lens to investigate the domain of culture, and in particular, the very suppleness of the culture that characterized late seventeenth-century Rome. In several examples, I juxtapose the desire to maintain genre, through status and definition, against forces that functioned to undermine a genre's fixity, exerted by those who found such manipulation a convenient or expedient end for social expression.

Opera's orbit – which exerts influence on, relates to, and refracts aspects of a larger musico-dramatic culture – conveys a unique angle of cultural history in Rome, and with a still wider span, reflects major shifts in the emerging eighteenth-century European cultural landscape. My attempt in this cross-reading of music and culture is to use the layers of analytical reciprocity between the selected domains as a means to deliver a more multifaceted account of this important historical juncture.

In the following chapters, I build a series of historical narratives, and explore a number of singular events, based on information culled from original research and also facilitated by other scholars' research published in source catalogues, appendices, and reference lists that include archival information and document transcriptions.[18] I draw upon a range of primary sources for my historical evidence. These include archival fragments taken from manuscript dispatches (*avvisi*) from Rome and other European cities, personal diaries, financial records, printed reports of official events (*relazioni*), printed books of theoretical or polemical treatises, printed libretti and musical scores (the latter mostly manuscript), printed images and other visual documents. However, this book does not aim to offer a broad historical view of Roman opera theater in the seventeenth and eighteenth centuries.[19] Rather, it seeks to fill an important lacuna in the scholarly literature by treating opera and musical drama as cultural and social phenomena, not only as objects for documentary or work-centered study. Admittedly, I am after something more inchoate than settled in this pursuit, in which I seek to maintain a peculiar tension. On the one hand, I have designed the separate chapters of this book around single genres: the oratorio, serenata, and cantata. I have organized the body of this book by these traditional genre titles, not to perpetuate the enclosures that genre as a concept privileges, but to acknowledge the fact that such categorizations and genre titles were seminal and effective within this early modern culture, in spite of their inability to hold to any real consistency, categorical protectionism, and enclosure. While each chapter recognizes a particular genre for its general characteristics, I also choose to access genre at the level of the individual event, when discrete moments highlight how the individual text and specific agents and critics interacted within the confines of a genre, its functions, and its expectations.[20] This allows a certain flexibility, where the focus on specific examples is not restricted to a single composer, patron, or setting, but rather underscores the eclecticism and variety of this musico-cultural landscape. Of course, each of the examples I present involves an act of interpretation on my part by the selection of events, discourses, and works that I examine as critical evidence and paradigmatic symptoms of the issues and period. This book does not seek a comprehensive treatment of all aspects of the genres and documents considered. Instead, I have made specific choices based on their relevance and evocation of salient trends. In all instances, I believe the examples selected are not merely representative of a specific genre, but deeply reflective of the era's debates and polemics.

The book proceeds from important foundations of history that are used to set the parameters for investigations in subsequent chapters, which constitute the body of the book. The order of genre chapters – oratorio, serenata, and cantata – is not inconsequential. I take on the oratorio first, as the most obvious (and yet problematic) contrast to opera; the serenata follows, as an intermediary genre whose secular nature makes the contrast with opera seem much less polarizing than the oratorio, yet whose forces for performance and political rituals shed important light on crucial debates surrounding opera; I end with the cantata and argue that this genre is both least like opera and, in significant ways, the most revealing of opera's orbit. Each chapter builds on the previous one, thus making this book not ideal for excised chapter reading without having the larger narrative trajectory in mind.

Chapter 1, "Enclosures, crises, polemics: opera production in 1690s Arcadian Rome," serves as the essential historical scaffolding of the book's narrative. Here I explore and review the various parameters of opera and its polemics, key developments of music and drama, along with papal history, socio-political crises, and the impulse for moral reform, as the necessary background for setting the broader cultural landscape of Arcadian Rome, but also for probing the layers of issues and debates crucial in the main body of the book. In this brief overview of the period, I make clear why I look beyond opera, and turn to the oratorio, the serenata, and the cantata as genres that illuminate an unquestionably influential opera culture, albeit an opera culture under considerable strain. This chapter thus builds a platform for the analysis and theoretical work I undertake in the chapters that follow.

The subsequent genre studies (chapters 2–4), though unique in their materials, investigations, and reflective conclusions, all follow a similar structuring device for their larger narrative. Each of these chapters begins by setting the various parameters of the genre's relationship to opera, or to the culture around it, of which opera was none the less an important aesthetic filter. I then turn to select readings, documents, or polemical tracts that serve as primary evidence for how knowledge of a genre may have been constituted, how it was remembered, what elements were highlighted or denied, and when possible, how critics, patrons, and authors of these genres came to negotiate its conditional and equivocal relationship with opera. With this knowledge as a foundation, I turn to descriptive examples that reveal such a genre in practice, and how its status as a performance, and as a devotional, political, or intellectual event, help to expose a more complicated rendering of that genre's categorical identity, its relationship to opera, and its signification as a larger cultural symptom of the period.

Chapter 2, "Disrupting the oratorio," considers the critical historical implications of opera's intersection with the oratorio and how that relationship would come to bear upon musico-dramatic culture at the close of the seventeenth century. In several ways the oratorio developed the most apparent oppositional relationship to opera with its devotional bent, sacred subject matter, and overt moral messages. Yet, despite its established distinction from opera, some works demonstrate how the late-century oratorio had readily acquired a more pronounced operatic expressivity. This fundamental duality endowed the oratorio with a marked set of tensions that would manifest in forms of discourse on the oratorio as well as in certain performed practices of the genre.

This chapter interrogates these qualities of tension, ambiguity, and contradiction by returning to Arcangelo Spagna, who, in his "Discorso intorno a gl'oratorii," published in *Oratorii overo melodrammi sacri* (1706), most singularly captures the oratorio historically as both a literary form and a musico-dramatic practice that clearly borrowed from opera. His discussion, however, reveals a certain measure of discomfort and conflict over opera's influence, and in this regard, we must come to see Spagna's voice as reflective of a larger contingent of artists, critics, moralists, and literati who either appropriated or vigorously debated opera's role in culture. Using Spagna as a starting point, I juxtapose his ideas and definitions of genre against the varied practices of the late-century vernacular oratorio, primarily because of the way it could test the boundaries between sacred and secular rituals. I focus on select events and musical works for non-devotional settings (specifically two well-known oratorios written and sponsored by Cardinal Pietro Ottoboni, and composed by Alessandro Scarlatti) that serve as examples through which to explore the oratorio's narrative and musical possibilities as shaped by the convergence of influences and forces of this historical moment. In my analysis, I consider how the oratorio helped to prefigure opera's eighteenth-century trajectory as musical drama increasingly turned away from the once privileged model of spoken tragedy and embraced a newer aesthetic of emotionalism versus reason, for which music became a more forceful arbiter of expression and meaning.

Chapter 3, "The serenata's discourses of duality," examines a particular historical juncture when patrons enlisted the serenata as a public performance (often as an occasion honoring a specific person or event) as a means to portray relationships of alliance and power. I pay special attention to the use and function of the serenata during the 1690s through the early 1700s, when local tensions arising from the shift in power from Spanish Habsburg to French Bourbon reflected larger conflicts brought about by the War of Spanish Succession. The serenata in Rome was thus affected by external pressures – political, social, and ideological – that seeped into its form and influenced the variety of its practices. I also argue, however, that the serenata and the systems of power that shaped it were intrinsically caught in opera's orbit, particularly in the Arcadian aesthetic polemics over word and music that influenced the serenata's narrative strategies. Though often staged in public squares and fortified with large instrumental forces, the serenata's essential expressive medium was more cantata-like, demanding a certain intimacy of listening. I consider how this quality re-emphasized the hierarchical relationship of poetry to music (in spite of instrumental music's nascent ascendancy in the period) as the source for the signification of meaning. Thus, even when sound functioned as the event's key symbolic element, the maintenance of poetry's elevated position continued to be particularly acute.

Using a close-up view of a highly celebrated 1704 event – the serenata *Le gare festive* by poet Giacomo Buonaccorsi and composer Pietro Paolo Bencini – this chapter examines how the serenata allowed for simultaneous but contrasting experiences, one ostensibly public, the other distinctly private. My concern is to probe the ambiguous role of music in the serenata's hybrid framework, and to explore how and why music in the serenata's bifurcated presentation was *both* accessory and pivotal for expressing the work's fundamental meaning. Ultimately, I argue that this ambiguity posed significant challenges to contemporary critics in negotiating the source of expressivity in musical drama.

I end the main section of the book with chapter 4, "The cantata, the pastoral, and the ideology of nostalgia," examining a genre that in some ways was the least like opera. This chapter moves from the public sphere of musico-dramatic performance to a more exclusive and intimate realm. Specifically, I concentrate my study around the context of Rome's Academy of Arcadians and explore how their cultural concerns and ideological leanings played a significant role in our understanding of the cantata's relationship to opera. I probe the role a pastoral literary inheritance played in the cantata's historicized legacy and chart how the Arcadians' reach for pastoral drama formed an inextricable link to the larger pastoral ethos that characterized their activities and permeated their agenda. My aim is to uncover how the pastoral and the cantata were similarly caught in larger debates over reform and cultural polemics aimed most directly at opera. This chapter, therefore, seeks to amplify a parallel embrace of the pastoral in *both* opera and the cantata, even if specific details of that embrace were different in each respective genre. In the end, I argue that the cantata may best reflect some of the most effective applications and yet glaring shortcomings of the Arcadians' pastoral reform.

Using the Roman environment and Arcadian criticism as a point of context, this chapter stresses the efforts to revive and retain certain of the cantata's legacies, especially the genre's courtly and pastoral associations. I argue that both of these legacies worked to create layers of opposition in the cantata, most distinctly the simultaneous embrace of complexity and simplicity, qualities that were grounded in a nostalgic idealization of this genre's cultural role. I examine how the cantata's appropriated associations – its fixed narratives, so to speak – were neither rigid nor stable, nor easily defined in binary terms, but rather revealed multiple configurations. These brief considerations of the cantata's potential variance in compositional style and practice are, however, juxtaposed against seminal discourses regarding the pastoral in this period. I situate the issue of the cantata's conceptual fixing upon a revealing document, Giovanni Mario Crescimbeni's *L'Arcadia* (1708). This crucial text reveals the importance of the pastoral for the Arcadians, not just as a style or form, but also as a deeper epistemological substructure, a tool to remake the present as a nostalgic revival of an idealized past. I argue that the cantata, the relationship between word and music, and opera reform play subsidiary roles in this work, but revealing roles none the less. I contend that the conception and treatment of the cantata by the Arcadians and other patrons in this period must be seen as a symptom of the entire troubled dimensions of opera's orbit.

The epilogue of my book in one way follows the final chapter of the book's core, but is also a moment for consolidation and closure. I return to the Arcadians and make a case that their peculiar institution and their ideological leanings provide a means to begin to understand not just the history of opera and vocal drama in this context, but also opera's cultural status during this historical transition from the end of the baroque into an early Enlightenment period. In these last pages, I choose to recast and revise our understanding of the Arcadian project and offer a view that contrasts with much previous scholarship, which has at times either overemphasized or underemphasized the Arcadians' importance. I argue that the Arcadians' influence on opera was much less than is typically understood, but that this lack of influence is also significant and worthy of attention. The Academy's deeply nostalgic turn may have symbolized an important and perhaps enduring aesthetic trope, harboring a nostalgia that is full of lessons pertaining to cultural crisis, but the views of the Academy remained largely ineffectual because the Arcadian design for opera and its reform was in large part eclipsed by more powerful cultural forces, which trumped the polemical, and essentially anti-modern, anti-Enlightenment position taken by prominent members of the Academy. Thus, the peculiar symbolic significance and practical insignificance of the Academy's posture towards the musico-dramatic aesthetic gives me the opportunity to restate the overarching contours of this study as they relate to the concerns around opera in Rome, and the extent to which opera's orbit influenced other genres. Finally, the epilogue also offers a chance to reach beyond the specific historical parameters of the book and point to larger challenges posed by opera that historically precede and follow the case studies presented. In this way, I offer cultural and historical "bookends" to situate *Opera's Orbit* within the broader realm of scholarship on early modern opera culture.

Opera's Orbit is ostensibly about a dynamic and vibrant context of musical culture of the late seventeenth and early eighteenth century, a period in which opera, one of the most important forms of musical modernity, brought both modern cultural desires, aesthetic movements, and political and hegemonic power into a peculiar dialogue. But to draw out the lessons here, this study is about more than periodizing opera and its relations to other music. This study also asks questions about the very legacy of musicology's inheritance – the problem of the isolated genre treated as unique and distinct. It opens up the question of what it means to isolate a musical form – as a singular genre – by asking us to consider the manner and practices in which genres are actually constitutively integrated, how they emerge in relations, how they draw upon, answer back to, and transform the inner operations of musical forms, and how they refract the cultural realities of engagement and exchange. In essence, this study speaks to that very horizon of aesthetic and cultural practices in which musical forms, even in their conceptually neat categories, betray boundaries and serve as mechanisms for ideological discourses. In this regard, what is made visible in the period of this study ought to remain just as much a viable problem of music study today.

1 | Enclosures, crises, polemics: opera production in 1690s Arcadian Rome

The carnival season in Rome during the year 1690 opened with a not-so-light touch of what many viewed as Venetian carnival splendor, using operas, plays, dances, and masquerades to celebrate this annual ritual. The festivities marked not just the season but also the inauguration of Alexander VIII (Pietro Ottoboni, r. 1689–1691), whose papal nephews took an important lead as artistic authors and cultural ambassadors of the season's entertainment.[1] It was in the pope's best interest to dominate Rome's cultural scene and to restore a measure of papal sovereignty by creating a sense of hierarchy between the sacred court and local power nodes of the lay aristocracy.[2] Banquets, music, and above all, opera were not just surface indicators of restored liberalism and pleasure, but political maneuvers meant to cultivate a sense of familial dynasty within Rome's cultural sphere, as well as to provide contrast to Pope Ottoboni's predecessor, Innocent XI (Benedetto Odescalchi, r. 1676–1689); these festivities would also place in stark relief Ottoboni's reign against that of his more conservative successor, Innocent XII (Antonio Pignatelli, r. 1691–1700). The incredibly short reign of the Ottoboni court, a "blip" on the wider historical screen, was a symbolic turning point marking the end of the seventeenth century and the close of the baroque age. We might well use the lens of opera to reflect this historic transition. This chapter provides a brief exploration of opera production in Rome during these very years.

Opera's history in seventeenth-century Rome is long, illustrious, and distinctly varied. Its early highpoints were largely shaped by sacred culture and papal patronage under the Barberinis and their later legacy.[3] Within these parameters of courtly patronage opera thrived as both recreative entertainment and ceremonial duty. It worked especially well as a platform to symbolize and constantly reaffirm the noble or sovereign status of those whom it celebrated. We must remember that the social, cultural, and spatial constitution of papal and princely opera in Rome was rarely restricted to a small set of recipients. Papal patrons and courtly princes, although they maintained a tradition of staging opera within their residences or personal theaters, were interested not merely in self-reflexive image building but also in displaying their power and beneficence to the outside world – a world that in Rome accommodated a wide range of local and foreign residents and visitors.[4] Thus, to apply but a single conventional binary of private versus public dimensions to describe an event like opera in this context misses the more complex signification of its performance.

However, the eventual diffusion of Venetian-styled opera, with its use of public theaters and its adopted entrepreneurial business structure and management, only reached Rome in the 1670s, under the patronage of the exiled Queen Christina of Sweden and Maria Mancini Colonna.[5] Both women were successful in marshaling their financial resources and social networks to persuade other nobles and wealthy clerics to support this endeavor, which was guaranteed through the license granted by Pope Clement IX (Giulio Rospigliosi, r. 1667–1669) just before his death. The Teatro Tordinona opened under the impresarial directorship of Filippo Acciaiuoli in January 1671, with a revival of Francesco Cavalli's *Scipione affricano.* Most of the works in the few seasons that followed were either similarly adapted and modified Venetian operas (several by Alessandro Stradella), or works by local Roman composers, primarily by Bernardo Pasquini.[6]

The Tordinona's future, at least at this point in Rome's history, was short lived. After the Holy Year of 1675 the theater was ordered closed once the conservative Cardinal Benedetto Odescalchi was elected pope later in 1676.[7] As Innocent XI, Odescalchi assumed a much more rigid stance on culture with a desire to direct a return to devotional austerity.[8] His efforts to influence public morality were without equal in the memory of most Romans of the period, and included a number of decrees against women's fashion, attacks on indecency in public art, the outlawing of gambling, and the condemnation of staged drama and music. Odescalchi's policy decisions did, however, point to reasons beyond his spiritual profile and desire for reform. We must recognize political and economic factors also, with the pope's deep involvement as an ally to the Imperial Habsburgs, and his commitment to use whatever resources remained in the nearly bankrupt Papal States for the battle against the Ottomans, a threat that was seen as aimed not simply at the Austrian territories, but at early modern Christendom as a whole.[9] These pressures, along with Odescalchi's general lack of interest in, even disdain for, secular art and culture, had significant consequences for the history of opera. For one, the pope's actions brought public theater to a sudden halt, but had the opposite effect on the subculture of private entertainment and opera production in Rome. It was Innocent XI's *withdrawal* from the Roman social scene that left an empty space, a space soon to be occupied by private individuals.[10]

In spite of Innocent's efforts to forbid theatrical representations, opera throughout the rest of the 1670s and 1680s continued to thrive in the private realm of Roman palaces, on the illustrious and sometimes quite elaborate stages owned by patrons such as Lorenzo Onofrio Colonna and his wife, Maria Mancini, Queen Christina, and the Marquis Pompeo Capranica. Thus, despite the conventional wisdom which argues that the upheavals of papal policies regarding opera (with frequent bans and prohibitions) were to the detriment of Roman theatrical life, the city's peculiar predicament and necessary pocketing of opera culture into various private corners had creative advantages. Above all, it allowed for a variety of opera models, a change from the more singular adherence to the institutionalized formulas that dominated Venice's theater scene. The diverse array of potential opera supporters helped promote this variety, with some who desired the more martial and imperial qualities of late-century Venetian opera, others with Spanish cultural leanings who drew on their native comedies or allegorical and mythological dramas to create some of more spectacular productions of these decades, and those who preferred the bucolic and amorous subjects of pastoral drama for a much lighter, stylized chamber experience.

Yet the private model for opera had its limitations. The spaces for production were necessarily small, limited by a household's seating capacity. And without the regular maintenance and continuity demanded by a business model for opera, private operas were consequently more intermittent, and less publicly driven. Alexander VIII understood well the advantages of a public opera house, how it could be used and what it could symbolize, as this chapter will later detail. What is important to underline here is that the opportunity to reopen the Tordinona recreated a public forum for opera, during a time when opera's cultural status and future course were on unstable ground.

In some respects, we might say that opera during the carnival season of 1690 continued to serve the same princely mechanisms of private patrons that it had before. During that season, for example, the Ambassador to Spain supported the colossal production of *La caduta del regno dell'Amazzoni*, performed on January 15 in the palace theater at the Colonna residence to celebrate a Spanish dynastic union.[11] *La Statira*, the work selected to inaugurate the January 5 opening of the Tordinona, bore some similarities to the work performed at the Colonna residence as it was not without its princely connections: the libretto for *La Statira* was penned by the pope's nephew, Cardinal Pietro Ottoboni, and the subject chosen, the life of Alexander the Great, exemplified generosity and clemency as intended symbolic associations to the papal family who supported this opera's production.[12] Though the opera was not counted as an outright success, its subject, as others have noted, was emblematic of a new age under way in Italian opera dramaturgy.[13] This was not the first time that this opera had been staged, but this 1690s version suggested a more enlightened and noble form of operatic dramaturgy that would usher in the new century, including such features as the removal of comic scenes, a modest cast size, the reduction of spectacle merely for the sake of spectacle, a plenitude of *da capo* or *dal segno* arias, the use of at least some arias as exit conventions, and most importantly, the adoption of heroism as a theme to embody noble dignity, personal sacrifice, and virtue – the kinds of enlightened actions that would later fill the *opera seria* stage in the eighteenth century.

There were important historical and cultural connections between this performance and Cardinal Ottoboni, and by extension, with the intellectual movements that had surfaced in Rome during this decade. Ottoboni was an acclaimed member of the Academy of Arcadians, a group that celebrated its official inauguration later that same year. As is well established in the literature, the Arcadians were by no means the first to condemn opera, or to re-evaluate its place in Italian literary history and its appropriate use on stage. But they were undoubtedly the most emblematic of opera's "second arc" – a period of flux, re-evaluation, and reform that spanned the last quarter of the century, through the early part of the eighteenth century – when a new or revised set of conventions were consolidated and settled into the next phase of cultural practice.[14] By the onset of the 1690s, the concern over opera and its reform was emboldened by specific figures and strengthened through the collision of historical events, political upheaval, and aesthetic movements.

Yet to consider opera's reform and trajectory in this period I explore a wider range of Rome's daily and seasonal practice of dramatic and semi-dramatic music as a way to uniquely capture opera's larger orbit. It is in these alternative realms to public and private theater that a fuller picture of opera emerges, in the realm of discourses that document the current and future status of musical drama, and through the example of non-operatic works that similarly reflect the challenges of mixing media, staging spectacle with sound, and locating the expressive source of meaning. As we will come to see, Rome was a perfect host of this larger continuum of musico-dramatic genres, a spectrum that captured the diversity, complexity, contradiction, and reinvention of opera's critical turn to its next phase of early modernity.

Enclosures

Beyond the few theaters that operated in Rome at the end of the seventeenth century, music, poetry, and drama were being combined, composed, and performed in a number of locations throughout the city. The conditions that gave rise to the cultural vibrancy of the arts and music, and specifically, to the ritual practices of oratorios, serenatas, and cantatas, are worth considering here, even if in brief. There is little need to rehearse in detail the seminal aspects and qualities of Rome's late baroque landscape, as several good sources have already done so.[15] But a few aspects are worth mentioning here as they set up and relate to the three main genres of the musico-dramatic spectrum under investigation in the following chapters.

Urbis et orbis: Rome was considered both a city and the world – a sacred, political, and cultural capital that drew people from near and far. It was the center of Catholic governance and a major destination for religious pilgrims. It boasted the highest concentration of high-ranking clerics, priests, and lay-men working for the church in various capacities. But it was also a nexus for foreign visitors, many of whom came as representatives of their respective countries and regions as cardinals, ambassadors, and legates. Rome was a city of opportunity, with institutions of education (colleges, seminaries, and universities) for the young, both of high and low background. It was a place filled with the establishments of stable employment, within churches, governing bodies, and courtly households. It was a city of both the poor and the very rich, though it is through the rich that culture was largely regulated. The noble aristocracy reflected the city's cosmopolitan nature, with local families residing near foreign visitors who had made Rome their home, either temporarily or permanently. These noble dwellings were political, intellectual, and artistic centers, places within which people were received, where politics were negotiated, where visitors were entertained, and like-minded residents of the city spent their leisure time discussing literature, rhetoric, science, antiquities, art, and music, as their Renaissance predecessors once did.

Rome's architecture and urban layout in this early modern period has been described as mirroring European politics, reflecting the diversity of residents and the tensions that arose from the proximity of these factions within the city.[16] Each neighborhood, or *rione*, reflected these identities and allegiances. Thus, the city did not belong to Romans only but reflected an emergent European cosmopolitism, filled with those who bought or rented illustrious *palazzi* as temporary bases, embassies, or micro-courts to manage their diplomatic business. Each of these venues was an important political arena that served as a cultural enclosure where power was displayed and political interests maintained.[17] Rome was also a city of churches, both large and small, on nearly every block or placed off the city's main squares. The most iconic of all sacred locations were St. Peter's (and its connection to the Palace of the Vatican), and the official papal seat at St. John Lateran (and its proximity to the pope's residence at the Lateran Palace).

Churches, confraternities, colleges, palaces, and theaters were mainstays of musical performance. Music and drama played especially important roles in many of these institutions' ritualized ceremonies, sacred devotional rites, or social gatherings. With regard to the genres studied in this book, particular institutions and locations were linked to specific rituals (some seasonal, some event-driven) that shaped the musico-dramatic experience for the attending listener and spectator. Oratorios were most often performed during the Lenten season at the city's several oratories, located next to major churches. At times the performance of oratorios found its way into the household routines and rituals of noblemen and clerics, both during Lent and at other seasons during the year. Serenatas, on the other hand, were usually a summertime activity, when warm weather permitted outdoor performance and grand spectacle; however, serenatas could be staged at other times of year, sometimes within residences, colleges, or other institutions. Their commission and organization were most often tied to set occasions, such as birthdays and name days, or dynastic or military events. Perhaps the most consumable form of semi-dramatic music was pieces associated with the cantata genre, which ranged from very elaborate semi-staged affairs (a type of chamber opera) to very intimate chamber performances that highlighted the talents of a particular soloist or set of singers. Though often a type of social diversion, cantatas were used to order, allow pause, and give shape to a number of gatherings, both social and intellectual.

Although each genre discussed above had a designated place and function, we must also recognize that on occasion their boundaries and definitions could become blurred, or they were inclined to multiple manifestations, sometimes despite what contemporary critics, theorists, and authors stipulated. I am particularly interested in the way a specific genre displays a number of oppositional binaries, which while seemingly oppositional, work more as unified dualities. Each chapter's narrative explores select contextual conditions and cultural or aesthetic debates that help condition these oppositions. Genre as structural and cultural formation provides a critical window on to these dualities and their broader significance to the issues, debates, and concerns that surrounded the musico-dramatic spectrum in this period.

The oratorio engages the most obvious and tenacious binary of sacred and secular through its relationship to devotion, as well as formal and structural influences borrowed from opera and similar musical forms and practices. The serenata is unique in its exposure of a public and private binary; however, I argue that this binary was problematized in practice, resulting in not just one or the other experience (public or private), but implying both simultaneously. The serenata genre reveals that we may do well to recognize oppositions as dualities. It is the syncretic view of the serenata, taking in its broad signification, that helps to explain its complex mechanisms of expression, some of which reflected crucial points of contact with opera and the debates over the signification of meaning in musical drama. Finally, in the cantata we encounter a juxtaposition of ancient and modern, of idealized notions of music and poetic expression that conflict with the actual and real mechanisms of the cantata's modern musical setting. This perceived binary is rooted in discourses that both assimilate and reject the influence and importance of opera. Moreover, the cantata's perceived association with the pastoral is most revealing of the past/present duality, despite, as we will see, the efforts of contemporaries to depict this duality as a simple and irresolvable opposition.

Each of these qualities discussed is not, however, limited in relevance to a single genre or the chapter containing it. In many ways such dualities are co-constitutive and traverse the larger musico-dramatic field. My intention is to explore these perceived binaries to underline instances of disjunction that erupt in a genre's practice despite the presence of institutional rituals and expectations that, in the end, erect a sense of categorical imperviousness. In all of these – sacred/secular, private/public, past/present – I look for traces of ambiguity, of evidence where such erected binaries reveal larger and more important instabilities at stake in this historical context. My inquiry inevitably returns to the following basic questions: who erects the categories and then denies the ambiguity, and what are the consequences in both musical and cultural practice that result from this phenomenon?

Crises

Rome's origins and history had always been integral to its identity as center of the Western Christian world. During the seventeenth century, the recognition of Rome's roots in a classical, sacred, and humanist past characterized the foundations of the city's emerging modernity as it reached closure of not only a long century, but a recognizable cultural period that

we have come to identify, at least by convention, as "baroque."[18] I recognize
the great challenge of parsing complex roles of government, social and economic life, church and monarchy, and trends in culture in Rome during the
closing decades of the seventeenth century, subjects that have been expertly
addressed many times and in numerous scholarly fields. My aim is not
to re-map this broad terrain but to speak to recognizable features of this
end-of-century juncture as they pertain to opera and the larger spectrum
of musical drama in Rome.

The late decades of the seventeenth century were years of socio-political
transition and crisis that marked a number of cultural arenas.[19] Nothing was
so momentous and sweeping as the transformation of the church, its powers,
influence, and status. The effects of this change were heightened in Rome's
symbolic location, and during a time of upheaval that extended well beyond
the church. There are a few important trends and issues worth noting. The
transition between centuries was a time and place of great reconciliation
between religion and secular culture, devotional practices and empirical
knowledge, and faith and rationality. Perhaps more than any other pope of
the period, Clement XI (Giovanni Francesco Albani, r. 1700–1721) ushered
in the new century with the goal of bringing harmony between Catholic
teaching and the new science of experimentation. Clement XI strove to
create an intellectual atmosphere in which a more rigorous and "scientific"
Catholic scholarship could thrive. He viewed history as an ideological tool
to excavate the church's origins, its early simplicity and purity, and its
nascent forms of effective proselytizing. These historical pursuits were seen
as directly applicable to the reform of church governance, the problems of
clerical wealth, nepotism, and worldliness that many felt had overwhelmed
the better practices of spiritual devotion.[20]

We must therefore come to see the church's brokering of spiritual life with
secular trends, along with its insistence and ardent support of devotionalism
and adherence to orthodoxies, as a reaction to the era's new epistemologies and political realities. The papacy could no longer boast of a role of
hegemony or even prominence in the greater political struggle for power in
Europe. Much of its resources and stature had been diminished throughout
the sixteenth and seventeenth centuries in a series of conflicts that were
played out between Europe's warring monarchies and empires. The late
decades of the seventeenth century in particular were marked by a sense
of ambivalence and instability as popes wandered among political affiliations, between French and Spanish crowns, and eventually, to the Imperial
Habsburgs and Bourbon sympathizers. The culmination of these tensions
was drawn out in the long War of Spanish Succession that was waged in

different corners of Europe between 1701 and 1714. It was during this period that we especially witness the papacy's struggle to maintain autonomy and sovereignty despite the more radical changes underway in shifting political and social structures.

A larger narrative that shadowed papal history in this period was the transition from old to new nobility, from a feudal organization of economy and politics (from which the Catholic Church profited handsomely) to the newer and more modern systems defined by an emerging public sphere. The more progressive, socially expansive public forum for governing society produced a number of trends. Regarding the parameters and definition of nobility, the transition of old to new was deeply disconcerting for the traditional elite, who now headed rapidly diminishing families, and who clung to the tradition and nostalgia of a receding past. Their retreat was palpable on a number of fronts, not just within the papacy and in government, but also in other cultural, intellectual, and aesthetic organizations. On all these fronts reform remained a primary concern.[21]

The linking of sacred and secular circles within which discussions of reforming religion and culture resounded frequently is an important connection to recognize. Several scholars have attempted to relate the roiling debates of reform within the Roman church (and its adoption of pro-Jansenist and anti-Jesuit rhetoric) to the intensification of concern over taste, especially within literary and intellectual societies whose focus was directed upon the return to a purer sense of *buon gusto*.[22] It is my aim here not to unpack the complex ties between religious and cultural reform, but to point to indicators of telling overlap that at the very least suggest how we must regard "reform" as a larger movement beyond the boundaries of specific social institutions. In fact, the points of contact between cultural and religious reform, and the polemics directed at theater and opera, suggest how a number of powerful Roman circles were likely interlinked. Take for instance the argument for relating a phenomenon like Jansenism to larger cultural movements in early Enlightenment Rome.[23] Hans Gross notes that the Jansenist movement in Rome (quite different from its context in France) was intensely focused upon the problems of popular piety in religion. These church reformers felt that Rome's characteristic outlets and rituals for religious devotion had lost their course, with congregants too distracted by secular pressures and temptations. Faith had been diluted, moral codes had become ambiguous, and what remained of spiritual life was directed towards outward manifestations of exuberance and spectacle. Congregants lived through their senses only, not through moral reason: "they had to hear, and see, and touch religion."[24]

The concern over corporeality and sensory expressionism was not limited to devotional practices, but crossed religious lines and poured over into similar secular debates on morality, the direction of culture, and even over the future of opera and theater. We will come to see how the broad-reaching impulses for reform and the more specific concerns over sensory expressionism found resonance not just with the treatment of opera, but also with several kinds of musico-dramatic genres, as tensions over moral principles (both religious and non-religious) shared a number of cultural and social domains. With these connections in mind, I return to Arcadia, the institution that best represents the polemical positions of reform as they relate to music and drama, and that helps to reveal the grappling of an elite class who often wielded protectionist ideologies against new domains of culture – whether secular, public, or more broadly modern in orientation. Viewing Arcadia's struggle and its many paradoxes across this book, we witness how the location and definition of "taste" was tested and eventually limited to the smallest social enclosures, where the desire to recuperate culture's most idealized origins was reflected in a nostalgia for a lauded but distanced musico-dramatic past.

Polemics: exploring Arcadia's rise

There are many versions of the rise of the Academy of Arcadians, and their impact (or lack thereof) on culture in early Enlightenment Italy. There are versions that originate in the primary source literature penned by Arcadians themselves, or by other contemporary Romans of this period, in later Italian literary histories from the eighteenth through the twentieth century, and more recently in a range of secondary sources that span the disciplines of literature, history, art history, sociology, and musicology.[25] For the features worth reviewing, we must look back some decades before the academy's founding, to the time of Queen Christina of Sweden and her private but well-known intellectual and artistic subculture made up of friends and followers. The Accademia Reale, the gathering Queen Christina sponsored and organized at the Palazzo Riario, ranged across subject matters and activities – from science to philosophy, literature, classics, and the arts – but always retained as a common thread the values of simplicity, purity, and reason, qualities felt to have been overwhelmed by the manneristic and spectacular features of earlier seventeenth-century poetry and rhetoric.[26] And though several of the guests and regular attendees were figures of high rank (including the then cardinal, Giovanni Francesco Albani, later

Pope Clement XI), Christina actively recruited the younger, lesser-known members of Rome's society, using the Roman colleges as a source of fledgling members.[27] After her death in 1689, several of these same dedicated followers founded the Ragunanza degli Arcadi, with the first official meeting in October 1690, initiated by the lawyer and poet Vincenzo Leonio and the prelate Giovanni Mario Crescimbeni.[28]

Crescimbeni's role in the Arcadian Academy and his cultural significance is worth some reflection. His claim to fame during the early years of the academy's development was as the Arcadians' "custodian," a role that was both directive and administrative. Not only did he collect dues, and organize, schedule, and lead meetings and events, but he was the academy's most dedicated scribe, taking notes, dealing with correspondence, and most significantly, recording academy functions and putting into print its aims and ideological positions.[29] Crescimbeni was also among the first historians of Italian literary history. His *L'istoria della volgar poesia* (1698) was an ambitious attempt to collect, catalogue, and define vernacular poetry from the mid-thirteenth century to the end of the seventeenth century.[30] A selection of Crescimbeni's publications serves as materials that reveal not just his reflections on literary history, but distinct viewpoints on the role of music in drama – and not only in opera, but in other related genres of the selected vocal music spectrum. They also provide traces of the Academy of Arcadians' aspirations and ideals, even if strongly filtered through the perspective of one figure. In this regard, Crescimbeni's desires and biases must be treated carefully. They are neither inclusive of all Arcadians, or all like-minded critics and polemicists of the period, nor are they necessarily an accurate representation of literature, drama, poetry, music, and vocal genres. At the same time, Crescimbeni's sheer prolificness, his historiographic impulses, and his intense commitment to literary reform and to running the Academy of Arcadians make his voice significant, even if problematic.

Crescimbeni's impact upon the academy was debated, even in his own time. Some regarded him as too heavy-handed and dogmatic in his leadership, which created a well-documented schism between him and a small group of dissidents who resented his dominance.[31] As the custodian and the academy's main historian, Crescimbeni was effective in pressing his own aesthetic preferences for a new poetic humanism. He understood well the importance of revival, of resuming dialogue and historical connection with the classics, and with later Italian poets inspired by this same ancient tradition. Such revival was seen as the most expedient but noble way to reroute literary history's more recent detours into Marinism. However, historical revivalism had several potential paths. Some within the Arcadian Academy believed that the best models for reform were the classical genres of grand poetry: odes, hymns, *canzoni*, and the more epic forms of declamation. Crescimbeni (and others), nevertheless, led their revival along a different path. Among models they favored were the fifteenth- and sixteenth-century works of Petrarch, Sannazaro, and Chiabrera, whose sonnets and *canzonette* embodied a lighter style, with emphasis on lyricism and the sonic qualities of the Italian language. Scholars have noted the particular significance of this latter emphasis.[32] In essence, it underlined a different historical lineage by favoring the Italian early Renaissance legacy over classical models, which were formal, complex, and lengthy in comparison with the short, lyrical, and sentimental poetry preferred by Crescimbeni's faction of the Arcadians.

Crescimbeni's leanings towards lyrical poetry created a conundrum, especially with regard to the musical setting of poetry and drama. In these lyrical models, the emphasis on "melodic" qualities, rhythm, and formal division appeared to conform naturally to the song forms and arias used in dramatic and semi-dramatic vocal music of the latter half of the seventeenth century.[33] Yet, neither Crescimbeni nor many of his colleagues were inclined to embrace the aria, opera's most representative form of expression, and, as the reformists of theater and opera argued, an element best reined in if poetry hoped to maintain good dramatic principles. This Arcadian preference for the lyrical aspects of poetry emphasized the qualities of grace, charm, sentimentality, and emotion – the delectation (*diletto*) of poetry. Those, however, who favored more classical models, and who also wanted to align poetry closely with philosophical principles of the ancients, were much more rationalist in their ideals – poetry as edification (*utile*).[34]

These two strains of poetic modeling help to intensify the peculiar conflicts of Arcadia's neoclassicism. Crescimbeni was respectful of classical sources, and likely viewed his modern Arcadia as a neoclassical continuation of ancient ideals, manners, and style in the most general sense. Yet, there are some scholars who note that Crescimbeni was no purist in his revivalist pursuits, acknowledging that the poetry of his day could never equal or surpass that of the ancients, and that slavish adherence to classical rules was both impossible and futile.[35] This interpretation renders Arcadian literature, and by extension Arcadia, as rife with contradiction, providing a considerably less one-dimensional view than is often considered.

Performing Arcadia

There are several sources that bear witness to Arcadia's contradiction, though a good starting point may be to survey the academy's basic practices. From the outset, the recreation of an idyllic pastoral atmosphere of ancient Greece was a characteristic feature of the Arcadian gathering. The use of natural settings (or rather, palatial garden settings) as a backdrop for humanist intellectual and social exchanges was not in itself a novelty. However, the dedication to this notion and the regular maintenance of this ritual by the Arcadians was indeed remarkable. Their gatherings varied in purpose – sometimes they met merely to socialize or to conduct the academy's business, but most importantly their gatherings offered an opportunity for the performance and recitation of literary compositions, with accompanying discussion and debate. Most of their gatherings were scheduled during temperate months (spring through early autumn) when convening outdoors was more comfortable. They referred to whatever meeting place they chose as the *Bosco Parrasio*, symbolically referring to the ancient and enchanted grove of Parrhasius, an Arcadian city located in the Greek Peloponnesus.[36] In actual practice, an appropriate garden location in urban Rome was not always easy to find. For the first few decades of the academy's existence this location often changed.[37] From late 1690 through 1691, the Academy of Arcadians used the gardens behind the Palazzo Riario along the Lungara, the deceased Queen Christina's former residence. A contemporary diarist attending the first gathering at this location depicted the event as follows:

The Accademia di Belle Lettere, or (as they call it) the Conversation of the Shepherds of Arcadia moved for the first time from the garden of Mattei Navicella to the garden at the palace of the Marquis Riario (now inhabited by Signor Pompeo Azzolini, the custodian of Queen Christina) at the Lungara, where Christina, Queen of Sweden, resided when she was alive. The gathering was held in a wooded garden where there was not even a chair, stool, nor a bench provided, so that the Academicians and the rest of the audience sat on the ground in a great circle, as the true shepherds once did.[38]

The Arcadian gatherings themselves were a type of drama. Members referred to one another as *pastore* or *pastorella* (shepherd or shepherdess) and they adopted nicknames from Greek and Latin sources, in part to indicate specific classical locations as their imaginary "homeland."[39] Acting as shepherds and nymphs, the Arcadians believed that they had turned Rome's wooded groves into an ancient *accademia*, in the manner of their Greek and Roman ancestors. They equated the recitation of pastoral or

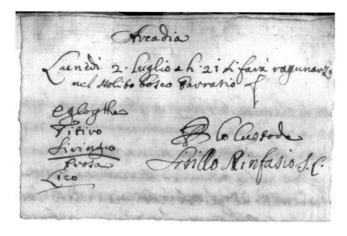

Figure 1 Announcement for an Arcadian gathering, July 2, 1691 (I-Ras, *Archivio Cartari-Febei*, Busta 103, fol. 145v).

amorous poetry and the contemplation of artifice, beauty, and grace in literary composition with the noble cultivation of eloquence and good taste. Above all other pursuits, literary reform was their primary concern. But in some respects, the Arcadians' idyllic role-play was tainted by certain realities of modern-day execution. Although their gatherings were meant to delight and inspire, in some cases listeners alleged that "compositions went on far too long." A contemporary witness reported that the prelates, who came in shorter dress, "found it was uncomfortable to sit on the ground."[40] It appeared to some that a return to the humble life of shepherds was an impractical notion, filled with romanticized nostalgia.

The Arcadians' interest in reviving the past also could be seen as part of a greater early modern interest in antiquarianism. In his study of seventeenth-century antiquarianism, Peter Miller indicates that the least discussed or appreciated tool of the antiquary is imagination: "No past fragments from a lost world could be made whole without the capacity to envision the whole."[41] For some antiquaries, historical recreation was an act that required a mix of history and fantasy, in some cases to such a degree that reality and fiction merged beyond any respective distinction. Imagining antiquity enabled the Arcadians to construct a pastoral world of their own. However, inherent to this creative process was the fact that visions of the past were inextricably imbued with the sensibilities of the present. Ultimately, the contradictions of past and present, and the influence this would have on their theory and practice, would strongly affect the Arcadians' program for literary and artistic reform. As we shall see, this would also profoundly influence their idealized conception of musico-dramatic representation.

We must recognize that Arcadia was not always unanimous in its ideals and proscriptions. Though the reform of culture and return to good taste via a revival of the past was certainly a rallying cry among Arcadia's members, diversity of opinion did surface. Probably the most famous internal dissension in the academy's early history occurred in 1711, when one of the founding members, Gian Vincenzo Gravina, angrily and publicly separated from the group to form his own "Arcadia Nuova."[42] Most scholars have framed this schism as a clash between Gravina and Crescimbeni over the academy's approach to literary reform. Some of those disagreements have been confirmed, but recent work by Susan Dixon highlights a further dimension to this troubled split, which cuts to the core of Arcadia's ideological tenets. Essentially, Gravina's outrage was over Crescimbeni's role, which, in the opinion of Gravina, had become too dominant within the academy. But Dixon argues that Gravina's challenge was not over distaste for Crescimbeni's leadership style or personality only, but directed more broadly at the academy's larger claim for democratic and progressive ideals.[43] And even if the whole affair was resolved in 1714 when Gravina left Rome for Naples, the impulse behind this schism suggests deeper and unresolved contradictions in the Arcadian project.

Dixon questions whether the Arcadians truly made good on their promise of progressivism. We see this best, perhaps, in the academy's approach to patronage. In theory, the founding members strictly forbade the association of a single patron with the academy, even if prominent nobles ostensibly took on such roles in their frequent sponsorship of Arcadian-associated events. For example, Cardinal Ottoboni and other like-minded patrons and supporters of music held frequent *conversazioni* in their private residences as unofficial offshoots of Arcadian gatherings. It is possible that privileging the few and the elite within the academy, which Crescimbeni may have encouraged, was an infraction that Gravina would have identified as undermining the academy's otherwise republican spirit. More dominant than the influence of any one noble member, however, was the papal court and its sway on Arcadia. As Dixon argues, the church's involvement, and clear favor for certain members of the academy, made any true progressive agenda and democratic governance difficult to realize fully.[44] This contradictory practice of progressive and conservative stances by the Arcadians, between democratic and elite governance, will serve as an important issue to consider in the context of understanding Arcadia and their aesthetic debates and polemics, especially as they affected musical drama.[45]

Pastoral, tragedy, and the operatic landscape: Rome in the 1690s

With the inauguration of the Academy of Arcadians in 1690 came a year of other firsts or significant revivals that would have lasting effect throughout the decade and beyond. Opera, as we know, reappeared in Rome with an emboldened presence following the change in papal governance and social politics. Starting with carnival, we might therefore begin by asking what entertainment pleasures theater-going Romans could have pursued within the walls of the papal city? What was the operatic landscape that characterized this moment? The inauguration of a new papal regime lifted what many Romans felt was a long-endured shadow of repression, ushering in a more open environment within which the secular pleasures of vibrant carnivals, games and masquerades, theater, and opera could thrive more publicly and easily. Yet the actual "public" who were able to attend any of the varied choices for theater during that 1690 season (or at most other times, for that matter) were expectedly limited. It is likely that this public consisted mostly of the privileged middle to high noble classes, ranging from those associated with princely families (local and non-local), to clerics, and foreign delegates accompanied by their monarchical-leaning entourages. During this season, some may have attended and supported student-performed dramas of the Roman colleges, typically religious or academic in tone, such as the mythological musical drama *Il Bellerofonte*, performed at the Collegio Clementino, complete with ballets and heroic battle scenes.[46] Another performance of the season included the private viewing of Philippe Quinault and Jean-Baptiste Lully's *Armide*, translated into Italian and hosted at the residence of the French cleric Cardinal Bouillon, before an audience of fellow cardinals and Roman nobility.[47] But the most lavish and coveted events of carnival that year were the competing performances of the two operas *La caduta del regno dell'Amazzoni* and *La Statira*, each of which I touched upon briefly at this chapter's opening. The performance of the *Amazzoni* opera was private, patricianly patronized, and a one-time ceremonial event, whereas *La Statira*, while fueled by courtly patronage, was presented as a carnival diversion to inaugurate the gala opening of Rome's only operating public theater, the Teatro Tordinona.[48]

These twin operas, marking the carnival that symbolized a new age for Rome, embodied an important past/present duality. The Colonna-sponsored production was reminiscent of Rome's more typical opera culture of the past several decades: privately sponsored within the confines of a noble palace, thus more exclusive in its audience, and demonstrating a

tighter hold on patron-based or familial court politics and propaganda. At
the same time we must recognize that despite the ostensibly courtly parameters of production and consumption, the Colonna opera house had long
set its sights on Venetian models of public opera.[49]

La Statira symbolized a somewhat different opera culture, but one in
transition. Like *La caduta del regno dell'Amazzoni*, it was admittedly courtly
oriented with equally propagandistic familial intentions. But the move on
the part of the Ottoboni family to stage the production in a public theater,
and not at the Palazzo della Cancelleria, Cardinal Pietro Ottoboni's residence
and the pope's de facto secular court, is significant. This marks the beginning
of a trend by noble patrons to abandon the private palace theaters as the
sole venue for opera, in favor of a more public forum, which may have been
viewed as a more effective medium of communication.

In his authoritative study on eighteenth-century *dramma per musica*,
Reinhard Strohm views the reopening of public opera houses in Rome in
1711 – particularly with the model of the Teatro Capranica – as a decisive
turning point towards public opera and an eighteenth-century opera culture, characterized "by aesthetic attitudes and practical conditions which
then formed a continuous tradition all over Europe."[50] He does recognize
1690 as a threshold for *dramma per musica*, when leading librettists, patrons,
and critics associated with the then nascent Academy of Arcadians chose
to depart from a more baroque aesthetic. But, as his analysis implies, this
transitory period was a difficult crossroads at odds with a true cultural break
from the past. It is with this crossroads in mind that I will underscore some
of the trends and hallmarks of Roman opera in the 1690s. What I hope
to show is the complexity of this transition, in which residue of the past
remained "sticky," even while considerable effort was placed upon opera's
renewal and departure. Opera's status as cultural practice and object of discussion in this period belies deeper discourses of cultural negotiation and
reform that extend beyond opera. Yet a concise overview of opera in this
period is a starting point for introducing some of these other critical voices.

Opera in Rome during the 1690s was characterized by fits and starts.[51]
It started strong – the opening of the Tordinona promised a shift towards
a more public manifestation of opera, an increasingly attractive option to
patrons busy competing for a wider platform to display ties to Europe's
political and monarchical dynasties, or to showcase innovations inspired
by reform aesthetics. The activities and productions at the two main public
theaters during these years – the Tordinona and the Capranica – reflected
these various political or aesthetic positions. For instance, Cardinal Ottoboni ordered a second performance of his work *Amore e Gratitudine* at the

Tordinona in 1691, the year after its premiere at the Cancelleria.[52] A work like *Amore e Gratitudine*, with its pastoral subject matter and *galant* tone, was an example of the kind of new reform libretti encouraged by leading members of the Arcadians.[53] In these early years of the academy, some members felt it important to perform such models of opera both within private confines, and also more publicly in the newly available theaters, as a means to circulate more effectively the artistic fruits of their reform.[54] As for the political side of public opera, dynastic families in Rome often used productions to advertise important political alliances or as displays of good will and neutrality. A report from January 1, 1690 makes particular note that the ambassadors of Spain, France, and Venice all attended the *commedia* at the Tordinona (likely for Cardinal Ottoboni's *Il Colombo, overo L'India scoperta*), a showing that resonated the political ties the Ottoboni family held with their native Venice, and also with the two crowns of France and Spain.[55]

Despite the utility and presence of opera in at least three public theaters operating during the 1690s (the Tordinona, Capranica, and the Teatro della Pace, which opened in 1694), the decade was not without obstacles to a thriving public opera culture. The carnival season of 1691 had a particularly poor showing of opera – likely an intentional pullback from the normal festivities by papal authorities to show penitence after a recent outbreak of plague.[56] Several operas were performed during carnival of 1692, although reports suggest a particularly unfestive carnival that year due to inclement weather.[57] Much had occurred to change the cultural scene in Rome during the preceding year, including the untimely death of Alexander VIII on February 1, 1691, and the subsequent election of Innocent XII, whose stance on secular culture and governing style marked a radical departure from his predecessor. Yet, despite the contrast of papacies and policies, opera in public theaters did not cease during the ensuing five years, even if it encountered occasional setbacks.

The years 1695–1696 were particularly active for opera, with the reopening of the Capranica in early 1695 after extensive renovation under the direction of Filippo Acciaiuoli. The operas performed in the remodeled Capranica did not appear to receive universal praise, even though the February production of *Nerone fatto Cesare* was conferred special recognition for its beautiful set designs.[58] In response, directors at the Tordinona took similar initiatives to refurbish and expand the theater, employing for the task the impresario Count d'Alibert, who in turn hired Carlo Fontana as architect.[59] For the grand opening, d'Alibert and the theater's patrons commissioned the 1696 Roman production of *Penelope, la casta*, which was applauded widely in news reports of that year, particularly for its scenes, machines, *intermedi*, and costumes, but less so for its music.[60]

The nature of Roman taste for opera during this period is important, but ultimately difficult to ascertain. A few significant trends are important to survey as a means to chart some of the tensions at work in the polemics over dramaturgical reform. In one respect, we can say that opera in public theaters during the 1690s often looked to a Venetian model, evidenced by borrowing of Venetian operas for the Roman stage or by operas that copied the Venetian style. Many of these operas were predictably historical and heroic, of the kind sought by Venetian audiences from the mid through later seventeenth century. For example, for carnival of 1694, patrons and directors staged a readaptation of Nicolò Minato and Francesco Cavalli's *Il Xerse* (Teatro Santi Giovanni e Paolo, 1654), with text modifications and score adaptations by Silvio Stampiglia and Giovanni Bononcini. The changes made for this late-century Roman production were mainly structural, including a reduction of the original work's recitatives, a doubling in the number of arias, and a change in aria placement so that they could function as dramatic exit pieces.[61] It appears that heroic narratives found continued resonance in this context, but that musico-dramatic ordering, structure, and production of performance in opera had clearly changed. At the same time, there are instances in which previously performed works from Venice and other northern opera capitals were largely untouched. One instance of this was the reproduction of *L'Orfeo* at the Teatro della Pace in February 1694. The opera was based on the famed work of Aurelio Aureli, first performed in Venice in 1672.[62] Aureli later adapted the work for a production at the ducal court at Parma in 1689, with modifications to Antonio Sartorio's original score made by the composer Bernardo Sabadini. From what we can ascertain, it was this Parma production that was presented to Roman audiences in 1694.[63]

It appears that the adaptation of Venetian works for the Roman stage was not a uniform or clear-cut process in either its justification or its approach. This is a topic in opera history that merits further investigation and scrutiny. For the purposes here, we might come to see how the diffusion of Venetian opera and its retranslation and translocation to Rome at the very least reflects an old/new dichotomy. Venice's opera culture, its works, its authors, and craftsmen were important models and symbols for Rome's princes and foreign delegates. At the same time, Rome had a long-standing tradition of private patronage somewhat at odds with the Venetian business model of opera, which included a highly developed impresario system. This type of organic entrepreneurship was not easily fostered in Rome; impresarios working the few running theaters in Rome were more likely to be beholden to the expectations of noble patrons and their primary needs as political players, not merely their taste as opera lovers. The Venetian model of opera, while symbolically the cutting edge of public theater, thus became mired in traditional private support systems that were deeply connected to Rome's aristocratic feudal legacy.

We must also be mindful, however, that this was not the only strain of opera permeating this landscape. Alongside these operas modeled on public theater performances were private operas that thrived in elite households, within the theaters of cardinals and nobles who often embraced a different kind of opera than the adapted Venetian versions. These were the venues where new reform principles were being put to the test. Reform principles did find their way to the public stage upon occasion, but the real home for opera's new path was in the protected noble space of the private theater. The leading supporters of these private circles for opera included some of the most influential figures of Rome's aristocratic network, including Cardinal Ottoboni, Prince Francesco Maria Ruspoli, and Maria Casimira, the exiled Queen of Poland, to name a few. All of these figures spent considerable sums of money supporting their commissioned operas, whose performances also offered opportunities for erudite discussions and private *accademie*. Among these exclusive circles, many of the ideas espoused by the leading literati of the Arcadian Academy were debated and put into practice, and a decidedly proscribed vision of opera's future began to emerge.

It is well known that Arcadians and like-minded reformists were highly influenced by French debates about spoken plays and issues of dramatic verisimilitude. The French tragedies of Pierre and Thomas Corneille and Jean Racine, among noted others, became models for librettists and Italian dramatists reforming their narrative and aesthetic approach. However, the exchange of models, especially within this Roman context, was particularly fraught. In one sense we see an emerging presence of French influence during these years, with the performance of Italian translations of French tragedies, particularly in the Roman colleges.[64] And yet, as Melania Bucciarelli's research shows, the reception of French influence bore the strains of critics who took offense at the notion of French hegemony in literary culture.[65] The Marquis Scipione Maffei, for example, felt it was of utmost importance to revive a reputable and performable tradition of Italian tragedy that could stand up to the French models. His idea was to return to Italian tragedies of the sixteenth and early seventeenth centuries, which were written in verse, a form long out of practice. Dramas in prose had since taken over, a fact that vexed many Arcadians, who felt that verse was the only means to mirror the decorum of classical tragedy. This switch to prose, argued Maffei, was largely due to opera's performance history and its links to the improvisatory traditions of theater.[66]

But another main culprit for the decline of good drama was the presence of music in drama. For Maffei, as for Lodovico Antonio Muratori, Gian Vicenzo Gravina, and several other Arcadians, music was an irreconcilable improbability – singing in dialogue seemed impossible to justify in the decorous and profound realm of tragic drama.[67] We must recognize, however, that on the issue of music different sides were taken. There were those who believed that music never had a place in tragedy to begin with, and expunging it was the only route to restore and resuscitate an Italian tradition to rival the French. Others disagreed, and believed the new initiatives of a *tragedia in musica*, spawned in the 1680s at the Grimani theater in Venice, offered a workable solution for the reformation of opera. For example, librettists such as Apostolo Zeno and Domenico David, along with Arcadian critics and opera practitioners such as Pier Jacopo Martello, made rebuttals to support the importance and use of music. They believed that if opera could be stripped of its irregularities and spectacular elements, then it would not necessarily contradict principles of verisimilitude, and could hold a reputable place among the literary branches of good Italian tragedy.[68] Among other Arcadians, however, a different path emerged altogether. Crescimbeni, Muratori, and to some extent Gravina believed that pastoral drama, with its non-historical subject matter, was the *only* viable solution. For one thing, the pastoral was vital to the Arcadians' agenda, since its historical and cultural heritage made it ideal for the movement's restorative program of literature. Moreover, the pastoral could better justify the pairing of music with drama. Like the French *tragédie lyrique*, pastoral operas could best contain the use and placement of mythological and spectacular elements, all plausible in an idealized pastoral world.

Yet the pastoral model for opera did not garner popularity as quickly or as thoroughly as was hoped. During the 1690s, there are few true pastoral dramas in Rome, the kind with small casts, sparse sets, and simple narratives focused on the melancholic expressions of shepherds in and out of love. Examples in this mold included Alessandro Guidi's *L'Endimione*, a *favola pastorale* that the Arcadians praised (and incorporated into their activities) for its novelty, fantasy, and ability to express things closest to nature, especially the concept of love.[69] Other examples worth noting include Carlo Sigismondo Capece's pastorals from the 1680s, including *Il figlio delle selve* (1687) and *I giochi troiani* (1688);[70] from the 1690s, there were Ottoboni's *Amore e Gratitudine* (1690–1691), Girolamo Gigli's *Amore fra gl'impossibili*

(1693), Crescimbeni's *L'Elvio* (1695), and Ottoboni's *L'amor eroico tra pastori* (1696), each of which kept to a true pastoral format and narrative style.[71]

However, many of the reform-oriented operas of the period were not pastorals in the strictest sense, and did not relate amorous tales of shepherds in their natural and bucolic settings. Canonical pastorals were mostly abandoned in the early eighteenth century, even by the Arcadians themselves, who seemed to have found historical sources and classical tragedy more compelling and less abstract than the predictable and fairly actionless bucolic plots of shepherds pining after nymphs.[72] In fact, it is in this period that we begin to witness a merging between the modern pastoral form (which, as a drama, found its roots in Renaissance texts like Tasso's *Aminta* or Guarini's *Il pastor fido*) and the classical model of tragedy or heroic history. As Susan Dixon explains: "The pastoral drama aspired to be tragedy, but the unsettling effects of fate were replaced by the protagonist's acceptance of divine will. Thus, the action always ended on a victorious note."[73] The main character of this hybrid style of drama (whether a shepherd or legendary or historic figure) was required to rise to heroic action and overcome obstacles by means of rational thought and moral action. Characters strove to be virtuous and not yield to instinct. They might find pleasure in the innocence of beauty, but love was not limited to mere romance; rather, it was equated with loyalty and was a symbol of God's perfection, not just the visceral passions of the mortal world.

Several operas from the period could serve as evidence in this regard. To take but one, the opera *Gli equivoci in amore, overo La Rosaura* (performed at the Cancelleria in 1690, and then later at the Teatro Capranica in 1692) is suggestive of this merging of forms and themes.[74] The opera is in three acts, with few major scene changes, many of which take place in natural settings, a garden or a forest. The cast is small: two sets of lovers and one servant: Rosaura (lover of Celindo); Celindo (lover of Rosaura); Elmiro (undiscovered brother of Celindo, but also in love with Rosaura, yet destined to marry Climene); Climene (bride-to-be of Elmiro); Lesbo (Celindo's servant). This classically set tale in the ancient land of Cyprus takes on a similar trajectory to stereotypical pastoral dramas depicting shepherds in love, but with important moral overtones. After the lovers have been variously tempted or confronted, Elmiro realizes that Rosaura will remain constant to Celindo, and thus he repents his transgression of both loyalty and honesty to his friend and brother, Celindo, and marries his intended bride, Climene. Ultimately, the message conveyed is that love is honored, dishonesty and presumption are punished, and the qualities of constancy reign higher than any other quality of beauty.

For the Arcadians, opera seemed an ideal vehicle to display the virtues they deemed significant, including justice and loyalty, humility and modesty, and natural simplicity. These were qualities that the reformists believed not only were necessary for the restoration of good literature (and thereby good taste), but also would help to establish a longer, universal reach for virtue and, essentially, enlightenment. Accordingly, many Arcadians, with an eye on the universal effects of reform, found in public theater not just the potential to communicate lofty aesthetic ideals, but also the possibility to modify social behavior through virtuous dramatic archetypes. What they did not account for, however, were the challenges of staging drama in less than ideal public spaces.

For one, public theaters did not, perhaps could not, run on the same systems of support and organization as private theaters. These presentations were not limited to the designs of nobly aspiring patrons and ideologues only, but were ventures to please a "public," whose tastes were mostly contingent upon their expectations for entertainment, which involved not just the reception of the drama and its ideals, but the visual and aural stimulation provided through stage sets, machines, ballets, and especially singers. Music and spectacle were thus hard to disregard, despite the Arcadian fear that the heightening of these elements marked a slippery slope to the over-the-top decadence of earlier seventeenth-century spectacle. Their concerns notwithstanding, it was the sensory elements of theater – scenography, staging, and music – that drew audiences, not the prospect of moral edification.

Public theater carried other risks as well. Conservatives cited the usual associations of general depravity, including secular immorality, licentiousness, and wayward youth. These concerns circulated in writings and tracts from the period.[75] These worries over opera were not limited to its content, themes, or reception, but also had to do with concerns over opera's performance in a public venue, a less-than-controlled social space that often brewed conflict and violence. In a recent essay by Margaret Murata, we learn that the most symbolically "aggressive" prohibition of opera – the demolition of the Teatro Tordinona in 1697 – was less about the prevention of opera per se, but rather, was instigated as a social mechanism for the "temporal-civil control" of theater spaces.[76]

Public opera thus had its many compromises. To start, it was beleaguered by papal and governmental threats of prohibition or closure more than private opera ever had been. And upon occasion, when bans did take effect, the citizenry felt a palpable impingement on, and discontinuity in, the vibrancy of Rome's musico-dramatic culture.[77] Even when opera could be performed freely, many Arcadians came to doubt that public opera, so riddled by compromises, was a deal worth making. Public-oriented opera used systems of production that were both similar to and yet significantly different from the preparations made for private opera. The operas performed within the walls of Ottoboni's palace or others like it were directed not at pleasing the wider public, but at satisfying the ideals of the patron and the patron's circle – be they Arcadian Academy members or similar elite invitees. Surely, Ottoboni, or any other noble patron of opera, wanted to please and entertain his/her guests. But in these privately circumscribed realms, there were no compromises, no ticket sales to maintain, and no theaters to pack throughout the carnival season. Finally, in the hurly-burly of the public sphere, with a greater mixture of class and type, there remained a lack of control over civil codes, a disregard for standards of etiquette, and, regrettably, the distinct possibility for violence. None of these were concerns at private palace theaters.

As in their Arcadian *Bosco Parrasio*, privately performed music and drama was removed from "the popular bustle,"[78] and was contained within increasingly smaller circles. We will come to see how this symbolic narrowing of dramatic representation was not limited to opera, but was a concern in a number of genre forums where music, drama, poetry, and allegory were combined. In fact, the retreat to smaller enclosures was not just symptomatic of Rome's entertainment culture, but reflects an enervated court society, waning and in crisis. Moreover, the negotiation between opera's impulse to find a public forum and its retreat to enclosures was not resolved in the 1690s, and remained a topic for debate well into the eighteenth century. For the purposes here, it is critical to recognize and stress the symbolic weight this tension carried in this Arcadian context, but also to consider and explore its resonance beyond the boundaries of opera to a wider orbit of music and culture.

Vantage points

As I move beyond opera to consider other forums for the representation of music and drama, we will come to see how the transitional nature of this end-of-century juncture affected the multiplicity of voices in dialogue. The simultaneity and juxtaposition of public and private opera, its license and prohibition, and the larger tendencies of progressivism versus regressivism in intellectual and aesthetic movements, are all characteristic of the contradictions that characterize this retrospective moment. Of all these contradictions, the tension between revival and departure from the past was especially profound. If the reform of opera meant charting a "new" direction, it also meant necessarily accounting for opera's lengthy and convoluted past, with both courtly and public origins. The intellectual, social, and aesthetic terrain of early Enlightenment opera was very different from opera of mid-century Venice, or opera of the post-Renaissance courts of Florence and Mantua. The revival of past principles and models could not easily emerge from a "cut and paste" technique, where Arcadian or like-minded reformers could simply choose the past they wished to evoke in their renewed visions for opera. Throughout its history, opera had acquired cultural encumbrances that could not be ignored or erased. Thus, as opera turned a corner from its baroque legacy to the "enlightened" road of the eighteenth century, it traveled with the burden of its own history that its authors brought to bear upon its re-envisioned status.

In his research on opera's reform and early modern dramaturgical theories, Piero Weiss emphasizes a pivotal decision, or rather a consequence that would affect the subsequent course of opera's history. He notes that critics and writers such as Crescimbeni, Gravina, and Muratori never saw the implementation of their prescriptions for reform, but instead witnessed the eclipse of their cherished "pastoral" opera by the more popular *tragedia in musica*.[79] What we must recognize, however, is that in this move from pastoral to tragedy, the lyricism embodied in pastoral operatic prototypes was not lost. That same lyricism, we will recall from earlier in the chapter, had been incidentally emboldened by the Arcadians' fervent support for sentimental lyric poetry, and the "melodic" sonnets and *canzonette* of their poetic Renaissance heroes. The ironic turn of the "failed" pastoral project was thus sublimated in the aria forms of *tragedia in musica*, whose authors/composers relied on short, lyrical aria moments for emotional and internal reflection upon the tragic qualities and heroic challenges of the larger drama.

Tragic opera, what would become known as *opera seria*, found its legs in this momentous compromise, portending opera's future, but also securing its historical legacy. Musical delight was not erased even during a time when the ideals of moral edification were given renewed emphasis. Moreover, the impulse to codify these musical moments into rationalized entities as a way to rein in poetic artifice presented its own contradictions. In essence, the desire to standardize arias into *da capo* form – largely a *poetic* choice, yet with significant musical consequences effected by the form's encouragement of regularized harmonic design and structural components of contrasting musical sections – helped to inspire a more lyrical and musical means of signification, less dependent on the poetry itself. We must come to see the role of music as emboldened through the shifts in poetic writing as the locus for underlining this trajectory. This was a phenomenon not limited to opera alone, but prevalent across the wider spectrum of secular vocal music. Above all, what is most ironic is that these poetic changes were in part marshaled by the very same critics who remained the most musically skeptical dramaturgical reformers. As their writings will expose, it was their *lack* of attention to music, through either ignorance or dismissal, which resulted in their own inability to see music imposing modernity and influence on opera – what would become nothing short of what Strohm describes as opera's "musicalization of the drama."[80]

The core of this study takes these very debates, their fateful decisions, and lingering anxieties and consequences, and displaces them outside opera within a selection of genres that best reveal the diffusion of opera's influence. These other genres are not just useful for purposes of comparison, but serve as strategic vantage points. With the oratorio, we will learn of its important alignment with the principles of tragedy and moral reason, despite its complicated aesthetic and stylistic propinquity with the lyricism and emotional expressionism of opera. More than other genres, the serenata presents an especially heightened role of music in its performance. This compositional feature arguably became the modern dimension that thrust the serenata from a genre resonant with Renaissance pageantry and spectacle, to one with the most cutting-edge dimensions of musical drama. The cantata reaches the very foundations of social and aesthetic upheaval taking place in this period, through its critics' desire to hold on to its chamber-like status and exclusively noble associations. The cantata's development in this period is in many ways the logical extension of the ideas of aesthetes who believed opera's social circles should remain elite and small. All of the genres to be discussed in the following chapters work in some sense as restorative impulses for reform, through either their reaction against or their appropriation of opera in its various ideological permutations. Thus, the conceptions of musical drama – as entities not fixed but in a process of transformation, debate, and negotiation – are best captured, not through opera alone, but through its moving orbit, its dynamic influence on other genres.

2 | Disrupting the oratorio

I

Of all the vocal dramatic music in early modern Rome that reflected opera's orbit, the oratorio looms large as a genre that was resolutely "anti-opera" in official function, yet was intimately bound with conceptions of the theatrical. The connecting points between the seventeenth-century oratorio and opera were therefore both obvious and yet problematic. On the surface remained the powerful demarcations of an oppositional relationship. When the papacy encouraged devotional activity the oratorio was frequently invoked as the kind of spiritual ablution ritual necessary to restore moral balance through instruction and penitence, with specific seasons, such as Lent, being more penitential than others. During such seasons opera was explicitly referenced as the sort of secular activity to ban, or which devotional acts – like oratorio performances – were meant to replace. But more than just replace, the oratorio was supposed to annul opera, to erase all that opera signified morally and socially. Yet, throughout this period, the oratorio had become closer in style and form to opera, even if the oratorio's purported devotional niche stood in marked contrast to opera's secularism.

The oratorio's impact upon the musico-dramatic landscape of late *seicento* Rome has been well documented, and the effect of opera upon the oratorio's development is often recognized. However, I argue that opera's influence deserves some pause. In several respects, the oppositional relationship of the oratorio to opera elucidates but also complicates the distinction and exchange between these genres. This chapter examines the interplay between the oratorio and opera and seeks to interrogate their opposition, all the while acknowledging the symptomatic force such opposition held within the Roman context.

Each genre examined in this book reveals the adaptation of a past history to newer practices as a genre transforms and encounters new pressures and ideological forces within each distinct culture of its authorship and representation. Between the late seventeenth and the early eighteenth century, the oratorio's status and function in Rome could not be divorced from a larger aura of "reform" that cut across secular and sacred boundaries and infiltrated the discourses of moral conservatives who sought more ascetic and severe religious practices, and of artistic and literary critics who argued for a return to the moralism, simplicity, and purity of past cultures as a means to renew their own. The continuity of oratorio devotional practices started to find new resonance in 1690s Rome, in an era of nascent Arcadianism, and of major upheaval within the spheres of papal reform and church politics. This period is especially revealing when we identify how opera's more recent troubled status intersects with the oratorio's historical legacy, including its roots in moral instruction and conversion. The long-held focus on morality and tragic elements as the oratorio's main dramatic subjects now collided with operatic reformers who sought similar, albeit secular, elements and stresses in their reshaping of dramatic literature. We must also recognize, however, that the oratorio composed in this historical transition was not the oratorio of its lauded past – the mechanisms of expression through musical forms had radically changed over time. Caught in the tide of historical legacy and larger cultural reform, the oratorio and opera formed a cultural alloy, two juxtaposed worlds – one half devotional and sacred, the other intellectual and secular.[1] Within this convergence of influences, the oratorio adapted to a variety of performance needs that captured a culture forced to negotiate the desires of worldly patronage and emboldened secularism, and one in search of conservative moderation, reform, and moral rectitude.

This chapter focuses on the vernacular oratorio of the late seventeenth century and how it came to embody a dual existence: one aspect emphasized continuity with the oratorio's origins, while the other emphasized displacement, or even a rupture with that trajectory as the oratorio increasingly felt the pull of opera's orbit. There were good reasons to insist that the oratorio maintain continuity with its devotional origins; perhaps most prominently it would reinforce the oratorio's function in social and cultural regulation. For decades, the oratorio served as opera's antithesis; maintenance and remembrance of that past was therefore symbolic and ideological. Yet, alongside this one-dimensional perspective that appropriated the oratorio to more socially rigid ends, there were many instances in which the oratorio defied categorical enclosures and displaced historical tradition and genre inscriptions with new rituals of performance, with diverse social, political, and aesthetic functions. This fundamental duality of remembrance and erasure endows the oratorio with a pronounced set of tensions but also a kind of malleability that is often overlooked.

Remembrance and erasure, I argue, are key components that shaped the oratorio's ambivalent relationship with opera, and present an antinomy that can be traced through the oratorio's representation in discourse and practice. For this reason, this chapter necessarily builds its momentum from selected discursive fields, first through an examination and return to a key critical reflection on oratorio practice penned by the cleric and librettist Arcangelo Spagna in the early eighteenth century. The analysis of his discourse sets the stage for exploring specific practices within the palace realm of Cardinal Pietro Ottoboni, whose Palazzo della Cancelleria served as an important venue for oratorio performances. Starting in 1689, and during the early years of the cardinal's sponsorship and authorship of oratorios, Spagna was employed as the cardinal's *maestro di casa*, and was listed as part of the household's ministry until his death in 1726.[2] We know little of the exchanges that occurred between patron and servant, or between these two fellow librettists and clerical men of letters over their aesthetic and functional aims for the oratorio's practice. By juxtaposing Spagna's arguments and discourse with Ottoboni's authorship and patronage (through a study of select oratorio events at the Cancelleria) I probe the oratorio's complicated relationship to opera. My objective is to embrace both Spagna and Ottoboni as figures whose words and deeds are each subsumed by mediating factors of critical events and historical change that mark this discrete period. With this analysis and comparison, I attempt to capture the sense in which the oratorio's continuities and discontinuities instigated a renegotiation of genre, and in the process affected how elements of the oratorio were remembered or conveniently effaced.

The research and analytical insights in this chapter owe a debt to the secondary literature, some of which has crossed similar historical terrain and/or cited the same primary literature and musical sources.[3] I have chosen to revisit some of these moments and works with a different purpose and framework in order to reveal the workings of the oratorio, not just as genre but also as *process*. It is in that process that I examine the oratorio's tension and contiguity with opera, and consider how such a merger reflects the workings of an inner circle of individual players, all in the act of resecuring their interpretive stake in directing culture. My emphasis will be on select examples that arose during the 1690s, though to understand important factors of this period, I frame these discrete events within a broad historical scope of the oratorio's intersection with opera.

Historical legacies

In early modern Italy, seasonal ritual had its importance and distinction, providing structure for the permission or prohibition of certain activities, and was created to direct social and moral imperatives for the general populace. The juxtaposition of the carnival season with the ensuing Lenten season highlights some of these distinctions and reveals critical dimensions for the intersection of sacred and secular music and culture. As was typical, operas and similar theatrical diversions were often permitted during carnival, whereas during Lent, oratorios and other devotional rituals were meant to replace all secular-based activity and entertainment. By the late seventeenth century, however, the clarity marking this seasonal and cultural juxtaposition had eroded. Oratorio performances were encouraged during Lent, but their platforms and locations for presentation, along with their orientation in meaning and ritual, saw a gradual change during these decades, reflecting qualities that often teetered precariously between the sacred and secular. In a recent study, Arnaldo Morelli calls our attention to the importance of palace-performed oratorios which, by being staged beyond the purview of a larger public (the majority of oratorios took place in the devotional spaces of confraternities), served noble households and their retinues as pseudo-sacred entertainment, offering an extension to the carnival season, not its negation.[4] These oratorios were rarely just devotional occasions; within this secular space they often served as a platform for a patron's political agenda, enabling high-profile socializing and networking, making for the kind of multi-gendered gathering familiarly associated with public and private opera, and similar recreation.[5] In fact, Norbert Dubowy offers the possibility that more people were introduced to opera's sounds and styles through public and semi-private musical devotionals like oratorios than through non-devotional performances in theaters or through the chamber performances of private salons and stages of noble palaces.[6] Moreover, the introduction to opera's conventions through the oratorio was not restricted to its audible elements only; there are many instances throughout the seventeenth and early eighteenth century in which the oratorio's rituals of performance lean quite closely towards more visually resplendent theatrical experiences.[7]

What is critical to emphasize, however, is that opera's fateful cut across the oratorio's path was not a one-sided collision but a slowly negotiated fusion with a long history. Morelli's scholarship has been key for tracing an earlier history. In his study of patronage in the Roman Oratory, Morelli provides a nuanced rendering of the ways in which sixteenth- and early seventeenth-century Oratorian fathers mediated, and sometimes vigorously debated, the inclusion of secular influences, including those musical, in the oratorio tradition.[8] The Oratorians had long seen music as a powerful vehicle to convey themes of devotion. Morelli charts a shift in the composition of the

oratorio's audience: from the late sixteenth century into the early seventeenth century the Oratorian rituals grew to include prelates and leading
nobles, a development with consequences for the oratorio's environment
and activities. This altered constitution of participants was correlated with
an increase in pomp and spectacularism, marking a departure from the more
modest and simple approaches of the early Oratorian fathers. The shift likewise affected musical repertoire, with two classes of oratorios emerging: one
characterized by simplified music and text for a larger, more diverse public,
the other by a more musically elevated and varied repertoire for a higher
socio-cultural level of audience.[9] The larger point revealed by Morelli is
the way in which the Oratorians confronted a divisive internal battle in
changing their artistic and musical practices. Despite the new variegated
repertoire, they still tried to maintain a level of sober simplicity at the core
of their spiritual philosophy. But, in the course of the seventeenth century,
that direction changed as competition for external patronage demanded
more elaborate and spectacular music. This meant that in the early seventeenth century the madrigal gradually came to replace the singing of *laudi*
in Oratorian exercises. Eventually, the madrigal form all but disappeared
(*c.*1640s), to be replaced by the monodic style of early musical drama and
related secular genres. A further consequence of the divergence of the oratorio from a simpler model was a growing sense that a congregation's own
musicians were not up to the challenge of this more elaborate repertoire,
and thus music was increasingly entrusted to professionals who worked in
the great churches and private residences of Rome.

The functional and aesthetic changes that came with adopting the new
"recitar cantando" did not come quickly or easily but required a series of
calculated steps that were not without controversy. Using a series of documents belonging to the Chiesa Nuova, Morelli reveals how the Oratorians
placed themselves in a compromising position. Even when internal dissent
surfaced over the degree to which spectacular music – secularly influenced
and novel sounding – had entered the oratorio, the ability of this music to
attract patronage and noble audiences made resistance ineffectual. A price
was to be paid for this external collaboration. Some of the fathers of the
Chiesa Nuova sorely lamented the entry of this "new air of worldliness
into the oratory," as it greatly diminished the tranquility of the meetings,
and placed emphasis on performance of newer dramatic-style music, at the
expense of sermons or other exercises.[10]

Although these alterations to the oratorio's presentation are most relevant to the Oratorian context of the first half of the seventeenth century,
they set a foundation for the secularization of music and for changes to

Oratorian conceptions of aesthetics and ritual in the latter part of the century. By the end of the seventeenth century any retreat from the newer musical changes made to the oratorio became increasingly difficult as dramatic music's influence across most sacred and secular vocal music gained permanence. Thus, after the passage of nearly a century, the conflict between those hoping to foster innovation and extravagance and those hoping to preserve modesty and tradition found new relevance in the closing decades of the century. While the oratorio shifted in sound and focus as it was appropriated for occasions beyond those purely devotional, papal austerity policies were instituted to counteract a culture perceived as too secular and deeply corrupt.[11] What is most critical for the purposes here, however, is to situate the oratorio's deepened affiliation with opera within a larger debate over morality that permeated much of the cultural discourse within Arcadian Rome. The issue of moral concern traversed papal cultural politics and was included as a theme in most contemporary aesthetic writings, especially those directed at the reform of theater and drama. It is in regard to the question of morality that the oratorio becomes ambiguously positioned as both a form of anti-opera (not just spiritually and seasonally, but now also literarily), and a genre that in practice had inevitably adopted and adapted the forms and aesthetic conventions of opera. We will see how this quality of ambiguity will come to bear significance in the words and deeds of critics, librettists, and patrons of the oratorio as the seventeenth century came to a close.

II

The oratorio and opera: revisiting Arcangelo Spagna's "Discorso"

There are few surviving discourses that trace the oratorio's history or its development, let alone that confront the oratorio's complicated but fundamental relationship with opera. The seventeenth century was not a period that treated music and genre relationships with much historical depth, and placing the oratorio in a larger musico-dramatic trajectory was by no means a priority of the contemporary literary figure, theorist, or critic who rarely addressed musical drama in any elaborate discussion except in the broadest outline. Even contemporary discussions of opera could hardly be called copious or comprehensive, in spite of the heated debates over the pairing of music with drama that took place at the turn of the eighteenth century.[12] The oratorio, like opera, involved a similar merger of poetic and musical composition, but its long-held association with sacred subjects and devotional activities and spaces usually excluded the genre's participation in debates over theatrical dramaturgy. There are exceptions, however. Recent scholarship has revealed or reanalyzed the exceptional cases in which the oratorio is referenced in the larger polemics over theatrical dramaturgy. For the purposes of my analytic contribution, some review of critical points in the scholarship is helpful for providing context to the specific arguments developed in this chapter.

In the rare cases known, it appears that critics who addressed the current state or future of dramaturgy sometimes invoked the oratorio during discussions of tragic drama, citing devotional themes and literary qualities as significant reasons to treat the oratorio as a musico-dramatic analogue to tragedy. Tragedy had become the preferred dramaturgical template for several early eighteenth-century poets and intellectuals committed to reforming opera and theater as a whole. It is worth considering the extent to which the oratorio, a homegrown Italian genre, might have provided a convenient response to French attacks on Italian opera. The oratorio was not a mere copy of French models of tragic drama (as the *tragedia in musica* might have been) but stood uniquely as a particular Italian solution for reforming music and drama.[13] Chief among the few who took up the oratorio in this spirit was Apostolo Zeno, whose writings Arnaldo Morelli examines to illuminate the poet's belief in the oratorio's theatrical potential.[14] In similar ways to spoken tragedy, Zeno found the oratorio literature to be filled with strong (biblical) figures who conveyed a sense of nobility of character. The genre's formal and dramaturgical concision also made the oratorio more readily capable of conserving the Aristotelian unities of action, time, and even place, and thus was an effective model for tragic drama, perhaps a better model than could be provided by other types of *melodramma*.[15]

The importance of considering how the oratorio could be conceived as a better model for opera's future is a topic to which this chapter returns. The point of Morelli's article is not so much to highlight Zeno or opera polemics of the early eighteenth century, as to reveal the similarities of ideas concerning tragedy and the oratorio identified in the earlier writing of Arcangelo Spagna, as was expressed in his 1706 "Discorso intorno a gl'oratorii," which prefaced his *Oratorii, overo Melodrammi sacri*.[16] Spagna's "Discorso," one of the few historiographic documents on the oratorio of the seventeenth century and thus cited frequently, has received new attention and important critical treatment by scholars.[17] Morelli's article explains that though Spagna's document heralds important shared qualities between the heroic style of spoken tragedies and the sacred style of oratorios, Spagna is careful to distinguish a specific kind of tragedy in this analogy, not the type modeled after Spanish comedies or romance novels containing complex and interlacing stories, but those of a Senecan flavor, with few interlocutors, and with a drama whose focus on the pathos of a single protagonist allowed for strong expression of the drama's sententious and moralistic tone. It was this other category of tragedy that best describes the template of stories – those such as Jephtha, Esther, or Judith – which worked most effectively as dramas for the tragic stage as well as for the sung oratorio.[18] What we gain from Morelli's study is a sense that the oratorio requires better placement within larger cultural movements that cut across sacred and secular divisions. Some of the changes made to the oratorio ushered in by Spagna and his generation (including the avoidance of intrigue and the privileging of storylines with simple, direct, and stoic themes) echoed similar ideas of reform regarding operatic theatrical dramaturgy that would begin to circulate in the early eighteenth century. In fact, Spagna was well acquainted with the central literary polemics of his day that affected both sacred and secular culture, even if his viewpoints and arguments were more rooted in mid-seventeenth-century aesthetics.[19]

The "Discorso" concentrates mainly on three central elements of reform which Spagna (in a gesture for his own self-promotion) argues were key contributions to the success and the perfection of the oratorio genre: the elimination of the external narrator (Testo), the adoption of a Senecan model of tragedy, and the use and maintenance of rhyme instead of the more widespread *versi sciolti* which were prevalent in late seventeenth-century musical drama. Spagna himself suggests that his choices for his own oratorio compositions were highly influenced by the generation of poets he encountered, including Giulio Rospigliosi, the embodiment of dramatic excellence for Spagna.[20] Mauro Sarnelli recontextualizes Spagna's mid-century literary sensibilities (which owed a debt to Gabriello Chiabrera, Fulvio Testi, and later Rospigliosi) and argues that they come into conflict with the trends in reform of the 1690s, such as those advocated by the members of the Academy of Arcadians, including Gian Vincenzo Gravina and Alessandro Guidi. Sarnelli explains that while Spagna embraced the Senecan tragic models of *his* generation, it was especially Gravina who had all but systematically demolished such models to create a different kind of tragedy.[21] Sarnelli argues that Spagna defends and attempts to rescue the aesthetic positions of the Barberini literary and intellectual circle, of which he himself was a member, thereby making clear his distaste for newer trends, especially those championed by key Arcadian figures. Spagna's treatment of the Arcadians is telling; he never condemns the group outright, but he never joins as a member, even though he is counted as a leading figure of the Accademia degli Infecondi, the group that helped to found the Accademia degli Arcadi.[22] Sarnelli's analysis helps to reveal the complexities in the intimate intellectual world of this context, showing that it was fraught with contradiction and generational conflict concerning poetic and dramaturgical aesthetics, even if the prevalent view was that drama ought to root its trajectory in classical models, not in opera as inspiration.[23]

As the recent attention reveals, Spagna's "Discorso" is rich in historical information but is also suggestive of important ideological implications. It is thus crucial to uncover Spagna's voice as a specific kind of agent relevant to the purposes of this study. His ecclesiastic position, coupled with an unusual exposure to sacred *and* secular music and theater traditions, along with his place within a collective mentality of cultural reform, makes his discourse valuable. It reveals how Spagna was caught in a historical web of contradictions, in which his discourse on the oratorio reflects a problematic ambivalence towards opera symptomatic of the era. I choose to revisit Spagna's "Discorso" with these qualities in mind, not to repeat the descriptive and analytic work already brought to this document, but to focus on the document's value for uncovering trans-genre tensions between the oratorio and opera. Spagna's may be one of the few (extensive) existing tracts on the Italian oratorio in this period. His writing calls for some reflection that highlights Spagna as a troubled voice among a larger contingent of artists, critics, moralists, and literati who attempted to discipline opera's influence by making sense of it, justifying it, or denying its overall effect.

Spagna confronts the opera–oratorio intersection by first addressing it historically. In fact, he freely admits the influence opera had upon the history and development of the oratorio, noting that "theatricalizing" devotional activity through poetry and music dates from the time of San Filippo Neri, the founder of the celebrated Congregation of the Oratory. Adopting certain theater practices and aesthetics was an effective means to an important religious end: to move the faithful, and to use the powers and persuasion of theater to direct attention to spiritual matters.[24] By acknowledging this process, Spagna suggests the necessary compromises the Oratorians made in their adoption of non-devotional music and theater practices in order to compete with the encroaching allure of secular culture. There is a telling aura of justification in rooting the oratorio's relationship with opera within imposed historical circumstances. Once that negotiation with opera had been made, Spagna appears to understand that he must unravel the ensuing history of the oratorio as one that *benefited* from opera's influence. He thus turns to the importance and usefulness of sacred opera as a model of influence for the oratorio. He views himself as an inheritor of this lauded literary tradition of sacred opera composition, epitomized by works such as *Sant'Alessio*, penned by the illustrious Rospigliosi and performed in the Barberini theater *c.*1631–1632. Although we assume that Spagna understood the difference in representation between truly staged opera (in the style of *Sant'Alessio*) and the visually unadorned oratorio, he still took to calling his oratorios "sacred operas" – a title he ostensibly treats without complication, as the combination of sacred subjects and musical drama had been made conventional by others before him.[25]

Historical precedence for Spagna becomes a powerful tool of explication. It also becomes a reference point of stylistic standards that it was essential to uphold. For Spagna, the insistence on maintaining the use of rhyme was a feature that could ensure a high level of erudition and poetic quality that had been sorely neglected in the operatic examples of his day. He criticizes opera librettists for their inconsistent standards when treating rhyme, using skill only in an opera's opening scenes, and then allowing a decline in quality as the drama progressed.[26] Johann Herczog speculates that Spagna's unfailing defense of rhyme may have betrayed "his fear that any minor or apprentice poet could turn his hand to writing oratorios."[27]

Though he placed great importance on the recitative, Spagna also granted a position of honor to the aria. When united with rhyme, musical harmony not only delighted the ear and dazzled the intellect, but could also quiet an audience and keep them in rapt attention, serving as an effective medium to convey the oratorio's moralistic content.[28] There is little doubt Spagna appreciated opera-style arias and their sway over audiences. We see this in his discussion of the use of the chorus in oratorios, thoughts that help to reveal his practical sensibility as a dramaturge.[29] Spagna argues that choruses do little to portray reflective moments of a drama and instead become displays of musical erudition, when a composer is able to show off his counterpoint skills. Spagna's concern is that not all in the audience would be capable of appreciating such compositional skill, and thus, he concludes it is wiser to end with a "light arietta" to please the audience more universally.[30]

Spagna did not, however, embrace the aria unconditionally. As we delve deeper into his discourse, Spagna's views on arias and their performance reveal cautiousness, ambivalence, even anxiety, as we come to see that the aria becomes a serious stumbling block for the oratorio's perceived distinction from opera. As much as they could be desired, Spagna admits that arias in form and function required strict boundaries. He found the *da capo* form unjustifiable because it encouraged length and repetition that not only confused and bored listeners, but also damaged the overall clarity of textual meaning.[31] For someone who embraced melodrama as an effective means of expression, Spagna reveals a notable sense of hesitation on the issue of music–word relationships. Arias were acceptable so long as they were meant to serve the text, not the other way around.[32]

It is difficult ultimately to chart the forms and approaches that Spagna sanctioned or actually attempted without also having in evidence the scores composed on Spagna's texts. Because *Oratorii, overo Melodrammi sacri* is often seen as a retrospective group of works, it is tempting to surmise that the newest formal, stylistic, and performative trends in musico-dramatic writing were less familiar to Spagna, although that seems unlikely. As an author of several types of melodrama, Spagna, at very least, would have been familiar with the directions musical drama had taken in the last half of the seventeenth century, directions which also influenced oratorio composers as they adopted a practice (or were encouraged) to write more arias, with lengthier musical episodes and embellishments, calling for more virtuosic singing.[33] For Spagna, singers were the guilty enablers of music's power to surpass text, working their tyrannical effects to seduce patrons and librettists through their fame as performers and with their vocal pyrotechnics. Rarely, thought Spagna, did such virtuosi display the "mature" ability of a cultivated performer who could delicately render emotive nuance, especially expressed in well-written recitatives.[34]

It is evident from these examples that in spite of Spagna's acceptance of, and even advocacy for, stylistic elements borrowed from opera, the influence of opera on the oratorio was not unequivocal. We have seen that on the one hand Spagna acknowledges that opera exerted a powerful pull on the oratorio. An inevitable negotiation with opera evolved, regardless of the internal desires of the Oratorian fathers to maintain the sanctity of devotional life, because opera's orbit coincided with the transformative direction of aesthetics and of culture as a whole. For the purposes of the cultural survival of the oratorio, it appears that Spagna understood that this was a necessary compromise. At the same time, we might imagine that Spagna would be resolute in arguing for the oratorio's maintained distinction from opera, based on his reflections and treatment of recitative and aria composition. He would likely encourage its authors to find a delicate balance between useful appropriation and careful disciplining of opera's influence. Here, Spagna's inclination towards genre distinction resonates with Ireneusz Opacki's theoretical notion of a "royal genre" – a genre to which all others are drawn. Simply stated, the oratorio had been drawn into the influence and sphere of opera, its activities, aesthetics, and culture.[35] But Opacki would be careful to stipulate that when a genre enters into "close

blood relations" with another genre, even a royal genre, it does not become
that genre, nor does it lose the distinguishing features that characterize it
as distinct.[36] The larger question is how a figure like Spagna distinguishes
those features, and in making such distinctions, how is the genre recast to
maintain its preferred conditions? In essence, what did Spagna wish the
oratorio could be?

It may be more conventional to read Spagna's "Discorso" for its historical definition and reflection on oratorio practices. But Spagna's words and
arguments are not the language of encyclopedic literature. My own interest
in reading this document is to forward a broader interpretation of its rhetorical thrust in order to see Spagna's words as reflective of the larger trends of
reform literature that circulated in this period in a number of literary incarnations. We see this revealed in Spagna's trepidation over arias, which is
less a concern over good dramatic composition than a broader yearning for
a future when oratorios and *all* musico-dramatic composition would hold
steadfastly to past principles of *prima le parole*. The aging canon was not
alone in such longing; his grief over the loss of the poetic word's primacy resonated with other turn-of-the-century reactionary critics, such as Giovanni
Mario Crescimbeni, or the more dogmatic Ludovico Antonio Muratori.[37]
Muratori sympathetically echoed Spagna, urging that music be reformed to
majestic and honest decorum, not like the current sacred poems called oratorios, which reveal how a different music has daringly made its way from
theaters into the sacred temples, and has "infected" the gravity of divine
practices.[38] Both Muratori and Spagna seemingly presumed that a puristic
oratorio practice – in truth, more reflective of mid-seventeenth-century
aesthetics and culture than of those from the later turn of the century –
could operate as universal practice, even when a conglomeration of devotional and non-devotional aesthetics had largely changed and reshaped the
oratorio's performative scope. Spagna's and Muratori's struggle to maintain
a sense of literary primacy in the theater and in devotional activities became
increasingly incongruous in a period and context where the demand for
high-quality music and vocal performance was pervasive, and certainly not
a new phenomenon.

For the purposes here, the larger question may involve exploring not
only how this phenomenon was registered in the oratorio, but how select
individuals – like Spagna, along with other critics, patrons, librettists, and
composers – accepted, denied, referenced, or processed this phenomenon in
light of the oratorio's opera-bound contingencies coupled with its otherwise
devotional history. Spagna offers an important perspective on this inherent
contradiction since his discourse transmits such tensions along a number of

historical planes. Spagna helps to reveal the manner in which the oratorio's troubled relationship with opera took on new registers at a time when the revision and reform of dramaturgical practices cut across several domains of culture. If for poets and literati the refinement of language was a means to recuperate Italian literary standards from decline, then for moralists and ecclesiastics a departure from operatic tendencies was also a way to restore a more sacred-bound conception of cultural practice. In several respects we see how Spagna's "Discorso" captures this intersection of moral conservatism, rising secularism, and cultural reform. We witness in the words of Spagna how he and others like him were in search of strategies to reconcile opera's influence over the oratorio with the desire to uphold and maintain the oratorio's sacred imprint and devotional legacy. But much of this process of historical *re*-negotiation depended upon how the oratorio was remembered, what was to be regarded as salient and crucial among its features, and what elements were deserving of stronger accents. It is as though the downplay of opera's interruption – in this retrievalist move – would allow for extravagant and secular tendencies to be reined in and disciplined. What is key to recognize and emphasize is that Spagna does *not* deny opera. His ambivalence is exemplified in the fact that he does not advocate (or believe in) a total erasure of opera's influence on the oratorio. Rather he appears caught between a realistic practice that complicates trans-genre distinctions, and a more nostalgic desire to remember the oratorio as a purer, simpler, and distinct poetic-musical ideal.

These desires were reflective of Spagna not only as an individual, but as someone whose views refracted those of the Arcadians who shared similar strategies of retrieval and maintenance. Though Spagna never joined the academy, his general ideational posture seems resonant with this group. In both cases – those espousing literary reform (as exemplified through lead-ing members of the Arcadians) and those espousing moralistic reform (as exemplified in Spagna's discussion of the oratorio) – *reform* as a word choice is somewhat misleading since the force and direction of either viewpoint was focused less on change per se, and more on retrieval. We must therefore come to read Spagna's impulse to recapture the oratorio's past as a larger restorative gesture, not just for the devotional practice of oratorios, but also for Italian musical drama as a whole. Though never actualized as a pro-posed statement in his "Discorso," one might still hypothesize as to whether Spagna regarded the oratorio as a possible model for theatrical reform, by exemplifying the oratorio's brevity of scope, moralism, and simplified yet elevated expression that he and others felt were missing in opera of the day.

Spagna's treatise thus serves to flag a number of broader cultural symptoms and dispositions that will be explored and revisited in the remainder of this chapter. The concern that the oratorio display or deny its opera-like features was certainly not new when Spagna published *Oratorii, overo Melodrammi sacri* in 1706. My objective is to push back these issues to the 1690s, a period when a number of conflicting interests coalesced, as expressed by patrons, composers, critics, and the papacy, who all in some sense reshaped the oratorio to renegotiate and control its relationship to opera in a number of divergent ways. The larger aim is to probe the significance of certain oppositions the oratorio developed, especially how the genre could articulate a kind of appropriated secular extravagance, while simultaneously maintaining qualities associated with devotional modesty and moral austerity.

In the following sections I build a case for exploration of select events that occurred within the (semi-)private setting of Cardinal Pietro Ottoboni's cultural milieu established at his palace residence. These events take place during a crucial cultural transition, when Rome encountered two diametrically opposing papacies – one extremely short-lived but festively vibrant under the leadership of Alexander VIII (Pietro Ottoboni, r. 1689–1691 – the great-uncle of Cardinal Ottoboni), the other under Innocent XI (Benedetto Odescalchi, r. 1676–1689) and his later successor, Innocent XII (Antonio Pignatelli, r. 1691–1700), who was especially committed to lifting ecclesiastical hierarchs from what he determined were the perilous depths of worldliness, and reaffirming austerity as a value for the culture at large. The oratorio's development and function in this vacillating turn-of-the-century period cannot be divorced from opera's own peculiar and troubled trajectory in Rome. This was a period marked by a sense of renewal during the short years of the Ottoboni papacy when opera returned to the public scene, followed by retreat, regulation, and prohibition of operatic practices under Alexander VIII's immediate successor. The handling of specific oratorio events during these years as managed by Cardinal Ottoboni's patronage proves to be a telling indicator of how the oratorio had developed malleable parameters of definition and practice in ways that did not seem to follow the kinds of strictures and genre maintenance reasoned by Spagna. In this important collision of discourse and practice we witness how the rhetoric of binary oppositions (secular versus sacred, or opera versus oratorio) was often powerfully deployed and yet concealed the more complex, exceptional, and adaptable qualities of the oratorio's cultural work within this critical period.

III

The oratorio in context: Ottoboni's *Sant'Eustachio* and the boundaries of genre

If the oratorio throughout much of the seventeenth century was defined in contrast to opera, then in the late century, during a period of more forceful ecclesiastic and moral reform, the opera–oratorio opposition was all the more intensified. There is an important irony, however, that emerges in this historical development. Rather than clarify the distinction and practice of the two genres, this rigidity of opposition notable in the period in effect complicated and blurred the boundary between opera and oratorio. I turn to the work of historian Renata Ago for a critical argument that may help to explain this phenomenon. In contrasting the austere papacies of Innocents XI and XII to the reign of Alexander VIII, Ago notes that historians have rarely delved deeply into the interplay between papal austerity and the political culture of the age. Her argument suggests that popes before Innocent XI pursued a monopoly of power through centralization of the production of artistic, cultural, and social events, whereas Odescalchi, Innocent XI, in the name of Christian piety and moral asceticism, relinquished festive occasions to lay nobility.[39] The oratorio provides a unique lens for exemplifying Ago's analysis. During Innocent XI's tenure, a new environment of secular repression appears to have reified the oratorio to some degree; oratorios did indeed proliferate in proportion to operas during Odescalchi's austere pontificate.[40] None the less, the ironic consequence is that the oratorio's greater ubiquity, along with its heightened symbolic opposition to opera, may have indeed encouraged papal regulators to ignore opera's influence on the oratorio, to turn a blind eye towards opera's traces. It did not appear to matter that the oratorio shared similarities with opera in its compositional construction, or in the details of its practice; what mattered was affirming its *historical* association with devotion and sacred culture. The result was that two distinct fields of the oratorio emerged: one that symbolically withdrew the oratorio from the present realities of its variegated practice; the other that shaped the oratorio around regulatory obstacles to fit the needs of a lay nobility, which, Ago notes, were now largely left unchecked. Perhaps we might come to see Innocent XI's critical withdrawal from the social scene as described by Ago as having helped to *widen* the gap in the oratorio's dual conception and practice, a tendency which had been present from the genre's early development when concessions to the pressures of secularization were first negotiated.

The oratorio's bifurcated nature often proved useful to patrons, especially clerical nobility whose social aspirations landed them in compromising situations when supporting opera and other festive entertainment.[41] The oratorio carried enough cultural capital as devotional ritual to efface some of the complications arising from the genre's less devotional potential. The hard language of contemporary edicts was often obfuscated in interpretation and practice. Crucial years followed Innocent XI's reign, when the Ottoboni papacy, short as it was, made the most of capitalizing on the vagaries of regulatory enforcement and legislative language. As Ago says, the papacies of Innocent XI and Alexander VIII could not better reflect diametrically opposed conceptions of the church and culture at large. The differences between these tenures were made manifest on the level of the festive and social, both important elements of papal sovereignty.[42]

Despite strong contrasts in leadership style and social politicking, Pope Alexander VIII was, at least at the outset, regarded in many ways as the inheritor of the legacy of Innocent XI. His election was unanimous in the conclave and he was embraced by the "Zelanti" for his dignity, morality, strength, and fairness.[43] Like that of his predecessor, his short papacy was focused on restoring the strength of the church and rights of the Holy See in the face of increased opposition and pressure from Europe's monarchal powers; the significant and effective difference was that Alexander VIII would do so through acts of conciliation, whereas Innocent XI worked from a position of inflexibility, a strategy that proved less effective.[44] But the Ottoboni papacy is remembered in cultural history less for its defense of church authority, than for its reversion to nepotism, building a familial dynasty through papal nephews, in a spirit akin to the years of the Barberinis, who employed familial connections to the pope to augment their prominence in Rome.[45] There is nothing equivocal about Alexander VIII's actions in such matters – upon becoming pope he summoned his relatives from Venice to Rome and placed them in important offices, bestowing upon them benefices that would provide great wealth and ensure their own longevity and future in the face of what he knew would be a brief papacy.[46] This turn of events would have significant consequences for the history of the arts, literature, and music, as it is well documented that Alexander VIII's great-nephew, Pietro, would become one of Rome's most beneficent and powerful patrons. Though he was elevated to cardinal and granted the position of the pope's vice-chancellor (a position he held for the remainder of his life), the young Ottoboni's true focus was less on ecclesiastical governance and directed instead towards his passions and pastimes as a collector, social intellectual, poet, and courtier.[47]

The Ottoboni patronage and artistic programs have received ample attention from a variety of scholars whose archival research and study of printed sources have done much to increase our knowledge of the papal nephews, especially of Cardinal Ottoboni and his impact on the Roman cultural scene in the last decade of the seventeenth century and first decades of the eighteenth.[48] However, for the purposes of this chapter, it is worth revisiting the early months of his great-uncle's ascendancy during which time the Ottoboni cultural agenda remained to be set, and when Cardinal Ottoboni took on the critical role of establishing his residence, the Cancelleria, as the secularized branch of the papal court. With the Cancelleria as their unofficial social headquarters, the Ottoboni family strove to bolster pontifical sovereignty and become the chief purveyors of cultural life in Rome. As was typical of the Roman environs of this time, the staging of private operas was an attractive, if not essential, symbolic gesture for asserting social status and displaying wealth. But operas staged by clerics were controversial, and if performed, they required careful management of presentation. In some instances, the need to uphold moral standards and messages, coupled with a desire to indulge social demands for secular entertainment, led to interesting outcomes. These events often purposely complicated the boundaries between sacred and secular, finding a peculiar balance between qualities that registered as operatic and those that were resolutely more devotional. A case in point emerged during the transitional months between the pope's inaugural carnival festivities and the ensuing Lenten period.

It is well known how splendorous and diverse was the entertainment that opened the carnival season of 1690. The papal nephews took an important lead in staging these events, both as artistic authors and as cultural ambassadors of the season's entertainments.[49] A few points, however, deserve special note. For one, it is important to flag the potential conflict that arose when Alexander VIII embraced such a festive cultural program. His permissive bent had its advantages, restoring a kind of splendor and vibrancy to Rome that many locals and resident nobility sorely yearned for during his predecessor's austere reign. There were also great personal and familial stakes in promoting the family's beneficence and status, although the air of worldliness that came with such activities and gestures had to be judiciously controlled. The immediate transition from the 1690 carnival season into Lent helps reveal the challenges of maintaining this precarious balance. For the purposes of this study, such a transition presents instances of exceptional genre manipulation, suggesting important consequences of the oratorio's contiguity with opera. I turn here to Cardinal Ottoboni's 1690 Lenten performance of *Il martirio di Sant'Eustachio* at the Cancelleria to observe how this work and its elusive genre identity illuminates the reworking of the boundary between opera and the oratorio, not merely for the sake of genre manipulation, but also for its utility of furthering the pope's political agenda.

Certain parameters of this event and the surrounding tensions are worth some consideration. As much as an air of festivity was established with the pope's opening carnival, it is also quite likely that in the ensuing Lenten period a retreat to a more somber tone of abstinence was expected. After all, the supporters of Innocent XI, the "Zelanti" who had promoted Ottoboni's pontifical appointment, did so on the grounds of his strong moral character, not his love of the arts.[50] At the same time, the social pressures for cultural ascendancy were strong, and it is possible that the papal family's careful selection of events for that first Lenten season was inspired by a need to reinforce their image as Rome's cultural leaders and most celebrated patrons, even of theatrical entertainment. For years, Roman opera culture thrived in the private households of the local aristocracy, with the Colonna theater among the most active and spectacular, especially during the later decades of the seventeenth century.[51] Opera at the Colonna theater stood as a model for noble entertainment, which though conducted in a private household, could symbolically convey its importance to a larger public. The Colonna family was also among the last true feudal families in Rome at the end of the seventeenth century, possessing economic, social, and political influence with which any papacy had to contend. It is likely that the Ottoboni nephews, and particularly Cardinal Ottoboni, entrusted with the promotion of the family's newfound social hegemony, made it their business to surpass other families, including the Colonna family, thereby recentering Rome's courtly culture around their own familial domain. This was especially critical in Rome, where the power dynamics between old and new aristocracy (and local versus non-Roman influence) affected papal governance.[52] The choices of musico-dramatic rituals during this first Lenten period may indeed reflect the Ottobonis' effort to establish a new order.

On Sunday February 26, 1690, Cardinal Ottoboni sponsored and presented *Il martirio di Sant'Eustachio* at the Cancelleria, with the libretto composed by the cardinal himself and the music by Flavio Lanciani.[53] It is difficult to assume a clear rationale behind the chosen subject of this work. St. Eustace's martyrdom was important to the church and to the cult in Rome devoted to him; moreover, the subject of St. Eustace had an intrinsic spectacular quality that was attractive to several seventeenth-century librettists, among whom were included Giulio Rospigliosi and Virgilio Mazzocchi, perhaps best known for their work *Il Sant'Eustacchio* (1643).[54] We also know

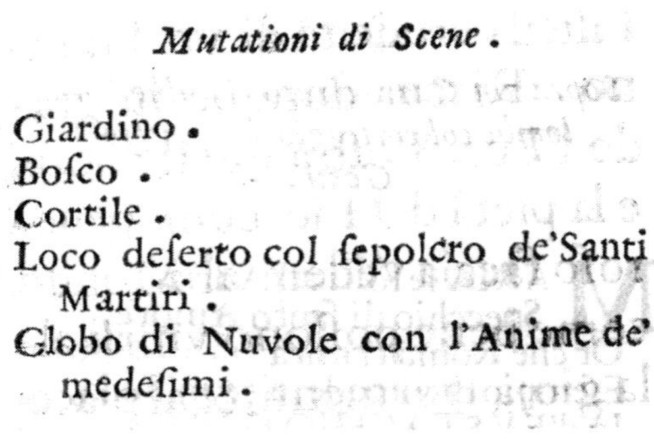

Mutationi di Scene .

Giardino .
Bosco .
Cortile .
Loco deserto col sepolcro de'Santi
    Martiri .
Globo di Nuvole con l'Anime de'
    medesimi .

Figure 2   Scene changes indicated in the libretto for *Il martirio di S. Eustachio, oratorio per musica*, 1690 (I-Rc, *Commedia* 81/1, fol. 5).

that Spagna composed a text based on the story of St. Eustace, collected in his second book of oratorios, *Il tronfo della fede nel martirio de'Santi Eustachio e compagni*. What is noteworthy is that Spagna considered his own version of *Sant'Eustachio* a "dramma scenico" (composed with a prologue and in three acts), though the published libretto suggests flexibility in performance as either an opera or an oratorio.[55]

As the first Ottoboni-sponsored performance at the Cancelleria, one possible interpretation could be that the story of St. Eustace, a martyred saint, stood as a symbol of generosity, good fortune, and unfailing faith, all features desirable for the Ottoboni papacy, with its hope of augmenting the pope's reputation as a restorer of public welfare.[56] For the purposes here, however, what is most interesting about this work and its performance is its quality of genre ambiguity, a trait that has not gone unnoticed.[57] From what we know of his dedication, Ottoboni underlined the appropriateness of a martyr story for the Lenten season.[58] And even if *Sant'Eustachio* was printed as an "oratorio," the cardinal conceived it as a dramatically staged work, complete with dancing and changes of scenery (see figure 2).

The production of *Sant'Eustachio* appears to have been well received. It was repeated several times during the remaining weeks of Lent and was sufficiently intriguing and important to have been mentioned in a number of sources, including news excerpts and letters. The cardinal's intentions appeared, however, transparent, as reports suggest that the oratorio title was merely conventional labeling for an otherwise staged *rappresentazione in musica*.[59] In some respects, *Sant'Eustachio* was *only* recognized as an opera, altogether dispensing with the work's alleged oratorio connection.[60] This oscillation in terminology is significant, and it would be wrong simply to dismiss *Sant'Eustachio*'s oratorio association as genre mislabeling, as some scholars have argued in their desire to define and solidify the stylistic boundaries between operas and oratorios.[61] The important issues in this case have little to do with internal stylistic properties of oratorios versus sacred operas. In fact, for the guests invited to the cardinal's palace who may have looked forward to an evening that resembled in form and presentation something closer to secular entertainment, such designations of genre may have mattered little, even if intuitively they understood the expected conventions of such specifications. But we might imagine that for the patrons, the oratorio's contiguity with opera was expedient and served as a powerful tool when considering the following.

For the Ottobonis, *Sant'Eustachio* and its ambiguous genre qualifications may have been critical for staging politics. To explore this idea, we must return to the months that preceded *Sant'Eustachio* and its performance. During their inaugural carnival, the Ottobonis were not the only family to stage opera. In addition to the gala performance of *La Statira* at the Tordinona, the other major theatrical event was the colossal production of *La caduta del regno dell'Amazzoni*, sponsored by the Ambassador to Spain and performed in the palace theater at the Colonna residence.[62] During the first weeks of Lent, the Ambassador to Spain had decided to restage this popular opera for private audiences. The ambassador's plans, however, perhaps were foiled as an *avviso* suggests that Alexander VIII specifically forbade the ambassador's opera until after Easter of that year.[63] Though it is difficult to truly probe the layered intentions of papal actions and official edicts, it does appear that in this case we might consider familial competition and the pope's desire to assert sovereign hegemony over powerful local nobility to have been operative factors. If this were indeed the case, then the sequence of events seems all the more telling. That the pope decided to prevent others from performing operas is one thing, but that members of his own family proceeded to prepare and perform an opera of their own during Lent under the provocatively thin façade of an "oratorio" title designation becomes much more noteworthy.

The significance of *Sant'Eustachio*'s oratorio designation cannot merely be passed off as an effect of the interchangeability of genre terms symptomatic of the period. In fact, it may tell a story of cultural politics, of social ascendancy, and of the intersecting and conflicting ambitions of Rome's aristocracy, as well as the essential role that opera played in such intersections, and the extent to which the oratorio had been drawn into this wider context and had become a malleable cultural form. The ritual of Lenten oratorios performed within the confines of private residences, often with the unstated aim of providing secular entertainment, can be traced to as early as the 1650s and possibly earlier.[64] *Sant'Eustachio* presents an interesting case because it was not composed as an oratorio per se. But the possibility of stylistic interchange between opera and oratorio in this 1690s moment is historically significant. This possibility represents an end point in the oratorio's long development, during which time operatic influences were internalized, and could be exploited or denied depending on performance context. The promotion and manipulation of an event such as *Sant'Eustachio* is a testament to the degree to which oratorios had become similar to opera, so much so that distinctions between the oratorio and opera could be treated in some instances as negligible. Most importantly, this example is suggestive of how knowledge of the oratorio may have been constituted. Here we have a compelling example of the way that agents – whom we can assume were well aware of the social utility of genres and the advantages that came with control over genre rituals – may have manipulated the range and flexibility of the oratorio. For Cardinal Ottoboni the ritual residue of the oratorio's devotional past was useful in so far as it suggested propriety merely through inclusion of the word "oratorio" in the work's title. The oratorio's historical scope as a genre was a powerful marker in negotiating the challenges and demands of performing *Sant'Eustachio* as likely more than a devotional occasion.

There are other considerations worth contemplating for the case of *Sant'Eustachio*. Even if the Ottobonis, for whatever reasons, did have carte blanche to perform operas in a Lenten season, perhaps a secular opera plot was not a natural first choice for the papal nephews. Arguably, the moral tenor of the story of a martyred saint was not only suitable for the Lenten season, but it also projected qualities of character and leadership this papal aristocracy desired and that served as an antidote to the blatant nepotistic maneuvers that were not well regarded by certain circles of Rome's dignitaries. It is also worth considering the possible historical connections of this event to past ones. Although the evidence is indirect, the Ottobonis may have shaped the performance and event of *Sant'Eustachio* to resemble the famed performances of other sacred operas sponsored by similarly "beneficent" papal sovereigns. An obvious example here is a work like *Sant'Alessio*, among the most memorable and celebrated events of the Barberini papacy, a work (as we know from Spagna) that served as a benchmark of dramaturgical, musical, and performative excellence even to this late period of the century. If we consider that crushing the competition in the arena of festive display was in part the Ottobonis' aim, then the spectacular and symbolic qualities associated with the legacy of events such as *Sant'Alessio* may have served as a motivation and model for the Ottobonis.[65]

What is most important about this single event is how it symbolizes the striking aesthetic juxtapositions in the oratorio of this period. After all, *Sant'Eustachio* is interesting not because it is really a sacred opera rather than an oratorio, but because it attests to the slippage that could exist between these devotional forms: an oratorio could flow somewhere between these two forms in style and practice, or could virtually become opera, in all but name. In fact, what we might characterize as the oratorio's two poles (secular extravagance at one extreme versus devotional modesty at the other) find new registers and configurations during this period, and in particular, within the circumscribed Ottoboni context where music, morality, politics, and social ascendancy – a hub of juxtaposed agendas – were constantly reshaped. The oratorio suitably reflects this assembly of depictions. Its inherited form, now all the more malleable, meant that the oratorio was able to accommodate a range of performative circumstances, which could be shaped by the degree to which the genre's respective poles were encouraged or restrained.

Works like *Sant'Eustachio* did not become the dominant form. Alongside examples of a few sacred operas were many occasions on which proper oratorios (unstaged sacred works divided into two sections) were performed on equal footing at the Cancelleria and in other similar private households. At the same time, these unstaged oratorios fulfilled a number of conventional roles, not just devotional or Lenten, but alternatively (and even simultaneously) courtly, political, intellectual, and social. What, then, were the remnants in these circumstances of a past oratorio ritual, and how were the elements of presentation, narrative framework, musical expression, and symbolic meaning reworked and rearranged in a context in which opera and oratorio had become so closely juxtaposed? A crucial level of the oratorio's generic and stylistic slippage was shaped by the construction of space; thus, one starting point is how the oratorio in such circumstances was aesthetically presented and visually "staged."

As witnessed in the case of *Sant'Eustachio,* the locale of the Ottoboni palace at the Cancelleria offers an unusually vivid glimpse into the cultural program of a patron who maneuvered a range of "staged" events with an aim of bolstering familial ascendancy and conveying noble grandeur. For this reason scholars of various disciplines have mined the archival traces surrounding this influential Roman household to uncover details that paint a picture of Cardinal Ottoboni's cultural life within the domain of the palace environment.[66] Maria Letizia Volpicelli has most thoroughly charted through documentation the many changes that took place at the Cancelleria in the cardinal's attempt to constitute within his palace the city's most important theater and the heart of Rome's cultural scene in these decades.[67] Yet Ottoboni's original plans for his theater would require revision and reinvention after he confronted several obstacles in the early years of its genesis. Tracing this process, we learn that the presentation of space became a means to construct and even mold various versions and ranges of "theatrical" activity. The oratorio was one of the cardinal's means to frame events that ranged from the semi-theatrical to the theatrical, and the genre's malleable signification – a complicated merging of both devotional and secular characteristics and associations – made it adaptable to conditional circumstances. The construction and manipulation of the theatrical space at the Cancelleria in the early years of the 1690s merits review for what it reveals about the different modes by which an oratorio could be constituted.

Staging the "theatrical" at the Cancelleria

The year 1690 becomes an important focal point for tracing Cardinal Ottoboni's theatrical program as he took on the role of the family's key cultural patron. Just in that first year of his great-uncle's papacy, opera performances at the Cancelleria outnumbered those at any other venue in Rome; between Easter and Christmas, Cardinal Ottoboni staged at least three different operas in his new residence.[68] During this period, the cardinal made use of the largest rooms in the Cancelleria for his opera productions, using temporary stages and seating for attendees.[69] It was soon clear, however, that the demand for more elaborate presentation of theatrical entertainment warranted a designated theater space. Cardinal Ottoboni and his father, Antonio, realized the advantages their own personal theater would confer. For one, private theaters rarely had to contend with the problems associated with larger urban gatherings, including the threat of unrest among spectators. Also, having one's theater adjacent to rooms and salons for after-performance refreshments and socializing eliminated any inconvenient changes from one location in the city to another.[70] But most importantly, privately owned theaters in Rome often seized the opportunity to stage operas outside carnival season, and to host such events throughout the year. By the spring of 1690, Ottoboni began making arrangements to build a permanent stage in what promised to be the most celebrated private theater in all of Rome.[71] It appears that Ottoboni had plans possibly to operate the theater as a commercial venture with the theater entrepreneur Jacopo d'Alibert.[72] Before this mission came to fruition and building was completed, however, the cardinal faced some unforeseen obstacles.

After months of preparation for the coming carnival of 1691, plans for the new theater at the Cancelleria were halted quite abruptly with the news of the death of Alexander VIII in the first week of February. Cardinal Ottoboni postponed all performances and officially announced his intention to mourn his deceased great-uncle for the remainder of that year. By the next carnival in 1692, cultural attitudes under a new papal leadership had shifted. It appeared that Innocent XII did not approve of the continuation of Ottoboni's theater project; the pope viewed the opera theater as not an appropriate institution for ecclesiastics to administer. Ottoboni dismantled the Cancelleria theater and terminated plans to build new theaters at San Lorenzo in Lucina (next to the residence of his uncle, Marco Ottoboni, at the Palazzo Ludovisi on via del Corso), and outside Rome in Albano, where the cardinal would erect a new church instead.[73]

Although Ottoboni was compelled to abandon his plans for an opera theater, dramatic-style entertainment at the Cancelleria did not cease; the cardinal sought alternatives. Within three years of the near-complete dismantling of his first theater project, Cardinal Ottoboni commenced new work, modifying the space and calling it *teatrino*, "little theater," or *teatro Novo dei Burattini*, "The New Theater of Puppets."[74] Though puppet dramas were not entirely exempt from papal oversight, it did seem that, in general, the absence of live actors/singers made them more acceptable and less susceptible to outright prohibition as live opera. Between 1694 and 1695, records show that Domenico Paradisi, the resident architect at the Cancelleria, transformed Ottoboni's theater to accommodate elaborate stage production with near life-size stick puppets used in the performance of musico-dramatic works.[75] The puppet theater and its productions had become the pet project of the cardinal. At least two works known to have been performed were set to sacred plots – *La Santa Genuinda* (*dramma sacro per musica*, 1695)[76] and *La Santa Rosalia* (*dramma per musica*, 1695)[77] – while another was set to a pastoral text: *L'amor eroico tra pastori* (*pastorale*, 1696).[78] These works were composed by the cardinal himself. With his theater transformed for puppets, Ottoboni successfully maintained his theatrical ambitions and the theater for which he played host remained one of the city's more important opera venues.[79]

What might these puppet productions have to do with the oratorio? In direct analysis, perhaps very little. Even though several of the puppet *commedie* staged at the Cancelleria were spiritual texts and stories of saints, stylistically they more closely resemble the *Sant'Eustachio* sacred opera model, with three acts, scene changes, the use of machines, and elaborated dramatic action. Once again, however, the importance of these juxtaposed and even interchangeable genres lies not necessarily in their internal stylistic character, but in their significance as performed event and calculated ritual. With the puppet productions, Ottoboni may have successfully bypassed most official prohibition by embracing a non-conventional, mechanical form of representation, thereby finding an unusual middle ground. This sort of maneuver and effort towards circumvention was common in this period, especially in a context marked by a deep sense of regulation, where inner/outer displays were highly shaped by political expectations and social norms. Within private palace walls, Rome's cultural elite had become highly skilled at designing their own performance solutions for events such as operas, ballets, masquerades, and other multimedia presentations by finding ways to exploit ambiguous boundaries. Beyond oratorios, we find a variety of creative solutions by patrons; for instance, in 1686, despite a papal edict prohibiting women from singing in public, we find reported in *avvisi* that Queen Christina commissioned a well-known singer ("la famosa Giorgina") to sing in several summertime serenatas performed outdoors in the queen's garden so that a larger public could enjoy "the harmonies" of Giorgina's voice even beyond the garden walls.[80]

We might come to define the oratorio as an example of this unusual "middle ground," a form with adaptable elements, which allowed it to run the gamut from opera-like ritual to devotional exercise, extremes that pulled in different directions, but served multiple needs. As others have noted, the Cancelleria offers a particularly rich locale for viewing the range and possibilities for presenting oratorios. In one celebrated case from 1705, the cardinal used the occasion of the August feast day of the Assumption of the Virgin to "stage" an oratorio – *Il regno di Maria assunta* – in the garden of the Cancelleria with a level of spectacle and pomp on a par with serenatas of the period.[81] Aside from the elements that were standard for such festive events, including numerous musicians, decoration, and lighting, a noteworthy feature at this performance was the hanging of a large transparent canvas depicting the Assumption of the Virgin, visual iconography of the oratorio's thematic essence. The visual association with the oratorio's theme and the iconographic depiction of action in an otherwise unstaged musical representation is an issue to which I will return. Here, it is important to observe the extent to which some oratorios took on theatrical gestures in their presentation.

For oratorios performed within the palace of the Cancelleria, the gestures were expectedly less grand, but at times similarly decorative and symbolic. We know that Ottoboni on occasion had his artistic staff prepare rooms for oratorio events.[82] It is likely that most pieces were performed in the Sala

Riara, the palace's largest room and major reception hall located on the *piano nobile*.[83] For more elaborate productions, the Sala could be transformed into a theater-like environment by erecting temporary seating and staging.[84] It is possible that Ottoboni ordered his staff to select tapestries or *arazzi finti* (canvases painted to mimic tapestries) to serve as iconographic backdrops for such performances, as described for the 1705 performance of *Il regno di Maria assunta*. Ottoboni may have used, for instance, tapestries from his collection depicting Old Testament narratives that were popular at the time, such as the stories of David or Judith and Holofernes, the latter being a favorite subject for two Ottoboni oratorios at the Cancelleria, to be discussed below.[85]

Spatial arrangements and décor can only tell us so much; in many respects, the room preparations and visual adornments made for oratorios at the Cancelleria were suited to a number of other musical as well as non-musical events. We must understand that spaces were constructed not merely by means of their decoration and arrangement, but also by the events that they were host to, and the rituals that would form their defining features and associative practices. To help parse the range of variation in palace-performed oratorios, which were as much inflected by external events and pressures as by internal compositional characteristics, we can turn again to Morelli's study. Take, for example, the elaborate "staging" of *Il regno di Maria assunta* during the summer of 1705. Much like a serenata, this oratorio served an overt political function, making direct gestures in its text for resolution among the warring monarchies over the succession to the Spanish throne.[86] Even palace oratorios prepared during the Lenten season rarely stood as self-contained and isolated works, but, as Morelli argues, were usually incorporated into a broader spectrum of activities sponsored by the resident patron. With Ottoboni at the Cancelleria, many of these activities were linked to the cardinal's erudite leanings and passion for music, two interests he married in his famed ongoing series of bi-weekly *accademie*. Morelli terms those *accademie* occasions at which oratorios were performed "spiritual academies." These events merged intellectual activity with the devotional season, and in presiding over them Ottoboni gained the support of Roman nobles who attended. The events might include, for example, an oratorio accompanied at intermission by a sermon or lecture, delivered by a well-known religious scholar or rhetorician.[87] Morelli cites a document from 1694 describing an oratorio at the Cancelleria that included a sermon by a Servite Father, who elaborated on the subject of Judith, the topic of the cardinal's oratorio.[88] The short length and convenient two-part sectioning made the oratorio an ideal choice for this type of hybrid academic gathering, which typically consisted of orations, sermons, or sonnets, inter-spersed with other instrumental musical interludes. Even when the practice of religious sermons fell out of favor, the two-part structure took on a new function, providing convenient pauses for festive intermissions with lavish refreshments.

Morelli concludes that from the early eighteenth century on, the oratorio in the Roman tradition progressively lost its devotional character and its function as a "spiritual academy," and increasingly served as secularized palace entertainment.[89] That may be true, though what seems noteworthy in this process is the persistent maintenance of genre and form. Whether tied to devotion and sermonizing or not, it appears that on some basic level the oratorio must have continued to serve the internal and external needs of the palace social sphere. Like the occasions for private opera, oratorios provided a venue to invite the outside in, to expose select guests to displays of beneficence and opulence in the hosting household, as well as to illuminate a patron's social and political affiliations through allegories subtly communicated by the choice of texts. What is telling is that the oratorio in this period did *not* become opera. Alongside three-act sacred dramas, patrons like Ottoboni continued to write and sponsor conventional oratorios, whose brevity and form must have appealed to the cardinal's and his audience's taste on some level. So, if the oratorio progressively dissociated itself from devotional associations and practices, why did the oratorio remain an oratorio?

The case of Ottoboni's and Scarlatti's *Giuditta* oratorios

It is difficult and rare to determine for any given oratorio performance of this period whether devotional or non-devotional activities took place alongside the musical performance, whether sermons were given or other, more secular orations were presented, or instead, whether reception ban-quets or intermissions were preferred. However, it is apparent that oratorios in this period did persist, even if their intention and style of presentation were gradually transformed within the private walls of Roman palaces. The Cancelleria oratorios performed during the prolific early years of Cardinal Ottoboni's patronage may help to tell this story.[90] From the few Ottoboni libretti we have, it does not appear that the cardinal necessarily followed Spagna's strict stand on the matter of rhyme, nor did Ottoboni shy away from opportunities to present textual settings conducive to aria writing. However, I would like to address the question of subject and its association to the aesthetic discourses and dramaturgical reform that Spagna discussed in his "Discorso intorno a gl'oratorii" of 1706. I turn here to a single case to address this question.

   Though it was not the only oratorio he wrote and sponsored, Ottoboni curiously took up the subject of Judith and Holofernes during his first decade as cardinal-patron more than once – first as librettist in his own version of *La Giuditta*, performed at the Cancelleria in 1694, then as sponsor of his father's libretto on the same subject, a second *La Giuditta*, performed at latest in the spring of 1697.[91] For musicologists, the great interest in the Ottoboni *La Giuditta* oratorios is that both libretti were set by Alessandro Scarlatti to remarkably different music.[92] There has been much said about these two scores and the contrast in their respective dramatic settings. Scholars speculate that the first *La Giuditta* (Naples) was intended for a larger audience and occasion, whereas the second *La Giuditta* (Cambridge) may have been written for a more intimate setting.[93] Certainly, it is in keeping with what we know about privately sponsored palace oratorios that circumstances for their presentation and performance could vary in intention and style.

   It is not surprising that the cardinal and his father found the Judith story compelling as an oratorio text. They were not alone. Musical and theatrical representations of Judith began to appear in the early part of the seventeenth century, and over time, these gained in popularity, especially as oratorios.[94] Judith's qualities of both chastity and sexual guile together with her traits of courage and aggression provided a subject rich with antinomic imagery of spirituality and worldliness. These contrasts lent the Judith story an inherent dramaturgical and musical malleability in oratorio settings. On some level, we could say this of several well-known biblical texts whose stories generated a series of oratorio works, albeit with diverse emphases. Not every version of David, Samson, Mary Magdalene, or Judith was the same; each librettist and composer drew out different nuances and qualities from these biblical templates. With the Judith story, the stress on eroticism, an effective means to the heroine's desired end, could have been particularly controversial.[95]

   The Book of Judith is an account of a Jewish heroine who uses deception and seduction to dupe Nebuchadnezzar's top general, the fierce and despotic Holofernes. With her nurse in tow, Judith crosses enemy lines to enter the Assyrian camp where she encounters Holofernes, flirts with him, watches him inebriate himself, then – at the moment when he is most vulnerable, in a tired, drunken stupor – she takes up his sword and decapitates him. With the general's severed head in hand, she departs for Bethulia having saved Judea from Assyrian invasion. In return, Judith is honored as God's devoted agent and Israel's fearless heroine.

For seventeenth-century critics and audiences, the means to Judith's heroic end was sometimes regarded as problematic. In 1675, one documented case suggests that an oratorio based on the Judith story was banned from performance at Santo Spirito in Sassia near Rome owing to the "amorous nature" of the text. The Passion story was chosen as a replacement, a performance believed to be far more appropriate to the occasion.[96] Arcangelo Spagna – though himself author of a *Giuditta* libretto[97] – generally steered readers of his "Discorso" away from erotic heroines. His recommendation was to avoid as much as possible any expressions of profane love, and thus, even when setting a story like that of Mary Magdelene, the key was to portray as boldly as possible her repentance and her acts of penitence and virtue, rather than her profane love.[98]

The Judith oratorios composed during the early years of Ottoboni's patronage allow us to view how the authors either embraced or avoided the question of spiritual restraint. Dubowy's analysis of the Ottoboni oratorios helps demonstrate the range of possibilities for portraying the erotic and heroic qualities of the story's female protagonist, demonstrating significant divergences between the two works. For example, the cardinal's *La Giuditta* (Naples) captures a strong, forceful Judith, who displays masculine and martial qualities, whereas Antonio Ottoboni's *La Giuditta* (Cambridge) tends to highlight the sly, coy Judith, who uses her feminine talent to fool a lust-stricken Holofernes.[99] It appears that representations of Judith could waver between the conservative moral terrain emblematic of most oratorios and the more liberal and profane world of opera. Nevertheless, it is possible that the strong, pious female exemplified by a figure like Judith still served as an antidote for the qualities embodied by the debased *prime donne* of the opera stage, especially during the later decades of the seventeenth century, when opera libretti had become particularly preoccupied with lascivious women and stereotypical erotic situations. Conservatives in Rome may have viewed Judith as a return to nobler theatrical heroines – women who clung to widowhood rather than succumbing to lust (even while exploiting lust to accomplish heroic deeds of faith).[100] Judith was traditionally seen as an example of noble Christian heroism, employing her faith to overcome heretical tyranny, irrespective of how librettists either exploited or suppressed the story's potential erotic nuances.[101] In fact, it is likely that the concern over the work's erotic reading was not nearly as important as the use of this biblical template to allegorize one of the story's dichotomies, Christian virtue and heroism versus Assyrian (i.e., Muslim) cruelty and hegemony, which held political currency during a time in which Rome and Catholic Europe were deeply embroiled in an effort to thwart Ottoman expansion.[102]

The subject of female agency in the seventeenth-century oratorio as compared with opera does deserve further scrutiny; the Judith story is but one recurring subject that could serve as an effective example.[103] In the case of the Judith oratorios performed at Cancelleria, the cardinal's intentions, or his interpretations of the erotic, heroic, or politically symbolic aspects of these works, are difficult to ascertain fully. For the purposes here, these two oratorio events are useful in addressing the question of heroism in musical drama more broadly, and in considering how the cardinal's predilection for the Judith story may have had strong resonance with other aesthetic currents that permeated this particular period and context. Recall Spagna's analogy between the oratorio and tragedy: both dramaturgical forms focused on distinctly singular protagonists who displayed nobility in character, and both adopted the moralistic overtones thought lacking in melodrama. Judith in the later *La Giuditta* (Cambridge) could be described as a more psychologically interior and introspective heroine who reflects on her motives, her effect on Holofernes, and the consequences of her act. The cardinal's first *La Giuditta* (Naples) captures the dichotomous qualities and antagonistic passions of virtue over vice, or good over evil, inherent in the Judith/Holofernes juxtaposition, as seen in other biblical subjects that had been adapted to oratorios and were well suited to the Aristotelian and catharsis-driven model of tragedy.[104]

There is an important, if unintended, connection worth considering here. The devotional oratorio and secular dramaturgical reform as separate and independent practices found a potent point of convergence during the waning years of the seventeenth century, perhaps especially effective within the palace context where rituals of devotion, Lenten practices, secular entertainment, and academic gatherings could mix with great fluidity. We cannot limit this phenomenon to the Ottoboni palace, yet the activities engaged there and the figures involved offer at least one venue in which such merging of rituals was likely to have occurred. We know that Ottoboni regularly held intellectual and social gatherings, his Accademie delle Belle Lettere e Musica, where many of the city's prominent literati and cultural critics (many of whom, like the cardinal, were acclaimed members of the Academy of Arcadians) convened. His oratorios performed during the Lenten season were, in all likelihood, integrated into these same academic rituals. It was also in this period in the 1690s that many of the figures associated with Ottoboni's *accademie*, and the social/intellectual circles of the Arcadians, were deeply invested in retracing Italy's literary history, and reconnecting to a perceived lauded past of high poetic style and dramaturgical form. Reviving and strengthening a tradition of Italian tragic drama (largely by following French models) was seen as a critical cultural direction.[105] We know that not all involved were convinced that opera was the appropriate medium for the future of tragedy. Within this network of literati, several harbored great doubts about opera and it is possible that a few began to recognize qualities in the oratorio that paralleled classical principles of tragic drama. Both tragedy and the oratorio centered on the protagonist's inner struggle, and in rendering this process, it appeared that both genres could display a wide range of the soul's passions (particularly those in dynamic opposition, e.g., virtue and vice) with a human intensity that was thought to be sorely missing from contemporary melodrama. In essence, the oratorio genre could have been regarded as a better expressive and dramaturgical model for charting a reformed musico-dramatic future.

We may not be able to link specific oratorio events, such as the Judith oratorios presented at the Cancelleria (whether performed as spiritual academies or as secular entertainment) with any particular reform discourse. Yet the confluence of these works, their chosen subject matter, the space(s) in which they were performed, the socio-cultural factors that shaped their presentation, and the agents and audiences who supported them were arguably conditioned by a similar collective mentality that consciously or unconsciously shared systems of representations (e.g., oratorios and tragic dramas) and certain values (e.g., religious and cultural politics along with dramaturgical reform) without the need to make these systems explicit. The question posed earlier of why the oratorio remained an oratorio in the context of the palace sphere, where form, style, and practice could acquire new parameters, takes on heightened significance when considered with these influences in mind. Genre maintenance in this respect requires further scrutiny and explanation. True, certain characteristic elements of the oratorio genre were curiously maintained despite the loosening of devotional strictures. Yet it is possible that what appeared to be maintained was actually reconceived to provide new meaning. The qualities and conventions that had been adapted to fit the oratorio's devotional rituals (its biblical texts, sententious tone, and two-part structure) were newly enlisted and conceptually transformed to serve as the basis of good tragedy; and the qualities of morality, stripped from a strictly devotional milieu, came to serve not only as religious edification, but also as broader *cultural* edification. Later, we will come to see that the very concerns and anxieties that arose in the context of the oratorio were also among the intersecting forces that affected the future course of musical drama.

I return to Scarlatti's two *La Giuditta* scores written for the Ottoboni circle at least in part to explore these questions. In doing so, I also introduce concerns that Spagna covered in his "Discorso" over the relationship of the oratorio to opera. My purpose in juxtaposing Spagna's anxieties with Ottoboni's selective practices is to reveal further how the oratorio in this historical context offers a lens for viewing many of the same polemics, apprehensions, and agendas that arose in the larger effort to direct the future course of musical drama.

IV

"Seeing" with the ear

When audiences or libretto souvenir seekers purchased Giacomo Komarek's print of Cardinal Ottoboni's *La Giuditta*, their eyes would have first met an iconic image: Judith, sword in her right hand, triumphantly raising the severed head of Holofernes with her left (see figure 3). There is something quite theatrical about this image, a striking quality of the print in light of the oratorio's actual *absence* of staging in performance. Readers are invited to peer behind the curtains, drawn back by majestic twin eagles. Below this proscenium stands Judith, front and center, with her neck brazenly exposed, and her dress skirt whipping around her body as if twisting in action. To her right lies the expired, decapitated general on his bed, with sword and shield at his feet, his trustworthy weapons that did little to protect him during Judith's apparently unassuming visit. In the distance, we see tents of the Assyrian army set upon the fields below Bethulia. Not all oratorio prints were as resplendent and theatrical as this one, though aspects of the engraving may partially mirror iconography that could have been displayed during oratorio performances. We know that patrons like Ottoboni often hung paintings or tapestries with select images of an oratorio's subject as a thematic backdrop to capture the story's great heroic moment. What appears characteristic of such images is the extent to which they evoked not merely a scenic backdrop but an actual symbolic moment of action linked to the moral or theme of the drama.[106]

Audiences holding the *La Giuditta* libretto adorned with its theatrical engraving were likely to have been somewhat familiar with the visual iconography associated with this biblical tale. During the early modern period, the Book of Judith inspired a number of artistic representations, several cultivating one or more of the story's various themes, but often focusing on Judith's heroic virtues and the moment of Holofernes' murder.[107] In some cases, the subject of Judith was represented by intimately personal

Figure 3 Arnoldo van Westerhout, engraving from the frontispiece of the libretto *La Giuditta, oratorio*, 1695 (I-Rc, Vol. Misc. 1638/5). This 1695 version of the title page is the same as the original version, first published in 1693 with the same engraving, copy held at I-Rn (34.1.ʟ.39/5). Franchi reports from his research that the oratorio was likely performed (and libretto sold) in a number of other cities; see *Drammaturgia romana I*, 664.

and voyeuristic interpretations, conveying cryptic messages known to the artist and to few others. The seventeenth-century painter Artemisia Gentileschi repeatedly returned to Judith's story for her most remarkable works, and her depictions of the story are perhaps the most violent representation of Judith's murderous act in all of baroque painting.[108] In the famous

Figure 4 Michelangelo Merisi da Caravaggio, *Judith and Holofernes*, c.1598 (Rome, Galleria Nazionale dell'Arte Antica).

Caravaggio representation of *Judith and Holofernes*, the murderess was modeled after Beatrice Cenci, a young Italian noblewoman beheaded for parricide (see figure 4). Some have suspected that the withered maid accompanying Judith in the painting could be Beatrice's mother and co-conspirator against her father's tyranny.[109]

The Caravaggio painting offers some useful points of analysis for considering the association of images in non-staged performances such as oratorios. Even if the artist had fallen out of circulation or had become less relevant by the latter part of the century, his painting serves as a prototype for understanding the physicality of this scene, and for the transformation of a hideous moment into pictorial splendor. Caravaggio's image delineates the symbolic polarities embedded in the story's structure: a pensive Judith stands erect, glowing and rising above a darkly shadowed, debased Holofernes, who struggles for his last gasp of life in excruciating torment. In this image, light contrasts with dark, heroine overcomes oppressor, and good prevails over evil. This visual example highlights the story's emblematic extremes, the same dichotomous qualities that inspired settings of oratorios and were associated with tragic drama in which contrasting characters and emotions were boldly delineated. Yet, in paintings like Caravaggio's, the graphic representation strikingly freezes the moment of murder. With one swift motion, Judith thrusts the sword through Holofernes' contorted neck, an action that is finalizing and brief. The painting's real horror lies in the fact that we see rather than hear the silence of Holofernes' scream. Using similar images, such as Caravaggio's *Testa di Medusa*, Slavoj Zizek describes such images as the "placeholder for a sound that doesn't yet resonate but remains stuck in the throat . . . the obverse of the voice that gives body to what we can never see, to what eludes our gaze."[110] In a fundamental way, much of theater, especially spoken tragedy, was grounded in giving body to what we can never see, a preference for the verbal account over the physical enactment of events. No theater practice in the seventeenth century would have permitted the enactment of murder onstage, as all horrific events, especially in tragedy, were relegated to the offstage world where violence, illness, sexuality, and all other "unseen" events could occur. As John Lyons writes, "One way of conceiving the offstage world is to picture it as the reality which is filtered to us through the stage."[111]

Yet for any playwright or librettist, the act of Judith beheading Holofernes was the ultimate dramatic moment – the symbolic placeholder of the story – and one that likely called to mind a powerful array of known imagery, allowing audiences to conjure a vivid picture of the unseen scene. For the oratorio author, the calling forth of powerful images was precisely what Spagna recommended, "to suggest in the minds of the listeners the theme being treated, which they can interpret and comprehend from the personages who speak, even if their figure is not exposed to the eye, but only to the ear."[112] In several ways, the oratorio thus had its advantages over staged theater. The absence of the visual broke down tragedy's onstage/offstage dichotomy allowing audiences to imagine the "unseen" *and* the "seen." Music furthermore offered an unparalleled sonic landscape that helped to paint the emotional nuances of verbal accounts and cued envisioned scene changes or imagined happenings.

In the case of an oratorio subject such as that of Judith, what then becomes the musical equivalent of the visual placeholder and the symbolic turning point of a work so controversially violent and sensual? In truth, Judith's act of murder – what seemed so attractive and effective as a subject in art – was, in large part, the least interesting moment musically. The murder scene in most scores is typically reduced to very little, a fleeting sonic trace, sometimes a simple jagged bass line to represent Judith's final blow. The visual medium can gloriously arrest this moment in time, capturing through pose, color, and motion all the allegorical nuances suggested in one moment of action. But the medium of music has a different goal. It works linearly, moving across time through the paces of this otherwise short-lived action. Conversely then, it is the buildup to this passing moment, the individual verbal accounts and dialogue between personages that provided the composer the musical "body" to constitute the emotional impact captured in visual shorthand in paintings or engravings of the time. In the oratorio, it is arguably the musical voice that gives body to the unseen, albeit with a different, but no less potent, form of expressiveness. We must recall how Spagna understood this, citing the aria for its powerful musical embellishment and ability to keep an audience in rapt attention.[113]

The oratorio thus presents some unique narrative considerations. Like operatic discourse, the late seventeenth- and early eighteenth-century oratorio had similarly wagered its aesthetic attraction upon the aria as the central node of dramatic interest. Yet, perhaps different from opera was the tendency for oratorios to be linked thematically to a single symbolic act rather than a complex series of moments, interconnected scenes, and subplots. In his study of the two *Giuditte* of Alessandro Scarlatti, Dubowy observes the dramaturgical and corresponding musical differences this creates. He explains that opera usually follows a livelier and more diverse rhythm of actions; the oratorio by contrast indulges in an elongated process of a more singular, emotionally wrought sequence, with a temporal structure that is much slower, to permit "the painting of an image of these dimensions," which, as he suggests, is not entirely possible in opera.[114] In essence, the oratorio (and similarly, tragedy) more extensively focuses its energy upon reflection, revelation, and catharsis, less so on action. It unfreezes the iconic dramatic moment and works up to it slowly by parsing through its layered allegorical dimensions and oft-used dichotomous symbols of good and evil. For example, the subject of Judith overcoming Holofernes does not exclude the finalizing violent act of decapitation, but it can distribute in a more complex way the notion of "doing violence" across the drama's reflective musical rendering. Using the cardinal's *La Giuditta* (Naples), we can affirm that tension builds not in the moment of murder, but in anticipation of violence embodied in an extended solo aria that unfolds during the internal monologue leading to Judith's final blow. As we see from the discussion of the musical examples that follow, the story's symbolic climax is expressed in the voice itself. Judith as heroine overcomes her enemy not really with the sword as much as through song.

In Cardinal Ottoboni's libretto, the "scenes" for this narrative take place alternately in the besieged Jewish community of Bethulia and in the camp of the Assyrians. In the oratorio's first section, Judith displays her moral virtue and courage in her resolution to confront the aggressive threat facing her

Example 1 Alessandro Scarlatti, *La Giuditta*: aria, "La tua destra" [1], 1694 (US-MT).

Giuditta	Judith
La tua destra, o sommo Dio,	[May your right arm, almighty God,
che ferir suole i tiranni . . .	which usually strikes down the tyrants . . .]

people. This first section also introduces Holofernes, in all his confidence and haughtiness, as the imposing Assyrian general. It is in the second section of the oratorio that all the awaited action takes place, specifically in the scene of climax between Judith and Holofernes. The events that precede Holofernes' murder follow the original biblical narrative: Judith seduces the general, but diverts his advances by persuading him to rest first. Putting Holofernes to sleep is therefore the pivotal plot device for Judith's action, but it also provides the occasion for musical embellishment as sleep or the realm of dreams had long been a means to justify song as lullaby in opera. Dubowy recognizes the power and utility of the onstage song or "realistic music" as one of several kinds of dramatic expression that oratorios adapted from musical drama.[115] In *La Giuditta* (Naples), Scarlatti employs onstage music not merely to justify singing through the rendering of a lullaby, but also to enact musically Judith's seductive and deceptive blow. She performs three songs in her attempt to lull Holofernes to sleep. The first, "La tua destra," is unusually discomfiting, since so little of the music cues the expected conventions of a lullaby. Dry and fatal broken chords fill moments of silence with an eerie suspense, and the alluring lyricism of Judith's melody is strangely out of phase with the beating pattern of the accompaniment, creating a sense of disorientation (see example 1).

Example 2 Alessandro Scarlatti, *La Giuditta*: recit. dialogue, "Troppo funesto,"
followed by the aria "La tua destra" [2], 1694 (US-MT).

Oloferne	*Holofernes*
Troppo funesto, o bella,	[My beauty, the tenor of this song
è del canto il tenor.	is too mournful.]
Giuditta	*Judith*
Son questi i voti	[With this prayer
che il popol di Giudea manda al suo Nume.	the people of Judea beseech their God.]

(*cont.*)

Example 2 (*cont.*)

Oloferne	*Holofernes*
Ma voti sparsi invano,	[But the prayer is said in vain,
se contro d'Oloferne	if the arrows in the hand of the Thunderer
crolleran del Tonante i dardi in mano.	will fall against Holofernes.]
Giuditta (aria)	**Judith** (aria)
La tua destra, o sommo Dio,	[May your right arm, almighty God,
che ferir suole i tiranni...	which usually strikes down the tyrants...]
Oloferne	*Holofernes*
Non so per qual cagione il cor s'affanni.	[I do not know why my heart aches.]

In reaction to this music, Holofernes becomes disturbed by the mood of Judith's ambiguous song, interrupting her and urging her to stop the disquieting melody. Judith, however, ignores the general's request and moves from directly addressing him to addressing God (see example 2). Holofernes provides a quick retort, attempting confidently to dismiss her prayers and to reassert his authority, though ultimately, his bravado is overcome by Judith's persistent lullaby. In fact, what occurs in this short sequence of dialogue and aria provides a persuasive argument for the power of song. When Judith's words are sung as recitative Holofernes apparently shows no fear of Judith's words, but when she resumes her incantatory music (a repeat of the first song, "La tua destra"), her lullaby penetrates his consciousness, making his "heart ache" in ways that her recitative failed to incite.

Less a lullaby than a provocation, Judith's musical supplication, through repetition, eventually acquires a particular force. Her song infuses Holofernes' heart and soul and overpowers his body. It gradually casts a spell and enchants him into a slumbering stupor, which Scarlatti captures in a simple chromatic descending bass line. At this point Judith's plot is nearly fulfilled, leaving only decapitation as her final act.

But before taking up Holofernes' sword, the heroine completes her onstage performance with a third and final song – a more complete, through-composed aria of "La tua destra," this time embellished with expanded instrumental accompaniment (see example 3). The additional orchestration of Judith's now complete aria fills in the stark and suspenseful pauses of the mere skeleton that made up the first two interrupted versions of "La tua destra." In this third rendition, Judith finally completes her thought, accompanied by flutes, strings, and continuo, which overlap in a layering effect to fill out the melodic architecture. Dubowy notes how this piece is "plurifunctional" – it merges the realistic lullaby music (happening in real time), with a kind of reflective monologue/dialogue (moved outside the temporal scope of the drama) as Judith debates the constancy of her courage while asking God for strength to finish her task.[116] What we should further consider is the way this aria moves internally to probe Judith's wavering spirit, her doubts, and private conflict, eliciting a less one-dimensional and more complicated conception of her heroism. More like the Caravaggio painting than the libretto engraving, "La tua destra" is a musical version of a pained Judith, with frightened scowl on her face, pulling herself to action.

But in a sense, hasn't Judith already completed the necessary act? Arguably it is her song that kills Holofernes as effectively as any single blow. It is through the suspenseful approach to Judith's act of murder that all aspects of this vivid symbolic moment are unraveled and complicated. Music invariably works as the essential catalyst, using multiple strokes to underscore Judith's deception, her aggression, her piety, her doubt, and her triumph; for Holofernes, music is the looming shadow of a danger and pain he cannot recognize but that, none the less, he can physically fathom.

Indeed, this first *La Giuditta* (Naples) makes a convincing case for the oratorio's aesthetic capacity for lingering reflection and potent catharsis. Moreover, it argues forcefully for music's particular effectiveness in relating drama. We see this most clearly in the parallel scene composed by Scarlatti

Example 3 Alessandro Scarlatti, *La Giuditta*: aria, "La tua destra" [3], 1694 (US-MT).

Giuditta	Judith
La tua destra, o sommo Dio,	[May your right arm, almighty God,
che ferir suole i tiranni,	which usually strikes down the tyrants;
in cimento così strano	grant this hand strength
doni forza a questa mano,	in this unwonted trial,
acciò tronco il capo rio	so that by severing the evil head
giunga fine a tanti affanni.	it may end our suffering.]

for the second *La Giuditta* (Cambridge) with libretto by Antonio Ottoboni. Like the first *La Giuditta*, Holofernes' sleep scene is the precursor and conduit to his ultimate murder. Yet the narrative progression to this moment is somewhat different. The intensified dynamic of the oratorio's smaller cast makes for a unique pacing and approach to the same story. In the first part, Judith and her Nurse debate the bold and controversial action Judith proposes, the section ending with Judith's arrival at the Assyrian camp and her first encounter with Holofernes. In this version of the story, Holofernes is more cunning and astute, recognizing Judith's ruse of seduction, yet admitting his own attraction. In the second part of the oratorio, he courts Judith, inviting her to his banquet table. After partaking in food and drink, he willingly gives in to Judith's offer to comfort him upon her breast as

Example 3 (*cont.*)

Example 3 (*cont.*)

he falls asleep. Again, Norbert Dubowy's analysis offers a useful guide for
understanding some of the music's compositional choices for this narrative
climax. He notes that in following the libretto, Scarlatti uses the same
convention of realistic music – a lullaby – to convey similar tension and
ambiguity as in the first *Giuditta*. But this time the protagonist does not
sing; instead, in response to Judith's request for assistance, it is the *Nurse*
who "sings" a gentle tale.[117] In her story, Judith's Nurse relates the account
of Samson's great downfall, the story of a man who also loses his power to
a woman while sleeping. Through the Nurse's parable the librettist stages a
critical moment of situational irony. He creates a *mise en abyme*, a powerful
interlude of reflexivity, by folding the nurse's narrative into the larger story
of the oratorio (see example 4).

In the narrative section that precedes the lullaby "Dormi, o fulmine di
guerra," the Nurse relates her tale as a recitative with obbligato accompaniment, which provides both expressive emphasis and yet a clarity of
execution that is all the more ironic when paired with the deceptive intention she and Judith share. More importantly, the Nurse delays her aria until
an essential musical moment. She turns to singing a lullaby in response to
Holofernes' distress at hearing her story, a gesture that is ostensibly meant
to be calming. Yet, with the biblical analogy of Delilah's lullaby to Samson

Example 4 Alessandro Scarlatti, *La Giuditta*: recit., "Canterò di Sanson, l'Ercole ebreo," and aria, "Dormi, o fulmine di guerra," 1697 (GB-Ckc).

Nutrice	*Nurse*
Canterò di Sanson, l'Ercole ebreo.	[I shall sing of Samson, the Hebrew's Hercules.
Ardea di fiamma impura per nemica bellezza	For an enemy beauty, a lewd flame
Sanson, cui diede il Cielo oltre natura	burnt in Samson, whom Heaven had given
pregio d'insuperabile fortezza.	an incomparable strength, surpassing all
Del crine, origin vera	natural forces. Delilah, by flattering him,
del suo vigor, potè scoprir l'arcano	discovered the secret of his hair,
Dalila lusinghiera.	the real source of his vigor.
Armò Parca omicida	The death-dealing Fate armed
di forbice la mano,	her hand with a pair of scissors;
e perchè non ardia	since she did not dare
troncar s'ei non dormia la fatal chioma,	to cut his hair while he was still awake,

(*cont.*)

| gli fe' guancial del seno ond'ei dormisse, | the Philistine siren made a pillow of her |
| la filistea sirena, e così disse: | own bosom to have him sleep, and said:] |

Oloferne

Che racconto funesto!

Holofernes

[What a woeful tale!]

Nutrice

Posa, posa, Signor, ch'e lieto il resto.
Dormi, o fulmine di guerra,
scorda l'ire;
già provasti ch'a ferire
l'arco e dardo d'un bel ciglio,
d'un bel guardo,
han vigor ch'i forti atterra.
Dormi &c.

Nurse

[Peace, my Lord, the rest of it is merry.
Sleep, thunderbolt of war,
forget your wrath;
you have already proved
that the bow and arrow of a fair eye
of a fair glance,
have as much strength as to fell a brave man.
Sleep &c.]

---

already embedded in the Nurse's previous narrative, Scarlatti uses the referential lullaby as the musical frame to stage the plot for Holofernes' murder.

Dubowy recognizes the sectional and conceptual break caused by the distinction between accompanied recitative and realistic song, the latter standing apart from any other solo in the score.[118] The aria's significance, however, deserves further elaboration. Several significant compositional choices and use of conventions help to efface a sense of time and place during this moment, such as the hypnotic ground bass ostinato that is heightened by the plodding note repetitions in the strings, along with the somnolent melody of long-sustained notes on "Dormi," that evolves into the gentle oscillation of the arpeggiated phrase on "guerra" (see example 4). These musical compositional elements unambiguously invoke a lullaby and appear to captivate the general, calming him, momentarily carrying him outside the context of the story, and inducing his slumber – he no longer seems disturbed by the tale and falls fast asleep. Using an ABA format, the aria's recapitulation of the "Dormi, o fulmine di guerra" section (the opening version of this music is shown in example 4) works to intensify the effect of temporal delay or erasure by recycling the same music. In fact, we might argue that this aria extends beyond the text and situational context. Its musical elements effectively work to daze the audience and compel them, like Holofernes, to forget what horror awaits outside the musically enveloping subconscious world of sleep. This oratorio reveals how music is all the more seductive, deceptive, and even horrific, not in how it depicts, but in how it *erases* the anticipated image of violence: with song, the visual template of murder momentarily disappears.

When we consider the *La Giuditta* examples in light of Spagna's position argued in his "Discorso," two points deserve some review. In one sense, Ottoboni and his father did not violate all of Spagna's principles. Yes, as in most vocal dramatic music of this generation, their arias were prominent and sometimes written in ternary/*da capo* form. However, we might also argue that, as librettists, they were not audacious in their use of song, and that they did seem to find literary reasons for musical expression and use of formal devices, with arias often effectively and delicately serving the given text. However, if for Spagna oratorios were a conduit to better listening practices, with their emphasis on what was not seen but what was heard, then the two examples discussed here present an interesting conundrum. The unparalleled sonic landscape now enhanced by a greater musical presence might well call forth powerful images and themes – of the kind Spagna hoped for – but music also had the potential to release a host of images, sensations, and ideas beyond the narrative framework. Worse yet (for someone like Spagna), in certain moments of the drama music might erode textual signification altogether.

Reflections

It is important to recognize how the 1697 *La Giuditta* (Cambridge) is somewhat unique in the oratorio oeuvre of this period. Several scholars have noted this; at least by comparison with the earlier Scarlatti *Giuditta* oratorio, this later one has a more focused, introspective, and more psychologically revealing tone, with a reduced cast of three, allowing for longer, singular moments of reflection that could be matched by musical embellishment.[119] At the same time, it is also critical to note that certain aesthetic tendencies recognized in Scarlatti's 1697 *La Giuditta* were not completely anomalous either. We could point to a number of oratorios from the period in which this compositional approach was prevalent.[120] Admittedly, the Book of Judith, with bold storylines of seduction and deception, lent itself well to musical discourse that displaced the action in favor of expression in song. The oratorio's particular qualities of heroism and reflection, and its depiction of strong contrasts of character and affect, evoked an important dramaturgical tendency that would come to shape the future of musical drama in the early eighteenth century. One could even argue that the oratorio registered these qualities before they were conventionalized in opera composition. In fact, the oratorio had long been a vehicle for dramatizing inner reflection, moral struggle, and emblematic qualities, either in narrative-driven libretti or in the allegorical meditations more prevalent in the earlier seventeenth century. By the end of the century, however, two factors external to the oratorio bore considerable influence on its modes of signification: tragedy and operatic language. The ever more pervasive interest in tragic drama during these transitional decades does seem to have deepened the oratorio's heroic and morally driven tendencies. This soul-searching introspection, captured vividly in singular moments of reflection, encouraged effective musical means for conveying emotion. As for all vocal dramatic music of the period, the aria had become the most powerful vehicle for relaying the soul's mixture of passions, and was the ultimate opportunity for musicality.

Yet tragedy and music were odd bedfellows. In one way, they seemed a perfect match: the reflective and contemplative qualities of the tragic narrative were ideal for musical settings. Music could take the most compelling dramatic moment of a tragedy and enhance, lengthen, even distinguish that moment's expressive force. It was these very qualities that Spagna noted while writing oratorio libretti, acknowledging the powers of musical expression not just in recitative, but also in the aria. Spagna also recognized the potential conflict music posed. As we know, he believed librettists should exercise restraint to limit the number of arias, make certain they strictly serve the text, and avoid any imposed musical demands (effected by singers) that lengthened text or took unnecessary repeats.

Spagna's concerns reflect both knowledge and denial of the oratorio's reconciliation with music. Let us return to the problems of denial; first, consider the knowledge Spagna had acquired. It appears he realized that a profound incompatibility existed between text and music. As literary drama, the oratorio, like tragedy, worked on the principle of instruction, in many cases using the concept of moral purification or catharsis, in which fear of the wicked and sympathy for the good were meant to be aroused in spectators. Yet, as Reinhard Strohm recognized in his discussion of musical tragedy, "this created an aesthetic difficulty. What had good and bad, right and wrong to do with music?"[121] Or more specifically, what would happen when music delighted *more* than it instructed? The anxiety expressed in Spagna's writing suggests that he shared this concern and that no matter the style of dramatic writing, or the direction of its intentions – spiritual, moral, cathartic – music threatened to eclipse prose, to disassociate itself from the direct tethers of word and engage its own sort of efficacy.

What is remarkable is that in spite of this potential conflict, Spagna wanted to retain a musical element in the oratorio, taking a line of argument similar to that of his contemporaries who argued for the viability of a *tragedia in musica*. The oratorio and tragic opera share important features. Many of the recommendations to reshape opera in a tragic guise – to avoid plots filled with complex intrigue, privilege stories with simple, direct, and stoic themes – were the same recommendations offered for the oratorio genre, which were accomplished more successfully and often with greater dramaturgical ease than in opera. In practice, however, neither the oratorio nor tragic opera really worked around the potential problem of musical excess. For opera, the dominating presence of music was unalterable. Even the most conservative librettists and revisionist critics hardly had the final word. Most succumbed to the pressures of singers and audiences, or to the commercial demands of patrons and impresarios for musically resplendent moments.[122] It might be thought that in Rome, where opera and other dramatic vocal music flourished beyond public theater, these pressures might be diminished. Yet even non-commercial and non-operatic environments sought to exploit the sheer power of music to move and delight. Consider the oratorio. The palace-performed oratorio in particular captures the two extremes of this conflict, heightening the genre's inherent tension between appropriated musical extravagance and its tradition of devotional modesty and moralistic proscription. Though tied to the notion of a "spiritual" exercise, oratorios were often multi-functional and could very well serve as entertainment while maintaining their categorical association with devotion.

Curiously, this was not how Spagna "remembered" the oratorio. From his perspective on morality and his exalted standards of dramaturgy, the oratorio could never be considered pure entertainment. And, most certainly, there could be no acknowledgment of any deeply revealing parallels between opera and the oratorio. If anything, Spagna's underlying rhetorical impulses might be read as a reform polemic symptomatic of the era, as a way to demonstrate how the oratorio could in fact exceed opera. With the spiritual, emotional, moral, and aesthetic compression it offered, the oratorio could remedy opera's failures and reform musical drama. Even if not specifically delineated in his prose, we might acknowledge that the spirit behind Spagna's essay is essentially nostalgic. It insinuates that the oratorio might indeed be the preferred conduit to a previous era. The oratorio harkened back to an earlier period when the sanctity of devotion and learned authorship were deeply protected, before the troubling aspects of opera's influence took hold. For Spagna, the memory of this past and the reality of current practice seem to meld precariously, allowing him simultaneously to assimilate and reject opera's cues, and to deny any real infractions of musical excess in oratorio writing of the day. Spagna's history is thus inherently selective. He presents the oratorio's historical development as one that purged and occluded the oratorio's other spheres of cultural work, when ritual ventured beyond the bounds of the strictly devotional.

The oratorio did indeed capture a range of discursive practices, tensions, and reconciliations emblematic of this historical moment. We need only to pair Spagna's historical enclosures with Ottoboni's more flexible practices in order to show how oratorios could be thought to remain seemingly immune from and yet participate in a more ostensible secularized presentation. The perception and use of the oratorio by these two men help to illustrate key cultural features that brought the genre into a contestable relationship to opera. Ottoboni pushed the undeniably fluid boundaries between opera and oratorio that Spagna sought to demarcate and reify. As seen through their respective orientations the oratorio allows us to view the convergence of multiple discrepant fields – conservatism, rising secularism, progressiveness, and reform.

If an oppositional relationship between the oratorio and opera was deepened in Spagna's rhetoric, for Ottoboni the areas of genre overlap provided opportunities to further his cultural, social, and artistic patronal agenda. Oratorios provided a platform for the dissimulation of opera by emphasizing the oratorio's difference of content, form, and devotional rituals; but when convenient, oratorios were also an opportunity for the *simulation* of opera's cultural capital for assumed grandeur. This phenomenon reveals the two distinct fields of the oratorio that emerged largely because a gap had formed between genre perception and genre practice. The inherent malleability embedded in the possible range of oratorio presentations and their respective meanings recalls Renata Ago's theory of "unchecked lay nobility," which may have resulted when conservative pontiffs willingly became out of touch with the cultural practices of their day in their desire to uphold a more singularly moral and non-secular agenda; festive practices had been relinquished to other nobility.[123] Ottoboni – even though holding a clerical title – had similar social ambitions at stake to those of other noble dynasties in Rome, especially when the protection of his family's papal sovereignty ceased. Like other nobles, any occasion of musical and artistic performance had potential social appeal. His status and cultivated taste demanded that all platforms of music and drama, devotional or not, were meant to be entertaining if they were equally to perform a social duty and function as a cultural commodity. This meant employing the most sought-after composers and the best singers to set and perform music regardless of its textual and affective medium. The key was that music was the main object of delight and entertainment regardless of the degree of devotionalism or secularism the event actually portrayed.

If both of Scarlatti's *La Giuditta* scores demonstrate important lessons, they serve as markers for the oratorio's narrative and musical possibilities as shaped by the convergence of influences and forces in this moment. In both versions, music provides a crucial dramatic role in particular circumstances of the narrative. Sometimes it conveniently obfuscates meaning, as in *La Giuditta* (Naples) when Judith's words in "La tua destra" take on a completely different cast when sung as aria than when conveyed as recitative. Holofernes hears and discerns Judith's speech clearly when expressed in recitative, but is overcome with emotion and confusion when her text is set to song. The effectiveness of Judith's aria, though tied to the specifics of the narrative in this "scene," is, however, largely symbolic. It may simply underscore the difference between speech and song, but on another level it also problematizes the distinction between what Downing Thomas characterizes as music that is "story-telling" (diegetic) and music that is "performance" (extradiegetic).[124] As he demonstrates in his treatment of French musical drama in the seventeenth and eighteenth centuries, opera continued to dismantle this distinction. For our purposes, we can see that the late seventeenth-century oratorio helps to herald this same moment and foreshadow future manifestations of this musico-dramatic phenomenon. When endowed with its own authority, music could effectively complicate the signification of words, and, depending on the situation, music might function dramatically as a narrative element to further the plot. Take the second setting of *La Giuditta* (Cambridge). In the Nurse's lullaby, performance begins to obscure story-telling when music overwhelms listeners with the extradiegetic, with decoration and embellishment of sound over word. Many thought the oratorio kept a safe distance from opera through its lack of dramatic presentation, costuming, and staging of marvelous effects. But what critics failed to account for was that the oratorio's stripped-down approach of "seeing with the ear" might also allow that ear to be distracted from the essential thematics, to wander away from moral messages to become enthralled sensually and to lose a connection to reason. The Nurse's lullaby ironically symbolizes this moment – dramatically and extra-dramatically – calling attention to music's ability to delight rather than to instruct, and to overcome reason with its appeal to the senses.

As striking as this moment is, and as modern as the musical mechanisms might be, the desired effect witnessed in the 1697 *La Giuditta* (Cambridge) actually had deep historical roots that are important to keep in mind. Morelli's historical research on the early Italian oratorio reminds us that the regard for music as an effective emotive medium was prefigured in the Oratorians' history as compared with other Catholic reform movements born in the same period. Using other historians' findings along with a number of primary sources, Morelli presents an illuminating view of the Oratorians' singularity when compared with the Society of Jesus. What he highlights is the diversity of both spiritual and functional dimensions between the Oratorians and the Jesuits: "the former characterized by familiar, immediate, spontaneous, open approach, the latter by an austere, gloomy, rigid, rational style, almost detached from the world."[125] When it came to art and music, what this meant was that the Oratorians tended to emphasize a deeper emotional level rather than an intellectual level, speaking more to the senses than to reason.

What the early Oratorians could not account for was the power of this emotional unleashing in the musico-dramatic context, its future resonance with the operatic trajectory, and what that trajectory would come to symbolize in a later generation steeped in reactionary conservatism. The emphasis on emotion over intellect and sensation over reason would produce a stunningly clashing effect when juxtaposed against the aims and rationalized procedures of late seventeenth- and early eighteenth-century tragic dramaturgy. Tragedy was imposed on musical drama from spoken theater to rescue musical drama, to rein in opera's pervasive wonder-driven allure (*meraviglia*), and to make the un-verisimilar and contrived seem more real. Compared with opera, the oratorio was more amenable to this dramaturgical prototype and could be seen as providing a model system for enacting this moment of reform. Yet in all of this lies an important irony worth probing. Tragedy may have *encouraged* rather than discouraged musicality, a development arguably contrary to Spagna's emphasis on the primacy of word and meter. Though acts of heroism were central to dramatic procedure, we have already noted the importance of premeditation and reflection upon those actions as key to tragedy's symbolic core. It is not that music was incompatible with this procedure. On the contrary, music arguably heightened such moments. But in emphasizing the need for reflection, music was often asked to do more work than words, bypassing or overwhelming text with emotion. It was not that music altered the need to reflect internally (already an integral element in both tragedy and the oratorio); it was the difference a musical setting could make to the significative process of that reflection.

It is true that with the process of secularization and the intense pressures felt in Rome during this period, oratorios began to decline in prominence, especially after the first few decades of the eighteenth century.[126] I would argue that what it is important to capture in this last flicker of the oratorio's Roman significance is not its longer-term persistence or relevance later in the eighteenth century, but how it served as a harbinger of things to come. In essence, the oratorio helps to prefigure opera's eighteenth-century trajectory when music becomes an arbiter of meaning, as opera turns away from the moral aims of tragedy to embrace new concerns of sensibility and feeling. The oratorio sits at this unusual crossroads in the ongoing debate of music and affect. However, it does not suffice to characterize this as a "fence-sitting" genre; rather, the oratorio was pressed to work the cultural tensions brought about by opera's rupturing impact. In doing so it harkened to a Counter-Reformation past in which emotional immediacy was encouraged as a practical device to entice listeners (many of whom were not restricted to an elite class) to devotional practices. That emotionalism, once a practical measure, became an element and posture distrusted by the cultural gatekeepers of the late seventeenth century. The oratorio had to work with both opera's enticing cultural power and its position as a moral and political aberration, and object of condemnation. In this turn-of-century context the oratorio emerges to take on the work of transformation, reaching for the emotional intensity made available through the tradition of literary primacy, yet converting those redemptive impulses into modalities that also augmented the progressive transition of music's growing centrality.

The musico-dramatic potential that we witness in the Judith oratorios was real, vibrant, compelling, and in several ways it was a result of this particular juncture that speaks of a history and foretells a future, as musical drama progressively tipped away from a dramaturgical framework of intellectually defined catharsis towards a renewed aesthetic of emotional immediacy whose foundation *was* music. Arguably, it is in the shadow of opera's transitional moment that the oratorio is given new birth. It is in the context of a cultural crisis that opera is singled out as problematic. In the wake of opera's formal stigma, the oratorio was subject to strategic revision, and then rehabilitated, redefined, and edified within a conservative reformist culture that also required recommitment to devotional culture. In edifying the oratorio, opera's weaknesses and strengths, its allure and stigma, and its effectiveness and shortcomings are brought into reflexive measure.

3 | The serenata's discourses of duality

I

Of all the musico-dramatic genres that developed and thrived in the Roman context, the serenata may be unique in its heterogeneity, where disparate elements from opera, oratorio, cantata, and instrumental music meet. Shaped like a cantata for two or more voices, filled with the kind of allegorical characters familiar to oratorios, using arias as a central mode of musical expression, yet having large instrumental forces as accompaniment to provide introductory, intermediate, or concluding narrative signposts, the serenata's confluence of styles and genres defies simple categorical ordering. At the same time, this extensive range of influences has much to tell. The serenata is distinctive among the vocal genres examined in this book because it often involved striking degrees of visual and sonic spectacle, with larger instrumental forces as part of its performance mechanism and mode of expression. Nevertheless, the musico-dramatic core of the serenata was more closely akin to similar vocal genres that were not fully operatic in narrative style and in formal presentation, but highlighted the solo voice or intimate dialogue in a musical format characteristic of much secular vocal music of the period. This chapter explores the degree to which the serenata's contrasting dimensions intersected with the larger aesthetic discourses concerning musical dramaturgy. Specifically, I use the serenata's elastic performance mechanisms to explore the significative conflict posed by an increased musical presence as embodied through instrumental sections and interludes. I argue that the juxtaposed elements of instrumental sound with a musico-dramatic texture (as controlled through a literary mode of signification) posed significant tensions that challenged contemporary critics on the sources of expressivity in musical drama. In essence, what made the serenata unique among similar genres is the degree to which music as a purely sonic element could function as a locus of meaning and thus challenge the semantic singularly of text. We will come to see how the serenata provides a different lens through which to review this central debate surrounding opera and music in early eighteenth-century Rome.

As the previous chapter did for the oratorio, this chapter treats the serenata as a site intersected by external pressures – political, social, and cultural – pressures that seeped into its form and shaped the variety of its practices. The serenata was performed in settings of which the character ranged from enclosed intimacy to full-scale public display, from the private environs and gardens of noble palaces, to the public squares of the city at large. Though the genre also had a life outside Italy, it flourished in the cities of Naples and Venice, and especially Rome, where the amplitude of musical forces coupled with social and political needs prompted the serenata's production.[1] However, the aims of this chapter are neither to define the range of this genre in any comprehensive way nor to detail the serenata's multifaceted history. In keeping with the period and locale under consideration, the chapter examines a particular historical juncture in Rome when the serenata as form was enlisted as practice, working to host events that served the needs of political and religious patrons and their relationships of power. For this reason, I narrow my interest to the more "public" face of the serenata. My focus will be on specific serenata events during the 1690s into the early 1700s, when local pressures resulting from the shift in power from Spanish Habsburg to French Bourbon reflected instability brought about by the War of Spanish Succession and tensions over conflicts of European monarchy. While I wish to consider the connections between the serenata and surrounding social and political tensions, I will not propose that these links are in any way rigid or absolute. Indeed, how a genre like the serenata comes to acquire a practice that reveals important relationships between systems of power is a complicated process. Cultural forms and practices often do emerge during periods of great upheaval for a dominant culture. So, what conditions – at least in the Roman context – allowed for a compelling fit between the serenata as an aesthetic form and the systems of power that intersected it? Using select historical cases, this chapter examines the circumstances that yielded such conditions.

As in the previous chapter, I begin this chapter by returning to contemporary sources. It is well established that the serenata worked propagandistically as political spectacle. This view is grounded in the writings of Giovanni Mario Crescimbeni, especially his oft-quoted remark from his *Commentari... intorno alla sua Istoria della volgar poesia* of 1702, in which Crescimbeni distinguishes serenatas from related genres by their presentation to a public audience, their evening setting, and their tendency to place on display ambassadors, princes, and other important personages in all of their splendor and magnificence.[2] The material on serenatas in Crescimbeni's volume is very brief, although his *Commentari* taken as a whole is an important turn-of-the-century cultural statement on the recuperation and centrality of Italian literature. In fact, the chapter in which the serenata receives mention attempts to define hierarchical values that governed the conditions of the lyrical and the musical. Much of the chapter acknowledges the involvement of music in genres used in festive occasions; however, Crescimbeni stresses the extent to which music in such instances must be treated as an accessory component, an element to be contained within the larger context of the event or of the text being heard. A detailed exploration of Crescimbeni's views on the relationship of music and poetry or other dramatic narratives will be treated more fully in chapter 4. For now, it is worth noting that the pronounced use of musical elements as employed in a genre like the serenata provoked controversy regarding the musicalization of drama. At the same time, this chapter recognizes the historical legacy of appropriating music both as sonic effect and as a key significative element in larger social spectacles. The serenata builds upon an early modern festive tradition of combining multiple art forms for propagandistic purposes. What changes (and what is debated) in these transitional decades between the seventeenth and eighteenth centuries is how music and other forms of media co-exist, interrelate, and compete for the expression of meaning.

In this manner, Crescimbeni's description of the serenata in his *Commentari* is valuable because he offers an account of how the serenata carried out *multiple* functions. As I shall argue, the serenata was drawn into a series of dual positions: it served private as well as public needs, and while it exemplified certain aesthetic tendencies of musical drama in this era, it also hosted powerful political impulses that transformed it into a larger social spectacle. We must therefore recognize the intricate overlap of aesthetic and political domains at stake in this discussion of the serenata. Later in this chapter, we will learn how the serenata's patronal circumstances fused absolutist politics with the larger cultural and aesthetic movements occurring in Rome, primarily led by the Arcadians. This intersection of circles – those literary and cultural with those papal, ambassadorial, and political – is vividly illustrated in the events, social performances, artistic intentions, and reception of a number of serenatas produced in this period.

This chapter thus turns from broader concerns to more specific observations. I consider the serenata's diachronic perspective and the genre's inheritances by tracing Rome's public serenata tradition from the latter part of the seventeenth century into the early decades of the eighteenth century. I direct my focus to a particular moment in time, to accounts of an early eighteenth-century serenata, *Le gare festive in applauso alla Real Casa di Francia*, by the poet Giacomo Buonaccorsi and composer Pietro Paolo

Bencini.[3] The events surrounding the performance of *Le gare festive* provide a close-up view of how the arenas of genre, musico-dramatic polemics, cultural aesthetics, and institutions of power coalesce during a moment of fragility over monarchal succession. In this context, I observe how this serenata takes on patterns and expressive structures that reveal its capacity to host and refract the political and cultural pressures that engulfed the site of its performance.

As a work and as an event, *Le gare festive* was by no means exceptional. By the first decade of the eighteenth century the serenata genre had been present for more than thirty years and was regularly performed by or for ambassadorial representatives residing in Rome. I look at *Le gare festive* and the events in Rome during 1704 to reflect on this long tradition and to consider the persistence of key features that tie the serenata's internal aesthetics to external social and political forces. Compared with other serenata events, *Le gare festive* is comparatively well documented by sources that help demonstrate the play-by-play unfolding of ceremonies leading up to the vocal and musical performance, suggesting some of the ways the event's discrete elements of spectacle moved through space and time. Understanding the details of *Le gare festive*'s ritual practice also provides a means to explore the serenata's aesthetic parameters. I probe how the process of ritual resonates with the narrative strategies used in serenatas. Of these strategies allegory was often the expressive core and catalyst for the public serenata's multifaceted performance. Like ritual, allegory served to isolate individual moments crucial for shaping the performance, and as a narrative strategy, it allowed the serenata to contain music and to mark its delivery as sonic symbol and referential agent in the libretto. The recognition of interplay between allegory and ritual will help to explain how the serenata ultimately allowed for simultaneous but contrasting experiences, one public, the other private. My concern is to use this duality to probe the ambiguous role of music in the serenata's multimedia context – how and why music in the serenata's public/private bifurcated presentation was *both* accessory to and pivotal for expressing the work's fundamental meaning. This exploration, however, goes beyond the serenata itself and considers how music's intensified function and potential for signification posed significant challenges to contemporary critics of opera and dramaturgy. These critics were eager to maintain word's directive role in musical settings despite the powerful expression allowed by distinct musical elements. Though an issue that cut across all musico-dramatic writing, the serenata's interpolation of instrumental *sinfonie* heightened this tension to the grandest proportions, largely because political crises demanded the efficacy of spectacular display. What it might be critical to recognize is how the fate of history – of monarchies, papal politics, and Europe's emerging modernity – did indeed have some effect upon the entertainment choices and musico-dramatic directions taking place, notwithstanding the technical and conventional developments specific to the intersection of instrumental and vocal repertoire already occurring. This aesthetic phenomenon – however unique in the serenata – would increasingly shape the future of musico-dramatic writing. Ultimately, the serenata provides another perspective for viewing the destiny of opera, whose orbit was caught in the very crossfire of historical upheaval taking shape in this period.

Sounding the serenata

In several respects, the serenata functioned as a type of dramatic cantata, and despite the numerous turns in its development, we will come to see how and why it largely remained this way. Vocal soloists in serenatas were typically small in number, were not usually costumed, and did not perform any stage action as part of their presentation. Yet a variety of conditions furnished the serenata with the potential for instrumental performance of comparatively grand proportions. Outdoor settings spurred an increase in the number of players to any given part; however, in general, instrumental ensembles accompanying vocal works became larger and more distinct from singers during the latter half of the century. In the most practical terms, serenatas acquired sonic power through "music," the instrumental *sinfonie* used to accommodate the genre's specific acoustic needs.[4] But the large number of musicians required for the serenata's *sinfonie* was also a symbolic marker of the grandeur of the event and of the wealth and influence of its sponsor. In a setting like Rome, the large scale of instrumental forces was made all the more possible by the excess of musicians seeking employment in the papal capital's many institutions (church, chamber, theater) where instrumental music played an important role.[5]

Music thus functioned as both a visual and an aural element in the serenata. The multitude of musicians was just as important to see as it was to hear, as emphasized by John Spitzer and Neal Zaslaw: "Rather than accompany the piece, the orchestra framed it . . . providing a visual backdrop for singers, orators, and other performers. The sudden entry, the full sound, and the unified execution of so large a group of instruments were a glorious special effect, like the fanfares and the fireworks at some of the same events."[6] During the public serenata music could be either constant or intermittent, its effect sometimes more visual than aural. The serenata's visual/aural delivery was expressed through the genre's concerto grosso organization (soloists to ripienists), of which the acoustical contrast (soft to loud) meant that separate segments of the audience could have engaged with or perceived music in different ways. Thus, for the general public, music was often an occasional special effect, limited to singular moments of the performance when music was made powerful both visually and aurally (e.g., when all fifty or so bows hit their strings at the same time). Sound coupled with "might on sight,"[7] the visual power of numbers in the serenata's instrumental section was viscerally effective if conceptually simple. As with fireworks, the aim of the *sinfonia* was to overwhelm audiences with the splendor of the event, and to bombard the senses through the sheer materiality of its presence. The force of music – its manifestation as a special effect – *was* the novelty of the occasion. However, its significance for the larger audience, as a gesture either of beneficence on a grand scale or merely one of festivity, was predicated on music's interaction with other aspects of spectacular display (colorful processions, brilliant lighting, pyrotechnics, etc.), in other words, elements that were highly visual.

We must come to see that the serenata's unique aesthetic dimensions are what largely enabled its enlistment in the political rituals governed by absolutism. Court societies had long demanded regal enactments of all sorts via highly scripted performances in order to present the social world back to itself in representative forms. In all cases, these displays were gestures to preserve order, power, and authority. The serenata was embedded in a culture that required such ideological rituals, and therefore, the serenata was also party to spectacles of power. An important qualification must be made here: what becomes the public serenata, as we see it take hold in Rome from the 1680s on, emerges because of its efficacy and viability as a form of political spectacle. In and of itself, the serenata as a musical form was not ritualistic, but it became a *vehicle* for hosting the rituals articulated by the reigning dominant culture.

The process of ritualizing the serenata opens a number of aesthetic issues worth probing. Foremost is the question of reception. The serenata, as we know, was adapted to fit the particular acoustic and spatial demands of an enlarged public forum. And yet the "public," for whom increased sound was intended, was far from an audience of social equals. The outdoor space of the public serenata included the elite participants who attended at the pleasure of the patrons and associates who commissioned the serenata. But the public setting for the serenata also included a broad swath of the less-than-elite classes, who looked on from a distance; they may have heard very little, but in their presence they served as symbolic recipients in these politically

Figure 5 William Reuter, *Celebrations at the Spanish Embassy on Piazza di Spagna*, 1662, depicting the public celebration of the birth of the Infante Don Carlos (Vienna, Akademie der Bildenden Künste, inv. 585).

motivated performances. It is important to note that the range of spectators who likely crossed the public arena of the outdoor serenata in Rome may have included more class types than was typical in seventeenth-century public theaters. In fact, it was not uncommon for contemporary writers of *avvisi* to report the occasional bouts of violence during serenatas performed in outdoor settings where the mix of crowds may have fomented social conflict. The William Reuter painting shown in figure 5 offers a glimpse of the motley collection of people who would potentially congregate in a larger public piazza, such as the Piazza di Spagna, where serenatas were frequently performed.

The serenata's aesthetic design thus raises an important contradiction as regards reception. The genre's visual splendor and musical accompaniment (the *sinfonia* that either opened the work or played intermittently during its performance) were its most obvious and symbolically significant features for the public at large. But the core of the serenata was essentially a series of unrhymed and rhymed verses delicately set above the support of continuo

instruments. Who actually took in the "real" serenata – the aspect that
conveyed the meaning of the text through the subtle rendering of its words
in both recitative and aria forms? To what extent was the public serenata
a case of unequal access, a reflection of the social conditions in which
audiences were convened? Public performances of the serenata combined
both a public and a private dimension that catered to a bifurcated reception
for those meant to perceive the serenata's deeper political message, and
those meant to witness grandeur and power in much less detail. After all,
if *universal* hearing were a central concern, then we might imagine the
serenata's performance configured differently, perhaps by having multiple
voices match the expressive force of multiple instruments.

We need to examine how the serenata's hybrid structure (the genre's
public/private dimensions as well as its cantata-like core with added large
instrumental ensembles) provides a framework linking the serenata's design
to surrounding political and social tensions. In doing so, we may come to
see the public rendering of the serenata as an event underlain by complex
processes. Though seemingly contradictory in its capacity to present a unified performance, the serenata enabled patrons to maintain an important
presentational tension. As a work of spectacle that juxtaposed public largess
with exclusivity, the serenata musically accommodated both mass audience
and privileged guests. In effect, the public serenata revealed the distance
between those who could access the more intimate orientation of the genre's
emphasis on text, which required a closer listening, and the remainder of the
public who primarily witnessed the grandeur of the spectacle. In this regard,
the power of the serenata's display was fitting in a society for which access
to cultural texts was highly stratified through both class prerogative and
literacy. The serenata's cantata-like core may have been retained for public
consumption so that a smaller, privileged audience could watch the public
watching *them* engage the serenata's intricate poetic and musical drama, as
though actors in the greater spectacle of representation and celebration of
court society.[8]

The forces that shaped the serenata's genre practice were heavily exerted
by regime politics. However, the serenata's hybrid structure and its potential
for simultaneous but contrasting experiences also reflect and help articulate
contemporary aesthetic debates, especially those grounded within the context of Arcadian Rome where the polemics of musical drama were timeworn.
As we know, at the heart of these late-century debates was a concern regarding the expression of word through music. It is perhaps not surprising,
even in the age of instrumental music's nascent ascendancy and increased

presence and function in musical drama, that concern for the primacy of word and text continued to be particularly acute. The relationship between voice and instrument or between word and sound is a familiar concern for the study of early modern opera. However, in discussions of the serenata – for which music was sometimes the heavyweight in the ring – music's role as an element in a multifaceted performance has been less thoroughly examined. Thus, while the serenata may have echoed the cantata most directly, its associations with opera may be most revealing for the cultural function the serenata was called to fulfill.

That said, the serenata was decidedly *not* opera. Though it often functioned as a replacement for opera during Rome's summer season, to see the serenata as merely a genre substitute misses a much larger and more significant issue. The serenata held important correspondences to opera and we will come to see that some of the debates over musical drama are uniquely "performed" in the serenata's distinct generic site. What is most effective is how in the serenata's public forum these aesthetic questions manifest themselves in exaggerated fashion through the widened contrast between the serenata's cantata-like core and its more grandiose casting of instrumental forces.

As with other genres investigated in this book, the serenata lacks a detailed trail of evidence linking it directly to opera. For descriptions of the serenata in its context, we have little more to rely on than traditional primary sources. Later in this chapter I will turn to a number of these documents, including fragments from newsletters, printed *relazioni*, and other documents of patronage, or to the serenatas themselves, which tell much through their narrative and musical expression. This will help to create an image of the serenata's design and performance practice, as well as suggest aspects of its reception and cultural practice. The serenata's links to opera are not always obvious; often they are revealed in roundabout ways, by indirect inference, or by omission. Thus, the serenata's links to opera may be understood to be more situational than programmatically intentional, producing dialogical connections that are inadvertent but none the less important in the overall interplay of the multiple musico-dramatic genres of the period. With this in mind, I return to Crescimbeni's remarks on the serenata, this time to place the author's comments in the broader context of his "Delle feste musicali, e delle cantate, e serenate" (On musical entertainments, and on cantatas and serenatas),[9] a short chapter belonging to the 1702 *Commentari*. Placing this genre definition in the context of a larger discussion of historical poetic forms will help to explain some of the features and problems of the serenata's multidimensionality.

II

"Delle feste musicali, e delle cantate, e serenate"

Crescimbeni's passage on serenatas is often paraphrased or explained as a fragment in isolation, following neat excision from the chapter containing it, with little or no effort made to place it in context.[10] There is something sorely missed by this dislocation since Crescimbeni's short comments on the serenata form but a single section of a more lengthy discussion on secular dramatic compositions for festive occasions. In what follows, I will place these remarks in the context of the *Commentari*, thus linking the meaning of this definition of the serenata to broader contemporary context.

At the beginning of Crescimbeni's chapter, he notes that festive entertainments – tournaments, jousts, dances, etc. – were often accompanied by music, which served to introduce or to facilitate the transition from one operation to the next.[11] As his title suggests, Crescimbeni separates cantatas and serenatas from *feste*. He makes this distinction primarily on poetic grounds, since cantatas and serenatas shared a similar mixture of rhymed and unrhymed verses and arias.[12] In making this distinction, Crescimbeni traces a particular historical trajectory, demonstrating how this poetry first arose in the seventeenth century, and how before that they used other, less structured forms like *madrigali*.[13] Crescimbeni is clear that cantatas and serenatas belong to this great lineage of Italian poetic history, and that they hold a high distinction among the variety of festive entertainments that he considers in his chapter.

Yet the serenata does present some suggestive correspondences to seventeenth-century *feste*, and not just to the cantata. In describing specific *feste*, Crescimbeni describes a spectacle-driven event hosted by the Prince of Brunswick, which was performed on the water at night. In several ways it shared noteworthy similarities with serenatas, including the use of light to splendorous effect, and the enlistment of large numbers of costumed musicians as part of the dramatic setting. Crescimbeni also describes an *Accademia del Disegno di Roma*, an event that was performed with some regularity on the Campidoglio celebrating the best painters, sculptors, and architects of the city, at which music and song were often present, including the use of "vaghe sinfonie" to introduce recitation and singing of poetry.[14] In these cases, the element of music played a significant but subsidiary role where it functioned as one element in a larger series of textual and visual displays. However, in the case of the serenata, one could argue that music was the main feature and the *raison d'être* for the performance.

So, what of the role of music? In the serenata, the distinct sonic element created by the serenata's instrumental ensemble, its relationship to the work's vocal rendering, and its effect on audiences remain contested. Among modern scholars of this subject, there are some who assert that music, though an important feature, was only one among many elements at play during a serenata. Gloria Staffieri categorizes serenatas such as *Le gare festive* with other complex multilayered political performances, the kind of public festival in which music likely occupied an ancillary position, indistinguishably intertwined with other spectacular, non-musical performative components.[15] Alternatively, Arnaldo Morelli argues that what made the serenata unique compared with other types of *feste* was, in effect, that musical performance was the event's central focus.[16] Both positions offer somewhat contrasting viewpoints regarding music's role in the serenata and its placement and expressive delivery in the process of performance. We might place this discussion as part of a more general debate concerning the status of music in a multimedia context. Does music commix with other elements? Does it remain subordinate to the verbal and visual? Or does musical sound, at least in the case of the serenata with its large instrumental forces, exceed other forms of expression?

The anxieties over word–music relationships form an important backdrop to the narrative ordering of Crescimbeni's chapter. The discussion of cantatas and serenatas, though seemingly appended to his chapter, nevertheless reveals links to other *feste*. With an increased propensity for vocal music to interpolate instrumental composition, it is possible that Crescimbeni felt it necessary to stratify the roles of significative expression. Even when an event focused more directly on musical performance (as with serenatas), music – in absolute instrumental terms – remained as accompaniment, meant to enhance texted phrases and facilitate transitions. Thus, for genres in which poetic style was seen as paramount and regarded as the continuance of a historical legacy, musico-cultural practices retained music as a subordinate element.

Indeed, there is an irony embedded in the serenata's performance design that is worth examining. Despite the fact that instrumental music was often strongly foregrounded and that the *sinfonia* itself sometimes took on dramatic roles, was music in the serenata emancipated from language? In her article on Corelli's composition of *sinfonie*, Gloria Staffieri addresses this question in broader terms by arguing that two simultaneous developments occur in the collision between texted vocal music and autonomous instrumental music.[17] While we may witness a departure of instrumental music in the 1670s and 1680s from the primacy of vocal music through the increased use of *sinfonie* in vocal mediums, the dominant cultural aesthetic still placed a higher value on poetry than on music. Even granting the ability of music to specify meaning through its structure alone, through the use of new concerto grosso techniques with dramatic contrast of forces and themes, or through counterpoint, homophony, imitation, rhythm, tempo, and dynamics, the purely tonal medium of music required words to offer a fuller and more specific representation. In fact, the significative potential of instrumental music was shaped by what occurred *first* in musico-dramatic writing, in which vocal utterances in arias were condensed into musical units to convey ideas or emotions via easily recognized musical structures and conventions. But even musical conventions applied to arias relied on words to identify the specific emotive content that such a musical symbol represented. Staffieri underscores the importance of the theory of affections in contemporary description of the development of vocal music, and notes that it could equally well have been applied to instrumental repertoire, to show how musical composition could have become an autonomous expressive form.[18] The process of stylizing instrumental language was a means to connect semantic labels embedded in the meaning of texts to distinct musical gestures. This would allow for audiences to be conditioned, guaranteeing that in the absence of words musical gestures would none the less call forth a host of semantic relationships cemented through word–music associations.

It is not surprising that Crescimbeni makes no mention of opera in his discussion of the serenata, even if we might consider it the proverbial elephant in the room. Although the serenata could function as a diversion for Romans during periods when public theater had been otherwise suppressed, contemporary audiences were unlikely to have confounded the two genres. In fact, the late-century serenata, at least in outward appearance and function, had less to do with contemporary trends in mid- and late seventeenth-century opera but, rather, harkened back to a pre-operatic era, a time of courtly spectacles when ceremonial performances of the sixteenth-century *intermedi* bore witness to the power of patrons through allegorically heightened forms of dynastic celebration merging sound with resplendent visuals in *tableaux vivants*.[19] But along with this courtly holdover, the modern serenata reached forward and embraced more progressive developments in instrumental composition through its use of the *sinfonia* and its virtuosic expressivity, which, in turn, were facilitated through the latest concerto grosso techniques. It is here that the diachronic dimensions of genre are instructive. The serenata's mixture of past and present influences may point to a more pervasive divergence between a receding court culture and an emerging modern public domain. When Crescimbeni discerns that the serenata serves a public function, we should note that it was "public" in a particular sense. Unlike opera, the serenata was not a form of public theater that was commodified through the sale of tickets, or that was shaped by entrepreneurial aspirations. Its public dimensions were manipulated to convey the sense of public space and public consumption, all the while steadfastly maintaining the social representation of courtly culture.[20]

Genre maintenance has important lessons to impart. The serenata did not become opera, nor as its own genre did it reconcile the disparity of its forces to accommodate more *fully* the reception of a truly public audience. Perhaps the maintenance of its intimate and cantata-like core functioned as a symbolic gesture of courtly protectionism, a symptom of an elite retreat, what Habermas describes as "the final form of representative publicness" reduced to "an enclave within a society separating itself from the state."[21] Through the serenata, and in the examination of its cultural articulations in specific settings, we are better able to understand the extent to which its aesthetic design was profoundly embedded in larger socio-cultural matrices. In the examples that follow, we will come to see how the serenata brokered a unique coalescence of factors, linking agents, institutions, and audiences to critical discourse, aesthetic norms, and musical forms, all in the moment of performance.

III

Inheritances

Rome in the 1690s was a time and location where the contours of political, social, and cultural conflict were largely shaped by events taking place throughout the rest of Europe. In every way, these events and their consequences were complex and detailed. As they regarded Rome, what can be said in short is that the church's influence – politically, economically, and socially – had been waning and the papacy was increasingly constrained to maneuver delicately between quarrelling absolutist monarchies and rising new capitalist economies.[22] These were circumstances that in large measure affected the direction of culture, the composition of rituals and events, and the performance of music. Regarding the specifics of the serenata, we can see that in the church's struggle to maintain influence of all types (spiritual as well as economic and cultural), clerical leaders often engaged in publicized, or sometimes clandestine, dealings with diplomatic envoys who had time-honored traditions of political and cultural representation in Rome. As historian Laurie Nussdorfer describes, ambassadors in early modern Rome constituted one of the primary "nodes of power" in the city.[23] The alliances forged between foreign diplomats and the papal court, including clerics with foreign ties to mother countries, and other important nobles with a mixture of national or cultural associations, were a means to effect change or strengthen entrenched positions. Seventeenth-century Rome was thus a political and social microcosm that mirrored the dynastic power-grab of European monarchical and imperial politics. The prominent players in this urban landscape included representatives from the Austrian imperial court, France, and Spain. The last two kingdoms were, by tradition, intensely competitive. Spain had long set its sights on Rome as a location to stage absolutist politics. In a recent monograph, Thomas Dandelet considers Spain's desire to Romanize its history, examining the symbolic relationship that developed between Spain and Rome during the early modern period. Dandelet alleges that Spain saw itself as heir to the Roman Empire: "The myth and site of Rome provided the Spanish with both story and a stage to reflect on their own destiny as the modern heir to the Roman empire."[24] France had similar aspirations. Since the end of the sixteenth century, France had been Spain's most formidable European rival, and as a competitor within Rome the French spent much of the next hundred years aggressively courting the favor of popes and cultivating as many pro-French allies as possible among local nobles.

Europe's political battles were made diversely manifest in Rome's public life, and the serenata ritual was but one occasion that drew upon some of the typical mechanisms and elements required for political spectacle in this context. Foremost among these was the symbolic appropriation of urban space. Most of the major European powers hastened to seize Roman residences and neighborhoods as their own, using space and architecture symbolically to create political territories with distinct geographical boundaries.[25] The Spanish, however, were the first actually to *own* a local palace and surrounding piazza, which gave them distinct advantage and permanency over other envoys who merely rented.[26] It was customary for patrons of both sacred and secular *feste* to use Rome's many piazzas and the roads leading to them as showcases for theatrically driven display. The Piazza di Spagna was among the grandest, flanked by an imposing hill (upon which the famous Spanish Steps were later built in the eighteenth century), which bordered one side of the piazza, upon the summit of which loomed large (symbolically, and somewhat ironically) the Trinità dei Monti, a church founded by the French in 1502 at the behest of Louis XII.

Not all serenatas of the seventeenth century were grand, public occasions. But among those that were, some of the most celebrated, documented, and memorialized in word and image were those that took place in the Piazza di Spagna. The surviving engravings which chronicle these events (for example, Gian Lorenzo Bernini and Giovan Paolo Schor's *Apparato e fuochi artificiali per la nascita del Delfino*, 1661; Filippo Schor's *Festa per la nascita dell'Infanta di Spagna*, 1681; Simon Felice del Lino's *Festa per la ricuperata salute di Luigi XIV*, 1687; Cristoforo Schor's *Festa in onore di Maria Luigia di Spagna*, 1687)[27] span the 1660s to 1680s and visually attest to the long tradition of French–Spanish one-upmanship that occurred in this venue.[28] The characteristic use of fireworks, lighting, theatrical machines, or temporary staging devices built to showcase the "innumerable" performers and famed solo singers was one of the features used by each faction to exhibit, as ostentatiously as possible, their ability to surpass the other through presentational flair.

The serenata was neither natively French nor Spanish,[29] but as a genre, it drew heavily from the political contests waged between the two monarchies during the latter half of the seventeenth century. The specific national influences on the serenata ritual, though important, are less of a concern here for my particular study; rather, I want to consider how external conditions characterizing this political rivalry, enhanced by the Roman locale, shed light on the manner in which the late-century serenata became an occasion increasingly ritualized through the use of elements borrowed from earlier serenata practice.

The pairing of grand spectacle with other forms of media had a long history in early modern Rome. The city's particular methods of civic and religious ceremony had descended from a broader Renaissance tradition, in which signification relied heavily upon a highly cultivated humanist frame of reference.[30] The sheer enormity of spectacle communicated simply and directly with a larger public, but the degree of interpretive depth demanded by allegorical forms of dynastic display required the literacy of an elite culture, highlighting what historian Peter Burke identifies as a symptomatic asymmetry posed by early modernity's two cultural traditions (those defined by upper classes, and the traditions forged by non-elite cultures).[31] In essence, Burke argues that the minority elite had access to *two* cultures, both elite and non-elite. And even though Burke notes that the upper classes gradually withdrew from participation in popular traditions in the course of the seventeenth and eighteenth centuries, their need publicly to maintain a "bi-culturalism" was arguably self-serving during the waning stages of absolute culture, during which time the maintenance of such a false binary served to augment further the distance between elite or private and public realms. Thus, the serenata drew upon the legacy of merging public spectacle, visual and sonic on a grand scale, with elevated courtly language – a blend of poetic styles in which pastoral and mythological references were part of the allegorical structuring, as was the visual lexicon of emblems and heraldic symbols. Despite the rise of opera and other genres of entertainment, courtly pageantry of this sort held strong; this form of expression was a tenacious symptom of a kind of elite conservatism that persisted and was even intensified in the Roman context.

Ambassadorial patrons residing in 1690s Rome built on the serenata's inherited traditions, but in these later years it was the Spanish in particular who exploited the genre's mechanisms to bridge external and internal cultures. Within the larger European landscape, Spain was facing the growing threat of French expansion. During the mid-1680s this reality had rapidly escalated when Spain lost significant territories to Louis XIV's army, which by that time had become the most powerful military force in Europe.[32] It was during this period of increased vulnerability that the Spanish used their presence in Rome more assertively and turned to cultural politics to enlist the support of locals to maintain their status as a power nation.[33] King Charles II gave generously to the Papal States. He faithfully embraced the annual and very public ritual of the presentation of the *chinea* – the gift of a white Neapolitan horse, a symbolic payment of feudal dues owed to the papacy for the fiefdom of Naples.[34] For Spain, the presentation of the *chinea* was a political opportunity to strengthen Spanish–papal relations publicly. It was also an occasion for Spain to exhibit locally cultivated alliances either by allowing Roman nobles themselves to make the presentation or by using their heraldic symbols in the *chinea*'s visually resplendent ceremony.

The serenata had much in common with the *chinea*. It allowed the Spanish to place their monarchy on display and to show favor to local alliances beneficial to their own political survival. As a ritual practice, it served to instantiate a key group consisting of internal (Roman) and external (Spanish) constituents. Building that relationship, essentially, using the serenata to display these alliances (often demonstrated in print through the serenata's dedication or by visible placement in performance of important associates next to the patron) allowed foreign delegates to flatter potentates and court their favor to lobby for the protection of the pope. The serenata was a platform designed to "perform" a sense of strength and stability of distinct but sometimes fragile relationships in an increasingly volatile political climate.

The serenata in the 1690s

The early years of the 1690s form a high point for the serenata in Rome, not because they were the most splendorous (the 1680s arguably may hold this distinction), but because of the increased connection of the form with cultural and political discourses. Considering the importance of alliances, it had long been in Spain's interest to establish a link with local aristocracy, especially with families that had significant property in Rome, such as the Colonnas, one of city's oldest noble families.[35] Spain had honed this partnership over many decades, but the crucial phase in the relationship occurred in 1681, when the then Ambassador to Spain, marqués del Carpio offered his niece, doña Lorenza de la Cerda, to Filippo Colonna, the son of the influential Contestabile Lorenzo Onofrio Colonna.[36] However, the alliance between the Colonnas and the Spanish envoys in Rome would reach a new level after 1687, when Carpio's nephew, Luis Francisco de la Cerda y Aragón, marqués de Cogolludo and Duke of Medinaceli, inherited the position of Spanish ambassador, and moved into the national residence on the Piazza di Spagna. The evidence suggests that the marqués de Cogolludo may have desired, especially in the first years of his ambassadorship, to make bold, public pronouncements of Spanish links to local culture via the serenata. The highpoint of his first year as ambassador included the August 25 celebration of the Spanish queen's name day (a tradition which preceded him) with the presentation of a public serenata, in this case, a colossal performance including a great array of illuminations, a large ensemble of musicians, and select singers displayed on a theatrically decorated platform before the Spanish Royal Palace.[37]

Thomas Griffin views Cogolludo's event as a possible response to a similar grand spectacle held earlier that year when, in April, Cardinal D'Estrées commissioned the serenata entitled *La fama festeggiante*, which included a *sinfonia* said to have been composed by the famous "Arcangelo Bolognese" (Corelli).[38] If indeed Griffin's hypothesis is correct, this case makes us aware of the extension of political rivalry to the realm of musical patronage. Using the Schor engraving shown in figure 6 as evidence, John Spitzer and Neal Zaslaw have suggested that the two solo violinists (placed apart from the other musicians, literally on a pedestal) who performed at the Piazza di Spagna serenata in August were likely Matteo Fornari and Arcangelo

Figure 6 Cristoforo Schor, *Veduta della piazza con la festa*, 1687 (S-Sk, PLAF 24:51). For further background on this image, see Fagiolo dell'Arco, *La festa barocca*, 538–539.

Corelli.[39] If true, this would attest to the degree to which Cogolludo, the new ambassador, in a climate of stepped-up rivalry with France, thought it imperative to enlist local musicians who not only symbolized the best of what Rome had to offer, but whose presence onstage served as a visible marker of wealth and influence.

The marqués de Cogolludo also found new reasons to hold serenata events. On August 10, 1688, he celebrated his ties with the Colonna family by offering a serenata to commemorate the feast day of San Lorenzo, celebrating the name day of Lorenzo Colonna, the Contestabile, and of Lorenza, the daughter-in-law of Lorenzo and the marqués's own sister.[40] The alliance forged between Cogolludo and the Colonnas was deepened further by the ambassador's relationship with his brother-in-law, Filippo, who provided a critical entrée for Cogolludo to Rome's cultural milieu. The two together would later become principal patrons of the Tordinona theater from 1692 to 1695.[41]

As ambitious patrons of the Tordinona, Cogolludo and Colonna engaged some of the best local and imported artists and literati working in Rome's opera circuit during the period. Among the most influential at this time were the reform-minded intellectuals whose concern with opera, drama, and aesthetics had been largely shaped by their association with the nascent but increasingly influential Academy of Arcadians. With this as a backdrop, Lowell Lindgren describes the encounter of these two patrons with the poet and founding member of the Arcadians, Silvio Stampiglia. Lindgren surmises that Cogolludo and Colonna were introduced to the librettist through Stampiglia's work on *Eraclea*, an opera scored by Giovanni Maria Bononcini, which served as Cogolludo's first sponsorship of an opera as ambassador in Rome and took place at the Tordinona in 1692.[42] After this production, the Spanish ambassador and Filippo Colonna regularly hired Stampiglia and Bononcini during the summer off-season, when operas and oratorios were not performed and serenatas took their place as summer entertainment. Each August from 1692 through 1696, Stampiglia and Bononcini wrote a serenata to honor Lorenza Colonna.[43] Additionally, the pair wrote a serenata in August 1695, *La notte festiva*, which had been commissioned by the marqués to honor his wife the ambassadress, Maria de la Nieves Téllez-Girón.

Thus, the events of the early 1690s gave Spain the opportunity to rehearse the diplomacy of alliance building and self-aggrandizement by means of music, drama, ceremony and spectacle, mainly in two Roman venues, the Spanish embassy and the Colonna residence. Their favored authors, Stampiglia and Bononcini, successfully merged socio-political and cultural demands as the occasion necessitated. Let us turn to the latter of the two demands, those that were cultural, to see what it may reveal about how opera's discourses shaped the serenata's performance and ritualization during this period.

The Stampiglia and Bononcini serenatas written for performance at the Palazzo Colonna share a number of traits, suggesting a preferred mode of expression that may have been called for by the particulars of this context. From what we can gather, these serenatas were performed in the palace courtyard before a select audience of nobles, dignitaries, and prelates that was none the less an audience too large for an indoor space.[44] Of the works for which libretti survive (all but the 1692 *La nemica d'amore*), the style of the Colonna palace serenatas is pastoral, using archetypal shepherd characters and standard plots of unrequited, lost, or reclaimed love commonly found in cantata literature of the period, and in pastoral opera endorsed by Arcadian intellectuals. Musically, the works are arranged much like cantatas, with the majority of the score consisting of solo *da capo* arias preceded by brief recitatives, with occasional duets, often with the last lines of the serenata as a full aria ensemble. Beyond the small group of continuo instruments to support the voices, larger instrumental music does indeed play a role, typically as a standalone prelude, using solo and tutti distinctions when such contrasts are needed. Otherwise, the orchestra creates segues between moments of monologue and dialogue in the form of brief ritornelli, and occasionally accompanies specific arias, sometimes as the full ensemble, but more often as the designated concertino. For the case of the Colonna serenatas, narrative elements of text, subject matter, and tone suggest that these serenatas, like standard cantatas, were more insular occasions, directed to audiences for which the pastoral world was an idealization of their own noble reality – a nostalgic construction in which poetry and music were as much a symbolic link to an ancient, enchanted past as they were to modern forms of entertainment. We will return to this aspect of nostalgic idealism in the following chapter.

Serenatas performed in a more public forum in this period – under conditions that demanded a more intensified political and social statement – were of a different breed. In this category is included the 1693 performance of *Applauso musicale*, a serenata performed in the Piazza di Spagna on August 5, to honor to the name day of the Spanish ambassadress.[45] Though the score no longer exists, scholars have speculated on the nature of instrumental music for the occasion, extrapolating from other manuscript scores and using indications from the libretto.[46] Staffieri is perhaps most illuminating regarding the music's potential for signification and use as a narrative device. In *Applauso musicale*, the indication and placement of a "Sinfonia melanconica" or a "Sinfonia allegra con Echi" suggest the extent to which such instrumental interludes in serenatas or oratorios were dramatic musical markers used to indicate a modification of the plot's expressive tone, a change of scene, or the entrance of a character, especially in the absence of staged drama.[47] Thus, the placement of autonomous pieces, even if brief, reveals a process of conceptualizing sonorous structures. For the public serenata, this process was often symbolically layered. On the most basic level, the act of underlining sound worked as a special effect, calling attention to itself and to its powerful forces or very mechanisms of expression. The narrative use of instrumental music, therefore, emphasized a profound semantic connection of music to text.

The year following *Applauso musicale*, the Spanish ambassador organized a similar serenata event on August 5, this time involving the librettist Stampiglia and the composer Severo de Luca, who had previously composed serenatas for the ambassador. In this work, *La nova gara delle dee*, the figures of Juno, Pallas, and Venus (a distinct departure from the shepherds of Arcadia) are used allegorically, modifying the basic template of their story to fit the event at hand – the name day of the ambassadress, and by proxy, the glory of Spain. It is possible that *Applauso musicale* and *La nova gara* were models for later efforts by Stampiglia with Bononcini. In 1695 both collaborated to write *La notte festiva*, a work that clearly adapted some of the elements and techniques of these earlier public serenatas – events at which the aesthetics of performance were shaped by the particular venue of the Spanish Piazza itself, the agents present, and the ideologies to be reaffirmed.

La notte festiva

The central elements of the serenata's narrative strategy are clearly discernible in *La notte festiva*. Written for three singers (the Night, the Moon, and Apollo), the serenata begins with a dialogue between the Night and the Moon, who compete to adorn an "Iberian Heroine" – the Moon with her rays and the Night with the embrace of enveloping blackness.[48] The real-life dedicatee, the Spanish ambassadress, is mentioned early in the piece, her name a poetic refrain that works as a structuring device conventional in this type of serenata. Reference and repetition publicly reinforced her association with the patron (in this case, her husband) and with his status, social connection, and political significance.

Night and Moon's opening duet has more than overt political significance. The poet's choice to personify these two aspects of nature alludes to the visual and spatial qualities of the serenata performance itself. An indivisible pair, the Moon and Night *are* what make the serenata exceptional: the night providing the "scuro" or necessary background for the "chiaro" or luminosity cast by celestial bodies above. This juxtaposition of dark and light is frequently highlighted in libretti and in documents that describe serenata performances. Both moon and stars and the countless lights illuminating the stage transform the serenata setting into a nighttime spectacle of light and shadows. On the one hand, the Night and Moon in *La notte festiva* are the narrative agents for the literal meaning of the drama. Their purpose (as they themselves explain) is to use their natural forces to adorn the dedicatee of the event. But the Moon is not just the Moon; it signifies more than a round orb of light in the night sky. As with all personified figures in allegories, Moon and Night have signification, though less explicit – to personify and embody the serenata experience itself, an experience marked by the extraordinary allure of nighttime, outdoor theater, and spectacle.

Following the opening, the next significant moment in the text is the entrance of Apollo, the most important of the three soloists. Apollo is introduced in a rather roundabout way. He is crept up upon by a scheming Moon who, along with Night, has resolved to steal Apollo's rays while he sleeps, allowing them to honor the name day of Maria more splendiferously. The buildup for this act of theft is charged with great anticipation and even humor (the Night plays the coward while the Moon is fearless). Most significant from a musical point of view, however, is how this moment of narrative tension is met with sonic reinforcement (see example 5).

As Night and Moon attempt to "enact" their suspenseful heist, a "solemn sinfonia" serves as an acoustic interruption to underscore the tension of the imagined scene, but more specifically to express a critical dramatic moment – the waking of Apollo. Without a complete score, it is difficult to make a comprehensive analysis of this section.[49] However, based on conventions drawn from other examples, the *sinfonia* referenced in the example in *La notte festiva* may have accomplished any of the narrative functions previously mentioned: it may have functioned to introduce this new character; it could have indicated a change of scene (perhaps with an implied image of the heavens opening or the sun rising as Apollo awakened); and it is possible it was used to express a specific tone important to that moment in the drama, perhaps the solemn, even slumbering quality of Apollo awakening after being disturbed from an otherwise peaceful sleep.

A closer examination of Apollo's first aria, "Or che il Sol dormendo," also sheds light on the narrative use of music in this scene. In this relatively brief ABA aria, the plodding pairs of stepwise descending bass notes in the continuo part against a mostly ascending vocal line suggest a sleep-aria quality for the opening section. And yet Apollo's pointed question, culminating on a half-cadence at the beginning of m. 4, creates a shift in tone, followed by a darker contrasting B section. In mm. 8–10 Bononcini portrays Apollo's intensified longing for sleep through a circle-of-fifths progression that eventually cadences on C minor, acting as a relative minor pivot back to the opening key and to the unanswered and insistent query: who awakens Apollo? Very little about this solo sets it apart from typical continuo arias of the period. What makes it worth examining in the context

Example 5 Giovanni Bononcini, *La notte festiva*: recit. dialogue, "Troppo vile sei tù," followed by the aria "Or che il sol dormendo," 1695 (I-Moe, Campori H.6.16).

Cintia	*Moon*
Troppo vile sei tù,	[You are too cowardly,
Non si ritardi più; Notte, m'aita.	let us not hesitate anymore; Night, help me.]
Comincia sinfonia grave.	[*A solemn sinfonia begins.*
Segue detta Sinfonia fino	*The said sinfonia continues*
à tutta l'Aria d'Appollo.	*until the Aria of Apollo.*]
Notte	*Night*
Parmi ch'egli si scuota.	[It seems to me that he's waking.]
Cintia	*Moon*
Non proferir più nota.	[Don't utter another sound.]
Notte	*Night*
Cintia?	[Moon?]

Example 5 (*cont.*)

Cintia	*Moon*
Sei pur molesta.	[You are bothersome.]
Notte	*Night*
Nascondiamci.	[Let us hide.]
Cintia	*Moon*
Non voglio.	[I don't want to.]
Notte	*Night*
Ecco si desta.	[There, he's waking.]
Appollo (aria)	*Apollo* (aria)
Or che il Sol dormendo giace	[Now that the Sun lies sleeping,
Chi lo toglie al dolce oblio?	who takes him away from sweet oblivion?
Ti sospiro ò càra pace	I long for you, dear peace
Del perduto sonno mio.	of my lost sleep.
Or che il sol dormendo giace	Now that the Sun lies sleeping,
Chi lo toglie al dolce oblio?	who takes him away from sweet oblivion?]

of this serenata is that the aria was likely to have been bracketed by "solemn sinfonie," whose placement and musical character set the emotional tone for the imagined "scene" and musically heightened the dramatic "entrance" and expression by Apollo in the narrative.

Apollo immediately takes on the lead role in the drama after his initial sleepy confusion. He forgives Moon and Night for their disturbance after hearing their reasons for waking him. He too is inspired to exalt the Ambassadress Maria, but by his own superior gifts: through song and poetry.[50] In fact, the remainder of the serenata takes a decisive Arcadian turn. In a dialogue between Apollo and the Moon, Apollo calls upon the Muses of his Thessalian Parnassus to perform song and poems to immortalize the ambassadress's supreme qualities further. The Moon adds to this by referring to "the beautiful Arcadia" where a thousand shepherds and a hundred nymphs and more, who raise their song in harmony and sing of things not vulgar, will also unfold their noble verses of immortal praise.[51] As much as *La notte festiva* was a tribute to the Ambassadress Maria, it was also quite likely an intended tribute to the Arcadian Academy and to the aesthetic standards they avowed.[52] This merging of associations is significant for understanding how the serenata's agentive dimensions in this period fused absolutist politics with larger cultural and aesthetic movements occurring in Rome. The Academy of Arcadians may have been dedicated to humanist endeavors, yet as an elite society it included some of the most influential power-brokers in the city, many of whom leaned one way or another toward the support of various warring European factions – biases that were not easily ignored. It was in the interest of the ambassador not only to know these players, but also to involve himself in their circles, to become a player among them, and the Arcadian Academy in the 1690s was the supreme vehicle for forging such alliances. True, the marqués de Cogolludo already had made contact with the Arcadians via Colonna, as well as through his support of the poet Stampiglia, a founding member of the academy. But he had yet to make his association official. On March 20, 1696, Don Luigi della Cerda was officially accepted as an acclaimed member of the academy, and given his own Arcadian pseudonym, "Arconte Frisseo."[53]

La notte festiva thus reveals an important interplay of discourses. Some involve the forging of intricate socio-political relationships that were deeply connected to the public serenata's ritualization, its use as a political tool, and how such demands affected the serenata's unique blending of traditions, both past and present. This serenata also provides a possible entrée into some of the concerns over audience reception and, moreover, into the aesthetic debates concerning musico-dramatic signification. Though he was a typical figure in late seventeenth-century poetry, Stampiglia's choice of Apollo as the most potent expressive force in *La notte festiva* was not merely coincidence. Apollo held great symbolic prominence for the Arcadians, as the paradigmatic Arcadian shepherd and poet.[54] In this performance, Apollo's role underscores an important point that Arcadian ideologues frequently made – that first and foremost, listeners of this performance were to be enchanted and persuaded by noble verse, rendered effectively, but carefully, via voice.

So where does that place music? How were the *sinfonie* of *La notte festiva* meant to function? If text was the central expressive force, in what ways was non-texted music meant to be heard? And what were the concerns and parameters of reception? Of course, these questions are difficult to answer definitively. Occasionally, however, there is a chink in the armor of contemporary accounts beneath which lie details, or at least hints, that allow us to better infer how genres like the serenata were understood, regarded, and used by their audience.

IV

The serenata's dual nature

On the night of August 24, 1704, the Roman nobleman Urbano Barberini, Prince of Palestrina, hosted and played an active role in the lavishly performed serenata *Le gare festive in applauso alla Real Casa di Francia*, authored by Giacomo Buonaccorsi, and scored by Pietro Paolo Bencini. Like many serenatas, *Le gare festive* was a public act calculated to strengthen alliances, in this particular case between prominent Roman nobility, Spanish delegates, and the recently empowered French Bourbon court. The fortuitous birth earlier that summer of the Duke of Brittany, Louis XIV's first great-grandson, provided Prince Urbano and his entourage in Rome an occasion to celebrate the Spanish–French alliance. Urbano Barberini, a patron with an illustrious familial and political heritage, dedicated his serenata to the Duchess Isabella Maria Giron, wife of the Ambassador to Spain, Francisco Uçeda; but the significance of the work's performance was essentially to honor the French crown, using the occasion of the duke's birth for staging politics.[55]

Documentation for the spectacle surrounding *Le gare festive* is detailed and rich in imagery: a magnificent cortège entered the Piazza di Spagna, guided by three nautically themed carriages, each gilded ship carrying brightly costumed instrumentalists, soloists, and singers, the final coach driven by the bejeweled and costumed Prince Urbano himself. Unfortunately, yet perhaps predictably, the moment of the serenata's music making is not described in the same detail as the lively pre-concert buildup. Aside from an acknowledgment of many instrumentalists and mention of solo singers, descriptions tell us little about how this serenata sounded, and about what people may have heard.[56] Symptomatic of most news literature in early modern Rome, descriptions of serenatas and the festivities surrounding them have a narrow expressive range. The inclusiveness of *Le gare festive* – "an infinite number of spectators of every class and gender"[57] witnessed the performance – was an element recorded in many contemporary descriptions of serenata performances, yet beyond that, little else was ever written. However, the descriptions are quite different when it comes to highlighting privileged guests and their involvement in the event. It was customary for documenters to detail the manner in which the most notable members of the nobility among the spectators engaged with the serenata, always from vantage points that were more privileged and advantageous compared with those of the larger crowd, and often in positions that visibly and dramatically placed them as part of the extravagant display.[58]

In his description of the performance of *Le gare festive*, the diarist Francesco Valesio describes the experience of viewing the serenata from various locations. His observations elucidate the interplay of the serenata as a cultural event and as political spectacle. They help to capture how the ritualization process can speak simultaneously to the immediacy of multiple audiences while bearing the ideological pressures of enacted regime politics. Valesio describes the manner in which the larger crowd accessed the serenata by filling the streets and pushing as close to the main square as possible. By contrast, the noble patrons and guests (including the Spanish ambassador, his wife, and the French Cardinal Toussaint de Forbin Janson) were strategically displayed beneath the balcony of the Spanish palace, a space that remained illuminated throughout the performance.[59] Valesio also documents that Urbano Barberini placed a number of open coaches in the piazza the preceding evening.[60] Like opera boxes on wheels, these coaches offered privileged and private spaces, separate from the masses that crowded the open piazza. The coaches' proximity to this serenata performance may have afforded a better view of the concert, and perhaps, a better chance to hear what *Le gare festive* offered – a musically charged event for which sound was a symbolic marker of wealth, power, and splendor. But was the focus of the serenata – in its real-time, outdoor performance – actually about *hearing* the music? It may be a truism that we cannot provide definitive answers to questions concerning early modern reception;

an attempt to parse the role of music in the serenata and its perception by audiences does little to contradict this assertion. As with other works designed for one-time occasions, serenatas were ephemeral events difficult to trace. There are moments, however, in the otherwise sterile language of conventional newsletters that shed light on the matter.

An *avviso* dated August 30, 1704 notes that the success of Prince Urbano's first performance of the serenata *Le gare festive* prompted the Ambassador to Venice, Giovanni Francesco Morosini, to sponsor a second performance in Rome's Piazza San Marco the following night.[61] The document also relates that the ambassador, who resided near Piazza San Marco, demonstrated his generosity by inviting the nobility of Rome to his residence afterwards for refreshments and "to hear the music."[62] This may have been newsworthy precisely because it demonstrated that all efforts were made by the patron (or his entourage) to ensure a positive experience for the exclusive circle of invited noble guests. Even though the *re-hearing* of serenatas does not seem to have been a common practice, Carlo Cartari (a consistorial lawyer and chronicler of Roman news) reports something quite similar for a serenata performed in 1687:

On that same Monday evening, his Lordship the Spanish ambassador in the usual piazza held, for the second time after his arrival, a public celebration for the birthday of the reigning queen. Built in front of the small piazza called Mignanelli in front of the ambassador's palace was a graceful theater made of beams, boards, and beautifully painted canvases ... Rising from the ground was a staircase divided in three levels on which were placed the musicians and instrumentalists of all sorts. Once the curtain was raised (as I said), they began a marvelous and full *sinfonia* and singing; but little of that could be heard because of the buzz of the crowds and noise of the many carriages. The performance ended at two thirty. But because those who were exclusively invited to the ambassador's palace could not enjoy the music, due to the stated reason, His Excellency rightly considered having it performed again in his palazzo, as was immediately done.[63]

Cartari's description of the noise and chaos, which prevented him and other nobles from *hearing* the serenata, is exactly the sort of news that less personal, official sources often avoided, but it is instructive for probing issues of reception.[64] At the very least, it suggests that occasionally (or perhaps even frequently) the public forum for serenatas was not always conducive to listening to music. It suggests that this venue was not primarily devoted to an appreciation of the inner craftwork of the performance, but instead privileged the visual, social, and public dimensions of the serenata's status as *event*. This possibility points us back to the question of whether hearing the serenata in its outdoor public manifestation was, in fact, a concern. On the one hand, that documenters would take the trouble to note the inability to hear might prove that in ideal cases audiences (that part of the audience that was better positioned) did hear the songs and *sinfonie* of serenatas, which were presumably the intended novelty of the event. It is also possible that Cartari's account, along with the *avviso* of 1704, points to a unique multidimensionality inherent to the serenata performance. In essence, both documents reveal a public-versus-private framework embedded in serenata performances; however, the evidence in these two cases suggests a more pronounced hierarchical relationship in that dichotomy (elite guests ranked above the general public), a hierarchy that is disclosed in these instances through the dual nature of the serenata's reception. The mass audience witnessed the serenata (with all its spectacular components) once, whereas the more privileged guests engaged with the serenata as a *two-part* experience – one outdoors in the piazza, the second immediately following but indoors in the more intimate space of a private room. The performances, as we might imagine, created very different impressions of hearing and perception.

For the official public event, what mattered most was that the serenata achieved its intended political goal which, in the case of *Le gare festive*, was for patrons and their entourage to celebrate their alliance with the French Bourbon court in front of the public at large who stood as audience and witness. The expression of such a political and diplomatic concept entailed a complex multilayered performance, in which instrumental ensembles and vocal arias were but one part of a series of displays that included processions, symbolic exhibitions of light and fireworks, along with other decorations, each discrete, yet enfolded into the allegory of the serenata's poetic conceit. The key to the performance's public effectiveness was to reduce the complexity of its narrative into coherent, well-honed messages. Don Handelman describes such statements as the hallmarks of "events-that-present," making visible and continuous "this quality of might on sight, of the presence of power" that "may overwhelm in its mass and magnitude."[65] In practice, patrons of serenatas may have been concerned with making the visible dimension of the public serenata at least as effective as, or perhaps even more splendorous than, the sonic one. Thus, the quantity of musicians on stage was not only a method to augment sound, but also a visible demonstration of largess. The visual presence of well-known solo singers was equally important, as much for their singing capabilities as for their status as the patron's collected objects.

It is likely that the complete experience of the serenata, including hearing and processing the sense of the text and music in coordination with all other visual forms of display, was reserved and intended for a smaller group of participants for which the dense concentration of symbols and their complex associations were meaningful. This more complete and sophisticated experience was intentionally exclusive, what Robert Darnton has recognized as "social order representing itself to itself."[66] Patrons and select guests were often seated in positions from which they might watch the masses watching them. In other words, their placement *within* the performance was meant to associate them with the spectacular events taking place. Thus, the loud and visually forceful impression made by the serenata's opening *sinfonia* was, in effect, a token of their status. For these privileged participants the serenata's orchestral impact was both a form of festive display and a socio-political statement, symbolically embedded in the meaning of the event, for which the serenata's musical drama was the interpretive vehicle. Patrons and their elite audience needed to experience two simultaneous levels of the serenata. One was immediate and palpable – the physical effect of music's limited though highly anticipated presence. The other required reflection and insight as to how spectacular effects acquired deeper meaning when linked to the subtle musical rendering of the poetic text. The first entailed a very visceral public experience, the second a more insular, interpretive experience.

From this perspective music was *both* a dominant element – the serenata's featured novelty – and an element subject to interaction with other forms of expression. For a general public music needed a visual platform. Even if the fifty or so musicians played little, their visual presence and prominent staging was a constant symbolic element. However, for an elite audience music also required a verbal context. The libretto served as the blueprint for the performance, which ordered and gave meaning to the serenata's special but somewhat detached orchestral effect. Text was this audience's directive for hearing the music and for intercalating its performance within the larger symbolic drama of the serenata. In short, the serenata appears to have worked its dual nature in simultaneous and interlocking ways. The serenata was directed in the service of both public and private consumption. It exploited spectacular elements as a means to reach the lower, public orders, but demanded a different sort of textualism to convey emerging political alliances to elite audiences.

Ritual and memory

The serenata's capacity to direct meaning to different audiences within socially specific settings is instructive for several reasons. In one sense, the dual functioning of a serenata facilitated a socially bifurcated musical performance. Yet it also served as an occasion to broker complex and fragile tensions associated with political upheaval. Indeed, the August 24 performance of *Le gare festive* in 1704 appears to have been a musical event and cultural moment largely overshadowed by political demands. To clarify the dual nature of the serenata further, we must consider the ways in which a work like *Le gare festive* was pulled into the arena of absolutist politics. This will allow us to see how the functions of the serenata were related to the pressures that influenced its performance, and moreover, how this event was largely shaped by serenata rituals that preceded it historically.

We begin with the setting: the summer of 1704 scorched Rome with a heatwave that lasted nearly two months.[67] Warm weather pushed residents into the streets, especially after dusk when cooler temperatures provided relief. City squares bustled with Romans gathering to take air and to attend *al fresco* entertainment provided by noble families. A favorite summertime custom was the flooding of Piazza Navona to refresh audiences while they enjoyed a variety of diversions. Warm nights were also ideal for the performance of serenatas. During the early years of the eighteenth century, the Marquis Ruspoli, Don Livio Odescalchi, the Duchess of Zagorolo, Cardinal Ottoboni, and Queen Casimira of Poland were among those who supported Rome's frequent summertime serenatas, sponsoring performances inside their palaces or within their private gardens. It is important to emphasize that these entertainments were not only welcome distractions from warm weather, but long-awaited pleasures that had been denied. With political tensions heightened by the War of Spanish Succession, Pope Clement XI cautiously retained the prohibitions of public theater mandated by his predecessor, Innocent XI, in 1698. When a severe earthquake hit Rome in 1703, Clement XI enacted a five-year ban on all public theater and secular entertainment during the ensuing carnival seasons.

In 1704 serenatas functioned as more than seasonal entertainment to pass warm evenings. In some ways, these serenatas were a musico-dramatic substitute for the loss of opera experienced during this period. Moreover, the serenatas of 1704 held important political capital as well. To the delight of Bourbon sympathizers living in Rome, the summer season coincided with the birth of the Duke of Brittany at Versailles on June 25. The infant duke lived less than a year and played no role in European politics except through his birth that summer, which was an occasion for the French court to promote Bourbon ascendancy at home and abroad.[68] Courting Rome for their needs was among the Bourbons' more important political endeavors.

The War of Spanish Succession left the French Bourbon and Imperial Habsburg empires battling for European dominance. France had always hoped to weaken Spain's prestige in Italy and equally had feared that the Imperial Habsburgs would reconstitute what Charles V once had. The acquisition of the Spanish throne after Charles II's death was a significant triumph, and meant that France could begin to acquire Spanish territories, including politically and militarily strategic lands in Italy. Most controversial was the question of the investiture of the Kingdom of Naples and Sicily: with the acquisition of the Spanish throne, Philip V claimed it as his, yet the Habsburg emperor forcefully protested, threatening to invade Italy if the Bourbons had their way. At the center of the conflict was the Roman papacy, who tried to play the part of neutral mediator. But Clement XI vacillated precariously, motivated by his trepidation at the emperor's boldness and, at the same time, his fear of Franco-Spanish power. As Christopher M. S. Johns concludes: "As a diplomat Albani [Clement XI] was both combative and indecisive, and in spite of protestations of neutrality, frankly pro-French and anti-Imperial and was, consequently, truly trusted by none of the powers."[69]

Despite its advantage with the pope, France's dominion was never truly stable. The larger conflict between France and Austria forced many Italian states to take sides despite the pope's plea for neutrality. The northern Italian dukes of Guastalla and Modena collaborated with the imperial forces, whereas the Duke of Mantua sided with the French. Savoy initially supported the French but later was aligned with the Austrians. Such shifts in alliances were also evident in Rome, where diplomatic envoys engaged in aggressive propaganda to sway resident cardinals and local nobility.[70]

It was during this period of intensified conflict that the French sought Rome as a site to re-establish their prominence and secure papal protection. Even though events between 1701 and 1703 worsened the breach between the pope and the imperial house,[71] the Bourbons continued to face some difficult challenges diplomatically and militarily. The most debilitating of events came late in the summer of 1704, just weeks before *Le gare festive*'s performance, when on August 13 the French suffered a decisive blow. Though they attempted to create a German power to rival the Habsburgs, Franco-Bavarian troops lost ground to the imperial army and were defeated at the Battle of Blenheim. It is unlikely that *Le gare festive* was organized in reaction to this event; Valesio's diary shows that the news appeared to have reached Rome only by 20 August.[72] When Cardinal Forbin Janson, acting French ambassador to the Holy See, received news of the duke's birth on 7 July 1704, he rushed to announce this in person to Clement XI, and received gold and silver medals in return.[73] City-wide festivities were soon organized to honor the birth; however, the more important subtext for these celebrations was the endorsement of Louis XIV's supremacy. We might imagine that by allowing such events to take place under his watch, the pope once more placed himself in a controversial position by violating a pact of neutrality during a time of war.

July and August of 1704 were filled with a number of activities performed as sacred ritual or secular entertainment, but which ostensibly were inspired by the duke's birth, and thus functioned as *Gallispani* (French–Spanish) dynastic propaganda. When we consider these events as rituals we need to be mindful of how ritual can be both time-specific and time-less. When time-specific, ritual may respond to a particular event, or to a broader sense of ongoing change and indeterminacy. As one example, on Sunday July 20 the mass at San Luigi (the French national church in Rome) was anything but ordinary. The church was ornately decorated and set with grand stages to hold eighty musicians who were to accompany a performance of the *Te Deum* following the mass. Among draped damask and taffeta were two portraits prominently displayed, side-by-side – one of the reigning pontiff, the other of the King of France. For the evening Cardinal Forbin Janson arranged to have a *macchina da fuoco* in the Piazza San Marco, with an architectural design that revealed the familial heralds of the Bourbon household, including that of the new Duke of Brittany. Rome's Spanish factions were asked to stage a similar set of performances. They too held a *Te Deum* on July 21 at San Giacomo degli Spagnoli. Later that day the Spanish ambassador prepared a *macchina*, this time flaunting the image of Fame flying through the air (proclaiming the duke's birth), while a rising sun (the symbol for the French king) triggered a pyrotechnic display.[74]

The repetitive visual imagery glorifying the Bourbon court was matched sonically in a series of serenatas performed that summer. For many of these we know little of the specific contents of the text or music, though the mere mention of patrons (Cardinal Forbin Janson, the Spanish ambassador, and other Spanish representatives) supports the possibility that *Gallispani* sympathizers used these serenatas to publicize Bourbon influence.[75] One serenata was particularly explicit. In the July 22 performance of Francesco Posterla's *La contesa d'onore*[76] the characters Glory, Valor, and Fame celebrate the auspicious news of the duke's birth and conclude the serenata with a rousing call, "Long live the Great Louis!"[77] The most sumptuous serenata honoring the Bourbon legacy was *Le gare festive*, which had been saved for the August 24 vigil of San Luigi so that the *Gallispani* could compound the political symbolism of the duke's birth with the celebration of the patron saint of the French monarchy, a feast that had long been commemorated in Rome with great ceremony.[78] It is essential to view *Le gare festive* not as an event in isolation, but as the significant end point of a larger arc that built up symbolic capital through a series of performances – visual, textual, and aural – each bearing characteristically repetitive gestures. *Le gare festive* exemplifies a particular kind of serenata, not one performed solely out of seasonal custom, but one enacted as ritual practice called upon to serve the increasingly troubled *Gallispani* dominion.

Le gare festive cannot be divorced from the political uncertainty of early modern Europe at the turn of the eighteenth century. Though the Bourbon Empire was in official ascendancy, it was undeniably fragile. In the last three decades of Louis XIV's reign, France had consumed a good portion of its assets and achieved no permanent stability for itself or the rest of Europe. The projected images of an empire in true ascendancy may not be as telling as the images conveyed during potential moments of weakness, when public displays of supremacy often can be repetitive and grand, as well as ostentatious and inflated. *Le gare festive* captured all of these qualities. Urbano Barberini spared no expense on ceremony and pomp. In fact, the diarist Valesio reveals his surprise when he reports that the prince, despite his indebtedness, managed to borrow a considerable sum to finance the lavish event. It appears that Urbano's spendthrift habits were well known, or at least made so by the publication of *Le gare festive*'s text, in which the phrase "con licenza de' superiori" (by the permission of the authorities) was allegedly substituted with the phrase "con licenza de' creditori" (by the permission of his creditors).[79] Aside from the patron's financial controversy, librettist Buonaccorsi reveals a further layer of concern regarding the extreme pomp and strong political overtones of this event, considering the tense conflict over Bourbon or imperial hegemony among Roman delegates. It is noteworthy that in his dedicatory letter to Urbano Barberini printed in the libretto, he asks for the protection of his patron from censorship.[80] Fiscal mismanagement and self-indulgence aside, we might come to understand Urbano's self-promotion as symptomatic of a growing fragility and insecurity for both courtly elites and monarchal hegemony. The recognition of this quality of decadence in the shadow of political uncertainty, as in the case of *Le gare festive*, is crucial to the understanding of the public serenata as ritual.

Although public serenatas were anchored to particular moments in time, their repetitive gestures and maintenance of acknowledged conventions preserved a sense of timeless endurance to give an impression of cultural continuity. As rituals, serenatas were inherently reflexive. While ostensibly designed for public response, we have already seen that the aesthetic mechanisms of serenatas may have spoken best, and most thoroughly, to the most insular subset of their total audience, those observers who most needed symbolic and historical reinforcement consistent with their understanding of the larger and shifting political horizons. In the absence of a truly stable and indisputable Bourbon hegemony, the serenatas written for their self-celebration required exaggerated and recurring markers to create a sense of social order. The patrons and architects behind the dynastic events of 1704 understood these conditions and parameters. They were the inheritors of a long history of ritual practice. Even if the content was Bourbon-directed, *Le gare festive* drew upon a distinct Spanish–Roman legacy. By 1704, what Bourbon agents needed most was to appropriate the memory of this legacy through continuity and ritual re-enactment. The Bourbons thus engaged in simple inheritance. In the absence of an unencumbered and politically expansive horizon, they continued with what had already proved culturally viable, and adopted the same forms, location, function, and elements of serenata practices. In this case, stasis was a more potent political force than radical change or novelty.

The ritual enactment of *Le gare festive* bears the essentials of these inherited characteristics while serving to symbolize a desired political continuity. As the patronal agent, Urbano Barberini maximized the symbolic link between past and present and connected Roman aristocracy, Spanish inheritance, and Bourbon hegemony.[81] It was quite fitting, then, that under his patronage the pre-concert procession that left the Palazzo Barberini on course for a climactic arrival at the Piazza di Spagna, the ritual site of serenata performances, also celebrated a Spanish–French coalition. Emblematic journeys were not uncommon in Rome.[82] Typical of feudal public ceremony and spectacle, which routinely carried out the work of social representation, this procession encompassed the very process of ritual's operational divisions by marking relations that unified locations and objects in space and time. Claude Lévi-Strauss suggests that ritual uses a procedure of "parceling out," which makes "infinite distinctions and ascribes discriminatory values to the slightest shades of difference."[83] The deliberate and repetitive procedures of ritual create the impression of slow motion and function as a deliberate control mechanism for ordering reality. Lévi-Strauss's insights into the functions of ritual can shed light on how *Le gare festive*'s symbolic array featured distinctions between types of gestures and classes of objects (including social agents as well as physical and material factors) that figure into the serenata's staging of social meanings.

Le gare festive's ceremony was an elaborate affair with each sequence of the procession symbolically ordered.[84] The first and second coach carried the musicians, each costumed with red and white tassels, the same decorations worn to war by soldiers of the two crowns. Both carriages were accompanied by fellow noblemen belonging not only to Urbano's social milieu but also to the circle of supporters of *Gallispani* politics.[85] Urbano himself drove the third coach, the focal point of the procession. Larger and more ornate than the previous two, this chariot held select noble guests, and pedestaled three singers,[86] who, like their fellow musicians, were adorned with white and red ribbons but otherwise costumed more elaborately. The separation of singers and instrumentalists in different carriages in the procession mirrors the distinction made in actual performance, when singers typically would be placed at the front of the stage, apart from the larger ensemble.

A central element of *Le gare festive*'s pre-concert parade was the symbolic use of light. Thirty torches carried by Urbano's uniformed footmen illuminated both agents and spectators as the procession moved through Rome's crowded streets. Light in the serenata (as in other nighttime spectacles) was often an indicator of beneficence and power.[87] Apart from the actual cortège, torches lined the streets leading to and around the piazza, tracing the pathway of the procession's approach, as well as outlining the shape of a theatrical arena. Torches also illuminated the insides of palaces, whose windows served as spaces for nobles, elite women, and guests to witness the events – and at the same time, to be witnessed by the masses of people filling the piazza below.[88] Light surrounded these windows and enshrouded the privileged few in a glow, making them part of the total spectacle, and at the same time distinguishing them as belonging to a private realm. Light therefore served as an important element, enabling and directing the audience's gaze by steering lines of spectatorship, parcel by parcel – from the procession, to the windows, up towards the balcony of the Palazzo di Spagna (on which stood the ambassador, his wife, and Cardinal Forbin Janson) – visually connecting this patronal network to the temporary staging area where the serenata was to be performed.

Valesio reports that once musicians and patrons settled into their respective positions, the musicians were given the signal to start.[89] Little else of the performance is discussed, and yet the foregoing details of ceremony – pre-concert procession, costuming, lighting, and ordering – and moreover this performance's specific placement within this historical time and space, are fundamentally connected to the serenata's aesthetic parameters. As we will come to see, the serenata libretto played its own role within the greater ritual, and it too parceled out elements resonant with ritual's logic of design and unfolding of events, helping to order music's delivery within the larger context of the serenata's ritual structure.

"Sound carriers" in *Le gare festive*

Serenata libretti were often loosely drawn from mythology or pastoral literature, and their frequent use of mythological and allegorical elements strengthened the link between ritual and text. Their plots typically lacked the intricacies of action found in opera libretti, and they often proceeded by means of an allegorical frame – a dominant theme – from which the interpretive leap to the personality or event commemorated could be easily made by culturally literate audiences.[90] *Le gare festive* is exactly as the title indicates, a festive contest, and thus fits the very popular contest formula used with great frequency in serenatas of the period.[91] The text is based on the mythological tale of the Golden Apple, or the Judgment of Paris; however, the poet Buonaccorsi reorients the plot to fit the occasion that this serenata celebrated. He begins *Le gare festive* after Paris's judgment has occurred but relocates the story from Mount Ida to Rome. He introduces a disgruntled Juno and a more tempered Pallas, who initiate the drama with expressions of dismay over their loss to Venus, who they feel has unfairly won the Golden Apple by seducing Paris. After brief exchanges and an aria sung by each deity, their laments are interrupted by the sudden appearance of Fame, the third member of the serenata's cast, a character not connected to the original myth. Fame's reputation in classical sources as a force for either good or evil is ambiguous and open to interpretation. Her enigmatic status and significance to *Le gare festive* therefore begs further scrutiny.

Fame embodied the image of a sound carrier in motion, a resonant creature whose many voices could not be ignored. Whatever she heard, she repeated first in a whisper to a few, then louder, more vigorously, and with many voices; her stories became rumors transmitted to many. Virgil first accentuated the goddess's extensive powers in the *Aeneid*. A giant bird-beast, Fame was created by Gaia (Earth) to avenge wrongs committed by the gods. Virgil describes Fame as moving swiftly and ceaselessly, shielded in feathers covering countless all-pervading eyes, ears, and mouths with multiple tattling tongues that shrieked through the night.[92] Ovid's opinion of Fame is more vague than Virgil's, although his description of Fame's dwelling in the *Metamorphoses* – a resonant palace of echoing brass, pierced with a thousand openings through which every voice could penetrate[93] – perhaps has more affinity with how Fame was visually and musically

Figure 7 Michel Angelo la Chausse, planning diagram for *macchina da fuoco*, printed in Francesco Valesio, *Diario di Roma*, 1704 (I-Rac).

portrayed, not only in *Le gare festive*, but in a number of events surrounding the duke's birth in 1704.

In this political context Fame was a positive force. For the July 21 *macchina da fuoco* sponsored by the Spanish ambassador, she was the visual centerpiece, flying with emblematic trumpet in hand, the sound device for transmitting Bourbon ascendancy to the four continents of the world.[94]

Fame became a theme that the librettist Posterla resumed in the serenata *La contesa d'onore*, performed on the following days. As a bird-like mouthpiece, she sings of taking flight, using her trumpet to spread the news of the infant's birth to the world.[95] In *Le gare festive* instrumental forces,

Example 6 Pietro Paolo Bencini, *Le gare festive*: sinfonia con trombe, 1704 (I-Rvat, Barb. lat. 4228).

particularly the effect of echoing brass, are also Fame's sonic and symbolic conduits. Through the allegory of Fame, instrumental sound takes on a prominent role in this serenata, serving as both a spectacular element occasionally placed in the foreground, as well as the central signifying vehicle for revealing the work's larger meaning and symbolic connection to the prescribed event.

Fame's first appearance in the drama is not vocally announced, but sonically suggested with the spontaneous intrusion of a brief *sinfonia con trombe*, five measures of brilliant fanfare that display trumpets prominently scored with string ensemble (see example 6).[96] This acoustic interruption expresses a critical moment musically and dramatically, and it also imparts an important visual dimension otherwise absent in the serenata. The image of Fame in motion – suddenly appearing from afar or descending from above – is suggested through sound, not sight, as would be expected from the serenata's action-less performance. In effect, music engenders Fame and it foreshadows the work's larger significance. Yet, for listeners distanced from the particulars of text (not just socially but literally), the sonic impact of this instrumental intrusion was likely without a specifically defined allegorical context. As with fireworks launched from a *macchina*, the *sinfonia con trombe* might have functioned for the broader audience as a sudden and momentary special effect, inspiring awe by allowing the audience to hear and visually witness the rendering of the ensemble's brief and unexpected fanfare. For the general audience, the sonic force of the *sinfonia* was an effectively direct and public aspect of spectacle. Only the libretto provided the interpretive springboard for listeners privileged enough to access it; they could read the *sinfonia* as part of the drama and perhaps come to understand its significance allegorically. Within the context of the serenata's plot, music is made diegetic. Upon hearing the *sinfonia*, Pallas equates the "warring trumpet" with Fame's approach.[97] She is the first to initiate a symbolic association between instrument and figure. Nevertheless, the relationship between Fame and her trumpets involves more than a literal substitution. The trumpets are not merely stand-ins for the goddess; they themselves become dramatic agents as is demonstrated in music example 7.

When Pallas's recitative ends, composer Bencini brings back the *sinfonia con trombe*, now shortened to a three-measure ritornello that introduces Fame for the first time in the *da capo* aria "Ad onta dell'oblio, mie trombe, non tacete" (Against oblivion, my trumpets, do not be silent), which she begins in measure 4. In the aria, what was the full *sinfonia* is now transformed into a series of fragments that are recalled or developed to accentuate the text and punctuate the end of Fame's vocal line. Set within this vocal texture, the simplicity of the fanfare is fragmented into something more complex for which instruments simulate dialogue with the voice. Fame is directive. Her first phrase is itself a trumpet-like fanfare, possibly a mimetic device to suggest how Fame "plays" one of the trumpets. The actual trumpet parts are abruptly cut off while she commands them to spread their blasts, the aural mechanism for extending praise for the infant duke. In measures 8–9, the first and second trumpets respond to Fame by sounding a series of high As, supported by the first and second violins, which adopt the trumpets' lead melodic material from the original *sinfonia*. In the measures that follow, obbligato parts respond similarly, but the trumpets play less of a role until each subsequent return to the tonic (m. 16, m. 22), in part because as natural instruments they lack the notes to play fanfares outside of the tone. However, Fame's repeated calls for the trumpets to participate are also thereby delayed, creating a sense of surprise each time this special effect is sounded, especially in measures 22–24 as the trumpets bring the first section of the aria to a brilliant close. The trumpets have become more than the goddess's representative symbol. Responding to her commands, they are Fame's sound carrier, her "echoing brass," which amplifies a single voice into many more powerful voices. This partnership between Fame and trumpets, between word and sound as dramatized in "Ad onta dell'oblio," will serve as the work's allegorical fulcrum to turn what was a Golden Apple spin-off into a story made relevant to the *real* occasion (with all its political references) that *Le gare festive* was to celebrate. Fame, who makes

Example 7 Pietro Paolo Bencini, *Le gare festive*:aria, "Ad onta dell'oblio, mie trombe, non tacete," 1704 (I-Rvat, Barb. lat. 4228). The music for the second stanza (mm. 25–38) contrasts melodically with the first and moves to the relative minor, as is typical in *da capo* form. Bencini closes the B section (mm. 36–38) with a similar fanfare for trumpets based on the motives used in mm. 1–3.

Fama	*Fame*
Ad onta dell'oblio,	[Against oblivion,
Mie trombe, non tacete,	my trumpets, do not be silent,
Spargete sì, spargete	spread out, spread out
I fiati alteri.	your proud blasts.
Festeggi il Prato, e il Rio,	May the meadow and the brook celebrate;
Ride la Terra, e il Polo,	the land and the sky laugh:
Dan moto al mio gran Volo	Supreme thoughts give motion to my
alti pensieri.	grand flight.]

an appearance as an outsider – the unexpected guest – will serve as the influential agent who turns the narrative to the event at hand.

At first, though, Fame's draw of attention creates controversy. Juno and Pallas rebuff Fame's sudden arrival, fearing the spread of the news of Venus's victory via the goddess's gossiping tongues. Fame, however, reminds them she is less interested in spreading rumors than in spreading praise. She urges the deities to turn their attention away from Paris's judgment, and to apply

Example 7 (*cont.*)

Example 7 (*cont.*)

Example 7 *(cont.)*

Example 7 (*cont.*)

their talents to nobler deeds, such as bestowing honor on the French king, whose name "resounds on such a fine day [the feast of San Luigi], festive and grand and adorned of beautiful glories."[98] Both women heed Fame's call and begin to sing the praises of Louis. Additionally, to honor the king, they agree to bestow upon the infant duke all that they had offered to Paris, a task they admit to be more valorous than the pursuit of beauty.

None the less, the festive expressions of Juno and Pallas are outflanked by Fame whose powerful trumpets are not merely glorifying, but also mnemonic. The tension between memory and loss forms an important theme in this serenata, as well as in the circumstances that incited its performance. The urgency and importance of Louis XIV's and the Bourbons' preservation was evident by 1704. Thus, for *Le gare festive*, the goddess's allegorical significance worked well. Fame's powers were thought to be transformative. In his epic *Thebaid*, the Roman poet Statius suggests that only Fame had the ability to remember princes and to make immortal the story of their lives.[99] Fame was thought to augment remembrance, and in *Le gare festive*, it is her trumpets who systematically amplify her message. As expressed in her aria, Fame uses music to stamp out oblivion.

This musical dramatization of ritual remembrance plays out sequentially in *Le gare festive*. Each major aria sung by Fame (placed more or less at the beginning, the middle, and end of the serenata), for which the notion of memory is directly involved, is scored with prominent trumpet accompaniment. In Fame's second remembrance aria, "Sì, che resisterà,"[100] the trumpets respond each time the goddess sings, "Yes, [Louis's great soul] will resist." Bencini creates brief echo effects by having the trumpet part reverberate the same cadential phrase expressed by Fame. Such moments are textually coordinated so that musical repetition and the trumpets' amplification of Fame's voice figuratively portray the thematic notion of resisting oblivion and spreading the king's memory in perpetuity, enacted through word and made more powerful through sound. For aria writing of the period, these musical approaches to text expression were not uncommon, but in *Le gare festive*, the meaning of the musical act had cumulative effect. To the audience for whom the libretto was intended, music was supposed to accrue sonic and symbolic capital. What starts out as a musical interruption, a simple *sinfonia con trombe*, far exceeds mere spectacular effect. Via the *sinfonia*, Fame's trumpets become the symbolic thread that ties the various strands of this allegory together. Even in her last monologue and the conclusion to the piece, Fame sings of taking flight with no fewer than a hundred trumpets.[101] As with her other "remembrance" arias, "Con cento trombe" is precluded by a brief orchestral fanfare, and the text is similarly marked with short trumpet responses. Fame's echoing brass, the serenata's ritual gesture, uses sound – one last time – to symbolically defy the loss of memory, as if to sonically fend off the potential decline of Bourbon hegemony.

Allegory and ritual

Along with other allegorical writings, *Le gare festive* operates by turning a conceptual system into a narrative one. Fame as metaphor for immortality is not signified in one particular instance; instead the metaphor is expressed in a series of moments over time. Allegory unfolds in a linear manner; its progressive amplification of a single concept, extended through repetition and embellishment, creates a vivid structural process.[102] Each narrative sequence of an allegory expounds the next, and yet the process itself is inherently fragmentary. While conveying a sense of temporal continuity, allegories can isolate individual moments, marking them as fragments in space and time. Furthermore, each instance in an allegory's unfolding reveals doubly articulated levels – the literal meaning and the symbolic meaning. That allegory organizes itself with reference to temporal axes is important for decoding the serenata's multilayered text and, more specifically, for understanding the narrative use and symbolic placement of instrumental music as a complex performative element.

Le gare festive illustrates this type of allegorical organization. As with most politically inspired serenatas, its narrative plot is relatively static and its theme is clear and repetitive. But the design and delivery of the libretto's didactic message involve the unique combination of distinct and directive structure coupled with subtler literary and historical references, which demand a sophisticated interpretive strategy. Audiences would have had to be familiar with the particulars of the Golden Apple myth in order to respond to Juno and Pallas's symbolic roles. The two bribe-makers (attempting to sway Paris) are transformed for this 1704 context into gift-givers (offering their exceptional qualities and military prowess to more worthy ends). The catalyst for their transformation is the figure of Fame, whose symbolic meaning in the weeks preceding the August 24 vigil of San Luigi was well rehearsed. Fame's qualities as powerful, all-pervading transmitter, using trumpets to blazon her message, constitute the necessary signifiers to transmit the allegory's secondary and more abstract layer of meaning. Fame effects power, Fame begets remembrance, Fame equals immortality. But this allegory is strictly circumscribed. Fame's abstracted associations are set within the confines of early eighteenth-century European politics. *Le gare festive*'s metaphor is ritualistically resonant. Each repetition and embellishment of Fame's significance is protracted over the allegory's sequential grid and gives structure to time. For the agents involved, they are present to reorient history and transform reality.

Fame's allegorical meaning is heightened through music. The *sinfonia con trombe*, like allegory itself, is doubly symbolic. It indicates the appearance of a new character, but its fanfare heralds more than entrance. Trumpets inaugurate Fame and they become her representative marker, but they also serve as the work's figurative device. Thus, each recurring fragment or memory of the *sinfonia*, however brief or transformed, is an aural reminder of the work's central concept. The trumpets' integration within each of Fame's remembrance arias reveals allegory's twofold significative process. On a literal level, Fame's arias mark time. Their prominent scoring serves to set sonic signposts during the allegory's unfolding. As recurring gestures, the arias help to give order and to underscore the allegory's implicit sense of structure. On a figurative level, we know that Fame's iterative expressions and their musical settings are integral for the allegory's meaning. These complete *Le gare festive*'s conceptual image of sound as a conduit for ritual remembrance.

There is, however, a consequence for allegory's distinct foregrounding of signifiers that in turn become vehicles for the larger story. The act of underlining a signifier accentuates its place in the allegory's narrative continuum. In *Le gare festive* the sounding of music *is* the story's signifying element. The work's allegorical process individualizes the music and thus breaks the sense of temporal continuity. Allegory brackets the *sinfonia con trombe* as an isolated event, which subsequently spawns a sequence of distantly resonant moments, recontextualized in aria format so as to dramatize the symbolic association between Fame and trumpets, between word and sound. Sounding the *sinfonia con trombe* underscores the serenata's duality. It sets that music apart from the rest of the serenata's sonic texture, and in doing so it marks the *sinfonia* as the accessory special effect, as well as the pivotal element for the work's interpretation.

Allegory aids the privileging of meaning as it facilitates and exploits the aural and visual potential of the serenata. In *Le gare festive* allegory parcels out music's performance as a material event. For the general audience the *sinfonia* works as a form of festive display, inspiring wonder through sonic force, but intensifying that impact through the ensemble's highly visual presence. For privileged participants the *sinfonia* functions on multiple levels. Through sight and sound, its performance is the event's most basic statement of wealth and power. But as a critical narrative element, the *sinfonia* demands more complex mechanisms of perception. It also requires interpretive integration in order to be "heard" within the story at large.

In effect, the serenata's narrative strategies resonate well with the serenata's ritual practice. Ritual embodies a logic of design similar to that embodied by allegory. It follows highly structured and standardized sequences. Formulas are repeated to reaffirm symbolic associations, and specific gestures are isolated in space and time to make the particulars of their elements plain. Lévi-Strauss recognized what appears to be a procedural problem in ritual that we can also apply to allegory. He notes "At first sight, the two devices of parceling out and repetition are in opposition to each other . . . but in fact, the first procedure is equivalent to the second . . . Ritual, by fragmenting operations and repeating them unwearyingly in infinite detail, takes upon itself the laborious task of patching up holes and stopping gaps."[103] For Lévi-Strauss, parceling necessitates repetition. In other words, to counter the isolation of the parceled event (e.g., allegory foregrounding the *sinfonia*), ritual has to make up the sense of temporal and conceptual separation through the parcel's continuous recurrence – the iteration and reiteration of the fragment. The correspondence between ritual and allegory is telling. In *Le gare festive* recurrence is linear, a series of sonically symbolic arias sung by Fame in which the allegorical theme (the triumph of immortality over obscurity) dominates the narrative. Ritual, says Lévi-Strauss, "encourages the illusion of moving back from the discontinuous to the continuous."[104] What Lévi-Strauss does not seem to address in stating this, however, is the possibility of divergent ritual experiences. If rituals are experienced uniformly, then the interlocking of sequences may be taken for granted conceptually. Again, allegory's lessons may prove useful here. Allegory involves an interpretive process that is *separate* from the creative process; that is, allegory is a specific method of reading in which moving between the text's literal and secondary meaning is necessary to obtain what is "other" – etymologically speaking, the ἄλλος of allegory. It is possible that ritual wields a similar sense of power through its structure.[105] Edward Muir contends that rituals "speak with many voices," and they can be ambiguous in their function and meaning.[106] In the case of the serenata, it may be that not *all* recipients were meant to hear *all* voices equally. Instead, it is more likely that the ability to apprehend ritual's interpretive continuity, and to move between the doubly articulated levels of the serenata's allegory, was intentionally limited to a privileged few.

Only those who navigate the layers of allegory's bifurcated structure can truly patch up holes and stop gaps, so to speak – that is, patching up holes and gaps is tantamount to grasping the cultural meanings that bind aesthetic proclivities and political pressures in the work of the serenata. In the opening years of the eighteenth century, elite members of a courtly society could not take social, cultural, economic, and political stasis for granted. It is not surprising that the anxieties over social change underfoot would find their sounding in the serenata's dual operations, in its broader reach as public spectacle and its more privatized and exclusive enclosures as ritualized allegory. As an integration of aesthetics and politics melded in musico-dramatic practice, *Le gare festive*, then, can be grasped as a cultural form that emanated from and addressed the wings of Rome's high court society as well as its troubled social representation.

Behind closed doors

Narrative choices in the serenata do seem to matter beyond the conventional and largely repeatable templates these libretti typically offered. We might do well then for reasons of comparison and for final reflections to return to the 1695 libretto of *La notte festiva* for this kind of examination. Recall that the emphasis of this narrative was placed upon Apollo and all that he symbolically represented in the development of that drama. And, as discussed, it is quite likely that the marqués de Cogolludo's serenata was meant as a tribute to his wife and, by extension, to the Spanish royal household, but it was also likely that *La notte festiva* was a homage to the Arcadian Academy and to the cultural aesthetics upheld by the society's ideologues. The personification of poetry through Apollo's role is indeed suggestive of this, as exemplified in the following.

At *La notte festiva*'s climax, in which all three figures (Apollo, the Night, the Moon) agree to give praise to the ambassadress, the librettist, Stampiglia, offers several telling directives through the character of the Moon: "Now, we should form gay voices of praise for such an illustrious royal woman, and create a verse appropriate to her great merit." The Moon then addresses the orchestra (characterized as genii, or spirits) and orders: "You, genii who follow our will, move your plectra now quickly now solemnly to form sweet harmonies, and please accompany the song with your playing."[107] Though clearly embedded within the particulars of the drama, we might come to see Stampiglia's line as also implicative beyond this work and even suggestive of the hierarchical dimensions between poetry and music. This short fragment is declarative: music is being asked to follow as an element controlled and exploited by the poets and makers of rhyme who occupy a higher position of expressive power. An important lesson may be gleaned from this moment. Even when instrumental music was foregrounded and took on a dramatic role within the serenata, it was not necessarily emancipated from text. Music may have functioned as the event's pivotally symbolic element, but sound was still kept on a tight leash. In essence, the detachment of music heightened by the serenata's symbolic mechanisms and contrast of dissimilar forces was often, if not always, reconciled through text, the blueprint for decoding music's delivery within the drama's larger allegorical context. Text provided the means to navigate between the serenata's doubly articulated sonic and significative levels.

This point aside, we must also recognize the more complex problem of access and reception in the serenata. As we well know, studies of reception of past musical cultures and contexts can hardly be conclusive. We may never know with certainty whether each serenata attendee placed as near as possible to the performance, or whether each guest invited behind closed doors to *re-hear* a serenata, actually decoded his/her experience of the music within the context of the drama and the event it celebrated. In fact, we cannot say just how frequent or routine re-performances of serenatas may have been, despite their mention in the 1704 *avviso*, or in Carlo Cartari's description of a 1687 serenata. Yet we might come to understand such evidence less as a standard than as an indicator that multiple versions of the serenata experience could exist, whether as two separate occasions in two contrasting spaces, or more likely, as simultaneous and overlapping experiences, each coded for different audiences and each addressing distinct social representations. My interest is to accept some inherent level of uncertainty in this matter and to turn instead to the serenata's performance (its structural peculiarities, aesthetic strategies, and cultural context) as an entrée to the realm of its reception and its role in the negotiation of aesthetic debates of the period. For the purposes of this discussion, perhaps the notion of "behind closed doors" works better if taken less literally and more as a metaphor for the kind of elusive boundary separation conditioned by the serenata's public/private dichotomy – a gesture that fundamentally shaped the delivery of the serenata's urban outdoor performance. It is not enough simply to consider the serenata as a practice that had a fixed moment, a fixed context, and a fixed quality of performance. Rather, the examples discussed here raise the question of how a serenata might occur as multiple versions conditioned by the contextual range of audiences and reception requisites, a phenomenon that may have been widespread, even if few documents attest directly to this.

When we consider the serenata's trajectory in the decades at the turn of the century under study, we come to view the ways in which powerful platforms of ritual designed to celebrate social and political solidarity often functioned in the absence of real unanimity and consensus.[108] Recalling Muir, rituals can "speak with many voices" and "can open up a labyrinth of dissonance rather than a neatly unified vision of society."[109] Strangely, scholars have paid little attention to the qualities of dissonance heightened by the serenata's ritualistic structure, made manifest through its dichotomous features (e.g., loud/soft, visual/aural, dark/light, distant/close, etc.). Guiding each of the serenata's varied oppositions are the distinct yet simultaneous spheres of "public" and "private," carefully constructed and manipulated by the hegemonic impulses of competing empires for which the dual nature of the serenata ritual was socially and politically expedient.[110]

The design of the serenata's performance reveals an important political dimension for which dichotomous structures and multiplicity of meaning may indeed indicate discrepant appropriations. The serenata's public sphere offered elite patrons an opportunity for the display of social order and image building. Such performances could be acts of consolidation or reinforcement of known political realities. However, serenatas often accomplished their best cultural work during times of instability when, as acts of beneficence, their allegorical portrayal of political ascendancy was self-validating. The serenata's tendency toward allegorical expression was not arbitrary. The use of allegory was fitting in moments of ambiguity, in the absence of clarity or consensus, during those times when the potential for "double-speak" (allegory's literal and figurative levels of signification) was especially opportune.

We should also remember that as a cultural form, the serenata was a product of patronage and thus subject to the greater social forces that patronage often accommodated. *Le gare festive* of August 1704 conveyed such currents. Its importance was engendered through the cultural hierarchy of patronage and its enlistment within a weakened absolutist regime. Though the serenata may have favored the intimacy of the smaller chamber venue and the corresponding qualities of privacy and exclusion, its performance also lent itself to a public domain, and to a suggested sense of inclusiveness. The serenata thus operated in its capacity to work several different boundaries, creating a multivocal performance shaped by these qualities of ambiguity. Above all, music as sonic expression appeared to straddle both sides of the public/private divide. In doing so, it was neither an ancillary effect nor the center of attention, but effectively both.

This last statement deserves some pause because it captures not just the flexibility and ambiguity of music's significative role in the serenata, but also how effectively this aesthetic condition of "straddling" speaks to this histori-cal moment. Music – as embodied in the accompaniment and instrumental interludes in serenatas – was neither fully directive nor fully submissive to the narrative-driven parameters of the serenata. In a genre that linked and superimposed a number of expressive elements (and in ways *differ-ent* from opera), we might come to understand that a profound aesthetic development was underway, but one that was in transition and therefore characterized by great tension. Crescimbeni, as we noted, provided an ini-tial clue: the serenata along with the cantata, he argued, was embedded in a larger and more powerful tradition of literary practice to which music was presumably best understood as ancillary. Respecting the longevity of history and tradition, Crescimbeni sought to continue the edification of the literary over the musical, with the latter filling a supporting role. Neverthe-less, even though Crescimbeni and some of his colleagues may have wished to see the role of music in this supportive capacity, the serenata also had the historical fate of emerging in a context of shifting social and political currents. As much as its aesthetic expositors embraced its formalist ele-ments and its function as musico-dramatic entertainment, the serenata was inadvertently pulled into powerful cultural currents where it was enlisted to carry out work beyond its specific musical dimensions. Along the way, ele-ments of musical independence became increasingly discernible; we see this especially in the case of *Le gare festive*, with the presentation and function of the *sinfonia* and the importance given to it in articulating the symbolic aspects of the performance. The *sinfonia* appears to have been assigned to convey certain duties of expressivity, but in a manner that (ironically) highlighted its capacity for aesthetic isolation, presaging nascent strains of autonomy. While the particular deployment of the *sinfonia* was still considered an adjunct to text – as ancillary, supportive, embellishing, and augmentative (but never authorial in itself) – it presents perhaps a harbinger of things to come. Thus, in the context of turn-of-the-century court society, the *interplay* of social pressures along with new developments in musico-dramatic and instrumental music composition allowed the serenata to host those emergent strands of musical autonomy, the very tensions that challenged the literary dispositions of Arcadian ideologues.

We must also recognize how the dualistic conditions that resulted from the serenata's narrative procedure and performance mechanisms similarly echoed another sort of tension emanating from the socio-political domains of culture. In fact, the peculiar insistence on the serenata's inherent dichotomies could be understood as endemic to a context dependent upon the control of social boundaries. As discussed, that which was presented as public and inclusive was really a pretense for affirming the underlying state of elite withdrawal from the larger and more popular public realms of culture and society. Though appearing to traverse the public/private divide with a kind of social "bi-lingualism" (in the Burkean sense), the upper classes who commissioned, sponsored, and required events like public serenatas ultimately remained withdrawn, if not literally, then at least symbolically.

The serenata provides a fascinating lens through which to view this socio-political phenomenon. As we have seen, events such as *Le gare festive* were not mere occasions for entertainment and they were certainly far more than simple opportunities to articulate a recognized musical genre. Through the serenata we witness how the insistent holdover of courtly ceremony and ritual were symptomatic of a context fraught with the crisis of impending socio-cultural transformation. The following chapter will further explore the phenomenon of withdrawal and nostalgia as seen through the Academy of Arcadians and their pastoral reform. What the serenata captures for us here are the powerful intersections of diachronism and synchronism that often traverse a genre. I have already made known the ways in which the serenata drew upon the legacy of its history, from its inspirational roots in a pre-operatic era when courtly spectacle was a necessary form of dynastic representation. Among the central elements of this form of signification was the use of allegory and ritual, the key components that shaped the serenata as form and as practice. But along the serenata's developmental arc music not only formed a distinguishing characteristic of its performance mechanisms; it became *the* central vehicle for its symbolic spectacle. Much of this was facilitated by a number of new compositional developments, some from the strictly instrumental arena of music, as well as those developments taking place in secular vocal music of the period. In this respect, the serenata quite forcibly embodied the dualistic condition of resistance and change that more broadly defined this historical period. Moreover, the serenata exposes the intersection of cultural life (dominated by the Arcadians' influence) with the ongoing political upheaval that had intensified during this era of monarchical succession and regime change.

The serenata also plays a critical role in reflecting opera's larger orbit. Even if the serenata's revelations were displaced beyond the actual environment of opera, the serenata did rehearse a number of core issues at stake in the debates about music, literature, drama, and signification that marked these turn-of-the-century decades. Opera had already made its debut as a predominantly public form. And, though its public status was controversial, critics who sought to reform opera (those within the Arcadian Academy in Rome or affiliated with satellite societies in other Italian cities) ventured that public theater could be a critical platform to elevate audiences morally and enact true literary reform. The public forum, however, proved to be an unruly arena to manage. Only in the case of events like serenatas – in which multiple audiences were addressed by carefully controlling and disseminating that which was ostensibly public and that which remained exclusive for elite consumption – could the sense of "public" be an expedient for propaganda and persuasion.

In the following chapter, we will learn how the warring dimensions of public/private would continue to plague opera's next directions. What the serenata lends to our understanding of opera's trajectory is a progressive transition within the multimedia complex of musico-dramatic expression. If vocal music helped instigate the emergence of an independent instrumental idiom, we also see how instrumental music shaped new potentials for expression within vocal music. This seemingly symbiotic relationship was not always fluid and not without contention. A re-shifting among the hierarchy of the arts, where music now ascended to a new rung on the ladder, would remain a major topic of debate. Within opera, instrumental sound coupled with increasingly stylized vocalization would certainly challenge the placement and expression of word in the larger scheme of musico-dramatic meaning. And, though opera was no longer dominantly allegorical (in ways that serenatas were), the "parceling" of music – perhaps embodied by an opening ritornello or melodic phrase – would gain significant symbolic strength. If the serenata demanded the grounding of text in order for the holes between symbol and meaning to be "patched up," it also provoked the question of a potential future where the gaps could remain unstopped, or at least open to other interpretive leaps of assumed meaning.

4 | The cantata, the pastoral, and the ideology of nostalgia

> I will be gone from here and sing my songs
> In the forest wilderness where the wild beasts are,
> And carve in letters on the little trees
> The story of my love, and as the trees
> Will grow the letters too will grow, to cry
> In a louder voice the story of my love.[1]
>
> Virgil, *Eclogue X*

I

Imagine a continuum with opera at one end and non-operatic vocal forms toward the other. It is likely that in moving away from opera, we might proceed in the order I have followed in this book: oratorio first – a seasonal, but devotional genre, divided into two sections resembling the separation of dramatic acts, using casts of representational figures that could include up to five to six singers; next, but not too far along the continuum, might be the serenata – also seasonally performed, though often for specific occasions, and compared with the oratorio, tending toward a more distinctly allegorical conception of drama, using at least two or three singers; and finally the cantata – which resembled some serenatas by employing few singers, though more often composed for solo voice, and set mythological and allegorical texts, albeit texts that were shorter, more simply performed, and least tied to occasional events. Indeed, the cantata may appear to sit more markedly toward the non-operatic end of this continuum.

What then might the cantata tell us about opera at the turn of the eighteenth century? Some things we already know, such as that vocal chamber genres always had a close relationship to opera, often aspiring to dramatic music. In several ways, we might say the early modern cantata worked like an opera in miniature. More conceptually focused and condensed, and usually stripped of any scenic presentation, the cantata in a most paradigmatic way projected the musical essence of operatic expression, the alternating unrhymed and rhymed verses of the recitative–aria complex, what others have termed opera's most essential and "minimum semantic unit."[2] But form, structure, and expressive conventions tell only half the story. Less obvious but more important for the purposes of this chapter is to pursue how such features of the cantata were possibly read, repressed, or reinterpreted by audiences, patrons, and intellectuals belonging to this Roman context.

It is important to acknowledge that making these connections is difficult since the evidence available is quite limited. This chapter focuses on select documents, figures, and events that help capture the ways in which genre distinction and genre blurring – specifically regarding the relationship between the cantata and opera – were acutely connected to larger aesthetic polemics and to opera's status as a cultural form in this period. What we might learn from this discussion is that the cantata's relationship to opera does raise a possible irony. As much as the cantata reflected opera's influence, to some the genre embodied a powerful contrast with and distinction from what opera signified. The cantata thus suggests *two* truths worth considering. Truth number one: the cantata was least like opera and furthest from what public opera symbolized to many critics of this period. Especially in a context such as late *seicento* Rome, cantatas were embraced as the antithesis of public entertainment; they retained a long-held association with private, exclusive circles within which the subtle and more abstract expression of vocal chamber music was duly sanctioned and privileged as noble entertainment. Yet, even if we concede that the cantata was least like opera, we will come to see that the cultural work it facilitated and its relationship to the rectification of opera bound it in a functionally close, if not intimate relationship to opera. Therefore, a second truth to consider: the cantata, in the end, may be *most* revealing and closest to opera in the way it refracted opera's discourses and recontextualized a number of contentious issues that surrounded opera during this time.

The aim of this chapter is to address the simultaneity and tension of both truths and to explore how opera's orbit in this Roman Arcadian context constructed one way by which to view the cantata's assimilation and rejection of opera's influence.[3] The cantata was not a monolithic form or genre. As shall be seen through the perception of the genre's historical legacy, the cantata revealed contrary and conflicting qualities, some derived from a more distant past and some defined by concerns that emerged during this late seventeenth-, early eighteenth-century juncture. I consider how the cantata's symbolic heritage as an elite and intellectually oriented chamber genre helped to thrust this genre into opera's path during a time and within a locale where opera could be characterized as wholly distinct from the cantata. At the same time, the cantata found itself in an intimately bound relationship to opera, not only through stylistic traits, but also through the pastoral, which several leaders of the Arcadian movement saw as *the* preferred template for musico-dramatic reform.

The Arcadian movement, and specifically, its influential writings by select critics within the academy, form a grounding from which to explore the cantata's contiguity with opera and how the cantata–opera relationship was negotiated by this particular influential context of patrons, reformers, and listeners. The pastoral, pastoral reform, and pastoralism more generally form a critical cultural (not just formal) link for exploring the intersection of the cantata with opera. Using Arcadia as a lens through which to view this intersection, this chapter considers how the qualities of nostalgia and idealization, as connected with the Arcadian pastoral agenda, played sig-nificant roles in the perception of genre relationships, and in creating an idealized operatic future. The cantata may have had an indirect effect in determining opera's historical course; none the less, when conceived as the pastoral essence of music and poetic melding (as suggested by specific Arca-dian discourses), its status and symbolic significance provides an important if not revealing counterpoint to opera's perceived trajectory. Ultimately, this chapter explores a critical symbiotic relationship between the status and perception of genre and the context of agents in part responsible for creating the discourses that surround genre. The fraught connecting points between the cantata and opera are revealed here through the cultural prac-tices and polemical writings of the Arcadians. At the same time, it may be that through opera, the cantata, and the points of intersection between these genres, we might equally capture Arcadia's internal contradictions and ideological conflicts. In either realm – the musical composition of genres or Arcadia as a cultural institution – the handling and use of the past becomes both a fount of invention as well as one of early modernity's most revealing obstacles.

Appropriating legacies

To begin, let us reconsider some parameters of the cantata as genre, and its location and function in this period in Rome. Even if a thriving vocal chamber music culture had long been a noted feature of Roman high society, by the late seventeenth century one could argue that cantatas in the papal capital had gained renewed cultural currency. Many composers made their fame and presented their best vocal-dramatic work in cantatas during a time when operas had become difficult or impossible to stage. While the occasions and rituals that called for cantata performance in this period were not new, it is reasonable to posit that the frequently imposed restrictions on operatic entertainment may have placed a new premium on cantata production – for both librettists and composers, as well as listeners.

We must acknowledge that cantatas also flourished in this context because Rome hosted a sizeable core of noble households, many aspiring to displays of great artistic patronage. Several of these noble patrons were engaged in the types of activities – diplomatic occasions, intellectual gatherings, high-profile socializing – where the presence of music as entertainment was an expected mark of noble grandeur and hospitality. A genre like the cantata offered a platform to exhibit the wealth and influence of patronage, be it through the financing of the compositional invention of a prized composer, or through the presentation of the even higher premium of famed castrati or female singers.[4] Again, the symbolic purposes and functions behind this activity were not in any way novel, but it is important to note that the pressures and needs driving such elite sponsorship helped to concentrate the cantata's presence in this circumscribed context and period.

What is more critical for the purposes of this chapter's investigation is to consider how the late-century cantata (especially by comparison to opera) might have been viewed as a symbol of constancy against a larger backdrop of instability that characterized opera culture within Rome. An operative concept to consider here is appropriation – the extent to which the cantata was enlisted to accommodate a range of conditions and tensions that had emerged in consequence of opera's troubled status in Rome. Even if indirectly, the cantata was tied to many of the underlying aesthetic debates about theater, drama, and specifically opera. Though the debates themselves largely emerged within the context of discussing literary history, or the future of drama, in several ways did they also reflect the sense of change and reform that cut across a number of cultural and social domains. We must understand how the cantata and its associations around 1700 evoked a mode of retrospection that harkened back to a time when cultural power was more exclusively sequestered within the domain of a presumably more stable court society. In this regard, we might conceive the cantata of this period as a nostalgic symbol, pointing to a past that was committed to privilege and to the cultivation of "good taste." This look back entailed the same historical landscape from which grew the Renaissance traditions of art, literature, poetry, and eventually, dramatic music. Both opera and the cantata were founded in this moment, when Neoplatonic notions of artistic unity bound music to word. At this inception the combined forces of poetry and music were often performed simply, in a chamber-like format, in a context not yet subject to the pressures of the public sphere or commercial incentives; such pressures would emerge only later, pulling music, drama, and poetry into a realm beyond the exclusive confines of noble society.[5]

In several ways, the cantata becomes an interesting trouble spot on the larger spectrum of musico-dramatic vocal types. In practice, the cantata frequently blurred lines between chamber and theatrical categories; it had long been a barometer for gauging opera's formal and musical development, reflecting several of opera's compositional devices, its structural and expressive conventions.[6] And yet, despite this interaction and strong parallel the cantata was often defined by its dissimilarity to opera, which helped to deepen notions dividing the genres. The comparisons between cantatas and opera, however, are limited since distinctions of difference do not always capture a complete representation of actual practice. Though the cantata was implicated in the oppositional rhetoric of binary terms with respect to opera, its elasticity as a genre reveals an altogether more malleable function. Intersected by an array of forces, the cantata in the Roman environment was a genre whose multiple configurations were often contradictory. We must, therefore, regard the cantata as a form that registered a number of vital, sometimes conflicting associations. Several of these associations were historically determined, and their potential for diverse meanings is worth some scrutiny in order for us to understand the cantata as a variegated concept. Two elicit particular focus. In one respect, the cantata was involved in a legacy of socially circumscribed production governed by an exclusive, private, and courtly tradition. The cantata also carried the weight of cultural content with a pastoral literary inheritance. The associations of courtly and pastoral are not mutually exclusive, but some distinction between them is worth noting.

In the case of its courtly tradition, the cantata belonged historically to an exclusive environment of elevated and expert taste that long marked courtly circles and intellectual academies in Italy. In his research on the mid-seventeenth-century cantata, Roger Freitas skillfully illuminates *why* contemporary elite audiences specifically prized cantatas and their texts. He explains that poets and composers subverted predictable conventions of music and text by inserting unexpected or ironic turns, thereby conveying novelty and wit to aristocratic listeners who valued ingenuity and challenge.[7] Like a number of courtly activities and competitions, cantatas in the seventeenth century grew to become another type of cerebral exercise, a demonstration of rhetorical gestures and musical inventiveness. However, the link of courtly connoisseurship to cantatas needs to be reconsidered carefully when situating the cantata within the very late seventeenth- and early eighteenth-century Roman context, particularly when accounting for the discourses taking place there. Though the cantata had always held the position of elite musical form for which qualities of rhetorical skill, complexity, and progressiveness were markers of similar noble exercises of leisure, the exclusivity of the genre held new sway in Rome's polemical environment. We must come to see the cantata in this context with expanded levels of signification beyond its status as an exercise in rhetorical play. Though the genre was rarely, if ever, mentioned in ongoing criticism of opera and its abuses, the cantata was inevitably, even if *indirectly*, pulled into its aesthetic debates.[8] This chapter narrows in on select critical sources that address musical drama more broadly, and I consider how these discourses indirectly comment on the status and possible idealization of the cantata within this period. An enlarged perspective of the cantata will reveal that the status of the genre, within this place and time, had undergone a subtle shift. Yes, the cantata continued to satisfy courtly demands for cerebral exercise and competition, but, by the turn of the eighteenth century, this defining feature of the cantata – its placement in a courtly realm of expert listeners – was lent renewed emphasis in response to the critical discussion surrounding opera.

Turning to aspects of literary content, the development of the cantata had long coincided with the rise in popularity of specific classically oriented literary genres, such as the bucolic or pastoral eclogue.[9] These Virgilian-inspired models are worth noting for the ways in which they shed light on the tenacity of pastoral literary traits that remained prominent in late seventeenth- and eighteenth-century cantatas. The brief quotation from Virgil's *Eclogue X* that begins this chapter speaks to a number of critical symbols historically appropriated by poets and cantata librettists reworking this subject throughout the early modern period. The notion of retreat to nature, what Virgil describes in this passage as "being gone from here," was an old metaphorical trope by which withdrawal to a pastoral world symbolized a return to simplicity.[10] The pastoral was also a conduit to the classical Golden Age, mythologized by Hesiod and given moral and political value during the Roman republic by poets like Virgil.[11] There are other symbols we find that abound in Virgil and in the works of his poetic disciples that acquired renewed import in cantata writers' neo-ecloguian revival. The theme of love remained a popular conceit, so much so that it also became the object of ridicule and satire, years before the Arcadian Academy heavily invested their energies in perpetuating pastoral themes and in creating the amorous world of Arcadian shepherds.[12]

In fact, the Arcadians played a significant role in the cantata's status as genre in Rome, and in the larger story of its bucolic legacy. The recurrence of conventional pastoral themes was not unusual in seventeenth-century drama and shorter poetic forms. However, the Academy of Arcadians' recuperative measures for Italian literature and its history renewed their interest in pastoral themes, which included the pastoral drama. We should note that the cantata – topically, poetically, and structurally – had most in common with the pastoral eclogue and less with actual pastoral dramas. As Ellen Harris explains, there are two distinct lineages of the pastoral tradition. One stems from the classical eclogue, and thus falls in the lineage of pastoral *poetry*, leading to such fifteenth- and sixteenth-century models as those penned by Angelo Poliziano, Jacopo Sannazaro, and Torquato Tasso. The other is that of pastoral *drama*, which was essentially modern and devised during the Renaissance, influenced by a number of sources, but fundamentally a tragicomedy in form, epitomized by the works of Agostino de' Beccari and later Giovanni Battista Guarini.[13] What unites both lineages is content and spirit, not form or presentation. The cantata was not a drama in the fullest sense, nor was it meant for theater. Although these formal comparisons can prove useful, we will depart from this line of inquiry so that we may pursue a broader discussion of the pastoral topos. It is critical to understand how the pastoral was enlisted in the effort to reform opera, theater, and culture, and how this effort paralleled the grander pastoral ethos that characterized the activities of the Academy of the Arcadians. In effect, though the pastoral had relevance for *both* opera and the cantata, it was the cantata that may have best reflected the most effective application and – at the same time – the most glaring shortcomings of the Arcadians' pastoral reform.

I will later revisit the significance of the "pastoral agenda" for the Arcadians' redirection of opera's course. For now, let us consider more generally how the Arcadians' proclivity for the pastoral aesthetic informed their polemic leanings. In arguing against the abuses of *seicento* poetry (and by extension, opera libretti), several prominent Arcadians recommended a simplification in dramaturgical practices, an adherence to the Aristotelian Unities, a reduction of unnecessary scenes, and a return to poetic elocution and rhetoric. Harris suggests that the cantata from this perspective appears to have been a wonderful fit.[14] Nothing could capture the simplicity of pairing music with word more vividly than the story of shepherds from Virgil's *Eclogues*, who engage in singing contests or give voice to poetic sentiment through musical renditions of tales of love lost or found. Seen in this light, we might imagine the late *seicento* cantata as the more effective vessel for containing if not fully realizing the Arcadian pastoral reform ideals, and consequently, for absolving musical drama of its operatic transgressions.

The romanticized aura of pastoral life – the image of shepherds extemporizing poetry and expressing themselves through song – extended beyond the discourses of reform and had an important role in shaping the Arcadians' ritualized gatherings. Giovanni Mario Crescimbeni described the group's regular meetings as *Giuochi Olimpici* in which Arcadia's shepherds fled to the "woods" (or rather, to the urban gardens of fellow noble patrons) to recite their compositions, and to restore the erudition of ancient Arcadia. He specifies that these games were a revival of ancient Greek practices; in the case of modern Arcadia, however, he notes they were exercises not of the body, but of the mind.[15] From what we can gather from Crescimbeni's publications as well as from the documents collected from the Arcadian archive (ranging from poetry, to prose, and prints), the recitation, and perhaps, even the *singing* of pastoral poetry as literary contests was a known, if not archetypal activity of the society.[16] Important to underline, however, is that the Arcadians' commitment to the revival of ancient culture, even if intended to have universal effect, was not intended for universal practice. That is, the games of the mind – the recuperation of erudition through recitation or singing of pastoral worlds – were both a redemptive act and a pastime limited to connoisseurs. The Arcadians were not the first to view such practice in this way. In his own bucolic writings Sannazaro suggested similarly that not everyone could journey to Arcadia. Such a transformation required expertise, training, and elevated taste, and it was to an audience with just these qualities that Sannazaro directed his own prose/poetry – to those who could follow his pastoral meanderings with the closest attention.[17]

This emphasis on exclusivity and connoisseurship has great relevance for the cantata, since we must also recognize how the activities of the Arcadians help to place in high relief an emerging opposition regarding the perception of cantatas in this period. Aside from the notion of complexity and demand for connoisseurship, cantatas (particularly those with a pastoral orientation) equally embraced the notion of simplicity – simple shepherds, simple poetry, and simple music. Simplicity thus resonated on several levels. It cut to the root of Arcadian rationalism that sought balance between nature and reason and countered the extravagance and wantonness of the age (symbolically identified by critics in contemporary poetry) through a leveling of imagination with intellect, and invention with verisimilitude. Poetic simplicity was therefore personified through a shepherd's life, in the models of idylls and eclogues in which the notion of plain and natural discourse was best spoken by the simplest of men.[18] The extension of this metaphor was well suited to the reform of musical drama, in which the multiplicity of character types, plot directions, and locations had made operatic drama anything but simple. The very quality of simplicity as yearned for by critics of poetry and operatic literature was a frequently noted feature in pastoral cantatas, where imagery of nature and shepherds converged with a pared-down dramatic approach and graceful lyric style.

Yet the apparent simplicity of the cantata was misleading; cantatas were often neither purely simple nor purely complex. In fact, complexity and simplicity were qualities that operated primarily not at the level of musical practice in cantatas, but at the level of abstracted discourse. Though seemingly oppositional, the qualities of simplicity and complexity were united by their reactionary stance against opera. A cantata's endowed complexity could be seen to *exceed* opera by elevating listeners to higher aesthetic standards, whereas a cantata's perceived simplicity – simple formats, few characters, and pastoral plots – was viewed as correcting some of opera's most egregious infractions.[19] If anything, the complex/simple binary helps to link the cantata to opera in a broader frame of discourses from which we may read how aspects of this binary were misread and manipulated for critical purposes. In essence, the discourses surrounding complexity and simplicity will reveal the larger conflict between word–music relationships and how these tensions were perceived from within and from outside the cantata.

We must acknowledge how moments of incongruity or asynchronicity between text and music (an idiomatic feature that could well have delighted expert cantata listeners) were not a new practice in late seventeenth-century cantatas, or in operas or other vocal genres. In fact, by the early eighteenth century, critics of opera – especially those who continued vehemently to guard the sanctity of word – had good reason to fear the deviance of music, and the power of "pure voice."[20] Yet these belated concerns remained primarily directed at opera, even though the phenomenon of emphasizing voice through song was established practice by 1700 for most musico-dramatic genres. The perception of the cantata genre during this time thus becomes a gauge for reading and rereading reactions to opera. And in this context of Rome, where we witness opera's problematic impact upon and across other musico-dramatic genres, we begin to see that the perceived inviolability of the cantata gives way to multiple appropriations as it is positioned to facilitate "complexity" *and* "simplicity." For aristocratic audiences with a penchant for intellectual challenge, cantatas that encouraged conflict between structure and sense or between word and music were likely to have been embraced; whereas for critics such as the Arcadian founders, all that might have mattered was the association of the cantata (absent any deep structural thinking) with its noble milieu and thus with a protected sphere of taste and decorum. What such critics seemingly ignored was the extent to which compositional and aesthetic complexity defeated the sense of a *fixed* notion of the cantata, especially one that embraced its "simple" and idealized pastoral origins – as though all pastoral cantatas followed the very same unadorned and idealized aesthetic. It is striking that the desire to fix the cantata form rigidly – whether in terms of its noble, pastoral heritage, idealized aims, or word–music relationships – was exceeded by the cantata's potential to sprawl. Although some of the critical discourse tried to narrow the cantata's behavior and significance according to limited principles, any given cantata's individual expression – what existed beneath discourses, within the music, and thus in the reality of practice – might suggest otherwise.

II

The cantata as discourse and practice

One of the unifying features of the vocal genres scrutinized in this book is that, in practice, these genres were inclined toward multiple manifestations of form and presentation, less rigid or one-dimensional than often is characterized. We witnessed this with the oratorio and its ability to service a variety of venues and rituals, and with the serenata and its potential equally to accommodate large-scale public spectacle and intimate chamber settings alike. The cantata also appeared in many guises and in many formats. As the seventeenth century progressed, it was not unusual to find contemporaneous examples of cantatas that were modest in forces – for one voice and continuo – alongside others that were scored for small orchestral ensembles, several voices, and with greater narrative scope. What was labeled a "cantata" was flexible, but the most extreme variants – those most chamber-like and those most theatrical – highlight an inherent tension and crucial duality that helped to determine the cantata's manifold representations.

There are many reasons why the cantata progressively adopted various formats. In some cases, it is likely that as composers tried their hand at producing music for the theater and honed their methods for writing operas, these new aesthetic, structural, and melodic approaches bled over into other compositions. The overlap of styles was inevitable; that this occurred we now consider established knowledge. However, in a context like Rome, we can also add that the possibility for overlap was heightened by conditions external to purely aesthetic choices and largely motivated by the politics of culture. We have already noted with the oratorio, and now likewise with the cantata, that there were reasons and opportunities to cloak the more theatrical aspects of a genre in a less dramatic guise. This was likely a response and temporary solution to the restrictive attitudes towards secular entertainment, specifically towards opera. The cantata's non-public and non-spectacular orientation meant that such performance could more easily circumvent prohibition despite changes to content or format that may have made any particular cantata less cantata-like.

There are potentially hundreds of Roman cantata performances from the decades spanning the turn of the eighteenth century for which conditions of patronage and politics helped to shape reception, and guided the casting of the cantata in one guise or another as a genre that either resisted or conversely adapted qualities of opera. Yet to determine this is difficult; in most cases, we know so little. Of all musico-dramatic genres, the cantata was *most* behind closed doors, steeped in allegorical symbolism the significance of which was difficult to interpret without the cultivated knowledge of an insider. Unlike the serenata, single cantatas were less tied to particular occasions or to regular venues. Scholars have painstakingly attempted to infer these details using a variety of techniques, for example, ascertaining when and for whom a composer wrote. The well-known composers and their cantatas are more thoroughly mined. We know more about the cantatas – their provenance, potential audience, and possible reception – of figures such as Alessandro Scarlatti and George Frideric Handel, and to some extent Antonio Caldara and Franceso Gasparini, than we know of the works of lesser-known Roman composers such as Flavio Lanciani, Filippo Amadei, or Carlo Cesarini.[21] Clearly, there is more work to be done in this area with results that promise to illuminate small corners of this otherwise opaque field of musical practice. But for the purposes of this study, I am interested in examining some of the cantata's appropriated associations – what we might call its fixed narratives – as a way to chart how the cantata moves beyond individual works or sets of generic traits, and resonates with trends of culture particular to this historical period. I am thus interested in the cantata at the level of the paradigmatic, through noted compositional representatives whose notoriety came partly because they captured particular qualities of the cantata as genre – qualities that were often in direct opposition to the perceived practice of opera.

Alessandro Scarlatti's reputation as a cantata composer was renowned; even if we believe today that some of his achievements are, in fact, mis-attributed, his skills as a cantata composer were in demand and earned him great esteem in his own time.[22] In his *Commentari . . . alla sua Istoria della volgar poesia*, Crescimbeni names Scarlatti as among the truly "good professors" from outside Rome who wrote cantatas in this period.[23] Scarlatti was noted for his learned style and his intricate settings of cantata texts, which garnered high praise after the competitive exchange of 1712 with Francesco Gasparini. In this exchange Gasparini sent Scarlatti a setting of the cantata text *Andate o miei sospiri*, to which Scarlatti responded with two different musical settings of the same text, the first in his usual style, the second with daring and more extravagantly chromatic harmonies appended with the following infamous warning: "written as an inhuman idea, and not for every professor."[24] Admittedly, the circumstances of Scarlatti's setting of these cantatas were exceptional, yet, even in a cantata written under more normal conditions, and specifically not set as a competitive exercise, Scarlatti often pushed toward using subtle but daring harmonic passages and intricate counterpoint. Take for instance the cantata *Al fin m'ucciderete*, which, judging from the number of extant eighteenth-century sources, may have been among Scarlatti's most widely circulated and best-known cantatas.[25] *Al fin m'ucciderete* is pastorally themed and tells of a shepherd's plaint over the loss of his beloved, Clori, who has apparently abandoned him. Structurally, the cantata is made up of a series of two recitative-aria segments (RARA), with each aria written in *da capo* form.[26] I focus here on the first recitative-aria segment, which sets up the emotional tone of the cantata: the unstable lover is tormented by the thoughts of his shepherdess's disloyalty; he pines to see her again despite the pain of rejection (see example 8).

In terms of the recitative, the musical setting abides for the most part by standard principles of text expression, using musical means to highlight a particular word, sentiment, or signification. Other conventions abound, such as setting the notion of distance, as expressed in the phrase "da me lontana" (m. 5), with an octave leap, or landing on a dissonant chord to heighten the tension of the lover's mental anguish. More unusual is the degree of chromatic intensity and tonal adventurousness we experience, especially at the end of this recitative. Scarlatti builds to this moment by creating dramatic contrast. At "Ma chi sa" (the text's proverbial turning point), our panicked shepherd starts to fear the worst, an imagined scene of his lover locked in gaze with another. Here more than at any other point in the recitative (see mm. 17–22), the music becomes stable, and notably bright with the move to the parallel major key. Melodic motion is direct, unadorned, and even assertively repetitive. Again, the worst scenario is cast: Clori's tryst with another is neither troubled nor fantastical, but is ostensibly clear and confident. Things begin to change quickly at mm. 22–23 when the shepherd returns to wondering what his Clori thinks of him. When the

Example 8 Alessandro Scarlatti, *Al fin m'ucciderete*: recit., "Al fin m'ucciderete o miei pensieri!"; aria, "Io morirei contento per non penar così," *c.*1702–1708 (GB-Lbl, Add. MS 31508). This transcription is based on the facsimile copy of *Al fin m'ucciderete* published in Malcolm Boyd, ed., *Cantatas by Alessandro Scarlatti*, Vol. XIII: *The Italian Cantata in the Seventeenth Century* (New York: Garland, 1986), 137–41.

RECIT: "My thoughts, you will kill me in the end! Clori is far from me, Clori, my idol. Oh, God, if only she could remember my constant love, if only my sighs could at least meet with a sigh from her beautiful chest. Oh, if only in this moment Clori would think of me, who thinks of her many and many times! But – who knows – she is perhaps now speaking with someone else, and at the same time he stares at her and she at him. And who knows, she may even love him having forgotten me. Do fly far from my mind, tyrants of my heart. If you torment me with such fierce suspicion, you will kill me in the end, my thoughts!"

ARIA: "I would gladly die, not to suffer thus. But I would like to see again for one moment she who first took away peace from my soul and then departed from me."

Example 8 (cont.)

Example 8 (*cont.*)

Example 8 (*cont.*)

unspeakable is said – that she no longer may love him – Scarlatti returns to a more tortured "voice," underscored by a daring series of dissonant wanderings through the recitative's conclusion (mm. 26–32), marked by diminished harmonies and occasional chromatic descent in the bass.

Aside from the degree to which Scarlatti probes distant and dissonant harmonies, the music in this recitative is rendered to articulate the poetic meaning. The same might not be said of the subsequent aria, "Io morirei contento." There is nothing obvious in the text to demand a setting replete with imitative counterpoint; this seems to be a personal compositional choice, one that Scarlatti often favored. Yet Scarlatti's musical approach does enhance poetic expression; however, he accomplishes this by reaching beyond the bounds of close word–music relationships. This is evident with the word "penar," the theme of suffering and pain that serves as the aria's central affective mode. "Penar" is not treated directly, as in strict word painting. Instead, it becomes a launching point for musical inventiveness, prompting a short sequential passage of suspensions in mm. 40–41 and motivic elaboration in mm. 47–51. This latter segment exemplifies an important point of divergence. The motivic play of repeated and moving seconds (initially inspired by textual meaning, perhaps to emphasize insistently the sentiment of pain) departs from its direct textual connection and begins to work more independently, on a level more musically than textually determined. Another example of this appears in mm. 57–58. Scarlatti chose to repeat this motive twice in connection with the notion of "seeing again" (riveder). Even though the repetition is not coordinated with that word or phrase, it is possible that Scarlatti found this choice worked better *musically*.

This increased assertion of musical distinction and signification was neither a new development nor one that was singularly honed by Scarlatti; in fact, by the early eighteenth century it was not uncommon. Yet the argument can be made that new standardization of *da capo* aria forms, with the structural components of contrasting poetic sections, helped to encourage musical means of contrast and signification. This change helped to increase music's self-sufficiency, in which an abstracted musical gesture could easily overpower the singular sign of a word or even verse. It is not that the *da capo* aria was the first to instigate what Mauro Calcagno describes as musical "dissociation" from verbal meaning – a tendency already evident in early seventeenth-century opera and related vocal genres.[27] None the less, we can make the case that the restricted schema of a tripartite form provided stable and conventional tonal architecture that opened other possibilities for musical development. This is indeed the case in "Io morirei contento" with the line "per non penar così," which Scarlatti uses as the aria's symbolic theme to launch a series of cadential prolongations of V^7–I, especially in m. 47 with the alternating B/C motive over V^7/i reiterations. He adds further emphasis and embellishment with a prolonged cadential extension in mm. 49–50, with alternating F/G vocal motives over iv^6/V reiterations. Thus, the long-anticipated return to the tonic (m. 51) – required to close the first section of the aria and continue to the next stanza – becomes musical grounds for the distinct intervallic repetition we hear play out in the voice. "Penar" may work as the aria's semantic signifier, but music, shaped by tonal pressures, arguably begins to supercede individual word painting, working to express pain, suffering, and tension in more substantive ways.

The move towards increased musical distinction and signification, as witnessed in this Scarlatti example and evident in many other cantatas, calls forth a number of salient issues related to reception and to the cantata's cultural significance around 1700. While I agree with Roger Freitas that, in general, most consumers of cantatas were literate, "attuned to poetry more than music," I believe that the conditions and criteria for engaging with cantatas may have been different in the late seventeenth and early eighteenth centuries than in an earlier period such as the age of *marinismo* when, as Freitas argues, the thwarting of musical expectations was linked to breaches of stylistic regularity (for example, lyrical closure to a passage of recitative, or new rather than recurring music to set a refrain). In this earlier period, what was important was not whether music reflected text so much as that music highlighted a subversion of poetic convention.[28] In the age of the *da capo* aria, the standardization of poetry made such rhetorical breaches somewhat rarer. In fact, a decidedly anti-Marinist stance that emerged during the last decades of the seventeenth century may have been a forceful influence for redirecting musico-poetic texts towards simplification and a sustained, not breached, regularity.[29] Music, therefore, had new roles to fill. Sometimes, within the confines of recurring, standard forms, composers reverted to music's most traditional rhetorical strategy – imitation, or word painting. But more often, they emphasized certain words by isolating them with heightened musical gestures. Or, more daringly, they used purely musical means, enlisting new configurations of tonal structure, sudden changes of key, dissonance, and changes of texture or of melodic line for more abstracted forms of expression.[30] It would seem that music's role would create new demands on audiences; that the appreciation of a cantata's complexity was found not merely in its poetic style, but in the distinct intricacy and density of musical expression.

It was a mark of distinction and elite status to be among those aesthetes who could appreciate the most demanding of cantatas. Recall that Scarlatti warned his readers (at least in the case of the famed *Andate o miei sospiri*) that his music was not for every (read "ordinary") professor. We could also argue that the association with complexity had significance beyond cantata composition per se, and in this period, formed part of a larger discourse that concerned musico-dramatic representation. In a context like Rome, it is possible that Scarlatti may have been appreciated by his patrons and audiences not solely for his intricate and academic musical style, but precisely because this stylistic orientation – most appreciated in chamber settings – could serve as a standard for the recuperation and reform of vocal drama.[31]

Scarlatti's reception outside Rome was markedly different. In fact, for non-Romans, it appears that Scarlatti's cerebral style for vocal dramatic music was insufficiently accessible, and that many of his opera compositions earned only mixed success in his own day. In Tuscany, Scarlatti's patron, Prince Ferdinando de' Medici, warned the composer against using a learned style, and urged him to write operas that were "more cheerful," in a style that was "pleasant and lyrical, not intellectual."[32] Similarly in Naples, a contemporary report suggests that Scarlatti's compositional style was too restrictive, appropriate for the chamber, but not for the theater. In a famous quote from 1709, the Neapolitan count Francesco Maria Zambeccari writes that, in Naples, Scarlatti's style was poorly received:

> his works are not popular because his compositions are too difficult and are things for the chamber, and thus in a theater they are not as successful. If one can appreciate counterpoint, then he will esteem them; but for a theater audience of a thousand people, not even twenty can appreciate or hear his invention, and for the others who don't get to hear something cheerful and theatrical, they get bored . . . in sum, Scarlatti's style for the theater is universally not appreciated, people want things that are merry and energetic, of the kind they perform in Venice.[33]

Scarlatti's music, and more importantly, "things for the chamber" symbolically became the opposite of that to which the creators of public opera aspired (things "merry and energetic"). These very analogies speak to an important comparative status that the cantata had acquired in its relationship with opera.

At the same time, "things for the chamber" were not limited to cantatas in a complex, learned style. Within the same circle of patrons and audiences in Rome were other cantata writers who set music to similar Arcadian-inspired poetry exemplified by *Al fin m'ucciderete*, though they were often regarded as using a different aesthetic approach. Recognized by Crescimbeni as among the best of the modern cantata writers was Giovanni Bononcini, a good contrasting example to Scarlatti by virtue of how critics and listeners viewed his compositional style.[34] More readily than Scarlatti and other contemporaries, Bononcini was recognized for his "agreable and easie style" and for cantatas that captured qualities of simplicity and grace.[35] This was not necessarily a universally held opinion, and a true close examination of Bononcini's cantatas fails to yield such a singular compositional approach.[36] Nevertheless, these associations of simplicity, elegance, and grace emerging from a range of sources effectively set certain impressions of Bononcini. We might come to see this style of cantata writing as resonant with broader discourses of criticism and reform of opera. If Scarlatti's cantatas could exceed opera in their loftier approaches and more cerebral demands, then a composer like Bononcini satisfied patrons and listeners who sought elegance, grace, and simplicity in opposition to an older opera style that they had spurned for its *unnatural* embellishment and dramaturgical unwieldiness.

Bononcini's early fame as a composer was in large part built on the success of his Roman cantata compositions; between 1692 and 1698 he composed for the circle of cardinals, princes, and diplomats – all members of the Academy of Arcadians – and later, between 1713 and 1719, following a post at the imperial court in Vienna, he served the Viennese ambassador in Rome, Johann Wenzell, Count Gallas, writing chamber works for the ambassador's intimate weekly gatherings.[37] Of his cantatas that survive, especially from the 1690s, many were written to pastoral texts with themes of love – usually sorrowful, but occasionally joyful – often revealing Bononcini's noted gracefulness. Several of these cantatas from the period showcase Bononcini's famed stylistic signature, but in parts; as a whole, it is more difficult to delimit Bononcini's writing to one type of compositional expression. Lowell Lindgren views Bononcini's *Ch'io ti manchi di fede, idolo mio?* (entitled *Bella donna costante*) as a paradigmatic example of Bononcini's divergent approaches in writing cantatas. The work itself was evidently popular: it survives in more sources than any other Bononcini cantata and thus serves well to illuminate aspects of his compositional style.[38] For my purposes, I am interested in noting the ways in which such a well-known work may have stood in contrast to a more learned, intellectual approach and thus encouraged the association of Bononcini (and a certain approach to cantatas in general) with simplicity and grace. Let us consider the opening recitative and aria for the cantata (see example 9).

The opening recitative is brief and to the point: in seven measures we are introduced to the shepherdess's concerns and her resolve to persuade

Example 9 Giovanni Bononcini, *Ch'io ti manchi di fede, idolo mio?*: recit., "Ch'io ti manchi di fede, idolo mio?"; aria, "Se mai tento col solo pensiero," *c.*1692–1698 (GB-Ob, Mus. d.20). This transcription is based on the facsimile copy of *Ch'io ti manchi di fede, idolo mio?* published in Lowell Lindgren, ed., *Cantatas by Giovanni Bononcini*, Vol. X: *The Italian Cantata in the Seventeenth Century* (New York: Garland, 1985), 16–18.

RECIT: "Could I ever betray you, my idol? Could I ever upset you in love matters? My heart is not so vile, I proudly have a constant soul and I am yours."

ARIA: "Beloved eyes, if I ever try to betray you with my thought alone, may the fiercest Fate let all the irate stars shine against me."

Example 9 (cont.)

Example 9 (*cont.*)

her lover of her constancy – reaffirmed by the arioso-like departure in measures 5–7 of cadential resolution.[39] But this conviction is soon destabilized by the musical setting of the first aria (in ABA form). Section A (mm. 8–17) is a series of a short, almost "breathy" motive that is introduced first in the continuo accompaniment, and then imitated in the vocal melody. Though the frequent use of rests creates an overlap of short phrases between voice and accompaniment (conveying the lover's doubts about her own constancy), the musical texture of the aria is clear. The simplicity and elegance attributed to Bononcini's style is exemplified here in very tonally directed musical phrases, using short scalar descents to propel the music forward, without more pronounced dissonant wanderings or unexpected leaps. Section B (mm. 18–59) presents a drastic contrast with a more rousing tone of the arpeggiated accompaniment that supports a significantly more florid vocal line, the darkened mode of the relative minor, and a shift to a 3/8 time signature,[40] even though contours of clarity are similarly maintained as in section A. There may be a distinct shift in texture and in rhythmic drive, but the elegance of Bononcini's diminutions remains intact: even when the "stars are angered" (le stelle irate), a move that could provoke all kinds of sonic havoc, Bononconi maintains a simplicity in texture and tonal structure that works to support and not overshadow the intensified melismatic lyricism of the vocal line. The kind of academic texture we find more typical in Scarlatti cantatas, a feature that contemporary opinion emphasized, is less evident in the opening of this cantata.[41]

Even if the cantatas by Bononcini and Scarlatti were never uniformly evocative of one singular quality, their tendency to capture either a quality that aroused cerebral contemplation or that which characterized expressive delight unearths an important and timeworn conflict for musico-dramatic reception in the age of reform. The aim to delight was never regarded in any neutral way during the history of early modern opera, and in the late seventeenth century, it could be seen as a motivation that was associated with opera's disreputable qualities as a commercial and crowd-pleasing commodity.[42] At the same time, the pressure to restore a sense of "good taste" (specifically in literature, but by extension in all arts) as inspired by late-century reform movements did not negate the importance of delight.[43] Pleasure found through artistic experience was encouraged as long as it was equally coupled with a sense of edification.

This question of whether to delight or inspire helps to capture another related dualism that was inherent to the cantata in this period. Though often perceived as contradistinct, the realms of theater and chamber proved to be intersecting influences and reference points for cantata writers. Let us for a moment recall the advice of the Medici prince and Count Zambeccari who advised opera composers to write in a merry, pleasing, and lyrical style, as opposed to a style suited for "things for the chamber." On the one hand, their advice resonated with the very qualities that reform critics proposed to help simplify opera, by paring forms down to their most graceful and lyrical essence, without being encumbered by convoluted narratives. Yet cantata writers *also* captured this same quality of "simplicity" in response to the pastoral texts they set to music. Consistent with the critical advice for opera, composers such as Bononcini and others wrote cantatas in this graceful lyrical style, sometimes more effectively than in operas. Not all cantata texts were set this way, as the excerpts from Scarlatti's *Al fin m'ucciderete* reveal by providing an alternative, if not counterexample, to this simplified mode. By contrast, a cantata such as *Al fin m'ucciderete* presents daring harmonics and textural density of a more intricate counterpoint that signified different possibilities for the cantata, underscoring its unstaged milieu, where the cantata remained an object of contemplation for noble connoisseurs. Important to recognize is that the qualities and stylistic markers of each category (chamber and theater) and each aesthetic tendency (to inspire versus delight) was evident in various degrees and measures across cantata writing of the period.

In essence, the seemingly divergent realms of theater and chamber tell us several important things about how the cantata's identity was shaped. Like simple and complex, the oppositional binary of theater and chamber was collapsible through the connection to opera. Whether a cantata's approach was more cerebral, complex, and chamber-like, or endeavored to simplify expressive means by following new trends in dramatic writing, each could be seen as a corrective – a means to elevate musical drama or directly repair it through reform proscriptions. Thus, the polarization of that which was operatically "lyrical" versus that which was "chamber-like" was a false opposition in practice. The cantata could be equally referential to theater styles as to "things for the chamber." In either case, what united these fronts was their mutual reflection of reform aesthetics in this period.

Though powerful in how it shapes perception, a genre's fixed narrative can be significantly different from that same genre's compositional practice. We need not look further than the two examples examined above to understand how cantatas in practice were not singularly one way or the other – graceful and elegant, or complex and cerebral – but often could be a composite of both qualities. In other words, music could be multiply positioned despite the desire to lock the cantata conceptually into a single category. Genre monolithism has always held a powerful position in a culture where transition and reform undermine a sense of desired stability. Though the cantata may have been treated as determinably located in space and function, and even inviolable in spite of opera's sway, the multiplicity of associations that intersect the cantata expose the degree to which a genre could be *variously* perceived to serve the pursuits of external agendas. In the following discussion, we witness the extent to which the cantata's externally determined associations help reflect the ideological leanings of Giovanni Mario Crescimbeni, the Academy of Arcadians' head custodian and strong proponent of theatrical reform. His marginal diversion into the discussion of a musical *accademia* will prove to be rich and revealing of the kind of genre scripting symptomatic of the period, in which the complex connecting points between the cantata and opera play themselves out.

III

Theorizing the Arcadian musical *accademia*: Giovanni Mario Crescimbeni's *L'Arcadia*

In 1708, Crescimbeni published *L'Arcadia*, one of the more unusual works in his oeuvre and a foundational text for the Academy of Arcadians. Starting with *La bellezza della volgar poesia* (1700), much of Crescimbeni's writing in these early years of the academy was dedicated to creating a national cultural heritage by documenting the history of Italian literature, with the larger aim of using this historiography as a tool to enact Arcadian reform. The academy's aspirations and ideology were less overtly addressed in such writings; rather, they more subtly manifested themselves within surveys and descriptions of genres and their historical roots, placing them squarely within select literary lineages. *L'Arcadia* was not this kind of literary history, but instead was meant to function as a history of the society. This was not the first time that a member of the academy (which, in printed matters, was dominated by Crescimbeni as academy "custodian") took on the task of recording the history of the academy's activities. *L'Arcadia*, however, presented a novel turn. In this unique publication Crescimbeni dedicated himself to a different kind of retelling of Arcadia's founding by writing a pastoral fiction, one that allegorized and idealized the society's connection to a classical past.[44] *L'Arcadia* will be taken up in more detail later; an important feature to highlight for now is that Crescimbeni chose to write the history of *gli Arcadi* not as an event-by-event chronology, but as a tale, a dramatization through parable of how and what (in so far as it mattered to the small circle of Roman intellectuals that included Crescimbeni) Arcadia came to be.[45] It is significant that Crescimbeni chose this work, with its unusual narrative strategy, as one of few writings to detail the setting and performance of cantatas. In what follows, I offer an overview, paying close attention to specific passages of Crescimbeni's two sections of chapter 7 of *L'Arcadia*, in which he discusses the performance and reception of a musical *accademia*.[46]

L'Arcadia is a quest narrative that portrays the story of a group of Arcadian nymphs who set out on a journey through the Arcadian landscape on their way to the Olympic Games, though in effect in search of knowledge.[47] On their way, they encounter shepherds (representing men of cultural distinction in contemporary Roman society) who lecture the nymphs on topics that range from poetry and art, to medicine, anatomy, botany, mathematics, history, and archaeology. These exchanges are punctuated by poetic recitations and by courtly games and entertainment as the nymphs journey from encampment to encampment (here again, the encampments representing specific Roman palaces). Crescimbeni indicates that as much as he wanted this work to be serious in tone, he would not exclude amorous compositions, so as to temper the more severe subjects of mathematics, philosophy, anatomy, and the like. The "Accademia in Musica" of chapter 7 served as a venue where these types of amorous compositions and pastoral diversions could be performed.

As the story in this chapter goes, the nymphs and an entourage of shepherds and shepherdesses are invited to the "Capanna di Metaureo," the "hut" of the Abbot Domenico Riviera, who has arranged the gathering. At the *accademia*, Alessandro Scarlatti (Terpandro), Bernardo Pasquini (Protico), and Arcangelo Corelli (Arcomelo) were said to offer their music as entertainment – a *divertimento* to pass the remainder of the evening. The naming of specific musicians is important for the way this moment of the story is rendered. Crescimbeni explains that the evening began with some confusion when members of the group proposed various entertainments but could find none that seemed appropriate. In response, Scarlatti is depicted as telling his fellow non-musician shepherds to leave the task of selecting pieces to the musicians of the group – "those who deal with such activity."[48] Whether fictionalized or not, Crescimbeni reveals a significant point here. He acknowledges the degree of prominence and respect as well as responsibility placed in the hands of the musicians who acted as "directors" of the *accademia*, and, as is well known, they were the only three composers to have been ever admitted to the Academy of Arcadians.[49] Other details are revealed in this moment. The *accademia* begins, we are told, with one of Corelli's famous and beautiful *sinfonie*, of the variety typically heard at actual *accademie* that Cardinal Ottoboni would have held at his private residence.[50] As Crescimbeni promises in the preface to *L'Arcadia*, real events and figures central to the rise and history of the academy are alluded to within this pastoral tale.

The section of this chapter that has sparked the greatest interest among music scholars, however, is the section that ensues, when Crescimbeni describes a dialogue between Scarlatti and the lawyer and poet Giambattista Felice Zappi.[51] In this instance, the author writes that Scarlatti (Terpandro) pulled from his bag a number of *canzoni* that he had set to music, with verses written by a fellow shepherd, Zappi (Tirsi), also present at the *accademia*. With this gesture begins a long competitive exchange between Terpandro and Tirsi over the merits of setting poetry to music. Terpandro begins the exchange, admitting to feelings of anxiety. Of the songs he has recovered from his bag, he worries whether their music will bring the shepherds the same pleasure as the verses.[52] In response, Tirsi pleads with Terpandro to set those verses aside and instead to choose others. The poet confesses that such compositions "were written to be set to music," and in fact, they were improvised hastily and experimentally at the very table of the composer who set them.[53] He thus expresses his concern that few of these songs would be suitable for the delicate taste of the outstanding literati, the shepherds at this gathering. What is important about this exchange is the portrayal of music's potentially damaging role. Crescimbeni, through Tirsi, suggests that poetry written for music (at least poetry improvised hastily in *this* way) is substandard, either not serious enough, or perhaps poetically compromised for musical purposes, rendering it inappropriate for the refined tastes of these listeners. Note here that he does not suggest that these cantatas are inappropriate as music, but that they are not suited to elevated and delicate tastes – in this instance, tastes more literary than musical.

Terpandro reacts to Tirsi's disclaimer by pointing out that the poet is too modest – even his improvised verse is more beautiful than the verse of others who have the benefit of time to apply their best efforts. What ensues, as Crescimbeni narrates, is a performance of Tirsi's texts set to what appears to be a solo and then a duo cantata, with Pasquini and Scarlatti alternately providing accompaniment at the harpsichord for each performance.[54]

The events of the concert become more remarkable when the issue of improvisation returns. Crescimbeni describes that during the singing of the last amorous duet, Terpandro notices from his harpsichord that Tirsi, though clearly engrossed by the performance, nevertheless seems lost in thought. The composer provokes the poet, trying to guess his thoughts, while Tirsi replies that he will tell Terpandro what he is thinking on the condition that they engage in an impromptu competition. Tirsi proposes to recite a new poem he has been composing inwardly if Terpandro immediately sets it to music following Tirsi's rules (the rules of poetry)[55] and performs it as a gift to this noble gathering so that the listeners may decide whether it is true that Tirsi produces such improvised *canzoni* so admirably.

Tirsi begins by reciting his aria verse, after which Terpandro, with amazing alacrity, rushes to set the words to music. Crescimbeni writes that following the performance of the aria, so much delight is elicited in the souls of the listeners, that they beg the shepherds for more. Crescimbeni's concluding narration following Tirsi and Terpandro's second aria provokes some interesting issues:

Everyone was overwhelmed to see how these two so excellent masters competed, one of poetry, the other of music; and their competition reached such a point that just as one finished the last verse of the new aria, the other completed the last line of his music. Now this new way of improvising a musical *accademia* so much pleased the party, that with that they completed their soirée.[56]

Here Crescimbeni highlights several aspects of the exchange between Scarlatti and Zappi. For one, the spontaneous creation of word and music is portrayed as a miraculously unified activity, with music flowing seamlessly out of the poetry of verse. However, we are never told much about the quality of these verses, or whether music always directly "obeyed" the poetic affect, or if it instead gained the upper hand. Unfortunately, we lack any specific means to help us better evaluate the details behind this creative process. We have no knowledge of a Scarlatti manuscript that set any of these texts by Zappi.[57] All we do know, according to this source, is that this manner of artistic creation pleased this audience and was considered to be a novelty, even though it is doubtful that such competitive exchanges were entirely new, or that the creative transaction between vocal music's contrasting media was so regularly and unfailingly integrated. What is most significant is that even in a document that acknowledges the transaction between composition, performance, and listener, little of detail or substance about the poetry–music relationship is revealed in the exchange between Scarlatti and Zappi.

I have chosen to re-examine this well-known passage from *L'Arcadia* not in hopes of finding new technical details of vocal music composition. Others have analyzed this passage and have noted that it is exceptional for the unique manner in which it evokes the atmosphere of the context in which Scarlatti's cantatas were born. Some have cautioned, however, that Crescimbeni's language in this instance appears particularly "flowery," betraying an overly ornamented narrative style.[58] Fabrizio Della Seta views the excerpt as exceptional for different reasons.[59] He contextualizes Crescimbeni's narration of a musical *accademia* within a broader evaluation of music's role in Arcadia. Based on study of documents in the Arcadian archive, Della Seta demonstrates an overwhelming *lack* of evidence for music's presence or importance within the Arcadian institution. The very act of admittance of musicians to the society was unprecedented, he claims, and the gesture was surely significant. Despite Crescimbeni's desire to establish a special musical group within the academy, the "Coro d'Arcadia" was never fully realized; furthermore it appears that Corelli, Pasquini, and Scarlatti actually requested their own admittance into the society. Della Seta finds it odd that among the documents in the archive there is little evidence of their compositions, or of any other music for that matter.[60] Thus, for Della Seta, the musical *accademia* and Zappi and Scarlatti's exchange fail to serve as normative evidence. The source merely serves to perpetuate the enigma of music's role in its lack of musical description, despite whether it directly or indirectly expressed the Arcadians' preferred pastoral modality, or reflected the society's cultural practices.

If we seek concrete evidence for music's value and aesthetic relationship to both the poetic and larger Arcadian ideals, then Della Seta may be correct; we are at a loss, for very little in Crescimbeni's rendering of the exchange between Zappi and Scarlatti over the creation and performance of cantatas provides such evidence. On these grounds, it would not be unreasonable to dismiss *L'Arcadia* as a source. But perhaps a conventional reading of documents for this kind of detail or substantiation is a wrongly directed approach in light of the peculiar kind of narrative constructed by Crescimbeni in *L'Arcadia*. In fact, it is entirely possible that in our search we should be less attentive to what this document affirms than to what it denies. But to read it this way means we must consider the musical *accademia* in the context of Crescimbeni's work as a whole.

Crescimbeni is forthright about his approach to *L'Arcadia*. In the preface, he states that he has chosen to depart from a simple historical account, and instead, has resolved to ornament this history and make it appear *other* than it is by disguising it as a tale.[61] For Crescimbeni, the classical and Renaissance pastorals are the stated models for such *favole*. In fact, he cites none other than Jacopo Sannazaro as inspiration for *L'Arcadia* and also as the source for the title, a point we might read both as a commemorative gesture and as affirmation of a link to a poetic and cultural lineage. Sannazaro's *Arcadia*

(1504) carries great significance for Crescimbeni, and his use of this work as a template underscores his connection to a host of Tuscan literary influences, above all Petrarch, and to the humanists' classical models for the pastoral topos found in Virgil's *Eclogues* and Theocritus's *Idylls*. Sannazaro may have served Crescimbeni in more specific ways, providing an example of the successful interweaving of prose with poetry and showing how past and present could be conflated. Among the greatest imaginative leaps for Sannazaro was the creation of Arcadia as a place in the mind, not limited to an imagined Grecian topography, but one that encompassed multiple times, spaces, and pastoral motifs.[62] Crescimbeni similarly erased temporal boundaries and distinctions. His representations of the academy's activities in *L'Arcadia* are cast dualistically as if happening in a distant past, yet also occurring in the modern present. He urges his readers to think of Rome as Arcadia, and Arcadia as Rome, blurring the differences between modern and ancient constructions.[63] Though their works are outwardly similar, Sannazaro and Crescimbeni none the less wrote with different aims in mind. Sannazaro's *Arcadia* was a self-conscious celebration of pastoral literature and a poetic tradition. Crescimbeni's *L'Arcadia* likewise commemorated poetic traditions, but it also served as a kind of manifesto, a declaration and guide to the academy's deeper ideological pursuits. Several scholars have noted the Arcadians' ideological tendencies, but few have probed those implications critically or considered their conflicting and antinomic qualities.[64] When the academy's ideological and cultural impact has been addressed, scholars typically choose sides: they either find the Arcadians' enlightened goals suspect and essentially ineffective, or they credit the society as an important source of progressive ideas within the otherwise oppressive confines of papal Rome.[65] The question of how to read the Arcadians' conflicting ideological tendencies remains a provocative challenge that I will revisit later. My immediate interest is to pursue how *L'Arcadia*'s narrative strategies and rhetorical techniques may come to bear upon the use of music within the society's activities, and the ways in which nostalgically imagining the past as the present served as both a polemical and an ideological tool for Crescimbeni and his circle of Arcadian critics. There is analytical utility in taking this position of the imaginary seriously. Surely, Crescimbeni's *L'Arcadia* is not valuable as a repository of fact-based evidence; but then again, nostalgia and formalist rigor never have gone hand in hand. His account of the musical *accademia* is neither founded upon any observation that can be documented, nor is it a recollection of an actual performance that we know took place – rather, it is an idealized construct. One could easily dismiss Crescimbeni's references to music and to the pairing of sound and word in cantata settings precisely because they have no bearing on the real or actual, but to argue for such grounds for dismissal may actually be to dismiss an important cultural grounding.

Nostalgia as ideology

Crescimbeni's musical *accademia* is but one of many vignettes in *L'Arcadia*'s complex and intricate narrative that introduces its readers not just to the history and diversions of Rome's Academy of Arcadians, but to the larger ideological construct behind *Arcadia*. In depicting his present environs of Rome as those of ancient Arcadia, Crescimbeni invites his reader to imagine this merger, to envision the past as present. To do so, however, requires a certain denial of historical evolution; and it is this process of denial that will more specifically come to bear upon the Arcadians' portrayal of opera and its relation to the cantata.

The impulse to restore a past in order to remake a present entails a purposefully orchestrated discontinuity. For some Arcadian ideologues, this might be symbolized in the disjointed swaths of history they chose to resuscitate and rewrite when tracing their own vaunted lineage; they leapt from the ancient pastoral writers to the time of Petrarch and Boccaccio, and later to Sannazaro and Tasso, but most importantly, they effected near complete erasure of the seventeenth century until that redemptive moment when Arcadia was reborn and the pastoral was re-embraced.[66] This process was an ideological mindset for the Arcadian founders. When Crescimbeni penned *L'Arcadia*, it allowed him carefully to spin together real names and places alongside fictionalized accounts and events that were shaped through a romanticized imagination of the past. In his work this strategy is not employed haphazardly; on the contrary, Crescimbeni judiciously applies this distortion of temporal boundaries to effect a pervasive sense of nostalgia throughout.

Though nostalgia is normally characterized as the longing for something real and familiar from a time gone by, it can also manifest as a longing for an *imaginary* past. It is often therefore not memory, but an idealization of memory in which the past is evoked, but either fictionalized or distorted by the gap between the real and imaginary. In Crescimbeni's hands, nostalgia becomes a powerful tool to create this ideal, preferred past and thereby deny competing histories. In parts of *L'Arcadia* here discussed we shall see how the pastoral becomes the locus of nostalgia and works a cultural strategy to distort history and transfigure events into a preferred ideological realignment.

The Academy of Arcadians was by no means the first such group to embrace the pastoral as an important literary style, but the centrality of the pastoral as a cultural formation vital to the academy's image building and polemics deserves further scrutiny. Among Arcadian thinkers, the pastoral was the modern conduit to a Golden Age. In classical sources, the Golden Age evoked a prestigious and exalted past of fertility and harmony achieved through the practice of simplicity. For Rome's modern Arcadia the pastoral was, furthermore, a link to a second "Golden Age," to the Renaissance, when crowning achievements in Italian literature took place. It was therefore viewed as a historical as well as literary benchmark to resurrect. Pastoralism and its historical significance worked as a discursive formation around which to shape attitudes, negotiate culture, and espouse political views. Modern Arcadians projected this pastoral notion of a Golden Age on to their noble pastimes, in conceiving themselves as shepherds and shepherdesses who romanticized a lauded past in their own image at each of their gatherings. And yet, we must recognize that even if their pastoral vision was one that operated to perfect and purify the world, the activism implied in such a mission was ironically thwarted by the marked tenacity and maintenance of past practices. Arcadia had long been a figment of writers' and thinkers' imaginations. It was the ideal idealized place. For this early eighteenth-century Roman enclave, rather than radical change, the pastoral offered symbolic protection in their otherwise shifting political and cultural landscape.

It is critical at this juncture to pull back momentarily and stress an important tension that arose within the Arcadian ranks of leadership and power. I have thus far discussed the Arcadians' pastoral vision and nostalgic posture mostly through the doctrines designed by Crescimbeni, who arguably controlled the academy's ideological direction during these years. However, his thoughts and positions were not without dissenters.[67] Of those, most famous was Ludovico Antonio Muratori, whose impatience with the Arcadians and their pastoral obsessions led him to propose his own academy that could more readily and directly address cultural, moral, and ecclesiastic reform beyond what he thought was the narrower and more self-absorbed version that Arcadia represented.[68] Even more rancorous towards Crescimbeni's dominance was the voice of Gian Vincenzo Gravina, who also complained about the Arcadians' frivolous preoccupation with lyrical poetry and pastoralism instead of the larger issues of morality, civic duty, and republican ideals.[69] Ultimately, Crescimbeni's nostalgic vision of Arcadia and his pastoral program held sway, regardless of these nonconforming voices; yet pastoral absorption had its consequences. It meant that for Crescimbeni and his followers their supposed parallel universe of past as present, Arcadia as Rome, ideal as real, became sets of dualities fraught with contradiction. In his discussion of Muratori's anti-Arcadian critical stance, Vernon Hyde Minor plumbs the essence of the Arcadians' problem in his paraphrase of Muratori's argument: "without balancing intellect, the fantasy cannot know the truth."[70] As Muratori's sentiments warn, imagination had its dangers. Left unchecked it ran the risk of going astray, and in this case, the nostalgic posture of Arcadia did not just idealize memory but had the tendency to distort reality as a consequence of its peculiar form of pastoralism.

There is much to learn from Crescimbeni's application of the pastoral as a nostalgic device to shape the ideological framework of *L'Arcadia*. Here, however, I would like to explore more specifically how nostalgic idealization frames the Zappi–Scarlatti exchange in Crescimbeni's section on the musical *accademia*. Much is at stake polemically in the author's pastoral fantasy in which a bucolic image is painted of shepherds in playful competition over the extemporization of poetry and music. Tirsi (Zappi) and Terpandro (Scarlatti) are depicted as conceiving and performing their respective arts as a perfect marriage of artistic languages. But Crescimbeni, through his characters' words, embeds an important subtext. What we witness here is a representation of both an *ideal* and an *exceptional* performance, one carefully tailored to the cultivated tastes of an esteemed audience; hence, an exchange that could never take place if governed by the ordinary standards of contemporary poetry, a sentiment spoken through Tirsi, but essentially conveyed by Crescimbeni. Recall that it is Tirsi's exceptional talents that truly bring pleasure to the audience. Despite its pretenses, no part of the shepherds' encounter is meant as a light diversion. There are clear workings behind this event, as it underscores how the redemptive aspirations of the Arcadian fathers enlightened these shepherds in their important abilities to create cantatas, not merely as products of diversion but as polemical templates of doctrine. Crescimbeni's ideological agenda has a heavy hand here as he idealizes the specific relationship between two crucial modalities: poetry and music.

Music, embodied by Terpandro, enters the scene in a privileged position; Terpandro gets first draw, pulling verses of his *own* selection from his bag. It is possible that in this instance, Crescimbeni gives a nod to the recent admission to the academy of Scarlatti and his honored colleagues, Pasquini and Corelli. Yet, as though such acclaim might go too far, Crescimbeni casts doubt and insecurity in the words of Terpandro via his concern over whether *his* music and *his* form of artistic expression will bring the same pleasure as verse will. In fact, Crescimbeni follows this turning point with a series of performed examples that emphasize a realignment of roles and an establishment of hierarchy. With an allegorical approach in mind, Crescimbeni proceeds with his word–music competition, which, perhaps not surprisingly, affirms the primacy of word: verses are recited and music is meant to follow. Though music has the first pass, it is made clear in this performance that text will reassert itself and music will accommodate. But, if poetry needs to lead music, how perfect then is the marriage of languages? Except for Crescimbeni telling his readers that the performance pleased listeners, we know very little about the aesthetic role the musical setting played. Della Seta suggests that the absence of such musical discussion is not casual. Though he admits the possibility that members of the society had taken great interest in and privileged music, he also notes that the Arcadians were not disposed to accord music any license of autonomy and independence from the domain of the word. Whether this was because musicians were viewed as craftsmen and not literati, or because music was placed at the bottom of the Aristotelian-conceived hierarchy of the arts, the Arcadian aesthetic did not accommodate music with any specificity.[71]

Crescimbeni's feigned fairness doctrine (as if music and poetry would each take turns) becomes a rhetorical sleight of hand, and before one knows it, hierarchies are fixed and the relationship of word and music as performed in the cantata has been realigned. Most important, however, is what is left unsaid. Poetry may have the upper hand but music's potentially independent powers of expression are left untouched. What to make of the possible but overlooked disjunction between poetry's signification and its relation to music? What happens when the perfect union is broken? To present some responses to this question, I wish to explore the manner in which Arcadia's nostalgic ideology further widens the chasm rather than repairs the perceived disjunction between poetry and music. In what follows, I explore the utopian pastoral vision of the Arcadian institution through a number of examples. Arcadia viewed as utopia may reveal how the society's discursive practices indirectly reflect the music–word disjunction.

A utopian Arcadia

In a 1973 article, sociologist Amedeo Quondam investigated the institutional qualities of Arcadia and the extent to which the academy's ideological leanings were less a vehicle for enlightened thinking than a stance supporting the implementation of papal cultural policy.[72] For Quondam, the Arcadians' actions and forms of control (which he notes in the early period from the 1690s to the early 1700s were largely shaped by the first custodian, Crescimbeni) were characterized by a hegemonic impulse, a desire to expunge competing socio-cultural movements. He interprets this move as shrewd and efficient, and yet equally revealing as an act taken during crisis in an attempt to recuperate a cultural history on the brink of extinction.[73] Here Quondam refers to the Arcadians' anxiety and reactionary intransigence towards a number of emerging late-century intellectual trends whose liberal and secular tendencies upended the Arcadians' conservative view (a view heavily influenced by the Curia's internal politicking) and threatened to extinguish their idealized past.

Quondam is not alone in reading the Academy of Arcadians as a vehicle for papal cultural policy rather than as a forum for unilateral progressive thinking. In his patronage study of art and cultural politics in the age of Clement XI, Christopher M. S. Johns offers a similar but somewhat more nuanced take.[74] His study points to important links between the cultural policies and political conservatism of Clement XI (Giovanni Francesco Albani, r. 1700–1721) and the Academy of Arcadians' reform mentality. For Johns, one reflexively shaped the other. Johns explains that as a young budding intellectual, the soon-to-be pope, Albani, frequented Queen Christina of Sweden's academy at the Palazzo Riario. As we know, his group was fiercely dedicated to the reversal of recent literary trends, seeking to expunge poetic affectation and excessive conceits, and thus advocating a return to a written tradition that esteemed simplicity and reason, values not unconnected to Christina's unwavering belief in papal Catholicism.[75] The emphasis on reason and the society's engagement with new empirical thought are provocative qualities when considered in this context. Along with literature, Christina's academy welcomed the participation of other artists, philosophers, antiquarians, and scientists, a tradition upheld by the Arcadians' subsequent reincarnation of Christina's gathering.[76] Even though much of the scientific discussion encouraged in Christina's (and later the Arcadians') circle echoed the impact of the scientific revolution sweeping Europe, the focus on empirical observation, as Johns argues, had non-scientific aims in mind. If anything, Clement XI and a number of very powerful intellectual colleagues within the Academy of Arcadians were challenged and threatened by the unarbitrated dissemination of knowledge represented by scientific and other revolutions, and were not uniformly inspired to follow them. Their engagement with a new intellectual landscape was selective. For Clement XI and those working with and under him, empirical research occasioned a radical re-evaluation of how the past could remake or, at very least, shelter and protect the present. In the guise of science, Clement XI's programs encouraged a re-evaluation of church history, the study of sacred antiquity, and the restoration of existing eccle- siastic monuments and art in Rome. Not since the Counter-Reformation had an outpouring of interest in the "sacred sciences" taken such hold, but now the difference lay in the approach: historical claims to the truth and the inevitability of Catholic hegemony were not enough; *empirical evidence,* early modernity's new rhetorical tool, had to be marshaled.[77] In Johns's esti- mation, this sacred agenda was equally tied to literary and cultural reform. After all, this was an "age of historical precedent and legitimacy" in which scholarly scrutiny applied to the restoration of the church's leadership in politics and culture simultaneously and reciprocally affected the Arcadian longing for an uncorrupted simplicity. Johns interprets the Paleochristian movement and Arcadianism as equally yearning for respective Golden Ages. He characterizes each as "an aggressive, primitivist movement [that] gen- erally sought to simplify modern culture by a return to origins, stripping them of the accretive artifice of time."[78]

It is important to realize the extent to which *both* the enlightened tools of a proto-modern intellectual rationalism, as well as the arguably irrational yearning for simpler and purer "truths" of an imagined and romantically primitive past, were equally symptoms of retreat. Both sides of this other- wise divisive opposition (that is, viewing such movements and institutions as *either* progressive *or* conservative) can be read as indicators contributing to the same cultural enclosure, enacted to protect the decidedly esteemed and shrewdly selective notion of cultural inheritance. Institutions like Arca- dia ironically engaged the tools of an emerging modern intellectual land- scape – be it archaeology, rationalistic philosophy, encyclopedic ordering, or other empirical approaches – to resist and deny the onset of the same modernity.

It is useful to embed these contradictions within the larger discourse that regarded Rome's Arcadia as utopia. Like Arcadia, utopias were imagined spaces typically conjured in reactionary moments when critiques of present circumstances spurred radical revision and reconception. The modern rise of rationality provoked a series of utopian discourses in Western culture, from those of Thomas More and Rabelais, to Tommaso Campanella and Jonathan Swift. Alain Touraine writes: "The voluntarism of utopia is abso- lute; it is as full of confidence in reason as it is critical of power and wealth."[79] However, it would be wrong to equate Rome's Arcadian movement with the kind of utopia imagined by Thomas More, for example, whose sixteenth- century rhetorical conceit gave rise to this literary genre. Serving as a cri- tique of the reigning order in England of his day, More's *Utopia* implied a construction of the future brought about by human effort. More argues for a diametric reversal of his reality, a rupture or break with the past meant to usher in a new (albeit imagined) social arrangement. This, too, is a move towards enclosure; after all, it is an island that More envisions. In that act of separation and isolation, More's utopia is also an escape from surrounding social conditions, an effort to abandon the socially dominant. But More's utopia envisions a future on the premise that the past and present are no longer livable. In this strong form, a utopia destroys memories of the past and realities of the present through what we might regard as political and/or cultural revolution.

Though traces of this utopia may resonate with aspects of a Golden Age idealization, the differences are noteworthy. The Golden Age is not attained through human effort, but is offered through divine intercession, a created earthly paradise filled with abundance, ease, and simplicity. This is nearer to the utopian vision of the Roman Arcadian leaders, who created their mythic utopia (of a noble savage bent) by "re-costuming" their present noble life as a romanticized Arcadian landscape, with shepherds who "labor" but never work in the true sense of the word. Their utopia was less about change than about maintenance in so far as Rome's Arcadia functioned as a *static* paradise in referral to and defense of the past. In this sense, the Arcadians were the kind of utopians to emphasize not so much radical anticipation as redemptive cultural work.[80] Thus, in a utopia tending toward nostalgia, ideological positions are compromised. The past is the idealized anchor of everything that was good, but it is also a heavy weight, an impediment to change or self-awareness by virtue of its longing for a time that no longer exists.

In memoriam

To understand the utopian dimension of the Academy of Arcadians, it is important to recognize that, traditionally, utopias have tended to be textual, consisting of things told but not seen. For the Arcadians, and especially for Crescimbeni, the imagining of Arcadia through the act of writing was their most powerful tool. The enchantment and ideological efficacy of juxtaposing the real and imaginary in a work such as *L'Arcadia* would be difficult to realize outside of text. In the hands of Crescimbeni, writing became a mechanism of control, as evidenced in the crafted tales of pastoral fantasies, as well as in the memorials and obituaries he meticulously collected, researched, ordered, and archived as an act of the society's self-preservation. This practice of commemoration and of archiving was an obsession for Crescimbeni and for his fellow Arcadian leaders. He felt it to be the principal objective of Arcadia to honor particularly its shepherds, both living and deceased.[81] He spent the next twenty years of his career commemorating the lives and deaths of important Arcadian members through two separate published series: *Le vite degli Arcadi illustri* and *Notizie istoriche degli Arcadi morti*.[82]

The *Vite* were propagandistic works, part of Crescimbeni's painstaking approach to promote the academy and establish the Arcadians' distinction and supremacy as compared with society at large. Each selected figure embodied the ideas, values, and accomplishments most cherished and espoused by Arcadian ideologues. The *Vite* were thus a means of commemoration and recollection, yet also a kind of ritual practice. Their accumulation and increase in number implied institutional success, but more importantly, their repetition reaffirmed a continuity with the past.

Ritual and commemoration permeated most aspects of the academy's activities, whether manifested in Crescimbeni's writing or his call to archive all things Arcadian, or in recurring ceremonies such as the *Annoverazione*, when new members were initiated, as well as the *Giuochi Olimpici*, which dramatically re-enacted the Arcadian vision of a pastoral life.[83] What was most important to achieve in such acts was a sense of preservation rather than of renewal, a comfort with the repetition of formula rather than a reinvention and new ideas.[84] Here again we can identify Arcadia's peculiar form of utopian rhetoric at work, in which ritualizing an idealized past may prevent actual change or renewal. Archiving, documenting, and ordering the past, though effective as empirical and rational approaches, may have encouraged a kind of cultural stasis, thereby diminishing the Arcadians' willingness to engage with other dominant trends of culture in this period.

We must also recognize that the act of preservation of the past took work, detailed work, on the part of Crescimbeni and his fellow Arcadian archivists who documented the members that embodied the society's ideals. Along with the *Vite*, Crescimbeni also collected a series of panegyrics in *Notizie istoriche degli Arcadi morti*, what he described as a tribute to Arcadia's "deceased children."[85] Each entry functioned as an obituary and served as yet another printed vehicle for the memorialization and the maintenance of social memory. In a sense, life and meaning were kept most alive through death, since efforts to recover, preserve, and continue the past were just as much acts of remembrance as they were rituals of termination, a freezing and halting of present time in order to dwell in more vast places of memory.[86] Crescimbeni's literary tributes inspired real epitaphs too, in the form of plaques (*lapidi di memoria*) that were ritualistically hung at Arcadian gatherings after 1698.[87] It was through these real and figurative monuments that Crescimbeni meant to immortalize Arcadia and to allow its pastoral world, and all that it had come to signify, to exist in perpetuity.

At the same time the creation of memorials reveals a conceptual conundrum that permeated the Arcadians' utopian stance. In the words of David Lowenthal, "monuments and memorials embellish the past by evoking some epoch's splendour . . . What most such evocations have in common is being made after the event; they celebrate the past in a later guise. And their form and features may in no way resemble what they were expressly built to recall."[88] If Arcadia summoned the past, it did so from the present. As obvious as this paradox may seem it reveals a critical disjunction at the core of Arcadia's ideological approach and belief system, at least that espoused by Crescimbeni and his followers. The past cannot become the present, nor can it erase the present; the present *is* the present. This was indeed the feeling of those critical of Arcadia's more extreme utopian and pastoral stance, who may have lamented a lost past, but chose classical models of literature and culture as a fount of sustenance and inspiration to reshape and redirect their *present* universe.[89]

Scholars have puzzled over Arcadia's many paradoxes, often with the aim of evaluating the society's efficacy and long-term effect on eighteenth-century culture and on the Enlightenment. There are a number of unsettled relationships (pastoral as urban, past as present, ideal as real) that one might argue complicated, even stymied the Arcadian movement, but also profoundly shaped its cultural practices.[90] My interest is less focused on the evaluation of efficacy, than on viewing such paradoxes as a telling symptom that helps to grasp more effectively the Arcadians' perspective on musical culture in their time, as well as reveal how such paradoxes cast an indirect shadow upon the relationship of the cantata to opera.

I turn to an iconic image, one that has been much scrutinized, to explore these unsettled but determinant contradictions that pervaded Arcadia. In 1725, Antonio Canevari and his assistant, Nicola Salvi, finished the drawings and plans for the construction of the Arcadians' permanent *Bosco Parrasio* (see figure 8).

For the first three decades or more, the Academy of Arcadians had no fixed meeting place, though true to their name, they typically convened out of doors in garden settings.[91] Finally in 1723, under the relatively new protector of the academy, King John V of Portugal, the Arcadians purchased land on the Janiculum and hired a fellow member, the architect Canevari, to design the garden and supervise its construction.

Figure 8 Nicola Salvi, after Antonio Canevari, *Gianicolo Bosco Parrasio*, Garden of the Accademia dell'Arcadia, 1725 (Accademia Nazionale di San Luca, Rome, inv. n. 2121).

The realization of this garden was a true climax in the early development of the academy. Not only did it fix a permanent meeting place – and thus give further credibility and symbolic weight to the Arcadians' presence in Rome – but it succeeded in achieving a physically real and symbolically significant retreat where these self-fashioned literati could meet, rehabilitate themselves, and find solace in their pastoral cultivation of good taste. The Canevari–Salvi drawing and plans were in fact inspired by the lead shepherd of the academy, Crescimbeni himself, whose rough sketch indicates that the physical shape of the garden and many of its decorative gestures were thoughtfully chosen with a sense of Arcadia's symbolic vision in mind.[92] Of most importance was the visual representation of ascent, that members entered the garden to climb up towards their final meeting point, the Arcadian amphitheater, where readings, discussion, and inspiration would be drawn from shepherds' pastoral diversions. Along the way, the idea was that Arcadians could meander up the hill, while taking in vistas, sensing the protection of their cherished woods, and envisioning their pastoral past as provoked by the classically inspired sculpture (for example, figures of Pan, Syrinx, Athena, Mercury, Apollo, Pegasus) that adorned the tops of the gates, the grottos and walls that marked the various landings, and the rotunda that crowned the very top.[93]

Significant in all of this is the fact that the plans of Canevari and Salvi (as inspired by Crescimbeni) were never *fully* realized by the time of the official inauguration of the garden in 1726. Lack of funds played an important factor as costs began to mount during construction. The garden, as it stands today, did retain a good deal of the original conception, including the central elements of the staircases, the amphitheater, and the adjacent *serbatoio* (which served as the archive of material holdings and an indoor salon during inclement weather or otherwise). Other features of the drawing, however, were never executed – notably the classically inspired sculptural plans, which were critical to lending this otherwise modern construction its symbolic connection to a mythological past. As Susan Dixon concludes: "The Arcadians could not have understood the significance of the statue of Apollo, nor the river gods of Mercury or Minerva, because they were not in the garden. The grotto of Alpheus was not operational to inspire any poet, and the picture gallery in the serbatoio was not in place to ensure the fame of deceased Arcadians." More serious, Dixon contends, is how the *ideal* garden was in conflict with how the Arcadians actually functioned, and what they accomplished. For all the grandness of notions this retreat inspired – pan-Italianism, republicanism, pastoral perfection, good taste, and classical revival – "the pragmatics and politics of Roman society in the early eighteenth century prevented closing the gap between the ideal and real garden."[94]

Retreat came at a cost. For some among the Arcadians it signified an unfortunate disengagement from the world, and perhaps a danger to distinguish and fluidly navigate between that which was idealized and the environment that was theirs. Canevari's unfulfilled design for the *Bosco Parrasio* is paradigmatic of the Arcadians' contradictions. Though a pastoral sanctuary idealized for its rusticness and simplicity, it was still a cultivated garden of modern construction superimposed upon nature. Here the rural and urban sit uncomfortably close, as do the juxtaposed realms of pastoral and modern. Despite the fantastical gestures that any sculpture could convey, the Arcadians' garden reveals two irreconcilable associations with time: the pastoral ideal is immersed in the image of historical time, whereas the modern realization exposes a break with time.[95]

Canevari's design for the *Bosco Parrasio* is not the only evidence of the conceptual split between classically inspired content embedded within modern form. And though it is difficult really to know how obvious this disjunction seemed or how self-aware the Arcadians may have been, in some ways we can identify the extent to which almost all their activities and ideological pursuits bore the same fissure of temporal disjunction and contradiction. If any medium of their choosing – be it art, music, architecture, or poetry – deployed a nostalgic revival of the past, it was through modern means. And even when that modernity was recognized, the society's more powerful nostalgic leanings made this distinction self-consciously difficult, if not at times impossible if the vision of Arcadia was to remain intact. Taking architecture, art, poetry, or music seriously – in the most realistic terms – would expose how their formal languages, structures, and means of expression were undeniably modern. Though the embodiment of a past/present duality was not uncommon in early modern culture, what is important to consider is how, for the Arcadians, the blurring of this division specifically affected the discourses that drove their reform efforts and influenced their perspectives on and reactions to opera and the role of music in drama. It is in this way that the idealization of the *Bosco Parrasio* (and its inherent contradictions) may indeed resonate with the Arcadians' idealization of musical drama.

When viewing opera we must not forget the power and importance that legacy and historical appropriation played in forming late seventeenth- and early eighteenth-century reform polemics. The Arcadians engaged in a kind of historiographic erasure by eclipsing opera's modern history, including its rise as a public form of theater with commercial concerns, and the poetic movements that formed its literary core. The pastoral channeled a different past, anchored in Italy's Renaissance legacy and its classical revivalism. It represented not just a poetic form or an appropriate setting for musical drama; it was also a consciousness and an ethos to live by, to experience on stage, to perceive in word and sound (as if any of this was actually possible). While some championed a pastoral solution, few Arcadian critics who addressed the future of musical drama carefully considered the compromises and contradictions that arose in "staging" the past through the realities of a performed present. As Daniel Chua reminds us, it was the visual form of opera that most obviously played out this split by compromising the "frontstage" mystification of an ancient world, with the knowledge of a "backstage" machinery that disenchanted this image by turning "the world into clockwork," and through "levers, pulleys and pumps . . . [made it] the site of modern science."[96]

If opera's visible traces of modernism meant that it could not easily fool the viewer, then we might come to understand how the invisible landscapes evoked by the pastoral cantata could more viably encourage a denial of past/present distinctions. Clearly the cantata was more amenable to the imaginary. Its simplicity of presentation idealized the best of what the pastoral had to offer: simple shepherds extemporizing and singing poetic amorous verses. However, we need only to return to Crescimbeni's rendition of the Zappi–Scarlatti moment to recall a deeper consequence of the cantata's signification. In Zappi and Scarlatti's exchange, the sense of a present reality is erased, hierarchies are asserted, and the centrality of poesis is strengthened in the cantata by eliding music's salience. Despite the reality of the cantata's modern musico-dramatic structures, its varied conventions of expression, and its presumed diverse reception, we see, none the less, that the idealized cantata was an over-coded genre. In all of its paradoxical simplicity and complexity the cantata was layered with historical legacy and, ineluctably, with opera's own troubled history.

IV

Opera's displacement

Cantatas may have served the Arcadians well in their pastoral fantasies and intellectual pastimes, yet we have come to learn how little they directly discuss the cantata, let alone its relationship with opera. The connections made in polemical discourses between the two genres are neither obvious nor explicit, and yet we know from Crescimbeni's discussion of the musical *accademia* in the seventh chapter of *L'Arcadia*, that the cantata was important, and may in fact symbolize more than pastoral diversion. For our purposes, the cantata uniquely functions as a mirror for opera's polemics, a reflection of qualities – stylistic *and* cultural – that represent the most idealized wishes of Arcadia's literary and dramatic reforms.

The polemical writings that address opera (via drama) are well known to scholars of the period; this literature has been much evaluated not only for what it says but for how such discussions of opera also fall short. We do not need explicit detail about opera and all of its practices to understand that at the very least, the most impassioned Arcadian reformers felt that the history of opera needed to be retold, rehistoricized, and redirected, in order to regain what felt like a lost historical trajectory. A variety of measures were taken, some effective, others less so; the critics and proponents of operatic reform were equally realist and idealist in their aims. As not uncommon for the period, their writings and ideas tended to elide, thwart, or idealize the element of music within their discourses. Yet, as we will come to see, music – as negated evidence – sometimes best revealed the limitations of a pastoral revival, and the complicated boundaries of a past/present duality. In all of this, the cantata worked as a site that reflected and appropriated opera's aesthetic struggles, the relationship between word and music, the question of authorship, and the crisis of a lost aesthetic unity.

From its beginnings, opera was as much about its discourses as it was about its practices. Renato Di Benedetto suggests that literature was part of opera's "genetic code," and it should not be surprising that a literary spirit – conveyed through copious polemical tracts, dedications, descriptions, critical commentary, even satire – infused opera's history and played a leading role in forging its cultural and social significance.[97] From its beginnings, the debates within Italy (largely penned by literati, *not* musicians) remained fixated on the task of marrying text to music, two central elements whose relationship was increasingly based on what some felt were unequal terms. Thus, the critical turn in the opening years of the eighteenth century presents a curious moment for opera's cultural history; curious, because the essential terms of the debate were in no way new but certainly were emboldened by new provocations. Polemical postures and cultural debate are often less about radical change and more about consolidation. And, sometimes, consolidation can signal a major gap between the perceptions of culture as filtered through discourse, and that same culture as determined through practice. But gaps such as these are significant to chart. Reactionary discourses may do little to alter the course of history, but they can be symptoms of larger cultural crisis.

The emerging autonomy of music within several facets of culture was a source of anxiety at the beginning of the eighteenth century. For Rome and for other European centers of culture, the dawn of the eighteenth century was a period when music would assume a relevance and cultural significance hitherto unknown. As a scholarly topic, music would not be a subject limited to specialist treatises, but would become a topic of discussion for intellectual circles, literati, polemicists, poets, and even musicians. Enrico

Fubini contends that as music emerged as a topic of discourse, "so too did the man of letters realize that music had become part of his world, and that the problems of music could and should interest him directly."[98] A new hierarchical rearrangement of the arts emerged in this period, with music assuming a more prominent position. This revealed more than aesthetic consequences; it disclosed other categorical shifts, since music's new prowess and stature signified new forms of authorial control and expressive agency, and it undeniably signaled changes in music's cultural institutions, their organization, power, and cultural reception. Opera served as an important catalyst during this period, so pivotal that its practices and discourses reverberated in other musical genres, such as the cantata. We must recall how the cantata registered a number of vital discourses outlined at the outset of this chapter; how in the minds of some, it captured a time when music and poetry were still creatively conceived within the bounds of courtly society. We also need to reflect on the ways in which perceptions of the cantata help to illuminate the conflation of an idealized past with a real present. We now understand how such enacted disjunction was a phenomenon symptomatic of the polemical ideology that marked this moment in time and that shaped Rome's most reactionary intellectual milieu. In recalling Crescimbeni's rendering of cantata creation and performance in *L'Arcadia*, we come to see how the cantata – not as artistic enterprise but as ideological posture – lived up to the desires of what most literati hoped opera could be.

But what did polemicists hope opera would be? It may be useful to invert the question and consider what they hoped opera would *not* be. Their view of opera was largely shaped by negation, the desire to rein in opera and perhaps reverse a number of its own tendencies. Mostly, they had hoped opera would not emerge as it did, especially throughout the first half of the seventeenth century, when it was increasingly nudged – in form, signification, and performance – beyond well-established rules and categories. During this period opera's expression of social representation expanded; it displayed a greater variety of subjects and characters. Opera narratives became increasingly complex and convoluted. Consequently, when opera intermingled the tragic with the comic, and the high with the low, literary purists saw that the cardinal rule of generic uniformity and cohesion had been transgressed. But above all, opera had accumulated conventions that fostered the increased presence of song, overwhelming audiences with music, thereby minimizing the importance of words, which the upholders of tradition felt were the only proper conduit to higher moral inspiration and qualities of good taste.[99]

Yet, with all the concern that music was changing drama, it is well known among scholars of this period that critical writings, in fact, take up very little about opera or music in any detail, especially when compared with the body of writing on spoken dramaturgy, which had an emphasis on theories of classical drama.[100] Italian literary figures were first and foremost concerned with literature, and – reacting to foreign, mainly French, criticism – with a critical rethinking of the entirety of Italian literary history. Opera's role in this discussion and in this revisionist moment is thus unusual. The reform of literature had little to do with opera in and of itself, or at least with changes directed specifically to its musical composition, but it did have much to do with the debates about and around opera. If modern Italian culture had discovered the conspicuous absence of a tragic theater tradition to rival the French, it was because opera, reasoned the Arcadian Academy, had usurped this role.[101]

Reactions to opera began to take several forms. Within the opera theater some made apologies by promoting reform. The most novel and lasting changes to libretto writing began in Venice, with the 1678 opening of the Teatro Grimani di San Giovanni Gristostomo, where librettists tried their hand at creating a new *tragedia per musica*.[102] It is not coincidental that these new changes to libretto writing took place during the same period as that in which the first Italian translations of French tragic masterpieces appeared.[103] But not all literati felt that music should have a role in tragic drama. Muratori famously denounced the use of music in tragedy. Of *tragedie in musica*, he said: "I would hardly dare to call such works [tragedies], since music as is used in our day, does not suit them (if they have to be perfect); indeed, it shrinks from them."[104] His sentiment is scarcely different from attacks by French critics, including Saint-Évremond and Le Cerf, who thought music should be completely removed from drama, and if not, kept to the barest minimum so that drama's actions and emotions remained mainly a function of its verbal elements.[105]

Aside from the adoption of tragedy as a model, another approach was taken in an effort to revitalize drama in Italy. Crescimbeni, along with several other leading Arcadian literati, believed that the only way to reform melodrama was through the revival of the *favola pastorale*, an important dramatic form we know had crucial bearing upon opera, though less directly on the cantata in this period, which was influenced more by the tradition of pastoral poetry as stated earlier in the chapter. For now we will put aside the cantata's connection to the pastoral and to the reformation of opera so as to focus on the interchange between opera and pastoral drama. What were the qualities of pastoral drama that could rescue opera from demise? Was music's role in pastoral opera as problematic as it was in tragic opera? The critic Muratori, along with his likeminded Arcadian colleagues, identified the pastoral, its tales with simple and credible plots, as the *only* drama where music might have a place, together with the use of dances, choruses, machines, and other spectacle.[106] Muratori, Crescimbeni, and, to some extent, Gravina attempted to trace a critical *Italian* lineage that belonged to the pastoral, yet their embrace of the pastoral was not solely an Italian reflex. Piero Weiss has identified French opera and French dramaturgical reform as key to the Arcadian move to pastoral models. While the Arcadians painted their embrace of the pastoral drama partly as tribute to the Renaissance legacy of drama, it was largely influenced by the French Lullian models of *tragédie lyrique* that had invaded the Italian peninsula. Looking to the French tradition of the *divertissement*, the Arcadians, like the French, found new justification for singing in drama, so long as subjects were invented, not historical, and were kept poetically simple to accommodate better the intrusion of other media.[107] This, they decided, was the only way to make the artifice of sung speech palatable, by pairing it with a poetic style specifically shaped to the needs of a musical setting.

The solution seemed easy enough and yet a continued discomfort and concern lingered over music's presence in drama. Crescimbeni's writings help to illuminate this unease. In *La bellezza della volgar poesia* (1700), he identifies the aria as opera's primary problem, because of the strain it places on dramatic verisimilitude. Though he cites a number of librettists whose works bring him pleasure, he admits that the world would be better off without melodrama.[108] However, in his *Commentari*, volume I (1702), written as a follow-up to *La bellezza*, Crescimbeni goes to great lengths to prove that his criticisms have been effective and that his recommendations are working. He notes that libretto writing has shown significant improvement, especially since the number of arias per opera had decreased, helping to keep dramas to a tolerable length.[109]

None the less, the heart of the problem did not go away. As Robert Freeman relates, Crescimbeni recognizes that "the poetry which is most *easily* set to music is apt to violate what he considers the tenets of poetic good taste."[110] The issue for critics like Crescimbeni and Muratori was that music was undeniably a central element of theatrical culture in their day. And unlike their Bolognese colleague, Martello – who accepted and even embraced music's pre-eminent position in theater and viewed the musico-dramatic librettist as a "versifier" and not a noble humanist poet – they appear to have wished that music was inessential, or better yet, as

Crescimbeni intimated, not there at all. Crescimbeni and his most sympathetic colleagues may have realized that opera would continue to thrive; some among them even confessed their enjoyment of it. But their ideal of theater culture was based on conceptions of ancient models, which held that music should meld flawlessly and unobtrusively with drama. Their deepest hope was that opera could recapture that expressive perfection, even if current practices of both literary and musical composition were the furthest thing from any presumably authentic, let alone known ancient model. A consequence emerges from this nostalgic viewpoint: by hoping to recapture a past no longer found in current dramatic practice, such critics appeared out of touch with the reality of modern drama and the conventional aesthetic taste of audiences. It took a dissenter like Martello to remind Crescimbeni and his fellow Arcadians (whom he condemned as nostalgic "humbugs") that music was the undisputed soul of theatrical performances of their day.[111] In essence, the critical literature that was most nostalgic in its prescription for reform was most remorseful about what musical drama had become. In considering this literature, we start to see a fissure emerge between content and form. Critics may have understood that, in theory, the connection to ancient traditions was through thematic content only, since the form of its expression was a modern conception.[112] Yet the temptation to allow content to distort form, so much so as to blur the modern side of this ancient/modern binary, appears to have been powerful.[113]

The Arcadians' pastoral posture affected the cantata in much the same way as it did opera, but the cantata perhaps more vividly discloses the hopeful intent for pastoral reform. In Crescimbeni's account of the Zappi–Scarlatti exchange, we have seen distinctions drawn between poetry written solely in the service of music and poetry written to *lead* music along paths to superior and noble expression. Several important parameters evolve here. As stated earlier in the chapter, a preferred hierarchy of the arts is established, with poetry reassuming the position of authority it once held when the idea for a modern drama with music was conceived. A realignment of the chain of command works well in a chamber genre like the cantata, nostalgically associated with an era when the courtly and private domains were the main institutions of culture. Crescimbeni's narrative suggests an important reversion to enclosures of musico-dramatic practice within the private, noble domain. He makes it clear that only the most outstanding literati among Arcadia's shepherds, those with the most developed tastes, could appreciate this elevated style of poetry, a style that would in turn elevate the quality of music, and by extension – the deeper subtext here – could redeem opera of its ills. If we attempt to understand the presumed extension of Crescimbeni's logic here, then we start to see how the preferred circles of performance for not just the cantata, but also opera, suddenly have become very small, perhaps as small as the most intimate chamber salon, a venue well suited for aesthetic compression and retreat. In the highly romanticized pastoral world of Crescimbeni's *L'Arcadia*, it is possible that the academy's leading ideologue found his best solution for opera's reform not in opera itself, not on the public stage, but in other realms of musico-dramatic expression where format, location, and historicized legacies were pre-adapted for the smallest circles of connoisseurs. Enveloped by the pastoral aura, the cantata could serve as a template for opera's recuperation. After all, it easily solved issues of length and adherence to the unities, and it displaced the need for spectacle. From this perspective, the cantata trumped opera, even pastoral opera, as the ideal incarnation of opera's reform.

Crescimbeni's idealization, however, and his desire to find resolution for musical drama, was ineffectual. In the same way that music never achieves a full and realistic discussion in his writings on opera, the same applies during this brief but revealing narrative regarding the composition and performance of cantatas as described in *L'Arcadia*. It is possible that the cantatas constructed by Scarlatti and Zappi in Crescimbeni's tale were nothing like, for example, Scarlatti's *Al fin m'ucciderete* or Bononcini's *Ch'io ti manchi di fede, idolo mio?*. The cantata, as with any genre, was never limited to any truly fixed conception, which makes such archetypal representation impossible. Cantatas were often composites of several qualities, difficult to pin down or limit within a fixed template of expression. Furthermore, a contradiction arises when examining the relation between the cantata's complexity and connoisseurship and its pastoral simplicity. How would a figure like Crescimbeni reconcile the standards of simplicity – in which pared-down texts were meant to encourage equally uncomplicated and graceful musical settings – with a propensity to encourage compositional complexity and to challenge listeners with complicated harmonic passages and contrapuntal textures? As discussed, the irony of reform (at least that which took hold) is that the regularization of structures as a means to tame "unnatural" poetic artifice also added new weight to the aria, and thus to music's significative independence. In a sense, the adopted "empirical" approach of regularizing and standardizing the form essentially undermined a true recuperation of a romantic, idealized history. The newly embraced *da capo* aria could hardly reflect a past; if anything, it forcefully underscored a thoroughly modern moment.

Unitary subjects

The contradictions that are rife in the treatment of the cantata, and more broadly, that are common in much early eighteenth-century polemical writing, are not surprising when we consider Italy's cultural posture. Fubini reminds us that Italy in the eighteenth century, more than most European countries, "remained anchored in the humanist tradition and in the concept of poetry's supremacy as an art form and as privileged mode of expression," making it difficult to accept opera and to tackle the perceived problems of music.[114] Not all literati of the eighteenth century held this position, however. Of the polemicists and critics who discussed musical drama, Gravina stands apart in this regard. He is remembered for his support in the 1690s, of the *favola pastorale*, and his placing of this genre on a pedestal as the preferred literary form of dramatic expression. But in the early years of the eighteenth century, Gravina becomes somewhat of an outlier, and eventually, a dissident within the Arcadian Academy.[115]

Gravina's internal split with the academy under Crescimbeni is revealed in a series of letters accounting for his "division" from Arcadia.[116] Compared with Crescimbeni and others with similar views, Gravina could not accept Arcadia as a fantastical recuperation of the past – "it was neither a republic nor a kingdom, like the old society has become, but simply a literary gathering."[117] His practical convictions and sense of reality were similarly revealed in his intellectual work from these years, especially in his concerns for dramatic verisimilitude and his interest in tragedy. His most entrenched positions are well summarized in *Della tragedia*, published in 1715.[118] Unlike many of his former Arcadian colleagues, Gravina did *not* choose to recognize any improvement to standards of Italian taste and to the state of literature during this period. Despite efforts towards reform, current theater, he thought, still lacked the necessary eloquence of ancient tragedy and failed to teach audiences virtues. Gravina heaped scorn on those involved with the theater, including librettists and reformists, for their glaring inability to correct moral corruption, a state of affairs he attributed to the eclipse of reason by the modern desire for pleasure.[119] There is certainly an element of personal affront we should account for in Gravina's cantankerous disavowal of Arcadia; after all, he was expelled from the academy. In the end, *Della tragedia* did little to alter the course of theater in Gravina's day or to make lasting impressions on practicing librettists.[120]

Gravina's views on music, however, are worth reviewing, in large part because he rarely takes on music in serious terms, and when he does so, reveals a more realistic and practical stance than most of his Arcadian colleagues. Gravina appeared to be unique in that he found little problem embedding music in drama, even though he recognized drama as ostensibly a non-musical form. He contended that classical tragedies were meant to have music in the scenes as well.[121] He asserted that even in antiquity, there were two distinct styles: one for solo declamation, and one for unison chorus; or, one that was closer to nature, as he claimed, and the other that was more artificial.[122] At the same time, Gravina was acutely aware of the indisputable temporal gap between ancient tragedies and the musical drama of his own time. He was critical of modern recitatives and arias, which he observed had diverged from the solo declamation and choruses of the past. In ancient theater, music was transformative, "exciting and calming passions, curing infirmities, and modifying behavior." Modern musical drama lacked such powers, he contended. He particularly objected to the rise of the aria, thinking it to be an overly decorative element obscuring the meaning of text and "erasing all semblance of truth."[123] However, unlike his fellow literati, especially those who blamed theater's ills on the inclusion of music in drama, Gravina unabashedly pointed an accusing finger at poetry. Here Gravina trips up Crescimbeni in his own argument. Like the custodian of Arcadia, Gravina believed music was the imitative follower of poetry. But as a shadow which follows suit, it is not surprising, he says, that "as poetry has been corrupted, so too has music."[124]

In Gravina's estimation, the purity of ancient music was lost, but this was not a loss he mourned. What he truly lamented was the loss of *unity*, the idea that a single author, as was the case in ancient tragedies, worked as the sole composer of poetry, music, and stage design to create a unified work.[125] He surely realized this was near to impossible in the modern world: few poets, if any, succeeded in writing music of the depth and quality of a Bononcini or Scarlatti, and though some of Scarlatti's poems were saved for the Arcadian archive,[126] as a musician he was unlikely to be in the social or financial position to commission his own music to set to his own libretti. Practicalities aside, Gravina recognized and lamented the growing division of labor, in which each element pursued autonomy.

As divisive as Gravina appeared, his privileging of the unitary subject was a foundational trope that united him with Crescimbeni. In fact, their similarities can tell us nearly as much as their differences. If we bring to mind Crescimbeni's account of the Zappi–Scarlatti exchange, we recall the degree to which cantata composition was said to have attained a sense of unified authorship, with music seamlessly following the poetry. But in actual practice, how closely did the music follow and in what ways? Crescimbeni's view assumes an imitative behavior of music towards text, a common assumption at the time. And yet, was music *always* to be the shadow that followed the poetic body? Arias written for Arcadian cantatas or musical dramas often achieved their best effect by maintaining a degree of autonomy from poetic discourse, and sometimes by using musical elements that had little to do with the sense of the poetry, or with a pastoral aesthetic. The truth is that Crescimbeni's rendering of music's seamless engagement with poetry was more ideal than real. The distinction between him and Gravina is that Crescimbeni believed such unity was revived within his cherished Arcadian circle, who saw to the recovery of such noble and elevated composition. Gravina saw through this ideal and understood the irreconcilable gap between ancient models and modern practice. In the end, Gravina's prescription for theater did not match that of the Arcadians; he did not believe music had no part to play in theater or that poetry was without sin in theater's fall. Perhaps more fundamentally, he denied the realistic possibility of fully recuperating a pastoral and ancient past and thus failed to participate fully in the Arcadians' romantic project.

What are the lessons here? Ultimately, it is the very *lack* of detailed discussion of music and text, or music and context, that actually tells us much about the cantata, the pastoral, and about Arcadia. There are likely a number of reasons as to why a more engaged and detailed discussion of music never happened in the Arcadian literature, among those critics who otherwise reflected on musico-dramatic forms but failed to address the role of music in any significant way. We might imagine that music may have been distant from these men of letters' expertise, an art form that could be idealized as an object of beauty, but whose workings were complex and misunderstood. Perhaps a detailed and forthright exploration of music's presence and transformative role in drama was best avoided anyway. The problem with music is that it helped to reveal the antinomic structure of the Arcadian cultural context. Except for their pastoral subject matter, the musical dramas and cantatas heard by Arcadians were essentially modern – content and form were not, and could not be, one and the same. Thus, the cantata's ability to resuscitate the past was no more possible or real than the Arcadians' invented pastoral surnames or pretend Olympic Games. We must see this contradiction as entirely resonant with Arcadia's inherent ideological paradox. Like their commemorative marble statues or Canevari's garden, music was reimagined as a monument to the past, regardless of its very real present.

In coming to view the cantata as a specific, even privileged kind of musical monument for the Arcadians, we have witnessed how one of their leading ideologues, Crescimbeni, reduced this musical genre to an idealized essence. In this process we have seen how the *ideal* cantata was caricatured and narrowed so as to deny or miss the genre's variable range of expression and practice. The cantata's manifold representations in form and style and in expression of sound versus word were a reality that to us now seems obvious – an effect of patronage demands, or of individual creativity and authorial choice, and due to the possibilities afforded by new aesthetic forces. This chapter's exploration of the examples by Scarlatti and Bononcini represents only one possible manifestation of cantata composition and performance. The solo cantata for soprano voice and continuo was certainly prevalent in this period of secular vocal composition, but there were many other examples of works categorized as "cantatas" that involved bigger forces, more singers or a larger ensemble accompaniment.[127] What may have been *da camera* in generic terms, and as defined by location and audience, may not have seemed all that chamber-like in style and sound. In this sense, the cantata often easily crossed the musico-dramatic genre spectrum and hovered alongside opera.

Despite a pastoral preponderance, the assorted cantatas that may have been heard in Rome's Arcadian milieu were not uniform or one-dimensional in musical terms. They encompassed a level of compositional variability that captured not just the conventions and innovations of the moment, but also the layers of history that connected the cantata to previous incarnations of secular vocal music, as well as later influences from opera and other related musico-dramatic genres. But we must remember that a genre is constituted by more than its internal formal characteristics. What made the cantata a cantata in the eyes and ears of Roman patrons and their audiences was just as much where it was heard, how it was contextualized, and *who* did the listening. The cantata's genre enclosures were equally defined by practice and location as they were by form and style. In this Arcadian milieu, the practice of listening to vocal chamber music was symbolically associated with the protected domain of the elite listener, where the cantata could be idealistically contained and a musico-dramatic pastoral vision could be best imagined.

In effect, the cantata's idealized essence was arguably opera's idealized essence as well. If all music and text could behave in the seamless unity described by Crescimbeni in *L'Arcadia*, with the proper balance of simplicity and complexity, to be appreciated by an audience who could discern such qualities, then good drama – and ultimately good taste – could be restored to culture. Yet, as we know, this was not how history unfolded. Operas that used a pastoral template akin to secular cantatas never really flourished beyond the initial experiments we see during these transitional decades between the seventeenth and eighteenth centuries.[128] The short, condensed, and abstracted format of cantata texts may have been ideal for pastoral poetry, but was not conducive to longer, sustained narratives demanded by full-blown dramas for the stage.[129] Moreover, opera could not be contained within the protected walls of the private chamber. It had taken on a public life all of its own; and admittedly, the public theater was a more effective stage for disseminating any prescriptions for reform. Opera did in fact undergo a set of changes in these years that influenced the dramaturgical, stylistic, and thematic propensities of operatic writing (both textual and musical). None the less, pastoralism was not the central force that shaped such change. Though the pastoral may have played a role in the discourses of reform, as an idealized model for opera, it ultimately failed.

The pastoral, however, does play a role in serving as the critical connecting point between opera and the cantata within this context and period. It was the cultural nexus within which these two genres collided, resonated with and against each other. It was a thematic reservoir for librettists and composers who set music to pastoral texts, but it was also the symbolic benchmark of literary excellence and purity in poetry, a poetry that critics thought could achieve verisimilar meaning when set to music. Moreover, the pastoral was also an imagined world where Arcadia existed, where it found its symbolic voice, where shepherds roamed, versified, and sang their souls. That the pastoral failed to sustain a proper reform of opera must therefore be seen as significant, even symptomatic of Arcadia's larger collapse. As the future of musical drama could not be restricted to the reduced format of the cantata experience, or contained within private walls only, so too would Arcadia eventually diminish in power, effectiveness, and stature instead of becoming the enlightened republican society that ideally it aspired to be.

The cantata therefore can and does embody two truths. In many ways, it was least like opera and furthest from what public opera symbolized to critics of the period; at the same time, we can also consider the cantata as perhaps the most deeply revealing in the way it refracted opera's discourses. At the turn of the eighteenth century, the cantata was pulled into opera's career and trajectory, by its appropriation into the larger debates over music's role in drama, its relationship with text, and its powers and possibilities for expression. The cantata's anti-opera status, ironically, was what made it the hopeful embodiment of opera's future: a future that ultimately never did happen.

5 | Epilogue

Rome in the late seventeenth century may not be the most obvious place from which to tell the history of opera; the locale does not make this task easy. Then again, even beyond Rome there is much about these transitional decades that makes opera's history difficult. Rome as papal capital was in many ways an epicenter for upheaval – political, religious, and cultural – that characterized other European cities, though in Rome opera culture was particularly affected by these instabilities, demonstrated by the enduring theater closures, prohibitions, and seasonal interruptions, which intensified at the transition from one century to the next. We have come to recognize that this environment had an important effect on musical cultural and history. When theaters were closed or performances forbidden, musico-dramatic entertainment in Rome did not cease but was re-channeled through a number of other arenas. Some of these cultural settings were devotional, others were secular, and almost all were private, exclusive, and in some way connected to the display of political sovereignty or social power and influence. Out of these circumstances emerged such a composer as Alessandro Scarlatti, whose production of cantatas was prolific, or George Frideric Handel, whose works completed in Rome include recognized masterpieces of vocal chamber music as well as oratorio compositions. Beyond those figures we canonize were many other well-regarded Roman and foreign composers and librettists who contributed much to this vibrant vocal music scene.

During the years this book surveys we witness how the entertainment of nobles through music, poetry, drama, and spectacle was ever-present. In its own way, opera also maintained a presence, despite its frequent absence during these years. Even when opera ceased production on the public stage, or remained only an intermittent pleasure of princes and clerics behind palace doors, opera's influence resounded. For many, opera was a topic of fascination or a point of concern and debate. Most importantly, it was an object of reform – perhaps *the* object of reform – for those focused on safeguarding Italian literature and transforming the future direction of culture. There was no way for contemporaries to write or recreate a history of drama and poetics without accounting for opera, even if that meant writing around opera.

Rome was not the only urban center in which a dialectic of reform took hold; however, the city's symbolic status as papal seat, its attraction to many cosmopolitan residents – courtly, wealthy, intellectual, and stewards of the church – make this particular capital a fundamental nexus for charting reform across the gamut of religion, politics, aesthetics, and society. The motivations for a "reform" writ large thus dominated culture during these years. Opera's appeal, its reception, and its pull as a center of cultural gravity parallel other issues at stake in Rome, from the weakening of church authority and the rise of secularism to the end of a baroque sensibility and the cultivation of a new enlightened aesthetic. Even the contemporary concern over authorship and poetics (as muddled as ever within the multimedia production of opera) can be read as reflection of a waning feudalism and humanist past. In many ways, this sense of a fated history fueled the impulse for a nostalgia that permeated Rome in this period.

These decades of opera's history in Rome are therefore a revealing historiographic moment. The act of historicizing opera was only possible given the luxury of time and reflection, from a perspective that took in the expanse of years, charting development and change. By 1700, historians, critics, and literati had the advantage of *some* familiarity with a century of opera and musico-dramatic traditions, though we must be mindful that the act of documenting and quantifying historical development with precision and comprehension was a modern tendency still in the making. The extent to which early Enlightenment historians and commentators knew opera's early or even mid-century history is difficult to determine. What few sources we have suggest an approach fueled by polemical arguments. Critics were concerned less about historical validity and more with the symbolic weight of specific aspects of a work or performance, a technique that works effectively when a more selective historical narrative is crafted. An obvious example of this approach is Giovanni Mario Crescimbeni's infamous attack on Cicognini and Cavalli's 1649 opera, *Giasone*.[1]

As we witness through the Arcadians, the recounting of opera's seventeenth-century history was largely a byproduct of a more expansive project to create a literary history, a phenomenon that blossomed by the century's end. Italy's traditions of poetry and literature had to account for the challenges of theatrical works and other forms of dramaturgy. Opera was not the only stage entertainment of the era, but it was privileged with an influence and popularity that fomented controversy, as this book has discussed. As a topic or a genre, opera often evoked a dualistic treatment. It was regarded either as a form with future promise or as a locus fraught with problems and pitfalls. Not all historians maligned opera's existence *in toto*, though most identified a critical turning point. For these critics, the fateful transition from the aristocratic and academic contexts of opera's early decades to the socially mixed urban arenas of the commercial theater marked a troubling historical trajectory.[2] It was this latter phase of opera that several turn-of-the-century critics and historians hoped to contain, reverse, or perhaps erase altogether. And as we have seen in earlier chapters, despite a variety of efforts to do just this – to clothe opera in pastoral prototypes, eliminate gratuitous spectacle, apply rigorous rules to the balance of music to word, or remake it as tragedy – the essential forms and characteristics of opera's history and practice could not be completely expunged. Opera inevitably traveled into a new century laden with its own considerable historical baggage.

This book's historical account of opera's influence, within this particular place and time, reveals its own idiosyncrasies and choices. In *Opera's Orbit*, I have attempted a critical account of opera's cultural impact in Rome during the epochal close of the seventeenth century. My focus has been both particular and broad. Regarding opera, I have favored broader strokes in order to maintain the "umbrella" of opera's influence as the book's primary portrait. I have treated opera as more than a form or discrete practice, but as a genre that becomes predominant over other genres and traverses a number of related domains. My approach to specific non-operatic domains, however, has been more particular than comprehensive, a way to root the reader into the deeper contexts of practice and discourse relevant to each genre. The analysis presented here in no way means to provide closure for the study of musical drama in Rome in the late seventeenth and early eighteenth century. On the contrary, my wish has been to reflect on the reasons why a broader selection of musical drama emerged during this period. My genre spectrum has served a purpose but does not cover the entire range of music where opera found influence. And for the genres I have chosen, my narrative has been limited to a selection of texts and examples, though in many regards, there is other work on the oratorio, serenata, and cantata yet to be done. Furthermore, I recognize that each of these three genres charts its own path into the eighteenth century, staking out a future or falling into decline. In some cases, they become important sources of genre-transference, inspiring the use of shorter plots, allegorical dramas, and chamber-like approaches in eighteenth-century opera. Yet in no other time than in the late seventeenth century does these genres' convergence in Rome, in a context of polemics, reform, and socio-political transformation, make their illumination as a spectrum across the orbit of opera so critical.

We could say of this larger orbit that opera held the most privileged position, the most *signorile* of all musico-dramatic forms. Yet, in practice, the distinctions between opera, serenata, oratorio, and cantata were often a function of performance ritual and venue only. On a fundamental level, the standards of setting poetic text in recitative and aria forms spanned a wide swath of the vocal music continuum. What distinguished a genre in prestige or event-worthiness was a genre's "dressing," the literary strategies it uses, and the degree to which it was "staged." In this regard, the genres studied in this book reflect opera's influence – though not just formally and structurally, but also practically as a model of aesthetics and performance. None the less, as the previous chapters demonstrate, the situation was not a simple case of lateral transference; the story of opera's orbit is one of struggle and contestation. In each instance, we have witnessed how opera's intersection with the path of each genre disrupted the continuity of that genre's singular identity and ritual practice. Opera was, in part, responsible for the transformation of the oratorio, the serenata, and the cantata. All the while, each of these genres (as shaped by those who authored their representative works) retained traces of its original function and singular identity. That combination of genre singularity and genre intertextuality endows these forms with the unique ability for mirroring opera, with a reflection that is both familiar and unfamiliar. I have used the oratorio, the serenata, and the cantata to illuminate opera's most prominent features, tensions, and debates, but I have also investigated this particular spectrum of genres as a way to explore opera's indirect wanderings that permeated this locale and period.

Each of the three genres surveyed presents a number of comparative impulses and reactions to opera. In doing so, they allow us to witness what conditions permit a genre to represent and circumscribe certain aesthetics, and what conditions make a genre vulnerable to contradiction and conflict. It would be easy to follow the more conventional path of treating genres as sites of control through the application of categories and generalizations that are in turn applied to single genre reflections. My aim, however, has been to place those same instincts against a different notion of genre, one that treats genre more as a problem than as a fixed entity of containment. I have searched for ways to relate how a genre's malleability and instability are not inherent to categorical traits and formal features, but result from agents who use, patronize, write, and perform such genres. My position has been to argue firmly how genres and genre relationships are fundamentally historical problems that can only emerge in socially, culturally, and historically specific circumstances.

One such circumstance, a centerstage of reflection in this book, is the rise of the Ragunanza degli Arcadi, the Academy of Arcadians. In a number of instances, this book surveys the manner in which the Arcadians' activities, predilections, and ideologies become representative of the era's reform *zeitgeist*. Their reach, as we learn, went beyond the opera theater and directly affected or resonated with a number of issues relevant to the oratorio, serenata, and cantata. However, as much as I highlight the Arcadians' role in my narrative – through their constructed events, writings, ideologies, and associations – I fully acknowledge that their effectiveness as agents of change has been questioned and widely debated, for reasons that are undoubtedly warranted. Although this issue is pertinent, I do wonder, none the less, what might be overlooked in choosing to frame the question as whether or not the Arcadian views were efficacious. In this monograph, the question I have pursued may not be addressed so plainly. Rather than determine whether the Arcadians were effective, I have looked for conditions that helped to shape and promote their nostalgic posture and efforts towards reform. By shifting the critical emphasis from cultural *solution* to *symptom*, I have discovered an ambivalence over their own visions of utopia. Choosing sides to determine their effectiveness or, alternatively, their ineffectiveness, overlooks this indeterminacy, this middle zone, where the Arcadian conundrum exists.

Upon closer viewing, the Arcadians struggled to reconcile their hopefulness for modernity with their impulse for retreat through obsessive memory work. As I have argued, the Arcadians could not remake or even escape their present by a constant recourse to the past. In large part, their projects and aspirations failed. And within the realm of literature and culture, we might also say that their reform of dramaturgy failed, too. In the end, the pastoral solution was short-sighted and short-lived, and opera would continue its course along the same lines of development, even if clothed in tragic models. Admittedly, the *tragedia in musica* did help to sediment and crystallize a new formula of dramatic narrative for opera. Repeatedly, in opera after opera, protagonists would be called to heroic action, asserting their better selves, guided by morality and rationality, while overcoming their base emotions. The Arcadians were neither the first, nor were they alone in the promotion of these dramatic models and enlightened ideals. In pressing their ideals, however, they overlooked a gaping incongruity of opera's reform. Emotionality and sensualism – those elements most crucial to deny and to sublimate – were allowed to enter through opera's significative "back door." Through music.

There are great ironies at work here. For one, music was essential to the bucolic landscape and to all things pastoral in activity and orientation. The pastoral fantasy envisioned shepherds and nymphs passing the time extemporizing poetry to music, through sounds evoking the very enchantedness of their utopian existence.[3] We have long apprehended that this pastoral world of sound, and its symbolism, inspired the first operatic creations, Apollo and Orpheus strumming lyres as an indispensable semiotic for their eloquent words.[4] Almost a century later, the Arcadians rendered the memory of this operatic history with unusual and fateful twists, primarily in an effort to devalue music's dramatic role. By the time of the Academy of Arcadians, music "assum[ed] the aspect of an inconvenient factor,"[5] as we have seen in our explorations of opera's intersection with other genres. This same problem would gradually and more forcefully emerge during the remainder of the eighteenth century, especially among French critics of opera who condemned music as the "disruption of poetics."[6]

The great paradox of Arcadia is that only through oversight, blindness, and failure was an effective, if unintentional, legacy secured. The Arcadians' inability to alter the course of musical drama in the manner that they intended underpins a crucial turning point in opera's history, as the form moves evermore towards a multimedia reality in which divisions of authorship are incontrovertible, and poetics have lost their dominant control over semantic content. I have made it known at several points that this major developmental transition long preceded the Arcadians; however, my interest all along has been not in "firsts," but in "after-effects," how the reception of the phenomenon tended to linger and beckon to the very articulations of contradictory ideals emblematic of this milieu.

Music's ambivalent status in these closing decades of one century and opening decades of the next permeates the musico-dramatic landscape within and beyond opera. Both in discourse and in practice my chapters help to reveal that music is often multi-positioned, *both* subservient to and at times also dominant over text. This straddled hierarchy for music would be accelerated by the increasing presence of the aria and the structural development of aria composition, important elements in what would become eighteenth-century opera's fundamental aesthetic "threshold."[7] Eighteenth-century opera scholarship has devoted much effort to this end, helping us to see and understand how thoroughly aria and voice would dominate the expressive and even social categories of Italian theater in the Enlightenment.[8] In the period considered here, however, we see that the ground was already rumbling; we witness these tremors in the anxieties over the aria and exclusive sections of independent music. If the Arcadians had had a better self-awareness and been more even-handed in their historical accounts, perhaps their knowledge would have revealed this trend, a development already underway prior to their emergence as commentators on literary and aesthetic politics. But those agents overwhelmed by crisis and transformation may have lacked the vision to read more deeply the traces of opera's past and to recognize more clearly the harbingers of what was to come. Opera surely had its encumbrances, but this historical weight did not change the fact that opera, perhaps in ironic testament to its pervasive pull across the musico-dramatic spectrum, was also adaptable and malleable. After all, it was opera's foundational seventeenth-century legacy from which future authors of opera borrowed, in order to reinvent the musico-dramatic experience in the century to follow.

Notes

Introduction: opera's orbit

1 In a recent essay, Margaret Murata expertly deconstructs the long-held binary that the history of theater in Rome is "simply a story of expansion under art-loving regimes and constriction under less liberal ones." What her essay reveals is that the prohibition of theater was neither consistently effective nor fully evidence of an anti-theater or anti-opera stance, but more largely related to the complexity of Rome's social context. See "*Theatrum intra Theatrum* or, The Church and Stage in 17th-Century Rome," in *Sleuthing the Muse: Festschrift for William F. Prizer*, ed. Kristine K. Forney and Jeremy L. Smith (Hillsdale, NY: Pendragon Press, forthcoming).

2 Many of the late seventeenth-century opera debates, and those specific to the Arcadian context, have been well rehearsed and re-evaluated in the scholarly literature, see, e.g., Robert Freeman's *Opera without Drama: Currents of Change in Italian Opera 1675–1725*, Studies in Musicology 14 (Ann Arbor, MI: UMI, 1981 [1967]); Renato Di Benedetto's historical overview in "Poetics and Polemics," in *The History of Italian Opera*, Vol. VI: *Opera in Theory and Practice, Image and Myth*, ed. Lorenzo Bianconi and Giorgio Pestelli, trans. Kenneth Chalmers and Mary Whittall (University of Chicago Press, 2003), 1–71; and Harris Saunders's dissertation, "The Repertoire of a Venetian Opera House (1678–1714): The Teatro Grimani di San Giovanni Gristostomo" (Ph.D. diss., Harvard University, 1985), which examines the reform crisis over opera within the late-century Venetian context. Melania Bucciarelli's *Italian Opera and European Theatre, 1680–1720* (Turnhout: Brepols, 2000) is among the more recent critical works to consider the importance of the Academy of Arcadians for the cultural poetics and aesthetic reform of opera at the turn of the eighteenth century.

3 Susan M. Dixon presents a quite thoughtful discussion of this topic and problem in her recent book, *Between the Real and the Ideal: The Accademia degli Arcadi and Its Garden in Eighteenth-Century Rome* (Newark, DE: University of Delaware Press, 2006), 52–53.

4 Vernon Hyde Minor, *The Death of the Baroque and the Rhetoric of Good Taste* (Cambridge University Press, 2006). See chapter 2, "*Buon Gusto*," 26–60 for Minor's discussion of the rise of a republic of letters in the late seventeenth century; and for his analysis of the Arcadians' impact, see chapter 5, "A Short History of the Academy of Arcadians," 115–126, especially 117.

5 See chapter 1 for a more extended discussion of the Arcadian debates over opera.

6 My use of "orbit" is inspired by and owes credit to Mikhail Bakhtin who uses the concept when discussing the modern novel: "In the process of becoming the dominant genre, the novel sparks the renovation of all other genres, it infects them with its spirit of process and inconclusiveness. It draws them ineluctably into its orbit precisely because this orbit coincides with the basic direction of the development of literature as a whole." From "Epic and Novel: Toward a Methodology for the Study of the Novel," printed in *The Dialogic Imagination: Four Essays*, ed. Michael Holquist, trans. Caryl Emerson and Michael Holquist (Austin: University of Texas Press, 1981), 7. However, Bakhtin's extreme elevation of the novel among other genres of literature is not necessarily an approach I seek to replicate for opera. Rather, I see his ideas as a starting point to provoke a new conceptualization of the web of genre relationships with opera, and to highlight how the dialogic relationships of genre serve as a means to read cultural process in this Roman and European nexus of early modern history.

7 When referring to non-operatic genres as "dramatic" or as "musico-dramatic forms," I am referring not just to a description of style but also to a manner of presentation. In these genres each singer (either solo, or two or more) usually functions in character, using words and emotions that are contained in some kind of plot, be it a short poem or a more elaborate story. In determining this approach I found Michael Talbot's period conception of "dramatic" based on eighteenth-century sources quite useful. See "The Serenata in Eighteenth-Century Venice," *Royal Musical Association Research Chronicle* 18 (1982): 9.

8 Lorenzo Bianconi proposes a model of "diffusion" to analyze the creation of a nationally based operatic system in the seventeenth century. He notes that it is through this negotiation of compromise that we might best understand the extent to which local operatic traditions were manipulated, transformed, or replaced by "Venetian-style" opera. "The Diffusion of Opera in Italy" in *Music in the Seventeenth Century*, trans. David Bryant (Cambridge University Press, 1987), 191.

9 My use of appropriation has been shaped by Roger Chartier's conceptualization of this phenomenon, in which he places appropriation "at the center of a cultural historical approach that focuses on differentiated practices and contrasted uses . . . appropriation really concerns a social history of the various interpretations, brought back to their fundamental determinants (which are social, institutional, and cultural), and lodged in the specific practices that produce them." See Roger Chartier, *Cultural History: Between Practices and Representations*, trans. Lydia G. Cochrane (Ithaca: Cornell University Press, 1988), 13.

10 Raymond Williams characterizes genre's residual imposition of abstract categories as a form of revived neoclassicism. Genres are thus reduced to abstract categorizations of a supposed single essence, which override the extraordinary variations (which for Williams are socially and historically determined) that

a genre holds together. See *Marxism and Literature* (Oxford University Press, 1977), esp. 182–183. His theories are further refined in *The Sociology of Culture* (New York: Schocken Books, 1982); see his chapter on "Forms," 148–180, esp. 148.

11 Critical discussion on genre remains surprisingly scarce in musicology, despite the important place genre holds as a tool for the field. Several scholars have explained this phenomenon as influenced by a nineteenth-century legacy, in which the emphasis on the autonomous status of musical works has been carried forth to the present day. The most persuasive and extensive writing on this historical aspect of genre and the eclipse of the social functionality of music has been by Carl Dahlhaus, see especially "New Music and the Problem of Musical Genre," in *Schoenberg and New Music*, trans. Derrick Puffett and Alfred Clayton (Cambridge University Press, 1988), 32–45. A small resurgence of genre studies in musicology was witnessed in the 1980s–1990s, among the most groundbreaking work on this subject being Jeffrey Kallberg's analysis of the rhetoric of genre in his study of Chopin. Kallberg has argued that in Chopin's milieu, genres were recognized by social convention and functioned as communication rather than as classification. See Kallberg's "The Rhetoric of Genre: Chopin's Nocturne in G Minor," *Nineteenth Century Music* 11, no. 3 (1987): 238–261; followed by his monograph, *Chopin at the Boundaries: Sex, History, and Musical Genre* (Cambridge, MA: Harvard University Press, 1996), in which he notes that at the time of this publication even an entry on "genre" was absent from *The New Grove*. Since then, Jim Samson has authored this entry in *The New Grove Dictionary of Music and Musicians*, vol. IX, ed. Stanley Sadie, 2nd edn (London: Macmillan, 2001), 657–659; see his bibliography for a sample list of recent research in musicology that tackles issues of genre. Allen Moore points out that until the 1980s, musicological research on Western art music tended to mix concepts of style and genre quite freely; after that point, musicologists have tended to use genre for external, socially conditioned distinctions of a work, and style for considerations of formal, internal features. See "Categorizing Conventions in Music Discourses: Style and Genre," *Music and Letters* 82, no. 3 (2001): 432–442. Only in a few recent dissertations do genre-theoretical approaches appear prominently. There has been a more forceful resurgence in genre-related criticism and an interest in genre's social and cultural contingencies outside Western art music scholarship, particularly in the fields of popular music and culture, film, media studies, sociology, and ethnomusicology. For a sample of this scholarship see, for example, Heather Sparling, "Categorically Speaking: Towards a Theory of (Musical) Genre in Cape Breton Culture," *Ethnomusicology* 52 (2008): 401–425; Fabian Holt, *Genre in Popular Music* (University of Chicago Press, 2007); Adam Krims, *Rap Music and the Poetics of Identity* (Cambridge University Press, 2000); Robert Walser, *Running with the Devil: Power, Gender, and Madness in Heavy Metal Music* (Hanover, NH: University Press of New England, 1993); Rick Altman, *Film/Genre* (London: BFI Publishing, 1999); Stephen Neale, *Genre*

(London: British Film Institute-Film Availability Services, 1980); Franco Fabbri, "A Theory of Musical Genres: Two Applications," in *Popular Music Perspectives*, ed. David Horn and Philip Tagg (Exeter: International Association for the Study of Popular Music, 1982), 52–81.

12 This quote is from Gary Saul Morson's essay, "Bakhtin, Genres, and Temporality," *New Literary History* 22, no. 4 (1991): 1071–1092, at 1074, referring to Bakhtin's concept of surplus.

13 Even though concepts of temporal evolution and transformation were central to many early modern genre theorists, it was only during the latter phases of Russian formalism that certain critics began to integrate a diachronic view (how a genre may modify in the course of its historical development), along with a synchronic view (the realization of a generic model in a specific place in time). Key among those were Vladimir Propp and Yuri Tynyanov who more intensely explored the historical dimension of literary genres. For further background, see Victor Erlich, *Russian Formalism: History-Doctrine*, 3rd edn (New Haven: Yale University Press, 1981); and Jurij Striedter, *Literary Structure, Evolution and Value: Russian Formalism and Czech Structuralism Reconsidered* (Cambridge, MA: Harvard University Press, 1989). These theorists, in their use of the adapted terms "synchronic" and "diachronic," are indebted to the pioneering work of Ferdinand de Saussure's *Cours de linguistique générale* (1916). A less systematic and perhaps more problematized vision of multiple temporalities at work in culture was inspired through Mikhail Bakhtin's engagement with the modern novel. For the most comprehensive of Bakhtin's writings on temporality and the novel, see "Forms of Time and of the Chronotype in the Novel," in Bakhtin, *The Dialogic Imagination*, 84–258.

14 Among Bakhtin's most insightful studies of genre interaction and influence is his 1941 essay "Epic and Novel," in *The Dialogic Imagination*, 1–40. Underlying much of his argument in this earlier work is Bakhtin's dialogic conception of language, whose implication for genre theory is addressed in his later essay "The Problem of Speech Genres," first written in 1952–1953, later printed in 1979, and more recently translated in *Speech Genres and Other Late Essays*, ed. Caryl Emerson and Michael Holquist, trans. Vern W. McGee (Austin: University of Texas Press, 1986), 60–102. Bakhtin's concept of "heteroglossia" emerged from his treatment of genres as dialogic forms. His later interpreter and advocate, Julia Kristeva, used the concept of heteroglossia as the basis for her own term "intertextuality," presented in her seminal essay, "Word, Dialogue, and Novel," in *Desire in Language: A Semiotic Approach to Literature and Art*, ed. Leon S. Roudiez, trans. Thomas Gora, Alice Jardine, and Leon S. Roudiez (New York: Columbia University Press, 1980), 64–91; this essay was originally published in 1969.

15 Drawn from Mikhail Bakhtin's "Response to a Question from *Novy Mir*" (1970), published in *Speech Genres and Other Late Essays*, 5.

16 Bakhtin, "Epic and Novel," 4.

17 Some members of the Russian formalist school took the notion of genre hierarchies and evolution into more extreme quasi-Darwinian terms, in highlighting concepts such as "competition" and "struggle of a genre's survival." For further background, see David Duff's concise but insightful section on Russian formalism in his "Introduction," in *Modern Genre Theory* (Harlow: Pearson Education, 2000), 6–8.

18 Key among these are Gloria Staffieri's collection of transcribed and edited *avvisi* in *Colligite fragmenta: la vita musicale romana negli "Avvisi Marescotti" (1683–1707)* (Lucca: Libreria Musicale Italiana Editrice, 1990); the appendix of documents from the Cartari chronicles compiled and transcribed by Arnaldo Morelli in "La musica a Roma nella seconda metà del Seicento attraverso l'Archivio Cartari-Febei," in *La musica a Roma attraverso le fonti d'archivio. Atti di convegno internazionale (Roma 4–7 giugno, 1992)*, ed. Arnaldo Morelli, Bianca Maria Antolini, and Vera Vita Spagnuolo (Lucca: Libreria Musicale Italiana Editrice, 1994), 107–136; the diaries of Francesco Valesio, *Diario di Roma 1700–1742*, ed. Gaetano Scano with Giuseppe Graglia. 6 vols: Vol. I: 1700–1701; Vol. II: 1702–1703; Vol. III: 1704–1707 (Milan: Longanesi, 1977–1979); sources related to specific patrons and their musico-theatrical activities, such as those by Hans Joachim Marx, "Die Musik am Hofe Pietro Kardinal Ottobonis unter Arcangelo Corelli," *Analecta Musicologica* 5 (1968): 104–177; Maria Letizia Volpicelli, "Il teatro del Cardinale Ottoboni al Palazzo della Cancelleria," in *Il teatro a Roma nel Settecento* (Rome: Istituto dell' Enciclopedia Italiana, 1989), II: 681–763; and Flavia Matitti, "Il Cardinale Pietro Ottoboni mecenate delle arti: cronache e documenti (1689–1740)," *Storia dell'arte* 84 (1995): 156–243; documents relating to specific composers or specific works by composers, such as the research on Alessandro Scarlatti by Roberto Pagano and Lino Bianchi, eds., *Alessandro Scarlatti: catalogo generale delle opere a cura di Giancarlo Rostirolla* (Turin: Edizioni Rai, 1972); Lowell Lindgren, "Il dramma musicale durante la carriera di Alessandro Scarlatti (1660–1725)," in *Le muse galanti. La musica a Roma nel Settecento*, ed. Bruno Cagli (Rome: Istituto dell' Enciclopedia Italiana, 1985), 35–57; and Frank D'Accone, *The History of a Baroque Opera: Alessandro Scarlatti's* Gli equivoci nel sembiante. Monographs in Musicology 3 (New York: Pendragon Press, 1985). Saverio Franchi, *Drammaturgia romana: repertorio bibliografico cronologico dei testi drammatici pubblicati a Roma e nel Lazio*, Vol. I (1600–1700), Vol. II (1701–1750). Sussidi Eruditi 42 and 45 (Rome: Edizioni di Storia e Letteratura, 1988–1997), is an indispensable source study and bibliography on dramatic texts and libretti of this region and time period.

19 Though not in the chosen purview of this study, I would add that such a project is sorely needed. For the history of theater in this period and locale, we are still beholden to studies that are in need of re-examination and revision, including the classic works on Roman theaters by Alessandro Ademollo, *I teatri di Roma nel secolo decimosettimo* (Bologna: Forni Editore, 1969; reprinted from Roman

edition, 1888), and Alberto Cametti, *Il Teatro Tordinona poi di Apollo*, 2 vols. (Tivoli: Aldo Chicca, 1938). Yet to be published is a study that systematically addresses the process of how late seventeenth-century Roman opera productions translated and reset Venetian operas to a new context, often by touching up libretti and adding new music.

20 The problem and controversy of relating individual texts to a larger category of genre has a long history in the literary and historical fields, emerging first in the nineteenth century with European romanticism's rejection of the neo-classical doctrine of genres, and manifesting later in the early twentieth-century manifestos and polemics of modernism (e.g., Benedetto Croce, *Aesthetic as Science of Expression and General Linguistic*, first published as *Estetica come scienza dell'espressione e linguistica generale: teoria e storia* [Bari: G. Laterza, 1902]). A more recent anti-genre stance (in argument for the individual text) is evidenced in Jacques Derrida's influential essay "The Law of Genre," in "On Narrative," special issue, *Critical Inquiry* 7, no. 1 (1980): 55–81, which also appeared in *Glyph* 7 (1980): 176–232. A different way to problematize genre and individual texts is argued by Ralph Cohen, "History and Genre," *New Literary History* 17, no. 2 (1986): 203–218, in which Cohen recognizes the autonomy of individual texts even if they are linked to larger generic categories. Essentially, he proposes that the importance of understanding generic purposes (why they happen) is made manifest through a *historical* study of individual texts.

1 Enclosures, crises, polemics

1 For contemporary documents that describe these events, see the collected news reports from the *Avvisi Marescotti* in Gloria Staffieri's *Colligite fragmenta: la vita musicale romana negli "Avvisi Marescotti" (1683–1707)* (Lucca: Libreria Musicale Italiana Editrice, 1990), 88–90. Staffieri makes particular reference to the *Mémoires de M. de Coulanges* (Paris: P. Didot, 1820) in which this French observer of the Roman scene notes the particular effect the festivities had upon the Roman nobility, who he claims were new to this sort of Venetian spectacle, but received it enthusiastically, none the less. See 89 n53.

2 The importance of papal sovereignty and its relationship with lay aristocracy in late seventeenth-century Rome has been explored in detail by Renata Ago, "Hegemony over the Social Scene and Zealous Popes (1676–1700)," in *Court and Politics in Papal Rome, 1492–1700*, ed. Gianvittorio Signorotto and Maria Antonietta Visceglia (Cambridge University Press, 2002), 229–246. See chapter 2 of this book for further discussion of Ago's argument, and my application of her theory to musico-dramatic patronage of the period.

3 Barberini patronage and influence has been a major focus in Roman opera scholarship; key among these studies are Frederick Hammond, *Music and Spectacle in Baroque Rome: Barberini Patronage under Urban VIII* (New Haven:

Yale University Press, 1994); and Margaret Murata, *Operas for the Papal Court, 1621–1668* (Ann Arbor, MI: UMI, 1981).

4 As an example, Lorenzo Bianconi and Thomas Walker, in their examination of the procedures of opera production in papal Rome under the Barberinis, note that attendance at these operas (specifically, they consider the 1637 production of *Chi soffre speri*) was likely through invitation to other clerics and Roman aristocracy, but that "Cardinal (Francesco) Barberini and Cardinal Antonio (Barberini) worked hard to accommodate as many people as possible, and it appears that the number of people amounted to 3500." See "Production, Consumption and Political Function of Seventeenth-Century Opera," *Early Music History* 4 (1984): 220.

5 Christina, the only surviving legitimate heir of King Gustav II Adolf of Sweden, converted to Catholicism, abdicated her throne, and arrived in Rome by 1655. Maria Mancini Colonna, the niece of Cardinal Mazarin, was the wife of Lorenzo Onofrio Colonna, an heir of old Roman aristocracy and grandee of Spain.

6 For a list of opera libretti from 1671 to 1674, along with relevant information regarding their provenance elsewhere, their publication in Rome, and their musical settings, see Saverio Franchi, *Drammaturgia romana: repertorio bibliografico cronologico dei testi drammatici pubblicati a Roma e nel Lazio*, Vol. I: *1600–1700* (hereafter *Drammaturgia romana I*), Sussidi Eruditi 42 (Rome: Edizioni di Storia e Letteratura, 1988), 429–476. For details of the Tordinona's history, see the still fundamental study by Alberto Cametti, *Il Teatro Tordinona poi di Apollo*, 2 vols. (Tivoli: Aldo Chicca, 1938); and also the more recent article by Andrea Penna, "Il primo teatro pubblico di Roma. Le vicende del Teatro Tordinona nel XVII secolo," *Studi Romani* 46 (1998): 227–268.

7 For evidence of Odescalchi's objection to musical comedies and the presence of public theater, see Arnaldo Morelli's transcription of documents (nos. 36–39, 41) from "La musica a Roma nella seconda metà del Seicento attraverso l'Archivio Cartari-Febei," in *La musica a Roma attraverso le fonti d'archivio. Atti di convegno internazionale (Roma 4–7 giugno, 1992)*, ed. Arnaldo Morelli, Bianca Maria Antolini, and Vera Vita Spagnuolo (Lucca: Libreria Musicale Italiana Editrice, 1994), 126–127. The Cartari chronicles also note the 1675 publication of a similar condemnation, the book *Comedio-crisis, sive Theatri contra theatrum censura*, by the conservative theologian, Girolamo Fiorentini. For a summary of this text, see Elena Tamburini, *Due teatri per il principe: studi sulla committenza teatrale di Lorenzo Onofrio Colonna (1659–1689)* (Rome: Bulzoni Editore, 1997), 235; and Ferdinando Taviani, *La commedia dell'arte e la società barocca. La fascinazione del teatro* (Rome: Bulzoni Editore, 1970), which provides a translation of the first part in Italian, 263–284.

8 Odescalchi was famously stern and devout, and as a strong defender of the church he became a vehement advocate of ecclesiastical and secular reform. Of particular note is that Odescalchi only accepted the election to the papacy on the condition that fourteen articles of reform already proposed during the last conclave would

be signed and sworn in by all the cardinals. These reforms included a general moral reform and the diminution of clerical luxury, among other items. For background on Innocent XI's reforms and the systems for their application, see Bruno Neveu, "L'esprit de reforme a Rome sous Innocent XI (1676–89)," *Dix-Septième Siècle* 50, no. 2 (1998): 203–218; and Stefano Tabacchi, "Le riforme giudiziarie nella Roma di fine Seicento," *Roma Moderna e Contemporanea* 5, no. 1 (1997): 155–174.

9 For studies that consider Innocent XI's policies regarding the Habsburg Empire, and his involvement in the anti-Turkish league, see the more recent work by Gaetano Platania and Joëlle Fontaine, "Innocent XI Odescalchi et l'esprit de 'Croisade,'" *Dix-Septième Siècle* 50, no. 2 (1998): 247–276; along with the more classic studies by Carlie A. Macartney, ed., *The Habsburg and Hohenzollern Dynasties in the Seventeenth and Eighteenth Centuries* (New York: Harper and Row, 1970); and Ludwig von Pastor, *The History of the Popes*, Vol. XXXII (London: Routledge and Kegan Paul, 1957), 38–167.

10 Ago, "Hegemony over the Social Scene," 238.

11 *La caduta/del regno/dell'Amazzoni/Festa Teatrale fatta Rappresentare in/ Roma dall'Eccellentissimo Signor/Marchese di Coccogliudo/Ambasciatore Della Maestà/Di Carlo Secondo/Rè Delle Spagne,/E Della Principessa/Marianna/ Contessa Palatina del Reno./Dedicata/Alla Maestà/Della Regina Sposa./[piccolo fregio]/In Roma, Per Gio: Francesco Buagni. M.DC.XC./Con licenza de' Superiori./ Si vendono in Piazza Madama da Francesco Leone.* The opera based on a New World subject (Antonio de Solis y Ribadeneyra's *Las Amazonas*, with libretto by Giuseppe Domenico de Totis, music by Bernardo Pasquini) was performed at Colonna's private theater on January 15, 1690, for the wedding of Carlo II, King of Spain to Princess Marianna, Countess of Reno. The production involved a formidable cast of singers and dancers and ostentatious intermezzi; notable features in this production included a subdividing globe, gem-studded coaches floating in water, and airborne carriages suspended above the stage. For background on the libretto and the work's first performance, see Franchi, *Drammaturgia romana I*, 621–623.

12 *La/Statira/Drama/Per Musica/Recitato nel Teatro di/Torre di Nona./L'Anno 1690./Dedicato/Alle Dame/Di Roma/[leone]/In Roma, Per Gio: Francesco Buagni 1690./Si vendono in bottega di Francesco Leone./Libraro in Piazza Madama.* Ottoboni's *La Statira*'s text is classically inspired and incorporates aspects of Plutarch's history of Alexander, along with stories added from Pliny. The story retells the battle between Alexander and the Persians, under Darius, his love for Statira, daughter to the Persian king, and his humane treatment of her and other Persian prisoners, as well as the complicated fate of their love. The story's culmination is a happy dénouement that exemplifies Alexander's magnanimous and noble behavior. The text was set to music by Alessandro Scarlatti. It was performed during the 1690 carnival on January 5, 11, and 24 and February 5, plus some additional performances, though its reception was mixed at best. In

the introduction to his edition, William Holmes reports that originally Ottoboni wanted to end the work with Fame descending on a stage machine while
singing the praises of the Ottoboni family, but his father persuaded him to take
it out of the production. For a history of *La Statira* as an opera and in dramatic
literature, see Alessandro Scarlatti, *La Statira*, ed. William C. Holmes, Vol. IX of
The Operas of Alessandro Scarlatti (Cambridge, MA: Harvard University Press,
1985), 6–7. For background on the libretto, see Franchi, *Drammaturgia romana
I*, 620–621.

13 See Tim Carter's essay, "Italian Opera after 1637," for this analysis and for further
discussion of *La Statira*, in *The Cambridge History of Seventeenth-Century Music*,
ed. Tim Carter and John Butt (Cambridge University Press, 2005), 270–277.

14 I borrow the idea of opera's moving arcs from Ellen Rosand's insightful description of opera's main two cycles in the seventeenth century: its first starting with
the opening of the first opera house in Venice in 1637 and moving through the
1670s; the second marked by the development of the reform movement, from
the 1680s and culminating with Metastasio in the eighteenth century. See *Opera
in Seventeenth-Century Venice: The Creation of a Genre* (Berkeley: University of
California Press, 1991), 3.

15 There are several sources that one could draw from a number of disciplines
with focus on Rome. A few studies by art historians have been particularly
useful in cataloguing and describing Rome's characteristic baroque aesthetic
and features, including the classic work by Maurizio Fagiolo dell'Arco and Silvia
Carandini, *L'effimero barocco: strutture della festa nella Roma del '600* (Rome:
Bulzoni Editore, 1977); Patricia Waddy, *Seventeenth-Century Roman Palaces:
Use and Art of the Plan* (Cambridge, MA: The Architectural Foundation, MIT
Press, 1990); and more recently, Stefanie Walker and Frederick Hammond, eds.,
Life and the Arts in the Baroque Palaces of Rome: Ambiente Barocco (New Haven:
Yale University Press for The Bard Graduate Center for Studies in the Decorative
Arts, 1999); in music studies, Hammond, *Music and Spectacle in Baroque Rome* is
a useful source, along with Malcolm Boyd, "Rome: The Power of Patronage," in
The Late Baroque Era: From the 1680s to 1740, ed. George J. Buelow (Englewood
Cliffs, NJ: Prentice Hall, 1986), 39–65.

16 See especially Joseph Connors, "Alliance and Enmity in Roman Baroque Urbanism," *Römisches Jahrbuch der Bibliotheca Hertziana* 25 (1989): 207–294; and
more recently, Laurie Nussdorfer, "The Politics of Space in Early Modern Rome,"
Memoirs of the American Academy in Rome 42 (1997): 161–186.

17 As one example, Thomas Dandelet examines the effects of French and Spanish
Habsburg conflicts on Roman urbanism between 1600 and 1700 in "Setting
the Noble Stage in Baroque Rome: Roman Palaces, Political Contest, and Social
Theater, 1600–1700," in Walker and Hammond, *Life and the Arts in the Baroque
Palaces of Rome: Ambiente Barocco*, 39–51.

18 There have been numerous studies on the baroque aesthetic that range in
discipline from histories of art, architecture, literature, music, to science and

philosophy. Among those that have been useful for my own research are Jon R. Snyder, *L'estetica del barocco* (Bologna: Il Mulino, 2005); Jonathan I. Israel, *Radical Enlightenment: Philosophy and the Making of Modernity, 1650–1750* (Oxford University Press, 2001); Andrea Battistini, *Il barocco: cultura, miti, immagini* (Rome: Salerno Editrice, 2000); Paula Findlen, *Possessing Nature: Museums, Collecting, and Scientific Culture in Early Modern Italy* (Berkeley: University of California Press, 1994); Renata Ago, *Carriere e clientele nella Roma barocca* (Bari: Laterza, 1990); Gilles Deleuze, *The Fold: Leibniz and the Baroque*, trans. Tom Conley (Minneapolis: University of Minnesota Press, 1993 [1988]); Lorenzo Bianconi, *Music in the Seventeenth Century*, trans. David Bryant (Cambridge University Press, 1987 [1982]); José Antonio Maravall, *Culture of the Baroque: Analysis of a Historical Structure*, trans. Terry Cochran (Minneapolis: University of Minnesota Press, 1986 [1975]); Fagiolo dell'Arco and Carandini, *L'effimero barocco*; Gino Stefani, *Musica barocca: poetica e ideologia* (Milan: Bompiani, 1974); and Walter Benjamin, *The Origin of German Tragic Drama*, trans. John Osborne (New York: Verso, 1998 [1927]).

19 There are a number of classic texts and more recent scholarship that help chart the socio-political and economic shifts in play during the early modern period, both across Europe and more specifically in Rome; a selection includes Fernand Braudel's classic Annales School three-volume study, *Civilisation matérielle et capitalisme (XVe–XVIIIe siècle)* (Paris: Armand Colin, 1979); and sociologist Immanuel Wallerstein's three-volume study, *The Modern World-System: Capitalist Agriculture and the Origins of the European World-Economy in the Sixteenth Century* (New York: Academic Press, 1974); for historical studies that consider the socio-political effects on culture and the arts, see Hanns Gross, *Rome in the Age of Enlightenment: The Post-Tridentine Syndrome and the Ancien Régime* (Cambridge University Press, 1990); Christopher M. S. Johns, *Papal Art and Cultural Politics: Rome in the Age of Clement XI* (Cambridge University Press, 1993); and Jeffrey Laird Collins, *Papacy and Politics in 18th-Century Rome: Pius VI and the Arts* (Cambridge University Press, 2004).

20 In this way, Clement XI followed some of the inroads made by his predecessor, Innocent XII, who had directed much of his attention to church reform. For further background on Clement XI's Catholic intellectual reform, see Johns, "Art, Science, and Idea in the Rome of Clement XI," in *Papal Art and Cultural Politics: Rome in the Age of Clement XI*, 22–38. For a recent study on the cultivation of scholarship among the religious orders in this period of the early eighteenth century, see Antonella Barazzi, "Una cultura per gli ordini religiosi," *Quaderni Storici* 40, no. 2 (2005): 485–517.

21 Peter Burke describes this phenomenon through his "withdrawal thesis," a sense that by 1800 most of Europe's highest classes (nobility, clergy) and merchant classes of professionals had relinquished any participation in popular culture to the lower classes. In part, he sees this as the elite's need to justify their privilege and exceptionalism during an era when a population boom, rise in

commercial economy, increased literacy, and forums for political expression had shifted culture away from feudal structures and their mechanisms of power and isolation. What he does stress is how this withdrawal was a gradual process starting from the late seventeenth century. See his chapter "Popular Culture and Social Change," in *Popular Culture in Early Modern Europe* (New York: Harper and Row, 1978), 244–287.

22 For a recent discussion of reform within the larger context of restoring an Italian sense of *buon gusto*, see Vernon Hyde Minor's chapter 1, "Cattivo Gusto and Some Aspects of Baroque Rhetoric," in *The Death of the Baroque and the Rhetoric of Good Taste* (Cambridge University Press, 2006), 4–25. Minor emphasizes that the Arcadians and others who reacted vehemently against baroque aesthetics and rhetoric were also taking aim at Jesuit poetics, and specifically that the Jesuit promotion of emotive expressionism was in fact *cattivo gusto*. He notes that several prominent Arcadians were in fact Jansenists, see 5–6. On the use of Jesuit aesthetics as propaganda during the baroque, see Evonne Levy, *Propaganda and the Jesuit Baroque* (Berkeley: University of California Press, 2004).

23 Jansenism, though originating in the writing of the Dutch theologian Cornelius Otto Jansen, found a particularly forceful context in seventeenth-century Paris among the theologians and writers Antoine Arnauld, Pierre Nicole, Blaise Pascal, and Jean Racine, to name a few. For a perspective on this religious-intellectual context in France, see Lucien Goldmann's classic study, *The Hidden God: A Study of the Tragic Vision in the Pensées of Pascal and the Tragedies of Racine*, trans. Philip Thody (New York: The Humanities Press, 1964), 89–163; for Jansenism as a particular Roman phenomenon, see Gross, *Rome in the Age of Enlightenment*, 270–285.

24 Ibid., 271.

25 For a number of these sources, see chapter 4 of this book.

26 On the establishment of Christina's academies, see Michele Maylender, *Storia delle accademie d'Italia*, Vol. I (Bologna: Capelli, 1926; repr. Bologna: Arnaldo Forni, 1976), 255–259; and Ruth Stephen, "A Note on Christina and her Academies," in *Queen Christina of Sweden: Documents and Studies*, ed. M. von Platen (Stockholm: P. A. Norstedt and Söner, 1966), 365–371; for some reflection on and reconsideration of the influence of Christina's academies as they regard music, see Arnaldo Morelli's "Mecenatismo musicale nella Roma barocca: il caso di Cristina di Svezia," *Quaderni Storici* 22, no. 95 (1997): 387–408.

27 As patron of the Collegio Clementino, Christina used her influence there, as at other schools, to attract the best students to her academy. Many of these students would be future members of the Academy of Arcadians; on the recruitment from colleges and the eventual involvement of these students within the Academy, see Ariella Lanfranchi and Enrico Careri, "Le cantate per la Natività della B.V. Un secolo di musiche al Collegio Nazareno di Roma (1681–1784)," in *Händel e gli Scarlatti a Roma*, ed. Nino Pirrotta and Agostino Ziino (Florence: Olschki, 1987), 304–305.

28 There were fourteen founding members of the original academy. For a description of its origins and institutionalization, see Crescimbeni, *La bellezza della volgar poesia* (Rome: Buagni, 1700), 217–230. For an overview on these early years of the Accademia degli Arcadi, see Francesca Santovetti, "Arcadia a Roma Anno Domini 1690: accademia e vizi di forma," *Modern Language Notes* 112, no. 1 (1997): 21–37.

29 Crescimbeni's writings were voluminous, in part a reflection of his extraordinarily long tenure as custodian (in theory, this was a position to be rotated every four years, though Crescimbeni held it for thirty-eight years). All the Arcadian records were initially organized and stored by him in an official archive, known as the *serbatoio*. Over time, when the managing of records and Arcadian publications became too onerous, new positions were instituted: the *pro-custode* (for administrative help), several *sotto-custodi* (to help organize the *serbatoio*), and eventually the establishment of a group called the *collegio* (for general running of the academy and its legislation). See Michel Giovanni Morei, *Memorie istoriche dell'adunanze degli Arcadi* (Rome: de' Rossi, 1761), 21–23.

30 Crescimbeni, *L'istoria della volgar poesia* (Rome: Chracas, 1698).

31 See the discussion below for further details about the 1711 Arcadian schism.

32 See Hanns Gross's discussion of these two strains in *Rome in the Age of Enlightenment*, 288–291; also see mention of the Arcadians' embrace of the Petrarchan sonnet in Susan M. Dixon, *Between the Real and the Ideal: The Accademia degli Arcadi and its Garden in Eighteenth-Century Rome* (Newark, DE: University of Delaware Press, 2006), 29; and Francesco Tateo, "Arcadia e Petrarchismo," in *Atti e memorie dell'Accademia degli Arcadi* 9, nos. 2–4 (1991–1994): 19–33, see n74 for a study of various Arcadian stances on the imitation of Petrarch.

33 For reflections on the effects of poetic change and formal conception as it affected musical settings (particularly of cantatas), see Carolyn Gianturco, "The Cantata: A Textual Approach," in *The Well Enchanting Skill. Music, Poetry, and Drama in the Culture of the Renaissance: Essays in Honour of F. W. Sternfeld*, ed. John Caldwell, Edward Olleson, and Susan Wollenberg (Oxford University Press, 1989), 41–51; also see Norbert Dubowy, "'Al tavolino medesimo del Compositor della Musica': Notes on Text and Context in Alessandro Scarlatti's *cantate da camera*," in *Aspects of the Secular Cantata in Late Baroque Italy*, ed. Michael Talbot (Burlington, VT: Ashgate, 2009), 111–134.

34 The terms *diletto* and *utile* were a well-known reference (before and during the seventeenth century) to Horace's *Ars Poetica*, in which he reflects on the aims and utility of poetry.

35 Vera Gaye, *L'opera critica e storiografica del Crescimbeni* (Parma: Guanda, 1970), 44.

36 Minor relates an important historical point about the reference to Parrhasius. He references the story by Plutarch that tells of the nymph Phylonome, who bore twin boys by the god Ares, but fearing her father's wrath, forsook the boys, leaving them on Mount Erymanthe. There, a she-wolf nurtured them until a

shepherd, Tyliphus, took them in, and named them Lycastus and Parrhasius. Minor's point is that the connection of this story with the legendary founding of Rome – creating a bond between Rome and Arcadia – is unmistakable. See *Death of the Baroque*, 142.

37 Dixon reasons that the frequent change in location was due to the academy's lack of a primary patron. Thus, they found several hosts to provide a garden space for their gatherings; the best of those included an open-air theater or amphitheater. She surveys the changing location of the Arcadians' gatherings in her chapter "The Ideal Bosco Parrasio," in *Between the Real and the Ideal*, 54–82.

38 "...l'Accademia di Belle Lettere, o sia Conversatione (come dicono) delli Pastori d' Arcadia, trasportata per la prima volta da Giardino de' Mattei alla Navicella al Giardino del Palazzo del Sig. Marchese Riario (habitato hora da S. Pompeo Azzolini custode della Regina di Svezia) alla Lungara, habitato mentre vivi, dalla Maestra della detta Regina di Svezia, Christina. Fu' tenuta in un Praticello ricoperto da gli alberi, nel quale non era alcunna sedia, ne' scabello, ne' banco; si che gli Accademici, e tutti gli uditori sedendo in terra formando un gran circolo, dissero all'usanza dei Pastori." May 27, 1691. *Archivio Cartari-Febei*, Busta 103, fol. 116v [I-Ras].

39 Every shepherd was given an Arcadian title in two parts: the first designated a name and the second a place or region of origin. For example, Alessandro Scarlatti in 1706 was given the Arcadian title Terpandro Politeio – Terpandro who comes from the region of Politeio in Arcadia. For Crescimbeni's alphabetical listing of all Arcadian shepherds (and their real identities) *c.*1700, see the "Catalogo de Pastori Arcadi," in *La bellezza della volgar poesia*, 231–251.

40 "...le compositioni riuscirono lunghi"; "...Alla Prelatura (che tiene in habito curto) dispiace il sedere in terra." *Archivio Cartari-Febei*, Busta 103, fol. 125r; fol. 146r.

41 Peter Miller, *Peiresc's Europe: Learning and Virtue in the Seventeenth Century* (New Haven: Yale University Press, 2000), 34. Also see Arnaldo Momigliano's foundational research on the topic of antiquarian research in the early modern period, as represented in "The Rise of Antiquarian Research," in *The Classical Foundations of Modern Historiography* (Berkeley: University of California Press, 1990), 54–79.

42 Most of Gravina's decisions are laid out in *Della division d'Arcadia, lettera ad un amico*, published anonymously in Naples, 1711; and *Della divisione d'Arcadia* written to the Marquis Scipione Maffei, published posthumously in Verona, 1726.

43 Dixon, *Between the Real and the Ideal*, 26.

44 Ibid., 15–16.

45 I take up this subject again in chapter 4.

46 *Il Bellerofonte/Drama/Da cantarsi nel Collegio Clemen-/tino nel Carnevale dell'/ Anno 1690./[mascherone]/In Roma,/Nella Stamperia di Gio. Giacomo Komarek,/ all'Angelo Custode 1690./Con Licenza de'Superiori.* See Franchi, *Drammaturgia*

romana I, 624–625. The music for this work was composed by Francesco Gasparini, see Lowell Lindgren, "Le opere drammatiche 'romane' di Francesco Gasparini, 1689–1699," in *Francesco Gasparini (1661–1727). Atti del primo convegno internazionale (Camaiore, 19 settembre–1 ottobre 1978)*, ed. Fabrizio Della Seta and Franco Piperno (Florence: L. S. Olschki, 1981), 178.

47 *Armida/Opera Musicale/Tradotta dal Francese, senza/mutar le note del Fa-/moso/ Gio. Battista/Lulli./[cesto con pomi]/In Roma, Per Angelo Bernabò 1690./Con licenza de' Superiori./Si vendono nella Libraria di Nicolò Corallo, all'In-/segna della Virtù, in Parione*. See Franchi, *Drammaturgia romana I*, 631–632. At least from Emanuel de Coulanges's point of view, it appears that French visitors to Rome observed that their Italian noble counterparts, though enthusiastic about the *Armide* production, still had little taste for the airs and style of French music. See the quoted passages from *Mémoires de M. de Coulanges, suivis de lettres inédites de M.me de Sévigné, de son fils, de l'abbé de Coulanges [. . .] publiés par M. de Monmerqué* (Paris: Imprimerie de P. Didot, 1820), 174; cited in Staffieri, *Colligite fragmenta*, 88–89, n50.

48 See pp. 22–23 for further details.

49 The Colonna theater, along with some of the public models of production in 1690s Rome, might well fit as an example of a "mixed model" (half-courtly, half-impresarial) identified and described by Bianconi and Walker, "Production, Consumption and Political Function of Seventeenth-Century Opera," 234–242. For a thorough study of the Colonna court theater, see Tamburini, *Due teatri per il principe*; on the more specific issue of operative patronage, also see Valeria De Lucca, "'Dalle sponde del Tebro alle rive dell'Adria': Maria Mancini and Lorenzo Onofrio Colonna's Patronage of Music and Theater between Rome and Venice (1659–1675)" (Ph.D. diss., Princeton University, 2009).

50 For the exact passage, see Reinhard Strohm, *Dramma per musica: Italian Opera Seria of the Eighteenth Century* (New Haven: Yale University Press, 1997), 2; but for Strohm's extended discussion of periodizing the genre and its departure from baroque traditions, see "Introduction: The *dramma per musica* in the Eighteenth Century," 1–29 and "A Context for *Griselda*: The Teatro Capranica in Rome, 1711–1724," 33–60. On the emergence of the Capranica theater, see Luigia Cannizzo, "Vent'anni di storia di un teatro romano: il Capranica (1678–1698)," in *Il libro di teatro. Annali del Dipartimento musica e spettacolo dell'Università di Roma 1990*, ed. Roberto Ciancarelli (Rome: Bulzoni Editore, 1991), 31–46.

51 There are few comprehensive studies that tackle opera production during this particular period within Rome, outside the classic, yet out-of-date studies focused on specific theaters, such as Alessandro Ademollo, *I teatri di Roma nel secolo decimosettimo* (Bologna: Forni Editore, 1969 [1888]); and Cametti, *Il Teatro di Tordinona*. More recent work has either surveyed or focused on select composers who wrote opera for the Roman context during these years, or key patrons working within this milieu; if theater-related, the research has been specific in topic and published as shorter, article-length studies. The unusual

conditions for opera during this transition between centuries and the particular qualities of Roman patronage, politics, and culture really do demand a more comprehensive and revisionist project.

52 *Amore/e Gratitudine/Dramma Pastorale/Posto in Musica/Da Flavio Lanciani/ Romano./Da recitarsi/Il presente Nuovo Anno M.DC.XCI./Nel Teatro di Tor di Nona./Dedicata all'Illustriss. ed Eccellentiss. Sig./D. Marco Ottoboni/Nipote di Nostro Signore/PP. Alessandro VIII./Generale delle Galere di S. Santità./ Duca di Fiano &c./[stemma Ottoboni]/In Roma, Per Gio: Francesco Buagni. M.DC.XCI./Con licenza de'Superiori.* Franchi, *Drammaturgia romana I*, 637. We know this work was penned by Ottoboni himself and signed in the dedicatory preface with his Arcadian pseudonym, "Crateo Pradelini." For the second publication of this libretto in 1691, the original allegorical prologue (whose allegorical characters Night, Love, and Apollo refer directly to the events surrounding the 1690 nuptials of Pope Alexander VIII's great-nephew Marco Ottoboni with Tarquinia Colonna) was taken out for the Tordinona production.

53 Crescimbeni honored Cardinal Ottoboni's works as exemplars of reform. However, it is not news to scholars of opera and drama of this locale that Ottoboni could never be counted an unqualified success as a poet. He may have been productive and persistent, but in truth, he was often criticized and ridiculed by Romans for his libretti. See Holmes, *La Statira*, 4. For a very vivid example of this criticism, see the evidence cited and transcribed in Maria Letizia Volpicelli's appendix of documents in "Il teatro del Cardinale Ottoboni al Palazzo della Cancelleria," in *Il teatro a Roma nel Settecento*, 2 vols. (Rome: Istituto dell' Enciclopedia Italiana, 1989), II: 694–697.

54 In 1692, the January reproduction of *La Rosaura* at the Teatro Capranica (text by Giovanni Battista Lucini, music by Alessandro Scarlatti), which was originally commissioned by Ottoboni in 1690 for a private performance at the Cancelleria to celebrate the double nuptials of Marco Ottoboni and Tarquinia Colonna, and Cornelia Zeno Ottoboni and Urbano Barberini, was later offered publicly by an associated intellectual society, the Accademici Uniti: *Gli equivoci/in Amore,/Overo/La Rosaura/Dramma per Musica/Di G.B.L./Da rappresentarsi dagli/Accademici Uniti/nell'Anno/1692./[cestino]/In Roma,/Si vendono in Piazza Navona nella Li-/braria di Carlo Giannini.* See Franchi, *Drammaturgia romana I*, 642–643.

55 See the *Avviso di Roma* cited in Cametti, *Il Teatro Tordinona*, II: 346. From December 28 through the first weeks of January the Tordinona staged *Il/Colombo,/overo/L'India Scoperta/Dramma Per Musica/Dedicato/All'Illustriss. ed'Eccellentiss. Sig. Principessa/D. Maria Otthoboni./Da Rappresentarsi/Nel Teatro di Tor di Nona/L'Anno M.DC.XCI./[stemma Ottoboni]/Ad istanza di Francesco Leone Libraro/in Piazza Madama./In Roma, Per Gio: Francesco Buagni.M.DC.XC./Con licenza de'Superiori.* See Franchi, *Drammaturgia romana I*, 636. The text was by Ottoboni (and signed as "Crateo Pradelini"), and music

possibly by Bernardo Pasquini, as suggested by Staffieri in her chronological table, see *Colligite fragmenta*, 234.

56 For evidence of papal prohibition during that season see the *Avvisi Marescotti* for January 6, 1691, 788, fols. 223v–224, in Staffieri, *Colligite fragmenta*, 96–97.

57 Rain and prohibitions may have appeared to dampen carnival, but clearly operas continued to be performed, as evidenced in the *Avvisi Marescotti*, 780, fol. 320v, in ibid., 102–103. According to source information, other operas aside from the 1692 reproduction of *La Rosaura* were performed, the two major productions being *Amor vince lo sdegno, overo L'Olimpia placata* (text originally by Aurelio Aureli and music by Domenico Freschi for a 1682 production in Venice, but adapted by G. B. Luchini, with acts recomposed by Alessandro Scarlatti in Naples in 1685, with new modifications for Rome by Francesco Gasparini) at the Capranica, dedicated to the Accademici Uniti; and *L'Eraclea, overo Il ratto delle Sabine* (text originally by Nicolò Minato and music by Antonio Draghi for a 1674 production in Vienna, adapted for Rome by Silvio Stampiglia, with musical modifications by Giovanni Bononcini) at the Tordinona. However, the most acclaimed of all productions was that of *L'Eudossia* (text by Alessandro Pollioni and music by Bernardo Pasquini), performed at the Seminario Romano.

58 *Nerone/fatto Cesare/Drama Per Musica/Di Matteo Noris/Da Rappresentarsi nel nuovo Teatro/degli'Illustrissimi Sig. Capranica/L'Anno M.DC.XCV./Dedicato/ All'Illustrissima, & Eccellentissima/Signora/La Signora/D.Felice/Ventimiglia/ D'Aragona Pignatelli, e Bar-/berini. Principessa di/Palestrina./[fregio]/Si vendono in Piazza Navona nella/Libraria di Carlo Giannini./In Roma, Per Gio: Francesco Buagni./Con licenza de' Superiori.* See Franchi, *Drammaturgia romana I*, 686. It appears that the Matteo di Noris libretto and the Giacomo Antonio Perti score from the Venetian production at the Teatro San Salvatore in 1693 were the texts used for the 1695 production in Rome; however, the stage design underwent major changes in the hands of Acciaiuoli (ibid.). Also see Staffieri's citation of *avvisi* and her citation of sources mentioned by Cametti and Ademollo about this and other opera productions during 1695, *Colligite fragmenta*, 121 n92.

59 Ibid., 122 n93.

60 *Penelope/La Casta./Dramma Per Musica/Da rappresentarsi nel nuovo, e/Famoso Teatro di Tor di/Nona l'Anno 1696./Dedicato/Alle Signore/Dame./[cherubini]/Si vende in Bottega di Pietro Leone/Libraro in Parione./In Rome, Pe'l Buagni. 1696/Con licenza de'Superiori.* See Franchi, *Drammaturgia romana I*, 700–701. Franchi reports that Matteo di Noris wrote the libretto for a 1685 production at the Teatro Grimano, with music by Carlo Pallavicino. For the Roman edition, Silvio Stampiglia was apparently hired to undertake some significant modifications to the text, which was set to new music by Antonio Perti. The public evaluation is evidenced in the following *avviso* from February 4, 1696: "Seguono le recite delle comedie con grande emulazione delli due teatri, ma quella di Torre di Nona trionfa, che è intitolata *Penelope la Casta*, mentre le scene, machine, intermedi, habiti, comparse et apparenze sono da farsi ad un imperatore e

conseguentemente superano il *Flavio Cuniberto* che si recita a Capranica, benché la musica di questo Teatro sii superiore sì come diversi recitanti." *Avvisi di Roma* [I-Rvat], Ottob. lat. 3361, 10r.

61 *Il Xerse/Dramma Per Musica/Del Sig. Nicolò Minati/Da rappresentarsi nel famoso/Teatro di Torre di Nona/L'Anno MDCXCIV./Consacrato/All'Ill.mo & Eccell.mo Sig.re/D. Antonio/Floriano/Di Liechtestein./Prencipe del S.R.I. di Nicolspurgh in Selsia, Duca/di Tropauu, e Iagendorf, Conte di Ritperg, Sig./Ereditario in Rumburgh, &c. Cavaliere del-/la Chiave d'Oro di S.M.C. e suo Amba-/sciatore alla Sede Apostolica./[leone]/Si vendono in Bottega di Francesco Leone/Librano in Piazza Madama./In Roma, per Gio. Francesco Buagni, 1694/Con licenza de' Superiori.* See Franchi, *Drammaturgia romana I*, 669–670. See Harold Powers, "Il Serse trasformato," *Musical Quarterly* 47 (1961): 481–492.

62 For more on this opera, see Ellen Rosand, "Il ritorno d'Orfeo: The Decline of a Tradition," in Rosand, *Opera in Seventeenth-Century Venice*, 388–391.

63 *L'Orfeo/Drama Per Musica./Da recitarsi nel Teatro della Pace/di Roma,/Il Presente Anno/M.DC.XCIV./Dedicato/All'Emin. E Rev. Sig./Il Sig. Cardinale/ Pietro/Ottoboni/[leone]/Si vedono in Piazza Madama da/Francesco Leone Libraro./In Rome, Per il Buagni. 1694/Con Licenza de'Superiori.* Franchi reproduces the dedication by Bastiano Ricci who confirms the Parma version was the one used at Teatro della Pace. See *Drammaturgia romana I*, 674.

64 Franchi's catalogue of libretti reports several works by Corneille and Racine performed at the Collegio Clementino towards the end of the decade, in 1699. See *Drammaturgia romana I*, 739–740.

65 *Italian Opera and European Theatre, 1680–1720: Plots, Performances, Dramaturgies* (Turnhout: Brepols, 2000), 81–89.

66 Melania Bucciarelli references Maffei's critique of opera's history as the reason for verse's decline. When early Italian tragedies, originally composed in verse, began to circulate in the reduced format of *scenari*, they were soon after subjected to improvisations by *comici dell'arte*, whose treatment was thought to be responsible for the degeneration of verse into prose. Ibid.

67 On the problems of verisimilitude in opera, see Scipione Maffei, *Teatro italiano, o sia scelta di tragedie per uso della scena* (Verona: J. Vallarsi, 1723–1725); Lodovico Antonio Muratori, *Della perfetta poesia italiana* Vol. II, ed. Ada Ruschioni (Milan: Marzorati Editore, 1972 [1706]); Gian Vicenzo Gravina, *Della ragion poetica*, Libro I, in *Scritti critici e teorici*, ed. Amedeo Quondam (Bari: Laterza, 1973).

68 For these contrasting viewpoints concerning the role of music, see Piero Weiss's "Opera and the Two Verisimilitudes," in *Music and Civilization: Essays in Honor of Paul Henry Lang*, ed. Edmond Strainchamps, Maria Rika Maniates, and Christopher Hatch (New York: Norton, 1984), 117–126; and "Teorie drammaturgiche e 'infranciosamento': motivi della 'riforma' melodrammatica nel primo Settecento," in *Antonio Vivaldi: teatro musicale, cultura, e società*, ed. Lorenzo Bianconi and Giovanni Morelli (Florence: L. S. Olschki, 1982), 273–296.

69 *L'Endimione/Di/Erilo   Cleoneo/Pastore   Arcade/Con/Un   Discorso/Di/Bione Crateo./All'Eminentiss. e Reverendiss. Sig./Cardinale/Albano./[cesto con fiori]/ in Roma,/Per Gio: Giacomo Komarek Boemo/all'Angelo Custode.1692./Con Licenza de'Superiori.* Franchi, *Drammaturgia romana I*, 641. The work was performed in the summer of 1691, during a July gathering of the Academy of Arcadians. Gian Vincenzo Gravina was among the first and most enthusiastic proponents of the *favola pastorale*, as expressed in his 1692 essay *Discorso sopra L'Endimione*, which was published with the Rome and Amsterdam editions of Guidi's drama, completed in collaboration with Queen Christina. For this essay in its entirety, see Quondam's edition of Gravina's *Scritti critici e teorici*, 49–73.

70 Carlo Sigismondo Capece was considered a favorite by Crescimbeni and received praise in Arcadian writings as one of the great librettists of his time. Bucciarelli describes his *I giochi troiani* as truly the first pastoral model that helped form the Arcadian notions of reform practices. See *Italian Opera and European Theatre, 1680–1720*, 111–118. Another important influence, though mostly through productions in Venice and other locations, was Apostolo Zeno, with works like *Gl'inganni felici* (1695), *Il Tirsi* (1696), and *Il Narciso* (1697). See Weiss, "Teorie drammaturgiche e 'infranciosamento,'" 290–292.

71 There were other non-Arcadian librettists during this period, both in and beyond Rome, who were involved in reform changes and in writing pastoral dramas. However, apart from Apostolo Zeno and a few other Arcadian poets such as Silvio Stampiglia and Carlo Sigismondo Capece, *only* Cardinal Ottoboni received regular praise by Crescimbeni for his pastorals, and for bringing back the elements of good taste to Italy, with use of choruses and adherence to the ancient rules (the Unities); likely, a necessary encomium for the cardinal's patronage. For evidence of Crescimbeni's praise for Ottoboni, see *La bellezza della volgar poesia*, Dialogo VI, 141.

72 There are exceptions, as noted by Strohm who recognizes a surge (and return) of pastoral popularity in Rome and elsewhere *c.*1710–1715. See *Dramma per musica*, 41. Also see Ayana Smith's recent article "The Mock Heroic, an Intruder in Arcadia: Girolamo Gigli, Antonio Caldara and *L'Anagilda* (Rome, 1711)," *Eighteenth-Century Music* 7, no. 1 (2010): 35–64, for an important discussion that underlines the exceptions to the pastoral, and even to strict tragedy as models for opera within this Arcadian period. Smith's detailing of the mock-heroic genre, through the case study of Gigli and Caldara's *L'Anagilda*, complicates the picture of reform aesthetics, and suggests that satire and parody of aesthetic movements, and more specifically of characterizing the "heroic" in opera, were alive and well.

73 Dixon, *Between the Real and the Ideal*, 32.

74 For information on these productions and libretti, see n54.

75 Contemporary writings that tried either to prohibit or to condemn opera often stressed the distraction of theater for the young, taking them away from their studies, devotional practices, etc., as exemplified in an *avviso* from January 8,

1684, collected in the *Avvisi Marescotti*, 787, fol. 70; likewise, we find in similar documents a concern that opera may be too satirical or dirty in tone, noted in an *avviso* from March 10, 1685, also collected in the *Avvisi Marescotti*, 787, fol. 185v; see Staffieri, *Colligite fragmenta*, 57, 63. For secondary sources that detail different qualities of intentions and language in theater bans, see Maria Grazia Pastura, "Legislazione pontificia sui teatri e spettacoli musicali a Roma," in Morelli *et al.*, *La musica a Roma*, 167–176; as well as Bruno Cagli's article on issues of prohibition of the stage and opera in the eighteenth century, "Produzione musicale e governo pontificio," in *Le muse galanti: la musica a Roma nel Settecento*, ed. Bruno Cagli (Rome: Istituto dell' Enciclopedia Italiana, 1985), 11–21.

76 Murata reveals that the demolition of the Tordinona in 1697 had much to do with a political dispute and violent outbreak at the Capranica, resulting in one death, which prompted the governor of Rome to close both theaters, even though some negotiations allowed for the Capranica to stay open, even after the Tordinona was closed. Murata points out that the violence that took place was not due to unrest among the lower classes, but occurred between members of elite classes who violated the ordinary decorum of civil society *because* the unbridled "codelessness" of the public sphere allowed for such transgressions. See "*Theatrum intra Theatrum* or, The Church and Stage in 17th-Century Rome," in *Sleuthing the Muse: Festschrift for William F. Prizer*, ed. Kristine K. Forney and Jeremy L. Smith (Hillsdale, NY: Pendragon Press, forthcoming). In the appendix of her essay Murata includes a transcription of the official papal notice. For further evidence announced in Roman *avvisi*, see the entries in the *Avvisi Marescotti* for August 24 and 31, 1697, 789, fols. 209v–211v, in Staffieri, *Colligite fragmenta*, 131–132.

77 Despite the fact that the Capranica was allowed to stay open, reports suggest that noble residents and patrons of public opera prepared to leave Rome for Naples immediately after Christmas of 1697, knowing that the following carnival would be more austere in entertainment. See details of this phenomenon reported in the *avviso* from November 30, 1697, collected in the *Avvisi Marescotti*, 789, fol. 236v, see Staffieri, *Colligite fragmenta*, 133.

78 In his address, *L'Arcadia restituita all'Arcadia* [Arcadia returned to Arcadia] (Rome: Gio. Battista Molo, 1692), the Arcadian intellectual Benedetto Menzini wrote: "Thus, by the name Arcadia, we mean to signify an honorable and civil assembly that, bearing us away occasionally from the popular bustle, turns the wooded groves into an academy and puts their innocent pleasures to good use by exercising our minds." For this English translation, see Brendon Dooley, ed. and trans., *Italy in the Baroque: Selected Readings* (New York: Garland, 1995), 609.

79 Weiss explains that a critical shift occurred when a high-profile librettist like Apostolo Zeno (who could not be accurately credited for reforming melodrama *alone*, but was clearly influential in his day) essentially abandoned the pastoral

version of opera by 1697 in order to write "tragedie cantate." He speculates that Zeno may have been "corrupted" by the desire to please his audiences and give them the heroism and tragedy they craved. See "Teorie drammaturgiche e 'infranciosamento,'" 292.

80 *Dramma per musica*, 15.

2 Disrupting the oratorio

1 For the concept of a cultural or intellectual alloy, see Roger Chartier, "Intellectual History and the History of *Mentalités* – A Dual Revaluation," in Chartier, *Cultural History: Between Practices and Representations*, trans. Lydia G. Cochrane (Ithaca: Cornell University Press, 1988), 39.

2 Arcangelo Spagna (1632–1726) was a priest and canon of the church who served three cardinals during his career in Rome (Franceso Barberini, Carlo Ciceri, and Pietro Ottoboni). Spagna is remembered by music historians primarily as a librettist and foremost authority on the oratorio genre as represented in his *Oratorii, overo Melodrammi sacri*, Vol. I (Rome: Gio. Francesco Buagni, 1706; reprint, ed. Johann Herczog, *Musurgiana* 25, Lucca: Libreria Musicale Italiana, 1993). Cardinal Pietro Ottoboni (1667–1740) was considered one of Rome's most influential patrons of music and other arts during the closing decade of the seventeenth century and for much of the first quarter of the eighteenth century. He was an active librettist of oratorios, cantatas, and operas, though likely owing to his ecclesiastical position, much of that authorship remained anonymous or was cryptically coded using a pseudonym. For more background on each of these individuals, see the references cited later in this chapter regarding their influence within this context and on the oratorio specficially.

3 Much of this scholarship is cited later in the chapter. Recent studies have recognized and confronted some of the unusual problems involved in studying the oratorio – a genre marked by a great variety of practices and quantity of works, but one in which historical circumstances have prevented the survival or even existence of detailed sources, both those descriptive and critical and those textual and musical. For a rich collection of recent essays that tackle questions of sources, production and patronage, local variation of oratorio practices, and relationships to other genres, including opera, see the two conference proceedings: Paola Besutti, ed., *L'oratorio musicale italiano e i suoi contesti (secc. XVII–XVIII). Atti del convegno internazionale, Perugia, Sagra musicale umbra, 18–20 settembre 1997*, in *Quaderni della Rivista Italiana di Musicologia* 35 (Florence: L. S. Olschki, 2002); and Saverio Franchi, ed., *Percorsi dell'oratorio romano, da "historia sacra" a melodramma spirituale. Atti della giornata di studi (Viterbo, 11 settembre 1999)*, in *Colloquia* 1 (Rome: Istituto di Bibliografia Musicale, 2002).

4 Arnaldo Morelli, "'Un bell'oratorio all'uso di Roma': Patronage and Secular Context of the Oratorio in Baroque Rome," in *Music Observed: Studies in Memory of William C. Holmes*, ed. Colleen Reardon and Susan Parisi (Warren, MI:

Harmonie Park Press, 2004), 333–351. Morelli reminds his readers that such ambiguities and concealments were characteristic of the baroque era as a whole, citing Rosario Villari, ed., *L'uomo barocco* (Bari: Laterza, 1991), ix–x, as further discussion. Specific details of Morelli's article and their relevance to this study appear in later sections of the chapter.

5 Several scholars have studied the political associations embedded in oratorio texts and their surrounding events, including William A. Broom, "Political Allegory in Alessandro Melani's Oratorio *Golia abbattuto*," *Journal of Musicological Research* 3 (1981): 383–397; both Victor Crowther's studies, *The Oratorio in Modena* (Oxford: Clarendon Press, 1992) and *The Oratorio in Bologna (1650–1730)* (Oxford University Press, 1999); Robert Kendrick, "Intertextuality in Scarlatti's Cambridge *Giuditta*," unpublished paper presented at a symposium on the oratorio at Northwestern University, Evanston, IL, 2000; Paola Besutti, "Oratori in corte a Mantova: tra Bologna, Modena e Venezia," and Saverio Franchi, "Il principe Livio Odescalchi e l'oratorio 'politico,'" both in *L'oratorio musicale italiano e i suoi contesti*, ed. Besutti, 365–422 and 141–258, respectively.

6 "Mai sono visti tanti Alessandro Magno e Nerone quanti Davide e Gefte" [Never were seen as many (representations of) Alexander the Great and Nero, as David and Jepthe]. From Norbert Dubowy, "Le due *Giuditte* di Alessandro Scarlatti: due diverse concezioni dell'oratorio," in *L'oratorio musicale italiano i suoi contesti*, ed. Besutti, 259.

7 As Robert Kendrick argues: "the obvious question of when a 'staging' might or might not be a staging is rendered complex by the use of some kind of scenic apparatus even in oratory halls and the like (a backdrop, a cloud machine, etc.)." "Devotion, Piety and Commemoration: Sacred Songs and Oratorios," in *The Cambridge History of Seventeenth-Century Music*, ed. Tim Carter and John Butt (Cambridge University Press, 2005), 364. For examples that detail such theatrically inspired "stagings" in the Italian practices of performing oratorios, see Howard Smither, *A History of the Oratorio*, Vol. I: *The Oratorio in the Baroque Era: Italy, Vienna, Paris* (Chapel Hill: University of North Carolina Press, 1977), 269; and Smither, "Oratorio and Sacred Opera, 1700–1825: Terminology and Genre Distinction," *Proceedings of the Royal Musical Association* 106 (1980): 88–104; along with Ellen Rosand, "Handel Paints the Resurrection," in *Festa Musicologica: Essays in Honor of George T. Buelow*, ed. Thomas J. Mathiesen and Benito V. Rivera (Stuyvesant, NY: Pendragon Press, 1995), 7–52. More recent scholarship that treats this question of the oratorio's "staging" and its secularized, even opera-like performances includes: Morelli, "Patronage and Secular Context of the Oratorio in Baroque Rome"; Besutti, "Oratori in corte a Mantova"; and Luciano Buono, "Forme oratoriali in Sicilia nel secondo Seicento: il dialogo," in *L'oratorio musicale italiano e i suoi contesti*, ed. Besutti, 115–139.

8 See Morelli's "'Il muovere e non il far maravigliare.' Relationships between Artistic and Musical Patronage in the Roman Oratory," *Italian History and Culture* 5 (1999): 13–28; and *Il tempio armonico: musica nell'Oratorio dei Filippini*

in Roma (1575–1705). Analecta Musicologica 27 (Laaber: Laaber Verlag, 1991), 29.

9 Morelli explains that although more complex than three-part *laudi*, these madrigals were not complex in their composition or in their use of difficult chromatics celebrated in the style of the *seconda prattica* of Monteverdi and his contemporaries. Rather, these madrigals remained "affixed to a pillar of Renaissance musical aesthetics: music is the vehicle of poetry." See "Relationships between Artistic and Musical Patronage in the Roman Oratory," 18–20.

10 Ibid., 25. In *Il tempio armonico*, Morelli uses a series of regulations and restrictions enacted by some of the Oratorians at the Vallicella and a series of decrees from 1643 and 1650–1651 to demonstrate the degrees of resistance mounted by members of the confraternity who felt betrayed by these moves towards secularization. A quotation from one particular father captures the degree of nostalgic despair that the negotiated deals with new musical practices and operatic influences brought to this cultural domain: "[Let not] the vanity of the music destroy the oratory's devotion, as in some places the devil has gained with our oratory in Rome, where we sweat blood to put an end to the disorders of the music and we suffer from it daily . . . [referring to the time and musical practices of Filippo Neri:] And when people say to me that now those times are gone, I sighing reply that this is the problem, that now those times are gone." For the full citation and transcription of Father Mariano Sozzini's commentary, see Morelli, *Il tempio armonico*, 185 (doc. 405).

11 For background on papal moral reform during these decades see chapter 1.

12 In his grand oeuvre historicizing Italian literary culture, Giovanni Mario Crescimbeni briefly addresses the oratorio, its history, style, and development. See his *Commentari del Canonico Gio. Mario Crescimbeni custode d'Arcadia intorno alla sua Istoria della volgar poesia*, Vol. I (Rome: de'Rossi, 1702), 256–258.

13 For more on tragic drama and reform *c.*1700, see chapter 4.

14 See Morelli's study of Zeno's writings for this analysis in "Oratorii ovvero sacre musicali tragedie?" in *Mozart, Padova e la Betulia liberata: committenza, interpretazione, e fortuna delle azioni sacre metastasiane nel '700*, ed. Paolo Pinamonti (Florence: L. S. Olschki, 1991), 275–287.

15 As evidence for Zeno's comparisons of the oratorio to tragedy, Morelli cites a letter by Zeno to the Marquis Giuseppe Gravisi from November 3, 1730 (reprinted in Guido Nicastro, *Metastasio e il teatro del primo Settecento*. Letteratura Italiana Laterza 33 [Bari: Laterza, 1973], 65–66), as well as Zeno's *Poesie sacre drammatiche* (Venice: C. Zane, 1735) [no specific pages indicated].

16 Spagna's "Discorso intorno a gl'oratorii" was printed as a preface to his collection of authored libretti, *Oratorii, overo Melodrammi sacri*.

17 Along with Morelli, see Johann Herczog's "Introduction" to the 1993 reprint of Spagna's *Oratorii, overo Melodrammi sacri*, ix–xxviii; and two more recent essays from the Viterbo conference, Franchi, ed., *Percorsi dell'oratorio romano:* Mauro

Sarnelli, "Percorsi dell'oratorio per musica come genere letterario," 137–97, and Oscar Mischiati, "La cantata secondo Erdmann Neumeister e l'oratorio secondo Arcangelo Spagna: una possibile analogia?," 95–98.

18 As comparative examples from spoken tragedy, Morelli cites the tragic works of Federico Della Vale whose dramas based on biblical and erotic themes mirrored the popular libretto subjects of mid- to later century oratorios. See "Oratorii ovvero sacre musicali tragedie?," 282.

19 In his recent essay "Percorsi dell'oratorio per musica come genere letterario," Mauro Sarnelli revisits Spagna's "Discorso" to uncover the fact that Spagna updated his work in 1714, and wrote a prefatory appendix to *Oratorii, overo Melodrammi sacri*. He uses this evidence to create a more rounded intellectual profile of Spagna. Not only was Spagna a significant figure in the powerful circle of Rome's literati, Sarnelli makes convincing arguments to recuperate Spagna from the view that his writings on the oratorio were merely dogmatic; Spagna was dogmatic at times but was not ignorant of the most current literary debates over reform.

20 We know that Spagna was well acquainted with the theatrical works of Rospigliosi, who, like Spagna, spent a long period of time in the service of the Barberini. For further background, see Herczog's "Introduction," xxvii.

21 See Sarnelli's citations of Gravina's *Delle tragedie di Seneca*, in "Percorsi dell'oratorio per musica come genere letterario," 152.

22 Contained at the end of *Oratorii, overo Melodrammi sacri*, Libro secondo, is a commemorative speech, *Origine de gl'Infecondi* (230–243), given to the Accademia degli Infecondi on July 25, 1700, discussing the group's activities and important role in recuperating ancient purity in literature and the arts. See the Herczog edition, 83–85.

23 Sarnelli also rightly notes that the reform ideas we tend conventionally to assign to the turn of the eighteenth century were well underway much earlier in the seventeenth century, when a move towards a more "moderate baroque" arose with the rejection of literary Marinism and the aesthetic of the marvelous. See "Percorsi dell'oratorio per musica come genere letterario," 141, as well as Sarnelli's citation of Franco Croce, *Tre momenti del barocco letterario italiano* (Florence: Sansoni, 1966).

24 "Discorso intorno a gli oratorii," in *Oratorii, overo Melodrammi sacri*, Libro Primo, 3 (Herczog edition, 7).

25 In the preface to *Fasti sacri* (Rome, 1720), Spagna's last publication, he refers to his two earlier books of oratorios as "sacred operas." Herczog suggests how this attachment to sacred opera (as a good model to follow) is indicative of a larger process of justification at work in Spagna's writing. He notes a personal unease behind Spagna's open admission that the oratorio had resorted to secular means to ensure its appeal to the faithful. His decision to abolish the narrator (Testo) and to make the oratorio more theatrical could be justified by showing how those compromises, in fact, predated his career as oratorio librettist (xxii).

The overlap of sacred and secular influences in genres like sacred opera and the oratorio deserves a more thorough investigation, especially when considering the possible contact and relationship between these two genre traditions. One recent example that questions the sacred/secular divide in sacred opera is Robert Kendrick, "What's So Sacred about 'Sacred' Opera?: Reflections on the Fate of a (Sub)genre," *Journal of Seventeenth-Century Music* 9, no. 1 (2003), available at http://sscm-jscm.press.uiuc.edu/jscm/v9no1.html.

26 "Discorso intorno a gli oratorii," in *Oratorii, overo Melodrammi sacri*, Libro Primo, 14 (Herczog edition, 9).

27 Herczog, "Introduction," xxiii.

28 "Discorso intorno a gli oratorii," in *Oratorii, overo Melodrammi sacri*, Libro Primo, 12 (Herczog edition, 8).

29 Perhaps this sensibility came from a wealth of experience; it is noteworthy that Spagna *did* compose libretti for comic operas, collected in his third book, *Melodrammi scenici* (Rome, 1709), including "Discorso apologetico della commedia," which can be described as a type of companion piece to "Discorso dogmatico." See Herczog's "Introduction," xxiv.

30 "Discorso intorno a gli oratorii," in *Oratorii, overo Melodrammi sacri*, Libro Primo, 16–17 (Herczog edition, 9).

31 Ibid., 19 (Herczog edition, 10).

32 Ibid., 18 (Herczog edition, 9); also see 21–22 (Herczog edition, 10).

33 It is likely that Spagna would have heard or seen examples by other oratorio composers of this generation, for example, those by Bernardo Pasquini, or Alessandro Melani, whose oratorios for Rome in the 1670s and 1680s captured the forms and styles of vocal dramatic writing (typical aria structures, affective gestures, and narrative conventions) prevalent in opera writing of the same period. For representative examples of this oratorio writing, one can consult the facsimile scores in the series, edited by Joyce L. Johnson and Howard Smither, *The Italian Oratorio 1650–1800: Works in a Central Baroque and Classic Tradition*, 31 vols. (New York: Garland, 1986), see specifically Vol. III, *Il sacrificio di Abel*, Alessandro Melani; and Vol. VIII, *Sant'Agnese*, Bernardo Pasquini.

34 "Discorso intorno a gli oratorii," in *Oratorii, overo Melodrammi sacri*, Libro Primo, 21 (Herczog edition, 10).

35 Ireneusz Opacki, "Royal Genres," trans. David Malcolm, in *Modern Genre Theory*, ed. David Duff (New York: Longman Press, 2000), 118–126. Opacki first published his essay as "Krzyzowanie sie postaci gatunkowych jako wyznacznik ewolucji poezji" [The hybridization of genre forms as a determinant of the evolution of poetry] in *Pamietnik Literacki* 54, no. 4 (1963).

36 Opacki, "Royal Genres," 122.

37 On the relationship between music and words as part of a larger criticism of opera, see Muratori's fifth chapter ("De' difetti, che possono osservarsi ne' moderni drammi") in *Della perfetta poesia italiana*, Vol. II, ed. Ada Ruschioni (Milan: Marzorati Editore, 1972 [1706]), 573–585.

38 Ibid., 576.

39 Renata Ago, "Hegemony over the Social Scene and Zealous Popes (1676–1700)," in *Court and Politics in Papal Rome, 1492–1700*, ed. Gianvittorio Signorotto and Maria Antonietta Visceglia (Cambridge University Press, 2002), 229–246; see especially 236–246.

40 Based on research conducted on the *Avvisi Marescotti*, Gloria Staffieri compares the mention of operas versus oratorios in the documents in the period 1683– 1707. Her table shows a spike in oratorio production from 1685 to 1689 while operas mostly remain at the same rate of production. See Staffieri, *Colligite fragmenta: la vita musicale romana degli "Avvisi Marescotti" (1683–1707)* (Lucca: Libreria Musicale Italiana Editrice, 1990), table 1, 39.

41 Contemporary news reports document many cases of censure for clerics who had supported or attended opera; these cases underline the inappropriateness of such public displays by clergy. As an example, see the *avviso* for February 6, 1694 that describes the pope's rigorous admonition of clerics attending opera. See the *Avvisi Marescotti*, AM 788, c. 486–487, in Staffieri, *Colligite fragmenta*, 112.

42 Ago, "Hegemony over the Social Scene," 243.

43 Ludwig von Pastor recalls that Pietro Ottoboni's name arose among the early selection of the 1689 conclave, in large part owing to his close relationship with and the respect he earned from Innocent XI. *The History of the Popes*, Vol. XXXII (London: Routledge and Kegan Paul, 1957), 532.

44 The biggest problem Alexander VIII faced in taking up the unfinished agenda of his predecessor was the restoration of peace with France after the scuffle over the Gallican Articles. He demanded that Louis XIV recant or confirmation of French bishops would not continue. Although Alexander VIII was known to make conciliatory gestures (often at the expense of the pope's other relations, i.e., with the Habsburg emperor), he took a firm stance with France, and Louis, faced with new difficulties against the Grand Alliance, conceded to the church. For details, see ibid., 539–555, especially 553. For a more general overview of papal relations with France and other dominant monarchies during this period, see Bruno Neveu, "Politique ecclésiastique et controverses doctrinales en Rome 1683 à 1705," *Bulletin de la Société d'Histoire Moderne* 74, no. 10 (1975): 11–18.

45 We should recognize, in light of Ago's analysis, how this move recaptured the papacy's centralization of cultural power that had been relinquished to lay nobility under the reformed emphasis on piety and asceticism of the Innocent papacies. In reference to the Barberini model of governance and sovereignty, see Laurie Nussdorfer, *Civic Politics in the Rome of Urban VIII* (Princeton University Press, 1992), especially 33–44; also Frederick Hammond, *Music and Spectacle in Baroque Rome: Barberini Patronage under Urban VIII* (New Haven: Yale University Press, 1994), especially Part I, 3–60.

46 See Ago's "Hegemony over the Social Scene" for an in-depth consideration of the social and political maneuvering and the eventual consequences of short papacies in the seventeenth century.

47 It is important to note that this tendency sometimes placed the cardinal at odds with his great-uncle, Alexander VIII, who on occasion was said to object to his nephew's behavior, as reports from the time attest. See Pastor's citation of a report penned by R. Pallavicini on November 26, 1689, in *History of the Popes*, Vol. XXXII, n1537.

48 For a sample of key scholarship on Ottoboni's patronage and involvement in music and the arts, see Sven Hostrup Hansell, "Orchestral Practice and the Court of Cardinal Pietro Ottoboni," *Journal of the American Musicological Society* 19, no. 3 (1966): 398–403; Hans Joachim Marx, "Die Musik am Hofe Pietro Kardinal Ottobonis unter Arcangelo Corelli," *Analecta Musicologica* 5 (1968): 104–177; Michael Talbot and Colin Timms, "Music and the Poetry of Antonio Ottoboni (1646–1720)," in *Händel e gli Scarlatti a Roma*, ed. Nino Pirrotta and Agostino Ziino (Florence: L. S. Olschki, 1987), 367–438; Maria Letizia Volpicelli, "Il teatro del Cardinale Ottoboni al Palazzo della Cancelleria," in *Il teatro a Roma nel Settecento*, 2 vols. (Rome: Istituto dell' Enciclopedia Italiana, 1989), ii: 681–782; Stefano La Via, "Il Cardinale Ottoboni e la musica: nuovi documenti (1700–1740), nuove lettere e ipotesi," in *Intorno a Locatelli: studi in occasione del tricentenario della nascita di Pietro Antonio Locatelli – 1695–1764*, Vol. I (Lucca: Libreria Editrice Musicale, 1995), 319–526; Franco Piperno, "Su le sponde del Tebro: eventi, mecenati e istituzioni musicali a Roma negli anni di Locatelli. Saggio di cronologia," in *Intorno a Locatelli*, 793–877; Flavia Matitti, "Il Cardinale Pietro Ottoboni mecenate delle arti: cronache e documenti (1689–1740)," *Storia dell'Arte* 84 (1995): 156–243; Edward J. Olszewski, "The Painters in Cardinal Pietro Ottoboni's Court of the Cancelleria, 1689–1740," *Römisches Jahrbuch der Bibliotheca Hertziana* 31 (1998): 119–212; Olszewski, "Decorating the Palace: Cardinal Pietro Ottoboni (1667–1740) in the Cancelleria," in *Life and the Arts in the Baroque Palaces of Rome: Ambiente Barocco*, ed. Stefanie Walker and Frederick Hammond (New Haven: Yale University Press, for The Bard Graduate Center for Studies in the Decorative Arts, 1999), 93–111; Olszewski, "The Enlightened Patronage of Cardinal Pietro Ottoboni (1667–1740)," *Artibus et Historiae* 23, no. 45 (2002): 139–165. More recently, Morelli's "Patronage and Secular Context of the Oratorio in Baroque Rome" addresses, albeit briefly, some important qualities of the Ottoboni patronage of palace oratorios. Outside of individual works (e.g. William C. Holmes's edition of Alessandro Scarlatti's *La Statira*, Vol. IX of *The Operas of Alessandro Scarlatti* [Cambridge, MA: Harvard University Press, 1985]) a more comprehensive and critical treatment of Ottoboni's palace theatrical program with thorough analysis of specific private operas staged there has yet to be undertaken.

49 See chapter 1 for further discussion and examples.

50 Pastor recalls the high moral character of Pietro Ottoboni by citing several archival sources as evidence for his conclusion. He writes: "Learned, blameless in his conduct, exceedingly prudent, he was regarded as one of the ablest, best informed and worthiest members of the Sacred College." See *History of the Popes*,

Vol. XXXII, 532. Beyond Pastor's documentary papal study, there is little in the scholarship in the way of a comprehensive study or single monograph dedicated to the papacy of Alexander VIII. Among the most recent essays and articles that cover papal politics during this period, see those collected in Gianvittorio Signorotto and Maria Antonietta Visceglia, eds., *Court and Politics in Papal Rome, 1492–1700* (Cambridge University Press, 2002).

51 For details and further references to the importance of the Colonna opera program, see chapter 1.

52 Ago argues that a shift in emphasis of governance with Innocent XI's "anti-festive rigour" and disengagement from local social politics is what added to the growth and prestige of the remaining old feudal families, like the Orsini and Colonna. Alexander VIII, by contrast, actively confronted social politics using his own family contacts and influence to help eliminate members of other families from centralized positions of prominence. See "Hegemony over the Social Scene," 240–241.

53 *IL / MARTIRIO / DI / S. EUSTACHIO / Oratorio / Per musica. / Dedicato all'Eccellentissima Signora / Principessa / D. Maria / Ottoboni / Nipote di Nostro Signore / Alessandro VIII. / In Roma, / Nella Stamperia di Gio. Giacomo Komarek / all'Angelo Custode. / Con Licenza de' Superiori.* The libretto is attributed to Cardinal Pietro Ottoboni (under his Arcadian pseudonym, Crateo Pradelini). Franchi notes two different versions of the libretto: one printed by Franco Buagni, 1690, held at Roma Naz. (34.2.A.30.5), with music by G. B. Bianchini; the other is published by Gio. Giacomo Komarek, 1690, and held at Roma Vat. Barb. JJJ v 21. Franchi notes that the characters, scene changes, and text are the same as in the previous version, but the prologue diverges; he makes no reference to the composer for this version. He refers to several exemplars of the Komarek version: another copy at the Vatican (Capp. v 708), at the Casanatense, and at the Conservatory in Brussels. See *Drammaturgia romana: repertorio bibliografico cronologico dei testi drammatici pubblicati a Roma e nel Lazio*, Vol. I: *1600–1700* (hereafter *Drammaturgia romana I*). Sussidi Eruditi 42 (Rome: Edizioni di Storia e Letteratura, 1988) 625–627. Staffieri in her chronology of performances for 1690 notes three different dates from the *Avvisi Marescotti* for performances of *Il martirio di Sant' Eustachio* at the Palazzo della Cancelleria: February 26, March 6, April 1. See Staffieri's chronology, *Colligite fragmenta*, 232. She cites Franchi's mention of G. B. Bianchini as a possible composer, but also notes that the score is likely to have been written by Flavio Lanciani; see her references; Fabio Carboni, Theresa M. Gialdroni, and Agostino Ziino, "Cantate ed arie romane del tardo Seicento nel Fondo Caetani della Biblioteca Corsiniana: repertorio, forme, strutture," *Studi Musicali* 18 (1989): 49–192; and the article on "Lanciani" by Lowell Lindgren in *The New Grove Dictionary of Music and Musicians*, ed. Stanley Sadie, 2nd edn (London: Macmillan, 2001), XIV: 206–207; the author documents that from 1688 to 1702, Lanciani served Cardinal Ottoboni as an "aiutante di camera," resident composer, musician, and

copyist, and set all or part of each of the six operas for which the cardinal had written texts, making him a likely candidate to have composed the work in question.

54 *Argomento/Del SANTO/EUSTACHIO/Attione In Musica./[vaso con fiori]/In Roma,/Nella Stamparia della Reverenda Camera Apostolica./M.DC.XLIII./Con Licenza De'Superiori.* See Franchi, *Drammaturgia romana I*, 251–252.

55 See *Oratorii, overo Melodrammi sacri*, Libro Secondo, 183 (Herczog edition, 75). Herczog's introduction explains that in the preface to his "Secondo Libro", Spagna considered this work an anomaly, but felt that despite its operatic characteristics, its sacred subject made it an appropriate fit in his collection of oratorios (xxvii).

56 St. Eustace (the name itself meaning "fruitful" and of "good fortune") was a second-century Roman general, who amid difficult tests of personal faith, remained strong and sacrificed his family and his own life to uphold his Christian beliefs. St. Eustace was later considered one of the Fourteen Holy Helpers and patron saint for difficult situations. See David Farmer, *The Oxford History of Saints*, 5th edn (Oxford University Press, 2003), 187; *The New Catholic Encyclopedia*, 2nd edn, Vol. V (Washington DC: The Catholic University of America, 2003), 836–837. On Alexander VIII's public welfare programs, see Pastor, *History of the Popes*, Vol. XXXII, 534–535.

57 Franchi, *Drammaturgia romana I*, 626–627; Stefanie Tcharos, "Beyond the Boundaries of Opera: Conceptions of Musical Drama in Rome, 1676–1710" (Ph.D. diss., Princeton University, 2002), 29–32; and more recently, Morelli, "Patronage and Secular Context of the Oratorio in Baroque Rome," 345, n62, who observes the similar genre interplay with *Sant'Eustachio*.

58 "Per adattarsi alle convenienze del tempo si rappresenta in scena un Martiro," from printed libretto of *Il martirio di S. Eustachio* (Komarek edition), by Pietro Ottoboni, held at I-Rc (*Commedia* 81/1), fol. 4v

59 The following letter recognizes how the work, an ostensible opera, was advertised "under the labeling of an oratorio": "Il Sig. Card. Ottobono (Ottoboni) domenica doppo pranzo fece sotto titolo d'oratorio una rappresentazione intitolata Il Martirio di Sant'Eustachio con balletti e mutazioni de scene..." Letter of Abbate Mancini, *Roma e Stato della Chiesa*, Mediceo 3956, Archivio di Stato, Florence, cited in William Holmes, *La Statira by Pietro Ottoboni and Alessandro Scarlatti: The Textual Sources* (New York: Pendragon Press, 1983), 84.

60 The following *avviso* does not even bother to mention the work's implied oratorio association: "Domenica il cardinale Ottoboni fece recitare una bellissima rappresentatione in musica intitolata il Sant'Eustachio, nel palazzo della Cancelleria con nobilissimi habiti, e vaghissime scene..." March 4, 1690, *Avvisi Marescotti* 788, fols. 148–149v, in Staffieri, *Colligite fragmenta*, 90.

61 Howard Smither argues that the term "oratorio" is misused for *Sant'Eustachio* considering the work's structural division into acts, the indications of scene

changes, and the alleged use of costumes by acting characters. Smither, *A History of the Oratorio*, Vol. I, 276.

62 See chapter 1 for details of this work and its production.

63 "Non fù sabato scorso rappresentata l'opera in musica dell'ambasciatore di Spagna, stante un ordine di Sua Santità per esser vicini li giorni santi, onde si è differita per doppo Pasqua." *Avvisi Marescotti* 788, fol. 152, in Staffieri, *Colligite fragmenta*, 91–92.

64 Morelli, "Patronage and Secular Context of the Oratorio in Baroque Rome," 335.

65 Herczog hypothesizes that Spagna may have had Rospigliosi's highly regarded *Sant'Alessio* in mind when constructing his *Sant'Eustachio*, since both works have similar first acts with luxuriant baroque settings, and allegorical representations of morality (Faith in Spagna, Religion in Rospigliosi), see "Introduction," xxvii.

66 Along with the references for Volpicelli, Mattiti, and Olszewski listed in n48, also see the classic studies by Emilio Lavagnino, *Il Palazzo della Cancelleria e la chiesa di San Lorenzo in Damaso*, I palazzi e le case di Roma 1 (Rome: Casa Editrice "Roma," 1924); Arnaldo Rava, *Il teatro Ottoboni nel palazzo della Cancelleria* (Rome: Reale Istituto di Studi Romani, 1942); and Armando Schiavo, *Il Palazzo della Cancelleria* (Rome: Staderini, 1964).

67 See "Il teatro del Cardinale Ottoboni"; and also Mercedes Viale Ferrero, *Filippo Juvarra, scenografo e architetto teatrale* (Turin: Edizioni d'Arte Fratelli Pozzo, 1970); and her more recent survey essay, "Stage and Set," in *Opera on Stage*, ed. Lorenzo Bianconi and Giorgio Pestelli, trans. Kate Singleton (University of Chicago Press, 2002), 60–65; Armando Schiavo, "Il teatro e altre opere del cardinale Ottoboni," *Strenna dei Romanisti* 33 (1972): 344–352; Salvatore Boscarino, "Juvarra scenografo del cardinale Ottoboni," in *Juvarra architetto* (Rome: Officina, 1973), 153–174; Henry Milton, *Filippo Juvarra, Drawings from the Roman Period, 1704–1714*, 2 vols. (Rome: Edizioni dell'Elefante, 1984).

68 The following operas occurred at the Cancelleria during the rest of 1690: on April 9, *La Statira* was reperformed; Lanciani's *Amore e Gratitudine* was performed during the fall; Scarlatti's *Gli equivoci in amore, overo La Rosaura* was also performed in the fall; and *Il Columbo, overo L'india scoperta*, composer unknown with text by Cardinal Ottoboni, was performed on December 28. See Franchi, *Drammaturgia romana I*, 633–636; Staffieri, *Colligite fragmenta*, 230–231. Also see chapter 1 for some discussion of these works.

69 See Volpicelli's appendix of documents for evidence of these preparations during this period, "Il teatro del Cardinale Ottoboni," specifically 690–694. Patricia Waddy describes how, in a typical Roman baroque palace, household furniture was rearranged by the *maestro di camera* according to the requirements of an occasion, and a specialized tradesman known as a *festarolo* or *banderolo* would choose and arrange ornamental hangings for wall embellishment to decorate palace walls. See "Inside the Palace: People and Furnishings," in Walker and Hammond, *Ambiente Barocco*, 28.

70 Volpicelli's research uncovers documents showing that Ottoboni's architects originally planned to construct the theater on the second floor, the level of the cardinal's private apartments, but altered these plans to place the theater on the third floor, in order to accommodate the height of stage and scenery, and that a separate staircase was put in for easy access to the theater. After socializing in the cardinal's apartments, guests could thus simply ascend the stairs and arrive in the theater for the evening's entertainment. See "Il teatro del Cardinale Ottoboni," 682.

71 See the references to a letter of April 29, 1690 from the *Avvisi di Roma*, Busta 67[66], Archivio di Stato, Modena, cited in Holmes, *La Statira: The Textual Sources*, 922. The exact date that the theater at the Cancelleria began operation is not clear from contemporary documents and letters. Saverio Franchi suggests the first performance would have been the oratorio *Sant'Eustachio* on February 26, 1690, *Drammaturgia romana*, Vol. II: *1701–1750* (hereafter *Drammaturgia romana II*), Sussidi Eruditi 45 (Rome: Edizioni di Storia e Letteratura, 1997), cvi. However, documents compiled by Volpicelli, "Il teatro del Cardinale Ottoboni," 689–692, and Holmes, *La Statira: The Textual Sources*, 91–92, indicate that in March–April 1690, only models of the theater had been completed by the architect, Felice del Lino (a pupil of Carlo Fontana), and even as late as October, set designs were still being painted. For further source details on the genesis of the Ottoboni theater, see Volpicelli, "Il teatro del Cardinale Ottoboni."

72 Drawing from contemporary documents, William Holmes indicates that Ottoboni had designs to replace the recently deceased Queen Christina as d'Alibert's partner. See his *La Statira: The Textual Sources*, 79.

73 "Il sud. Card. Ottoboni mutando registro in luogo del Teatro per le Commedie ha risoluto di fare una bella Chiesa nell sua Abbadia di Albano. Vi sono molti i quali credono che il Papa gli habbia fatto dire che i Teatri non sono da ecclesiastici . . . il detto Card. Ottoboni già ha dato principio à far disfare il suo Teatro nella Cancelleria, e non vuol più che si faccia l'altro à San Lorenzo in Lucina benché già ne havesse fatto fare il disegno." *Avvisi di Roma* March 12, 1692, I-Rvat (*Ott. lat.* 3279), fols. 218r–221v.

74 Starting as early as March 1694, documents mention various tasks undertaken for "il teatrino," and in April, after the construction of the theater's skylight, documents start to refer to the theater as "teatro Novo dei Burattini." For a collection of documents on Ottoboni's puppet theater, see Volpicelli's appendix of documents, "Il teatro del Cardinale Ottoboni," specifically 703–725. Also, for a general introduction to the development of mechanical theater in Italy, see Michele Rak, "Le macchine comiche: il sistema del teatro meccanico nel Settecento italiano e alcuni documenti romani di fine secolo," in Volpicelli, *Il teatro a Roma nel Settecento*, Vol. I, 259–319.

75 See Volpicelli appendix, "Il teatro del Cardinale Ottoboni," 711–715, for mention of Paradisi and other traces of evidence of puppet construction.

76 *La Santa Genuinda overo L'innocenza difesa dall'inganno/Dramma Sacro per Musica/L'Anno MDCXCIV/Dedicato all'Eminentiss. e Reverendiss. Principe il Signor Card. Pamphili/In Roma, Per il Komarek. 1694,* libretto copy from I-Rn (*Stampati-Libretti* 34.1.ғ.31/2), 1; score composed for Act I by Giovanni Lorenzo Lulier; Act II, Alessandro Scarlatti; Act III, Carlo Francesco Pollarolo (D-Mbs, F-Pc, GB-Lbl). Volpicelli's collected documents show that preliminary work and copying for a "rappresentazione S. Genuinda" began during 1694, but that it could have been performed for the carnival season of 1695, see "Il teatro del Cardinale Ottoboni," 706. An *avviso* from January 15, 1695 likely refers to the Santa Genuinda puppet performance: "Ieri sera il Card. Ottoboni fece fare la sua Comedia in Musica de Pupazzi con un gran concorso." *Avvisi di Roma,* I-Rvat (Ott. lat. 3359), fol. 24r.

77 There appear to have been two initial versions of this work: one for Christmas 1695, *La Santa Rosalia / Dramma per Musica / Per Anno 1695 / In Roma, MDCXCV / Per Gio: Giacomo Komarek Bohemo alla Fontata di Trevi,* libretto copy from I-Rn (*Stampati-Libretti* 35.9.к.18/2), 1; the other in January 1696 under a revised title, *La Costanza nell'Amor Divino, overo La Santa Rosalia / overo La Santa Rosalia / Dramma Sacro per Musica / Per l'Anno MDCXCVI / In Roma MDCXCV / Per Antonio de Rossi dietro San Silvestro / in Capite à Strada della Vite,* libretto copy from I-Rn (*Stampati-Libretti* 34.1.ᴀ.6/7), 1. For the 1695 production, Staffieri lists the possible composer of the score as Padre Palermino (= B. Aliotti), *Colligite fragmenta,* 252; the score for *La costanza nell'amor divino, overo La Santa Rosalia* had Act I composed by Severo de Luca; Act II, Flavio Lanciani; Act III, Francesco Gasparini. For brief mention of this work, see Lowell Lindgren, "Le opere drammatiche 'romane' di Francesco Gasparini, 1689–1699," in *Francesco Gasparini (1661–1727). Atti del primo convegno internazionale (Camaiore, 19 settembre–1 ottobre 1978),* ed. Fabrizio Della Seta and Franco Piperno (Florence: L. S. Olschki, 1981), 174–175. Volpicelli's collected documents show that work on a "commedia S. Rosalia," was in progress during much of 1695, see "Il teatro del Cardinale Ottoboni," 707–708. An *avviso* from December 31, 1695 reports a puppet performance of a *commedia* at the Cancelleria, which may have been the first *La Santa Rosalia:* "Nell'ultima festa di Natale fu recitata in musica nella Cancelleria una Comedia spirituale con Pupazzi da bravi musici dell'Em.mo Ottoboni." *Avvisi di Roma,* I-Rvat (Ott. lat. 3359), fol. 85v. The *avvisi* during carnival of 1696 seem to refer to more than one puppet *commedia,* but it is likely that the *avviso* of February 4, 1696 could be a post-Christmas follow-up performance of *Santa Rosalia,* although perhaps this one was the revised version, *La costanza nell'amor divino overo La Santa Rosalia:* "Il S. Card. Ottoboni ha fatto (line over word) la recita della seconda Comedia in musica nel suo Teatro de Pupazzi." *Avvisi di Roma,* I-Rvat (Ott. lat. 3361), fol. 10r.

78 Hithero considered lost, a manuscript copy of Ottoboni's *L'amor eroico tra pastori* has been recently identified in the Fondo Campello at Perugia, see Melania

Bucciarelli, *Italian Opera and European Theatre, 1680–1720: Plots, Performers, Dramaturgies* (Turnhout: Brepols, 2000), 113 n28. The score allegedly composed by Carlo Francesco Cesarini for Act I; Act II, Giovanni Lorenzo Lulier; Act III, Giovanni Bononcini. For information regarding further revisions and extant arias from 1705 and 1708, see "Bononcini," by Lowell Lindgren, *The New Grove Dictionary of Music and Musicians*, ed. Stanley Sadie, 2nd edn (London: Macmillan, 2001), III: 874; and his "Le opere drammatiche 'romane' di Francesco Gasparini," 176–177. Ottoboni's pastoral was highly praised as an exemplar of dramaturgical reform by Crescimbeni, who called it "the first to concern itself once more with the old rules, introducing choruses and other qualities pertaining to good comedy." See Robert Freeman's translation of Crescimbeni's *La bellezza della volgar poesia* (1700) in *Opera without Drama*, Studies in Musicology 14 (Ann Arbor, MI: UMI, 1981 [1967]). The work was also praised in a printed sonnet, "Alla Sublime Idea dell'Autore Della Pastorale intitolata L'AMORE EROICO TRA PASTORI, Rappresentata mirabilmente da figurine, in Roma l'anno 1696," I-Rvat (Ott. lat. 3361), fol. 1r.

79 An *avviso* dated March 10, 1696 reports the success of the year's carnival; the machines and stage scenes at the Tordinona received special praise as did the music heard in operas at the Capranica. After the puppet opera hosted by Cardinal Ottoboni at the Cancelleria, the cardinal was said to have lavished guests with copious refreshments: "Hà riportato nel passato carnevale applauso per le machine et apparenze l'opera del Teatro di Tordinona, e per la musica quella di Capranica, et è stata molto piaciuta l'opera de burattini fatta rappresentare dal cardinale Ottoboni nel palazzo della Cancelleria con l'invito di cardinali, cavalieri e dame, havendo fatto dispensare copiosi rinfreschi." *Avvisi Marescotti* 789, fol. 69v, in Staffieri, *Colligite fragmenta*, 124, who notes that this work was probably *L'amor eroico tra pastori* also mentioned in Marx, "Die Musik am Hofe Pietro Kardinal Ottobonis unter Arcangelo Corelli," 150, doc. 101b.

80 See the excerpts 41, 45, and 46 of the *Avvisi Marescotti* transcribed in Staffieri, *Colligite fragmenta*, 69–71.

81 *Il regno di Maria assunta in cielo, oratorio per musica (2p)*, Rome, de Rossi, 1705, see Franchi, *Drammaturgia romana II*, 34. The libretto was penned by Ottoboni with music by Alessandro Scarlatti. For descriptive details of the work and its performance see Morelli, "Patronage and Secular Context of the Oratorio in Baroque Rome," 347; and his "Alessandro Scarlatti maestro di cappella in Roma ed alcuni suoi oratorio: nuovi documenti," *Note d'Archivio per la Storia Musicale*, n.s., 2 (1984): 134–135.

82 For example, we know payments were made on March 31, 1691 to the *maestro di casa*, Arcangelo Spagna, and the resident architect, Felice del Lino, for chimney and/or fireplace cleaning at the Cancelleria, and also for the cleaning and preparation of the fireplace mantel in the room where the oratorio theater was constructed. See transcription of relevant documents cited in Volpicelli, "Il teatro del Cardinale Ottoboni," 693.

83 Olszewski examines Cardinal Ottoboni's use of decorative arts for staging oratorios in the Cancelleria, and suggests that it was possible that Ottoboni used the
Sala Riaria's balconies as platforms for singers and musicians. See "Decorating
the Palace," especially 95.

84 See the *avviso* from December 9, 1690, in the *Avvisi Marescotti*, 788, fol. 215,
Staffieri, *Colligite fragmenta*, 95.

85 Olszewski describes how Cardinal Ottoboni inherited some forty tapestries
from his great-uncle, Pope Alexander VIII, and also commissioned new ones
from the San Michele tapestry workshop in Rome. He hired Domenico
Paradisi to paint a series of *arazzi finti*, between 1689 and 1693, of Old
Testament subjects, and scenes from Tasso's heroic poem, *Gerusalemme liberata*. In 1694, Ottoboni acquired a tapestry depicting the subject of Judith:
"*2rLa Giuditta / Arazzi dell'Eredità Nini / Pezzi N.8 Alti l'uno Ale n.6 ¼*,"
I-Rvat (*Computisteria Ottoboni* 30), fol. 187. This would have been during
the same year that his first *Giuditta* oratorio was performed. Details on this
work cited below. For further background see Edward J. Olszewski, "The
Tapestry Collection of Cardinal Pietro Ottoboni," *Apollo* 116 (1982): 103–111;
see Appendix II, 111 for the specific reference to the *Giuditta* tapestry. Also see
Edith Standen, "Tapestries for a Cardinal-Nephew: A Roman Set Illustrating
Tasso's *Gerusalemme liberata*," *Metropolitan Museum of Art Journal* 16 (1982):
147–164.

86 See "Patronage and Secular Context of the Oratorio in Baroque Rome" for
selection from the text of *Il regno di Maria assunta*, including references to
the War of Spanish Succession. As further background on the possible political
function of the oratorio within this particular Italian period, consult the cases
described and analyzed in Broom, "Political Allegory in Alessandro Melani's
Oratorio *Golia abbattuto*," and Saverio Franchi, "Il principe Livio Odescalchi e
l'oratorio 'politico.'" in *L'oratorio musicale italiano e i suoi contesti (secc. XVII–
XVIII). Atti del convegno internazionale, Perugia, Sagra musicale umbra, 18–
20 settembre 1997*, ed. Paola Besutti (Florence: L. S. Olschki, 2002), 141–258.
For comparisons of the oratorio with the serenata's intended narrative and social
function, see chapter 3 of this book.

87 Morelli cites, among many examples, the palace oratorios under Queen
Christina's sponsorship, which he aptly describes as "a sort of spiritual academy
that invariably included the recital of a sermon (entrusted to a renowned
preacher) inserted between the two music sections, in accordance with the
custom established by the Oratorians." See his "Patronage and Secular Context
of the Oratorio in Baroque Rome," 336.

88 The article cited is from *Foglio di Foligno* (Orietta Sartori, "Notizie di interesse musicale in un antico periodico a stampa: il *Foglio di Foligno*," *Esercizi Musica e Spettacolo* 16–17 (1997–1998): 107), and the work referred to
was likely to have been *La Giuditta*, the music for which was originally composed by Alessandro Scarlatti, though this document notes the music was by

Bernardo Pasquini, who Morelli believes added additional pieces; see Arnaldo Morelli, "Gli oratori di Bernardo Pasquini: problemi di datazione e di committenza," in *Percorsi dell'oratorio romano: da "historia sacra" a melodramma spirituale*, ed. Saverio Franchi (Rome: Istituto di Bibliografia Musicale, 2002), 67–94.

89 Morelli, "Patronage and Secular Context of the Oratorio in Baroque Rome," 350.

90 Using the available lists of data provided in Staffieri's "Cronologia dello spettacolo romano," in *Colligite fragmenta*, 230–265 (for oratorios performed between 1690 and 1700), along with the oratorio libretti listed in Franchi, *Drammaturgia romana*, the appendices in Marx, "Die Musik am Hofe Pietro Kardinal Ottobonis unter Arcangelo Corelli", and Volpicelli, "Il teatro del Cardinale Ottoboni," we gather that the oratorios performed at the Cancelleria were not all that frequent, but that Cardinal Ottoboni also took the opportunity to have his oratorios performed in other locations, such as other private residences, or at the Roman colleges.

91 The first *La Giuditta* penned by the cardinal was initially performed on March 21, 1694, the fourth Sunday of Lent, in the Palazzo della Cancelleria. For further details, see the excerpt of the *Avvisi Marescotti* 788, fol. 502, in Staffieri, *Colligite fragmenta*, 115. The work was originally intended for Lent of 1693; however, Ottoboni's libretto was finished only in late February of that year, leaving Scarlatti little time to complete his score for Lent. For details of the preparation and delay of *La Giuditta*, see Morelli, "Alessandro Scarlatti maestro di cappella in Roma ed alcuni suoi oratori," 131; Roberto Pagano and Lino Bianchi, eds., *Alessandro Scarlatti: catalogo generale delle opere a cura di Giancarlo Rostirolla* (Turin: Edizioni Rai, 1972), 282–283. Subsequent performances of this work seem to have occurred, even ones in which new music by other composers was added, see Morelli, "Patronage and Secular Context of the Oratorio in Baroque Rome," 346. In his study on the circulation of the oratorio in Italy during the seventeenth century, Morelli documents a series of works under the title *La Giuditta*, with music by A. Scarlatti (Rome, 1693–1696; Naples, 1695; Vienna, 1695; Florence, 1700), see "La circolazione dell'oratorio italiano," *Studi Musicali* 1 (1997): 144–145. The manuscript text of Pietro Ottoboni's libretto is held at I-Rvat, Ott. lat. 2360. The first known copy of the score of this first *La Giuditta* is in Naples (I-Nc); another score was found in Morristown, New Jersey (US-MT), see Margery Stomne Selden, "Alessandro Scarlatti's Oratorio *La Giuditta*: A Communication," *Journal of the American Musicological Society* 22 (1969): 305. We know much less about the actual premiere of the second *La Giuditta*, the text of which was composed by Antonio Ottoboni. Staffieri suggests that as early as 1695, the *La Giuditta* performed on Sunday March 13 and Wednesday March 16 (first at the Cancelleria, second at the residence of the Marchesa Buongiovanni) was the second *La Giuditta* version penned by Antonio

Ottoboni, and re-scored by Scarlatti, see *Colligite fragmenta,* 251 (and she later reports another performance of this other *La Giuditta* at the Casa Vidman, performed by Ottoboni's singers and musicians, see 159). However, Michael Talbot and Colin Timms report that an autograph manuscript copy (GB-Ckc) of the second *La Giuditta, a tre voci* (whose libretto location they list as I-MAc, Mozzi-Borgetti [Correr 466], 351–367) is dated Rome, March 1697, see "Music and the Poetry of Antonio Ottoboni (1646–1720)," 401. Furthermore, Marx reports a citation for copies made for a "Giuditta a tre" (with the same personages in Antonio Ottoboni's libretto) recorded in Pietro Ottoboni's "Computisteria," see "Die Musik am Hofe Pietro Kardinal Ottobonis unter Arcangelo Corelli," 151.

92 Alessandro Scarlatti (1660–1725) attracted the attention of the most influential supporters and promoters of music during this era, and he was among the leading composers who wrote cantatas, oratorios, serenatas, instrumental music, and operas for the Roman Arcadian milieu, though much of his career success also occurred in Naples. See several of the following references for key bibliographic sources on Scarlatti, especially those regarding his oratorio composition.

93 Lino Bianchi published both versions of *La Giuditta* in modern edition: Alessandro Scarlatti, *La Giuditta,* in *Gli oratorii di Alessandro Scarlatti,* ed. Lino Bianchi (Rome: De Santis, 1964); *La Giuditta di "Cambridge,"* in *Gli Oratorii di Alessandro Scarlatti,* ed. Lino Bianchi (Rome: De Santis, 1966). From this point on, I will refer to both scores by their traditional association with their library locations (Naples and Cambridge). For further treatment of Scarlatti's *Giuditte,* see Bianchi's *Carissimi, Stradella, Scarlatti e l'oratorio musicale* (Rome: De Santis, 1969); and "Dall'oratorio di Alessandro Scarlatti all'oratorio di Handel," in *Händel e gli Scarlatti a Roma,* ed. Nino Pirrotta and Agostino Ziino (Florence: L. S. Olschki, 1987), 79–92; also see David Poultney, "Scarlatti and the Transformation of the Oratorio," *Musical Quarterly* 59 (1973): 584–601; David Swale, "The 'Judith' Oratorios of Alessandro Scarlatti," *Miscellanea Musicologica* 9 (1977): 145–155; Eleanor Selfridge-Field, "Juditha in Historical Perspective. Scarlatti, Gasparini, Marcello, and Vivaldi," in *Vivaldi veneziano europeo,* ed. Francesco Degrada (Florence: L. S. Olschki, 1980), 135–153; Giorgio Mangini, "*Betulia liberata* e *La morte dell'Oloferne*: momenti di drammaturgia musicale nella tradizione dei 'trionfi di *Giuditta,*'" in *Mozart, Padova e la Betulia liberata: committenza, interpretazione, e fortuna delle azioni sacre metastasiane nel '700. Atti del convegno internazionale di studi 28–30 settembre 1989,* ed. Paolo Pinamonti (Florence: L. S. Olschki, 1991), 145–172; and more recently this author's "Beyond the Boundaries of Opera," 53–84; and Norbert Dubowy, "Le due *Giuditte* di Alessandro Scarlatti," 2. The *La Giuditta* works of Scarlatti have clearly received ample discussion; my contribution in this chapter is not to repeat these analyses, but to take some of the observations made in earlier scholarship and newly apply them within the context and argument of this book so as to reveal

the oratorio as a broader cultural form and a critical lens for viewing opera's trajectory in this period.

94 In 1626, Cardinal Francesco Barberini reported a performance of a *La Juditta* that he heard at the Medici court, and Frederick Hammond notes a reference to a "La Juditta d'Andrea Salvadori," from 1626, in a collection of various manuscript items held at I-Rvat (Barb. lat. 3839), see *Music and Spectacle in Baroque Rome*, 184 n2. There is also evidence of another Judith text, entitled *comedia sacra*, that remains from a 1644 performance at the Seminary of San Pietro in Rome, and appears to have been staged in three acts with a cast of fifteen performers: *Argomento / Della / GIUDITTA / Comedia Sacra / Latino / Recitata da gli Alunni del Seminario / di S. Pietro. /* [stemma del Seminario] */ In Roma, Appresso Manelfo Manelfi. 1644. / Con licenza de' Superiori.* For further details, see Franchi, *Drammaturgia romana I*, 255. More importantly, the Judith and Holofernes story appears to have become more widely set as an oratorio text during the later seventeenth and early eighteenth century. In his study on the circulation of the oratorio in Italy during the seventeenth century, Arnaldo Morelli documents a number of works based on the Book of Judith. See "La circolazione dell'oratorio italiano," 144–145. Besides those by Scarlatti, other works listed are: *Giudith*, music by Giovanni Paolo Colonna (Modena, 1684); *Bettuglia liberata*, also G. P. Colonna (Bologna, 1690); *La Giuditta*, music by G. Fabbrini (Siena, 1693, 1697). Others not listed in Morelli's appendix occurring between 1685 and 1700: *La Giuditta*, music by M. A. Ziani (Mantua, 1686); *Juditha*, music by Gasparini (Rome, 1689). See Claudio Sartori, *I libretti italiani a stampa dalle origini al 1800* (Cuneo: Bertola & Locatelli, *c.*1990–1994), 336–337.

95 As a biblical text, the Book of Judith has frequently raised controversy in several historical contexts, with the recognition of Judith's prayer for God's blessing to deceive Holofernes as the basic moral flaw of the book. The Book of Judith is a deuterocanonical book included in the Septuagint and in the Roman Catholic and Eastern Orthodox Old Testament of the Bible, but excluded by Rabbinical Jews and Protestants. Protestants do not refer to any such texts as deuterocanonical; they are either omitted from the Bible or included in a separate section designated separately as "Apocrypha." See introduction to Book of Judith, in Bruce M. Metzger and Roland E. Murphy, eds., *The New Oxford Annotated Bible with Apocryphal/Deuterocanonical Books* (Oxford University Press, 1991), 20. The question of Judith's erotic potential and her status as a female protagonist as portrayed specifically in oratorios has received some commentary, though a more thorough study has yet to be undertaken. Judith's erotic qualities have been more comprehensively pursued by art historians, including Margarita Stocker's feminist reading of Judith in Western culture in *Judith: Sexual Warrior: Women and Power in Western Culture* (New Haven: Yale University Press, 1998); and Mary D. Garrard, *Artemesia Gentileschi: The Image of the Female Hero in Italian Baroque Art* (Princeton University Press, 1989).

96 Evidence documented in the *Ephemerides cartariae*, March 28, 1675, I-Ras
(Archivio Cartari-Febei, Busta 72), fol. 27 (cc. 1–1v), and cited in Arnaldo
Morelli, "La musica a Roma nella seconda metà del Seicento attraverso
l'Archivio Cartari-Febei," in *La musica a Roma attraverso le fonti d'archivio.*
Atti di convegno internazionale (Roma 4–7 giugno, 1992) ed. Arnaldo Morelli,
Bianca Maria Antolini, and Vera Vita Spagnuolo (Lucca: Libreria Musicale
Italiana Editrice, 1994), 125–126.

97 *L'Amazone/Hebrea./Nelle Glorie/di/Giuditta./Oratorio III./a cinque,* listed as the
third oratorio in the 1708 publication of *Oratorii, overo Melodrammi sacri.*

98 "Discorso intorno a gli oratorii," in *Oratorii, overo Melodrammi sacri,* Libro
Primo, 18 (Herzog edition, 9).

99 Discussed by Dubowy, "Le due *Giuditte* di Alessandro Scarlatti," 264–265.

100 Wendy Heller identifies virtuous figures such as Veremonda, the heroine of
Veremonda l'amazzone di Aragone (Venice, 1653), or *Zenobia* (Venice, 1666),
as women in mid-century opera who neither offered danger through seduction, nor were the embodiment of female power. See "The Queen as King:
Refashioning Semiramide for *Seicento* Venice," *Cambridge Opera Journal* 5,
no. 2 (1993): 113; and more recently "Semiramide and Musical Transvestism,"
in Heller, *Emblems of Eloquence: Opera and Women's Voices in Seventeenth-*
Century Venice (Berkeley: University of California Press, 2003), 220–225. In
general, Paolo Fabbri charts opera's departure in the 1670s–1680s from libretti
that demonstrate erotic type-casting for female characters to other alternatives,
see "Il gusto erotico," in Fabbri, *Il secolo cantante* (Bologna: Il Mulino, 1990),
293–300.

101 Lino Bianchi also suggests that for Roman audiences, Judith may have engendered associations with other contemporary female figures and famous Roman
patrons, such as Queen Christina, Olimpia Aldobrandini, and the Queen of
Poland: Pagano and Bianchi, *Alessandro Scarlatti*, 276.

102 In 1683, Innocent XI initiated a new Holy League (comprising the Holy Roman
Empire, the Venetian Republic, and eventually Poland and Muscovite Russia)
to stand against the Ottoman Empire through the 1680s–1690s until the League
prevailed at the Battle of Senta in 1699, and the Ottomans were forced to sign
the Treaty of Karlowitz. For further background see Asir Arkayin, "The Second
Siege of Vienna and its Consequences," *Revue Internationale d'Histoire Militaire*
46 (1980): 107–117.

103 Another example that touches upon this issue is Susan McClary's approach to
Stradella's *Susanna*, in "Turtles All the Way Down (On the 'Purely Musical')",
in McClary, *Conventional Wisdom: The Content of Musical Form* (Berkeley:
University of California Press, 2000), 1–21.

104 Along with Judith and Holofernes, Morelli cites the incorruptible John the
Baptist against the highly sensualized Salome, noting that the central oppositional dynamic in these canonical oratorio subjects was paradigmatic in tragic
dramas. See "Oratorii ovvero sacre musicali tragedie?," 282–283.

105 Reinhard Strohm adds the following in his discussion of the adoption of tragedy by *dramma per musica*: "The seventeenth and eighteenth centuries regarded the theatre as a moral institution, which was not allowed to cease education and morally improving the spectator ... Beyond that, however, there was the Aristotelian idea of 'catharsis' (purification) through the arousal, in the spectator, of fear of the wicked and sympathy for the good. It gave the theater an ethical purpose, one almost comparable to socially established laws." "*Tolomeo*: Handel's Opera and the Rules of Tragedy," in *Dramma per musica: Italian Opera Seria of the Eighteenth Century* (New Haven: Yale University Press, 1997), 210.

106 For example, at the acclaimed 1708 production of Handel's oratorio *La resurrezione*, held at the Marquis Francesco Maria Ruspoli's Palazzo Bonelli, a large painted backdrop was similarly displayed depicting the moment when Christ's resurrection is announced, with an angel telling Mary Magdalene and Mary Cleophas that Christ has risen from the dead. For descriptions of the performance décor and arrangements, see Rosand, "Handel Paints the Resurrection," especially 9–10.

107 Margarita Stocker discusses several artistic representations of the Judith story throughout history. Among artists in the Renaissance, she notes that the sculptor Donatello (1386–1466) used Judith as an icon for the city of Florence, her heroic actions symbolizing the free republic. In other later paintings of the period she was sometimes classicized, as in Antiveduto Grammatica's (1571–1626) version, with Judith represented in antique armor and helmet, drawing comparisons to Athena, the classical female warrior. Renaissance painters of northern Europe were particularly attracted to the story's erotic qualities and often portrayed Judith as courtesan, as in examples by Dutch artist Jan Metsys. See *Judith: Sexual Warrior*, especially 67–86.

108 For studies of Judith by Gentileschi, see Garrard, *Artemesia Gentileschi*; and Ward Bissel, *Artemisia Gentileschi and the Authority of Art* (University Park, PA: Pennsylvania State University Press, 1999).

109 A great deal of scholarly literature has considered this painting, and more generally, the place and influence of Caravaggio's art in his own time and beyond. For a recent collection of essays that interrogate aspects of Caravaggio's biography and his art's later influence, see Genevieve Warwick, ed., *Caravaggio: Realism, Rebellion, Reception* (Newark, DE: University of Delaware Press, 2006).

110 Slavoj Zizek, "'I Hear You with My Eyes' or The Invisible Master," in *Gaze and Voice as Love Objects*, ed. Renata Salecl and Slavoj Zizek (Durham, NC: Duke University Press, 1996), 93–94.

111 John D. Lyons, "Unseen Space and the Theatrical Narrative: The 'Récit de Cinna,'" *Yale French Studies* 80, *Baroque Topographies: Literature/History/Philosophy* (1991): 71. In *Aesthetics of Opera in the Ancien Régime*,

1647–1785 (Cambridge University Press, 2002), Downing Thomas further clarifies this convention in tragic theater by describing the distinction between conceptions of horror and terror made by contemporary French theater critics: "Horror was a violent and visceral reaction and was to be avoided in tragedy; terror, however, was grounded in an intellectual identification with the tragic characters and had, at least potentially, salutary moral consequences" (166).

112 "Discorso intorno a gli oratorii," in *Oratorii, overo Melodrammi sacri*, Libro Primo, 7 (Herczog edition, 8).

113 See n28.

114 Dubowy, "Le due *Giuditte* di Alessandro Scarlatti," 265.

115 For further details on these aria types, see Dubowy's list, in ibid., 266, though clearly he is most interested in the importance of realistic song, which in both *La Giuditta* oratorios will function as a crucial dramatic peak for the dénouement to occur. In asking whether this approach is isolated to this particular subject and these settings, Dubowy notes that Scarlatti culminates the main action in *Caino* with two arias of realistic song, 269.

116 Ibid., 267.

117 The elderly nurse found in operatic dramas was a familiar stock figure from spoken theater and *commedia dell'arte*. This figure often lent dramas a sense of comic relief, or as in this case, authority and power, which is why it is significant that she is given the role of "singing" Holofernes to sleep. For further background on the presence of nurses in sleep scenes, see Ellen Rosand, *Opera in Seventeenth-Century Venice: The Creation of a Genre* (Berkeley: University of California Press, 1991), 338–342.

118 Dubowy, "Le due *Giuditte* di Alessandro Scarlatti," 268.

119 Among those who probe this quality in some detail are Dubowy, "Le due *Giuditte* di Alessandro Scarlatti"; and Swale, "The 'Judith' Oratorios of Alessandro Scarlatti."

120 A number of examples might effectively demonstrate similar features of affect and composition noted in the 1697 *La Giuditta*. Other Scarlatti oratorios written in the same period or composed after 1697 contain comparable narrative moments that demanded inner reflection enhanced through musical settings; the same could be said of the vivid musical settings of similar reflective moments found in the two Handel oratorios composed for Rome. It is less important here to create a list or catalogue of such examples, than to underline the prevalence, even conventionalization, of this approach during these years.

121 Strohm, "*Tolomeo*: Handel's Opera and the Rules of Tragedy," 210. Though Strohm discusses this particular aesthetic problem in the context of *dramma per musica* of the early eighteenth century, we can see how these same problems are prefigured through the association of the oratorio with tragic drama in earlier decades.

122 For an example of a librettist who expressed misgivings about succumbing to such pressures, see Freeman's discussion of Apostolo Zeno's response to Ludovico Muratori's criticism in *Opera without Drama*, 29–32.

123 See pp. 60–61 for previous discussion.

124 Thomas, *Aesthetics of Opera in the Ancien Régime*, 7.

125 See "Relationships between Artistic and Musical Patronage in the Roman Oratory," 14, for which Morelli cites A. Zuccari, "La politica culturale dell'Oratorio romano nella seconda metà del Cinquecento," *Storia dell'arte* 41 (1981): 81.

126 Morelli notes this curtailment was particularly swift regarding the practice of palace oratorios. He cites Saverio Franchi's *Drammaturgia romana II* as a source for charting the chronology of musical entertainment, including oratorios printed in Rome during the first half of the eighteenth century. See his point discussed in "Patronage and Secular Context of the Oratorio in Baroque Rome," 350–351.

3 The serenata's discourses of duality

1 Regarding Rome and Naples, the most comprehensive study to date of the serenata in the late seventeenth and early eighteenth century remains Thomas Griffin's "The Late Baroque Serenata in Rome and Naples: A Documentary Study with Emphasis on Alessandro Scarlatti" (Ph.D. diss., University of California, Los Angeles, 1983); also see Griffin's "Alessandro Scarlatti e la serenata a Roma e Napoli," in *La musica a Napoli durante il Seicento. Atti del convegno internazionale di studi (Napoli, 11–14 aprile 1985)*, ed. Domenico Antonio D'Alessandro and Agostino Ziino (Rome: Torre d'Orfeo, 1987), 351–368. Regarding Venice, the most comprehensive work has been undertaken by Michael Talbot whose scholarship has also helped define the genre, see "The Serenata in Eighteenth-Century Venice," *Royal Musical Association Research Chronicle* 18 (1982): 1–50; also "Vivaldi's Serenatas: Long Cantatas or Short Operas?" in *Venetian Music in the Age of Vivaldi*, ed. Michael Talbot (Burlington, VT: Ashgate, 1999), 67–96. Some of the more recent studies on the serenata both within and beyond Italy include Norbert Dubowy, "Ernst August, Giannettini und die Serenata in Venedig (1685–86)," *Analecta Musicologica: Veröffentlichungen der musikgeschichtlichen Abteilung des Deutschen Historischen Instituts in Rom* 30, nos. 1–2 (1998): 167–235; Hans Joachim Marx, "Bemerkungen zu szenischen Aufführungen barocker Oratorien und Serenaten," *Basler Jahrbuch für historische Musikpraxis* 23 "Barockoper: Buhne – Szene – Inszenierung" (1999): 133–150; Carolyn Gianturco, "The 'Staging' of Genres Other than Opera in Baroque Italy," in *Music in the Theater, Church, and Villa: Essays in Honor of Robert Lamar Weaver and Norma Wright Weaver*, ed. Susan Parisi (Warren, MI: Harmonie Park Press, 2000), 113–129; Malcolm Boyd, "The Italian Serenata and Related Genres in Britain and Germany: Some Observations," in *Giacomo Francesco Milano e il ruolo dell'aristocrazia nel*

patrocinio delle attivita musicali nel secolo XVIII, ed. Gaetano Pitarresi (Reggio Calabria: Laruffa Editore, 2001), 515–527; Brian Trowell, "*Acis, Galatea and Polyphemus*: A 'serenata a tre voci'?" in *Music and Theatre: Essays in Honour of Winton Dean*, ed. Nigel Fortune (Cambridge University Press, 1987), 31–94; and a collection of essays edited by Siegfried Schmalzriedt that consider Handel's 1708 *Aci, Galatea e Polifemo* in *Ausdrucksformen der Musik des Barock: Passionsoratorium, Serenata, Rezitativ. Veröffentlichungen der Internationalen Handel-Akademie* (Laaber: Laaber Verlag, 2002); along with Wolfgang Ruf, "Dramatik und Lyrik in den Oratorien und Serenaten Handels," *Göttinger Händel-Beiträge* 9 (2002): 21–36. The most current publications have emerged from a 2003 conference recently published as *La serenata tra Seicento e Settecento: musica, poesia, scenotecnica. Atti del convegno internazionale di studi (Reggio Calabria, 16–17 maggio 2003)*, 2 vols., ed. Nicolò Maccavino (Reggio Calabria: Laruffa Editore, 2007). Of especial relevance from this collection are the following essays: Louise Stein, "'Una música de noche, que llaman aquí serenata': A Spanish Patron and the Serenata in Rome and Naples," Vol. II, 333–372; Michael Talbot, "'Loving Without Falling in Love': Pietro Paolo Bencini's Serenata *Li due volubili*," Vol. II, 373–396; Teresa Chirico, "L'inedita serenata alla regina Maria Casimira di Polonia: Pietro Ottoboni committente di cantate e serenate (1689–1708)," Vol. II, 397–450; Nicolò Maccavino, "La serenata a Filli *Tacete aure tacete* e altre serenate datate 1706 di Alessandro Scarlatti," Vol. II, 451–522; Elena Tamburini, "Luoghi teatrali per la serenata nella Roma del Seicento. Il falso convito di Gian Lorenzo Bernini," Vol. II, 523–546. For a recent general survey, see my "The Serenata in the Eighteenth Century," in *The Cambridge History of Eighteenth-Century Music*, ed. Simon Keefe (Cambridge University Press, 2009), 492–512.

2 "Ora sì fatte cantate, quando si mettono al pubblico, soglion farsi di notte tempo, e si dicono Serenate; e molte ne abbiamo ascoltate, che sono state fatte con soma magnificenza, e splendor da gli Ambasciadori, e da altri Principi, e Personaggi di questa gran Corte." From Crescimbeni's *Commentari del Canonico Gio. Mario Crescimbeni custode d'Arcadia intorno alla sua Istoria della volgar poesia*, Vol. I (Rome: de'Rossi, 1702), 241. As a whole the *Commentari* functioned as a detailed compendium of definitions of Italian poetry that followed the author's attempt at a comprehensive history of Italian literature, *L'istoria della volgar poesia*, first published in Rome in 1698.

3 Buonaccorsi, a Florentine poet, was admitted to Rome's Academy of Arcadians in 1692 (Pseudonym: Astilo Fezzoneo); he authored several serenatas and oratorios performed in Rome during the early eighteenth century. Bencini (*c*.1670–1755) is listed as composer in two separate manuscript scores of *Le gare festive* (I-Rvat, Barb. lat. 4179 and 4228; however, a manuscript hand notes on the first folio of 4179 that the opening concerto for this version was by "Sig.ʳ Carlo Ferrini Virtuoso del Sig.ʳ Prencipe di Palestrina"). Bencini had already set texts by Buonaccorsi, for example, the oratorio *L'innocenza protetta* commissioned by the Confraternità della Pietà dei Fiorentini in 1700. In 1702 he was considered

by the Arcadian custodian, Giovanni Mario Crescimbeni, as one of the great master composers for the court of Rome. See *Commentari*, Vol. I, 239–240. By 1703 he was working as *maestro di cappella* at the German church of Santa Maria dell'Anima. For recent scholarship on Bencini's compositional career, see Jean Lionnet, "Introduction" to *La Cappella Giulia*, Vol. I: *I vespri nel XVIII secolo*, ed. Jean Lionnet (Lucca: Libreria Musicale Italiana, 1995), xxvi–xxix; as well as his entry on Bencini in vol. III of *New Grove Dictionary of Music and Musicians*, ed. Stanley Sadie, 2nd edn (London: Macmillan, 2001), 224–225; Rainer Heyink's article, "Pietro Paolo Bencini, 'uno de' più scelti maestri della corte di Roma,'" *Händel-Jahrbuch* 46 (2000): 101–124; and most recently, Talbot, "'Loving without Falling in Love." For a short commentary on *Le gare festive* and a translation of the Valesio description of its performance, see Malcolm Boyd, "Rome: The Power of Patronage," in *The Late Baroque Era: From the 1680s to 1740*, ed. George J. Buelow (Englewood Cliffs, NJ: Prentice Hall, 1993), 60–63. Also see my "The Serenata in Early 18th-Century Rome: Sight, Sound, Ritual, and the Signification of Meaning," *Journal of Musicology* 23, no. 4 (2006): 528–568, which provided some of the material and inspired part of the analysis that forms this chapter.

4 Franco Piperno clarifies the term "sinfonia" and the range of its use in the late seventeenth-century context to mean (1) a composition of many instruments juxtaposed against other vocal pieces; (2) an independent instrumental work; (3) an instrumental work written to accompany a vocal piece, and functioning as introductory or interlocutory material. See "'Anfione in Campidoglio': presenza corelliana alle feste per i concorsi dell'Accademia del Disegno di San Luca," in *Nuovissimi studi corelliani. Atti del terzo congresso internazionale*, ed. Sergio Durante and Pierluigi Petrobelli (Florence: L. S. Olschki, 1982), 151–208; see esp. 163–164. Also see "La sinfonia strumentale del primo Seicento," *Studi Musicali* 4 (1975): part 1, 145–168; 5 (1976): part 2, 95–141; and Peter Allsop, "Problems of Ascription in the Roman Sinfonia of the Late Seventeenth Century: Colista and Lonati," *The Music Review* 50, no. 1 (1989): 34–44.

5 Mention must also be made of the profound influence on instrumental writing, the rise of large ensemble music, and in general, the prominence of string playing and virtuosity of Arcangelo Corelli's presence in Rome. In his history of deceased Arcadians, Crescimbeni acknowledges that Corelli was the first to introduce to Rome the concept of the "sinfonia" consisting of such number and variety of instruments; see *Notizie istoriche degli Arcadi morti*, 3 vols. (Rome: de'Rossi, 1720), Vol. I, 250. On Corelli's orchestras, see Franco Piperno, "Le orchestre di Arcangelo Corelli," in *L'invenzione del gusto: Corelli and Vivaldi*, ed. Giovanni Morelli (Milan: Ricordi, 1982), 42–48; Peter Allsop, *Arcangelo Corelli: New Orpheus of our Times* (Oxford University Press, 1999), especially 27–66, 139–52; also John Spizter and Neal Zaslaw, "Corelli's Orchestra," in *The Birth of the Orchestra: History of an Institution, 1650–1815* (Oxford University Press, 2004), 105–136.

6 Spitzer and Zaslaw, *The Birth of the Orchestra*, 123.

7 A term used by Don Handelman, in *Models and Mirrors: Towards an Anthropology of Public Events* (Cambridge University Press, 1990), 41.

8 It is important to note that most other baroque festivities and spectacles had by this time lost much of their public character. Joust, dance, and theater had begun to retreat from the public sphere into the enclosures of the protected private world of nobility, what Jürgen Habermas interprets as symptomatic of absolutist exclusion in the face of an emerging, modern public state. Faced with this predicament, it is surprising that the public aspect of the serenata persisted in the Roman context, and in fact, became more prominent still. See the section "Remarks on the Type of Representative Publicness," in Habermas's *The Structural Transformation of the Public Sphere: An Inquiry into the Category of Bourgeois Society*, trans. Thomas Burger, with assistance from Frederick Lawrence (Cambridge, MA: The MIT Press, 1989), 5–14.

9 Chapter XII in Book IV of Crescimbeni's *Commentari*, Vol. I, 236–241.

10 See n2 for the quotation of this passage.

11 Crescimbeni, *Commentari*, Vol. I, 236.

12 Ibid., 240.

13 Ibid. For background on the historical traditions of poetry and music in this period, see Robert Holzer, "Music and Poetry in Seventeenth-Century Rome: Settings of the Canzonetta and Cantata Texts of Francesco Balducci, Domenico Benigni, Francesco Melosio, and Antonio Abati" (Ph.D. diss., University of Pennsylvania, 1990).

14 Crescimbeni's *Commentari*, Vol. I, 238, 240. For background on the Accademia del Disegno performances, see Piperno, "'Anfione in Campidoglio," as well as the same author's "Musica e musicisti per l'Accademia del Disegno di San Luca (1716–1860)," in *La musica a Roma attraverso le fonti d'archivio. Atti del convegno internazionale (Roma 4–7 giugno, 1992)*, ed. Arnaldo Morelli, Bianca Maria Antolini and Vera Vita Spagnuolo (Lucca: Libreria Musicale Italiana, 1994), 553–563.

15 In *Colligite fragmenta: la vita musicale romana degli "Avvisi Marescotti" (1683–1707)* (Lucca: Libreria Musicale Italiana, 1990), Staffieri organizes references to musical activities found in her compiled transcriptions of the *avvisi* by genre/function categories. Though she lists certain serenatas in her "Scheda 3: Serenate, trattenimenti musicali, feste da ballo, conversazioni, recreazioni," she places those serenatas intended for public festivals in her "Scheda 5: Feste pubbliche con presenza musicale," for which she notes music occupies a more ancillary position (20).

16 Arnaldo Morelli, "La musica a Roma nella seconda metà del Seicento attraverso l'Archivio Cartari-Febei," in Morelli *et al.*, *La musica a Roma attraverso le fonti d'archivio*, 114 n23.

17 See Gloria Staffieri, "Arcangelo Corelli compositore di 'sinfonie.' Nuovi documenti," in *Studi corelliani IV. Atti del quarto congresso internazionale (Fusignano,*

4–7 settembre 1986), ed. Pierluigi Petrobelli and Gloria Staffieri, for the series Quaderni della Rivista Italiana di Musicologia 22 (Florence: L. S. Olschki, 1990), 349–350.

18 Ibid. For a comparison of similar ideas, though argued through a different frame of analysis, see Gary Tomlinson's chapter "Early Modern Opera," in *Metaphysical Song: An Essay on Opera* (Princeton University Press, 1999), esp. 42–61.

19 In his descriptions of tournaments, jousts, carousels, and other public spectacles, Claude Ménestrier credits the Italians with providing the sixteenth-century model for later stagings of courtly spectacle. See especially his "Inventions ingénieuses pour les spectacles publics," in *Traité des turnois, iuostes, carrousels, et autre spectacle publics* (Lyon, 1669), 1–8. For more on the *intermedio* as a form of courtly festival, see Iain Fenlon, "Music and Festival," in *Europa Triumphans: Court and Civic Festivals in Early Modern Europe*, Vol. I, ed. J. R. Mulryne, Helen Watanabe-O'Kelly, and Margaret Shewring (Burlington, VT: Ashgate, 2004), 47–55.

20 The serenata's "publicness" appears to embody all three of the central features that Lorenzo Bianconi clarifies as endemic to "public" music: "attributes of authority, pedagogical requisite of the ruling classes, and instrument of propaganda and persuasion." For Bianconi's nuanced reading of "public" and "publicity" as a dynamic concept in the seventeenth century, see "Musical Publicity," in *Music in the Seventeenth Century* (originally published in Italian as *Il Seicento* by Edizioni di Torino, Turin, 1982), trans. David Bryant (Cambridge University Press, 1987), 65–73: for quotation, 65.

21 Habermas, *The Structural Transformation of the Public Sphere*, 11. Also see Peter Burke's description of this same phenomenon in his chapter "Popular Culture and Social Change," in *Popular Culture in Early Modern Europe* (New York: Harper and Row, 1978), 244–287.

22 See chapter 1 for further background.

23 See her specific reference to Rome's cosmopolitan political culture in *Civic Politics in the Rome of Urban VIII* (Princeton University Press, 1992), 39–40.

24 Thomas Dandelet, *Spanish Rome 1500–1700* (New Haven: Yale University Press, 2001), 202. Though the book emphasizes Spain's hegemonic intentions in Rome, the author carefully depicts a Spanish–Roman relationship based on trade of favors. Spanish ambassadors, courtiers, and clerics offered protection and wealth (in wide-ranging forms of patronage) to the Papal States, in return for favors and concessions made to their king. The attraction for Rome in this exchange was a gain in political and economic stability, as well as cultural and religious influence within and beyond the Italian peninsula.

25 Here it is useful to call upon art and architecture historians who have surveyed the effects of civic and religious politics upon Rome's early modern urbanism; see chapter 1 for key sources on this subject. Specific to the matters discussed here, see Thomas Dandelet, "Setting the Noble Stage in Baroque Rome: Roman Palaces, Political Contest, and Social Theater, 1600–1700," in *Life and the Arts in*

the Baroque Palaces of Rome: Ambiente Barocco, ed. Stefanie Walker and Frederick Hammond (New Haven: Yale University Press for the Bard Graduate Center for Studies in the Decorative Arts, 1999), 46, for a more focused study on the effects of French and Spanish Habsburg conflicts on Roman urbanism between 1600 and 1700.

26 In 1647, the new Ambassador to Rome, Inigo Veles de Guevara, Count of Oñate, bid on the Monaldeschi palace, which the Spanish had been renting since the 1630s. Through a series of complex negotiations, the palace and four houses next to it were purchased to form the first embassy owned by a foreign power in Rome. For details, see Dandelet's *Spanish Rome*, 205; for the classic historical study of the piazza, also see Luigi Salerno, *Piazza di Spagna* (Naples: Di Mauro, 1967).

27 Several of these images have been reprinted in a number of publications. However, for a source that contains a reprint of the four mentioned here and a thorough cataloguing of their documentation along with similar images, see Maurizio Fagiolo dell'Arco's *La festa barocca. Corpus delle feste a Roma*, Vol. I (Rome: De Luca, 1997), a revised and enlarged edition of his and Silvia Carandini's *L'effimero barocco: strutture della festa nella Roma del '600*, Vol. I, catalogue (Rome: Bulzoni Editore, 1977). For images listed above, see *Festa barocca*, 409, 512, 533, 539. In *The Birth of the Orchestra*, Spitzer and Zaslaw point out how such images of serenatas used a "telescoping" convention typical of engravings in this period, in which *all* significant aspects of a performance were included in a single picture. The authors note that fireworks were rarely set off simultaneously with musical performances, unless during percussion and brass fanfares. See 123.

28 For a survey and catalogue of descriptive accounts of these serenatas which serve to show how this genre could be used to amplify nationalist sentiments, see Arnaldo Morelli's transcriptions of Carlo Cartari's *Ephemerides cartariae* in "La musica a Roma," especially document 7 (121), the *relazione* describing the 1661 "festeggiamenti per la nascita del Delfino di Francia," in which the author identifies the singers as the great castrati Giuseppe Vecchi and Giuseppe Fede, who Morelli adds, were supported for this event by the Francophile Cardinal Antonio Barberini; and also document 57 (130) describing the 1681 *Serenata a tre* sponsored by the Spanish ambassador, the marqués del Carpio, who purposely organized his serenata to honor the name day of Marie Louise of Orléans, Queen of Spain, on the very feast day of San Luigi, the French national celebration.

29 In her recently published essay on the serenata and its Spanish patronage, Louise Stein makes it clear that the serenata was not native to Spain. Her research examines those of Gaspar de Haro y Guzmán, marqués del Carpio (Spanish ambassador in Rome from 1677 to 1682), and argues that as a patron, Carpio maintained a strong Spanish aesthetic in the entertainments he sponsored and offered. Thus, even for a *non*-Spanish genre like the serenata (which was not

among the ambassador's favored entertainments), his inclination was to maintain Spanish influences, revealing the extent to which, as patron, he probably directed some of the creative and musical choices with a surprisingly heavy hand. See Stein, "'Una música de noche, que llaman aquí serenata.'" In "Fêtes et traditions espagnoles à Rome au XVIIe siècle," in *Barocco romano e barocco italiano: il teatro, l'effimero, l'allegoria*, ed. Marcello Fagiolo and Maria Luisa Madonna (Rome: Gangemi, 1985), 117–134, Martine Boiteux may be correct to note that documentary evidence of the period highlights the Spanish propensity for extensive forms of illumination (i.e., candles, torches, and fireworks) (119). I believe, however, that this characterization may simplify the extent to which certain traits and conventions were specifically Spanish in the Roman context.

30 Fenlon, "Music and Festival," 47.

31 Drawing on social anthropologist Robert Redfield's theories of the "great and little tradition," respectively elite and non-elite cultures (*Peasant Society and Culture* [University of Chicago Press, 1956]), Burke refines and complicates this binary by asserting that Redfield's definition is both too narrow and too wide. It is too wide because it treats popular culture too monolithically and homogeneously. It is too narrow because it denies the possibility of upper-class participation in popular culture. For Burke's complication of early modern's "bi-culturalism," see *Popular Culture in Early Modern Europe*, 23–64, esp. 28–29.

32 After the six treaties of Nijmegen (1678–1679), Spain ceded Burgundy and parts of Belgium to France, and in 1686 joined the Holy Roman Empire, the German lands, and Sweden as the League of Augsburg in defiance of French military aggression.

33 Stein's research on the Spanish patronage in Rome reveals an important contrast between Carpio and his nephew Luis Francisco de la Cerda y Aragón, the marqués de Cogolludo, who assumed the role of ambassador in Rome in 1687. The heavy Spanish influence that had characterized much of Carpio's entertainments had given way in this period under Cogolludo to one that was more Italianate, demonstrating a propensity to appropriate local customs as a path toward smoother and more fluid diplomacy between the Spanish and Roman aristocracy. See "A Spanish Patron and the Serenata in Rome and Naples," 352–353.

34 Dandelet suggests that the *chinea* and other such ceremonies dramatized the notion of Spain acting in the role of dutiful son fulfilling his promise to the demanding papal father (*Spanish Rome*, 6). He offers specific instances in which Spanish monarchs achieved better "good son" status as compared with France; for example, in 1687, when Innocent XI abolished the autonomy and diplomatic immunity of neighborhoods around embassies. France was outraged and reacted with heightened aggression, whereas Charles II made sure to have his envoys compliantly follow papal orders (*Spanish Rome*, 212–213).

35 Dandelet characterizes this relationship as particularly fragile but extremely strategic. From as early as the mid-sixteenth century, Spanish monarchs realized how important it was to maintain noble privileges of Roman landowners, such as the Colonnas who owned large territories in the Kingdom of Naples. The relationship was a delicate balance of powers: keeping the Colonnas happy allowed the viceroy to maintain stability, and yet controlling the lands of powerful Roman nobles was a large favor Spain offered the papacy, whose rule was frequently threatened by prominent local families with independent interests (*Spanish Rome*, 49). For a history of the Colonna family, see Filadelfo Mugnos, *Istoria della augustissima famiglia Colonna* (Venice: Turrini, 1658); Domenico De Sanctis, *Columnensium procerum imagines, et memorias nonnullas* (Rome: A. Bernabò, 1675); and Prospero Colonna, *I Colonna dalle origini all'inizio del secolo XIX* (Rome: Serono, 1927).

36 Lorenzo Colonna was a powerful figure in both Spain and Rome. He held the prestigious position of viceroy of Aragon, grand constable of the Kingdom of Naples, from 1679 to 1681, and in 1682 he opened a private theater within his palace in Rome, which inaugurated an important venue for musical drama and theater culture in the papal capital during the conservative reign of Innocent XI Odescalchi (1676–1689); see chapter 1 for further details. The Spanish did not always embrace Lorenzo's cultural influence in Rome wholeheartedly. Art and theater historian Elena Tamburini notes how the marqués del Carpio was often in subtle competition with the Contestabile, and capitalized on opportunities to outdo the Roman prince with his own entertainments, dramas, and musical spectacles at the Palazzo di Spagna. See *Due teatri per il principe: studi sulla committenza teatrale di Lorenzo Onofrio Colonna (1659–1689)* (Rome: Bulzoni Editore, 1997), 14.

37 Morelli's transcriptions of Cartari's chronicles ("La musica a Roma," doc. 65, 132), Staffieri's transcriptions of the *Avvisi Marescotti* (*Colligite fragmenta*, 78), along with Griffin's excerpts of documentation ("The Late Baroque Serenata," 120–129) all testify to the grandeur of this occasion. Griffin proposes that Cogolludo's serenata, *Applauso musicale à 5 voci*, was likely composed by Bernardo Pasquini (evidence includes the fact that the *Applauso musicale* libretto mentions a "Reina Ibera," a clear reference to Queen Marie Louise; see 127). For details on this last point and the problem of the serenata's authorship, see Morelli, "La musica a Roma," 115.

38 The full quote is republished in Renata Bossa, "Corelli e il cardinal Benedetto Pamphilij. Alcune notizie," in *Nuovissimi studi corelliani. Atti del terzo congresso internazionale (Fusignano 4–7 settembre 1980)*, ed. Sergio Durante and Pierluigi Petrobelli (Florence: L. S. Olschki, 1982), 218–222 (cf. Morelli, "La musica a Roma," 116, and n7). This performance is famously rendered in the engraving by Vincenzo Mariotti, *Il colle di Trinità de' Monti con la festa*, 1687; for further background see Fagiolo dell'Arco, *La festa barocca*, 532–534.

39 The authors suggest that no accounts mention Corelli specifically, but that given his pre-eminent position, it would be difficult to imagine that anyone else had organized and directed an orchestra quite so large as for this occasion. Spitzer and Zaslaw, *The Birth of the Orchestra*, 122.

40 Our understanding is that this serenata was *Cantata per musica a tre voci*, a work scored by Severo de Luca with libretto by Francesco Maria Paglia (both well-known artists working within the Roman milieu); see Griffin, "The Late Baroque Serenata," 145–146, for further details of this performance.

41 In his dissertation "A Bibliographic Scrutiny of Dramatic Works Set by Giovanni and his Brother Antonio Maria Bononcini" (Ph.D. diss., Harvard University, 1972), Lowell Lindgren notes that Cogolludo inherited one of the largest fortunes in Spain upon the death of his father in 1691. Lindgren proposes that this inheritance gave the ambassador the resources to become a principal patron of the Tordinona; similarly, Filippo could also afford to patronize public theater, as he inherited the Colonna fortune upon his father's death in 1689.

42 *Eraclea, o vero Il ratto delle Sabine* was first penned by librettist Nicolò Minato and composed by Antonio Draghi for a 1674 performance in Vienna. Lindgren explains that the extent to which the text was altered by Stampiglia or the number of changes and additions to arias by Bononcini is not known. Lindgren cites a number of *avvisi* which attest to the extent to which the 1692 version was seen by audiences as a failure, in part because of the work's length and tedious musical setting. Silvio Stampiglia (1664–1725) was a well-known librettist of this era, writing oratorios, serenatas, and operas (some as resettings of previous works, others as originals). His success as a musico-dramatic poet made him one of the most sought-after librettists of his time. Giovanni Bononcini (1670–1747) was the son of the composer, theorist, and violinist Giovanni Maria Bononcini, and became a string player, singer, and eventually renowned composer of vocal dramatic music. His success with opera eventually made him famous throughout Europe and he was regarded as the touchstone of Italian taste and a new musico-dramatic style that began to coalesce around 1700. For the most comprehensive discussion of Stampiglia and Bononcini's artistic relationship, see Lindgren, "A Bibliographic Scrutiny of Dramatic Works," 22–40; regarding *Eraclea* see 29; on their collaboration on serenatas in Rome, see especially 34–40.

43 *La nemica d'amore*, 3vv, Palazzo Colonna, August 10, 1692; *La nemica d'amore fatta amante*, 3vv, Palazzo Colonna, August 10, 1693; *La costanza non gradita nel doppio d'amore d'Aminta*, 3vv, Palazzo Colonna, August 17, 1694; *La notte festiva*, 3vv, Piazza di Spagna, August 5, 1695; *Amore non vuol diffidenza*, 3vv, Palazzo Colonna, August 10, 1695; *Amor per amore*, 4vv, Palazzo Colonna, August 10, 1696. Lindgren reports that the serenatas were likely to celebrate the name day of Colonna's and Cogolludo's wives, or also may have commemorated their wives' birthdays: August 10 for San Lorenzo; August 5 for Santa Maria delle Neve. Lindgren, "A Bibliographic Scrutiny of Dramatic Works," 36.

44 My survey of descriptive documentation in *avvisi* for these dates indicates that, except for the 1692 performance of *La nemica d'amore* which was held "in casa del contestabile," these were performed in the courtyard of the palace, which Lindgren notes was located in the Piazza Scossacavalli, ibid. An *avviso* describing the 1695 performance of *Amore non vuol diffidenza* is particularly instructive for understanding at least some parameters of the organization, attendees, and even tone of the event. As was typical of *avviso* language, the document stresses the high quality of the guests, by including specific names of some of the invitees, their connections to each other and to the patrons, where some were placed to view the performance, and how they were lavished afterwards with fine refreshments. For the original documentation of this *avviso* for August 20, 1695, see Staffieri, *Colligite fragmenta*, 122.

45 *Applauso musicale a quattro voci, al Giorno Natalizio dell'Illustrissima & Eccelentissima Signora D. Maria de Giron, e Sandoval, Duchessa di Medina Celi Ambascitrice di Spagna, &c. Parole di Francesco Maria Paglia, Musica di Gio: Lorenzo Lulier, Concerti d'Arcangelo Corelli, Che lo consacra a Sua Ecc.za* (Rome: Komarek, 1693). The copy of the libretto cited here is preserved in I-Rc, Vol. Misc. 1646.

46 In particular see Hans Joachim Marx, "Unveröffentlichte Kompositionen Arcangelo Corellis," in *Studi corelliani. Atti del primo congresso internazionale (Fusignano, 5–8 settembre 1968)*, ed. Adriano Cavicchi, Oscar Mischiati, and Pierluigi Petrobelli (Florence: L. S. Olschki, 1972), 53–61; Gloria Staffieri's article "Arcangelo Corelli compositore di 'sinfonie,'" includes the most recent discussion of *Applauso musicale*, see 339–341.

47 Staffieri, "Arcangelo Corelli compositore di 'sinfonie,'" 339.

48 *Cintia*: "D'un Eroina Ibera/Cintia risplender brama/Più del'usato ancor." *Notte*: "E à celebrarne il nome/La Notte cieca, e nera/Vol cinger l'altre chiome/D'insolito splendor." The copy of the libretto cited here is preserved in I-Rc, Vol. Misc. 1645.

49 Only two arias from this serenata score remain: "Fece un misto di Gigli" and "Or che il Sol dormendo," I-Moe (Campori H.6.16), fols. 65–71r, 81–82r. No other parts or instrumental sections survive. I am grateful to Professor Lowell Lindgren for pointing me to the specifics of this reference.

50 *Apollo*: "Su la gemmata mia cetra d'oro/L'Eccelsa Donna io canterò,/E cinto il crine d'eterno alloro/L'alte sue glorie sentir farò." I-Rc, Vol. Misc. 1645 (6), 10.

51 The following are excerpts from this dialogue: *Apollo* (recit.): "Io Signor delle Muse/Sul Tessalo Parnasso/A immortalare i pregi suoi supremi/Da loro ordir farò Canti, e Poemi." And then followed an excerpt within recitative sung by *Cintia*: "Là nella bella Arcadia/Serbo mille Pastori/E cento Ninfe, e cento,/Che in soave concento/Di cose non volgari ergono il canto,/Questi d'immortal vanto/Spiegheranno alti metri." I-Rc, Vol. Misc. 1645 (6), 13–14.

52 It is worth noting that libretto copies of both *La notte festiva* and *Amore non vuol diffidenza* were saved in the Arcadian archive, what Crescimbeni called the

serbatoio. See I-Ra, *Accademia Letteraria Italiana-Arcadia*, Ms.5.156, 242r–249v; Ms.5.157, 150r–257v.

53 See Crescimbeni, *L'Arcadia del Canonico Gio. Mario Crescimbeni* (Rome: de'Rossi, 1708), 345.

54 For the significance of Apollo to the Academy of Arcadians, see Susan M. Dixon, *Between the Real and the Ideal: The Accademia degli Arcadi and its Garden in Eighteenth-Century Rome* (Newark, DE: University of Delaware Press, 2006), 63; and Vernon Hyde Minor, *The Death of the Baroque and the Rhetoric of Good Taste* (Cambridge University Press, 2006), 143–144.

55 The work's title page reads: "In applauso alla real Casa di Francia con occasione della nascita del serenissimo Duca di Bertagna, festeggiata dall'illustriss., ed ecellentiss. Signore, il signor principe di Palestrina D. Urbano Barberini Grande di Spagna di prima classe, e Cavaliere del Toson d'Oro. Cantata a tre voci dell'abb. Giacomo Buonaccorsi. Dedicata all'eccelentissima Signora, la signora D. Isabella Maria Giron duchessa d'Uzeda ambasciatrice di Spagna." The copy of the libretto cited here is preserved in I-Rli, 171.I.19.

56 Several different *avvisi* document aspects of this serenata, including: I-Rvat (Ott. lat. 2732), 164r–v; I-Rsc (35.A.16), 67v, 69r; I-Rn (fondo Vittorio Emanuele 790), 362r–v, transcribed in Staffieri, *Colligite fragmenta*, 158–159; Francesco Valesio's *Diario di Roma*, Vol. III: 1704–1707, ed. Gaetana Scano in collaboration with Giuseppe Graglia (Milan: Longanesi, 1977–1979), 150–154 (hereafter cited as Valesio, *Diario di Roma*). Valesio's *Diario* provides the most detailed account of *Le gare festive* and of the 1704 events surrounding the Duke of Brittany's birth. I draw some of my translations of Valesio from Thomas Griffin's "The Late Baroque Serenata." Much of this excerpt is also translated by Boyd in "Rome: The Power of Patronage," 61–62.

57 "Nella sera in Piazza di Spagna al Sereno dell Stelle e senza altra luce si radunò un meraviglio di Popolo infinito d'ogni condizione, e sesso, e quantita di Carozze, invitato da una SERENATA del Sig.re Prpe. di Palestrina." *Avvisi di Roma*, August 30, 1704, I-Rvat (Ott. lat. 2732), 164r.

58 Regarding such accounts, Michael Talbot adds that the emphasis on purely visual aspects of production reflects a society with little access to visual reproduction of important events, which therefore relied more heavily on mental reconstructions of visual images based on verbal description. See "The Serenata in Eighteenth-Century Venice," 15.

59 Valesio, *Diario di Roma*, 153–154.

60 Ibid., 152.

61 We cannot rule out the possibility that the Ambassador to Venice acted as co-sponsor of *Le gare festive*. Carolyn Gianturco reports in her article "Cristina di Svezia scenarista per Alessandro Stradella," in *Cristina di Svezia e la musica. Convegno internazionale: Roma, 5–6 dicembre 1996* (Rome: Accademia Nazionale dei Lincei, 1998), 45–70, that serenatas sometimes were repeated several times by allied patrons. In the case of Alessandro Stradella's *Vola, vola in altri petti* (1674),

Gianturco notes that the coaches which carried the singers and instrumentalists for the serenata served as both staging device and a means of transport from one palace performance to another (46).

62 "Nella sera di detto lunedì fu dal sopraddetto principe di Pellestrina replicata detta serenata nella piazza di San Marco avanti il palazzo dell'em.mo di Boves (Gianson) coll'intervento di molti personaggi havendo anco dato il modo all'ambasciatore Veneto che stà vicino, d'usare la cortesia de rinfreschi con la nobiltà di questa città accorsa in sua casa *per udire la musica*." August 30, 1704, Staffieri, *Colligite fragmenta*, 158–159 (emphasis added). It may be worthwhile discussing briefly whether both manuscript versions of the score, Barb. lat. 4179 and Barb. lat. 4228, are linked to the two performances of *Le gare festive*. Although the opening *sinfonie* of the two manuscripts differ in music and instrumentation (the one by Carlo Ferrini in 4179 is scored for two trumpets, two "violini del concertino," two "violini del concerto grosso," "basso del concerto grosso," "basso del concertino"; the other by Bencini is scored for two trumpets, two oboes, two violins, bassoon, "violone," and harpsichord, with indications in the score as to when certain sections are to be played by soloists only), they both suggest a concerto grosso organization. The remainders of the serenatas are similar, except for two arias in Barb. lat. 4179, which Lionnet suggests have been transformed; see "Introduction" to *La Cappella Giulia*, xxviii. Lionnet appears to believe that 4179 is the definitive score, though he provides no evidence in support of this hypothesis. While it is true that 4228 reveals modification (Lionnet lists this version as Barb. lat. 4227, which is in fact a different work by Bencini, *Aminta e Dori, Cantata a due con violini*), there is ultimately no proof that such changes were made in response to the patron's demands, or theoretically, because of a change in venue: from piazza to piazza, or from outside to inside.

63 "La sera stessa di lunedì, questo Sig. Ambasciatore di Spagna nella Piazza solita fece per la seconda volta, dopo il suo arrivo, allegrezze pubbliche per l'anniversario della nascita della Regina Regnante. Era stato fabricato un gratioso teatro di travi, tavoli e tele ben dipinte nella Piazzetta che si dice de' Mignanelli avanti al Palazzo dell'Ambasciatore . . . Da terra sorgeva una scalinata divisa in tre gradi ne' quali stavano musici e suonatori di tutte sorti d'istromenti. E levata (come ho detto) la tenda, si diede principio alla sinfonia che riuscì piena e maravigliosa, ed al canto; ma questo poco si poté sentire per il bisbiglio e rumore del popolo e delle carozze. Durò tal funzione fino alle due hore e due quarti. Ma perché quelli che dimoravano nel Palazzo dell'Ambasciatore non havevano (per la detta causa) potuto goder la musica, fu stimato bene da S. Ecc.za farla di nuovo sentire nel proprio palazzo, come immediatamente si eseguì." *Ephemerides cartariae*, August 25, 1687, I-Ras (*Archivio Cartari-Febei*, Busta 96), 21r–v. A section of this source is cited in Morelli, "La musica a Roma," 132.

64 See Morelli's "La musica a Roma," 109. In his introduction and overview of Cartari's chronicles, he notes that although organized in the manner of

contemporary *avvisi* (weekly news journals), these documents reveal a more personal view of the events taking place around him, so that the news of the time is interspersed with his own life history, his career as a lawyer, his intellectual and recreational activities, and occasionally his view as a listener and spectator.

65 Handelman, *Models and Mirrors*, 41.

66 Robert Darnton, *The Great Cat Massacre and Other Episodes in French Cultural History* (New York: Vintage Books, 1985), 124; quoted in Handelman, *Models and Mirrors*, 41.

67 In his diary Valesio indicates that excessive heat began as early as July 6, 1704; not until August 30 does he suggest that the city finally cooled due to heavy rainstorms. See his entries, 160, 188.

68 Griffin, "The Late Baroque Serenata," 432.

69 See Johns's "Introduction," in *Papal Art and Cultural Politics: Rome in the Age of Clement XI* (Cambridge University Press, 1993), 1–12; for quote, 2.

70 For further details on mounting tensions in Rome and key diplomatic players, see the classic rendition of Clement XI's history in Ludwig von Pastor's *The History of the Popes*, Vol. XXXIII (London: Routledge and Kegan Paul, 1957), 1–34. Carlo Vitali, in "Italy – Political, Religious and Musical Contexts," in *The Cambridge Companion to Handel*, ed. Donald Burrows (Cambridge University Press, 1997), 31, affirms an important point: "it is probably misleading to interpret the taking of sides by Italian nobility" as "not a matter of ideologically motivated loyalty but rather one of steering a sometimes erratic course between complicated dynastic or family interests."

71 For example, imperial troops invaded Ferrara in 1701; also in that same year a plot was hatched for Neapolitan malcontents to rise against Bourbon domination; and in 1703 when Leopold renounced his rights to the Spanish monarchy, he elevated the status of his son from archduke to King Charles III of Spain, and demanded that the pope recognize this action.

72 See the entry for "Mercordì 20" as well as the insertion of a "Breve, e succinta relazione della gran vittoria ottenuta contra Gallo-Bavari dalle Armi Imperiali," *Diario di Roma*, 148–149.

73 Ibid., 118.

74 For details see Valesio's description for "Domenica 20 luglio," ibid., 124–125, 130.

75 Griffin has compiled a summary of the known data concerning all serenatas heard in Rome during 1704. See "The Late Baroque Serenata," 453–455.

76 *La contesa d'onore* (Rome, 1704); the copy of the libretto cited here is preserved in I-Rc, Vol. Misc. 1645 (35). Though we have no known record of the music, a document reports that Alessandro Scarlatti likely composed the work and that "the famous Arcangelo" (Corelli) performed it with harmonious instruments and beautiful playing: "[la Serenata] e posta in Musica dal Sig:re Scarlatti, ambi Uomini di grido, et i Musici furono Cecchino, Momo, e Pepe di S:M . . . La

quale serenata fù dalla Virtù del famoso Arcangelo accompagnata da armoniosi strom:ti, e da vaghe sinfonie." *Avvisi di Roma*, July 22, 1704, I-Rvat (Ott. lat. 2732), 146v.

77 The same *avviso* notes that the last refrain "Viva il Gran Luigi, Viva!" was repeated twice by people attending the serenata, who filled the streets, roofs, and windows of the grand piazza. Ibid.

78 For general background and documentation on the regular celebration of the Festa di San Luigi, see Jean Lionnet's thorough study, "La musique à Saint-Louis des français de Rome au XVIIe siècle," *Note d'Archivio per la Storia Musicale*, n.s., Anno III, 1985, Supplemento, première partie; Anno IV, 1986, Supplemento, deuxième partie: les documents (Venice: Fondazione Levi).

79 For details of Valesio's comments on Prince Urbano's financing of *Le gare festive*, see *Diario di Roma*, 152.

80 "Nondimeno considerando ella, che potrebbe esser tacciata di troppo animoso ardimento, viene ora à porsi sotto l'alta Protettione dell'Eccelenza Vostra, da cui spera difesa dall' altrui censura, e merito per esser gradita." I-Rli, 171.I.19, 3–4.

81 These same links are exemplified by the way Urbano lists himself on *Le gare festive*'s title page (see n55): Prince of Palestrina (the third generation of an inherited principate through his grandfather Taddeo Barberini, nephew of Pope Urban VIII, and of a family with Francophile leanings), Grandee of Spain and Knight of the Golden Fleece, both illustrious Spanish titles. In this period, however, it was known that Spanish grandees *now* would be recognized as peers of France, a result of the War of Spanish Succession. See Angelantonio Spagnoletti, *Prìncipi italiani e Spagna nell'età barocca* (Milan: Mondadori, 1996), 239–240.

82 Of all Roman cavalcades, the *possesso* was perhaps the most symbolic, in which the elected pope made his symbolic journey across Rome to take possession of the basilica of San Giovanni in Laterano. For a detailed analysis of this ritual in the context of the Barberini papacy (1623–1644), see Frederick Hammond, *Music and Spectacle in Baroque Rome: Barberini Patronage under Urban VIII* (New Haven: Yale University Press, 1994), 43–47.

83 Claude Lévi-Strauss, *The Naked Man*, trans. John and Doreen Weightman as Vol. IV of *Introduction to a Science of Mythology* (New York: Harper & Row, 1981), 672–673. Cf. Handelman, *Models and Mirrors*, 10.

84 For details see Valesio's description for Sunday August 24, 1704, *Diario di Roma*, 150–154. For the purposes of this discussion I have drawn from Griffin's translation of the document. "The Late Baroque Serenata," 445–447.

85 According to Valesio, these included the Marquis Maculani, Pompeo Capranica, and the Marquises Bongiovanni (father and son).

86 "... the daughter of Laura who lives opposite the Palazzo Chigi on the Corso, Cochina of the Monti household, and a young girl belonging to the same princess, the daughter of a carpenter." Griffin, "The Late Baroque Serenata," 446.

87 As previously noted, the Spanish in Rome were noted for their extravagant use of light for visual effect. In 1687, the Spanish ambassador de la Cerda, the marqués de Cogolludo, was said to have surpassed his predecessor and uncle, the marqués del Carpio, through his use of illumination. For evidence, see the *avviso* excerpt for August 30, 1687, *Avvisi Marescotti* 787, fols. 426r–427r; Staffieri, *Colligite fragmenta*, 78.

88 An *avviso* reports that the palace of the Ambassador of the Veneto was particularly well lit and filled with noble onlookers: "La Piazza, e le strade erano coperte di Popolo vago di vedere la comparsa degl'avventi tre Carri Trionfali, e li Palazzi intorno ad essa pieni della maggior nobilità, particolarmente quello del Signore Ambasciatore di Veneto, che si vedeva di dentro tutto illuminato." *Avvisi di Roma*, August 30, 1704, I-Rvat (Ott. lat. 2732), 165r. Focusing on Venice, art historian Eugene Johnson connects illuminated palace windows to the emergence of the "opera box." His research details how palace courtyards and public squares where private and civic spectacle took place served as models for the emergence of opera theaters. See "Jacopo Sansovino, Giacomo Torelli, and the Theatricality of the Piazzetta in Venice," *Journal of the Society of Architectural Historians* 59 (2000): 436–453.

89 Griffin, "The Late Baroque Serenata," 447.

90 It is important here to clarify the otherwise elusive meaning of allegory as it relates to the serenata. In his *Handlist of Rhetorical Terms*, 2nd edn (Berkeley: University of California Press, 1991), 4–6, Richard Lanham refers to Graham Hough's "clock diagram," or rather a continuum of various types of allegory. Hough provides a useful analysis that fits the serenata well: "Half-way between symbolism and naïve allegory we have what I will call emblem or hieratic symbolism. It exists largely outside literature – its special field is iconography and religious imagery. There is a tendency for symbolism to become fixed; the image shrinks and becomes stereotyped, and theme expands." Hough, *A Preface to* The Faerie Queene (London: G. Duckworth, 1962), 110–111. Also helpful is Michael Talbot's grouping of serenata narratives into four main types: (1) the rare work in which topical allusion is wholly absent; (2) when the allusion is external to the plot, occupying a detachable *licenza*; (3) when the allusion is intrinsic, but reserved for the dénouement (the kind we see applied in *Le gare festive*); (4) when the allusion is pervasive and may provide the starting point for the whole work. See "Vivaldi's Serenatas: Long Cantatas or Short Operas?," 77–78.

91 The other common formula was that of the quest, as described by Talbot as "better suited to straightforward encomiums. Here the characters, who reinforce rather than refute one another's observations, discover by stages the identity of the hero who is the object of the search." See "The Serenata in Eighteenth-Century Venice," 15.

92 "As people fable it, the Earth, her mother, / Furious against the gods, bore a late sister / To the giants Coeus and Enceladus, / Giving her speed on foot and on

the wing: / Monstrous, deformed, titanic. Pinioned, with / An eye beneath for every body feather, / And, strange to say, as many tongues and buzzing / Mouths as eyes, as many pricked-up ears, / By night she flies between the earth and heaven / Shrieking through darkness, and she never turns / Her eyelids down to sleep. By day she broods, / On the alert, on rooftops or on towers, / Bringing great cities fear, harping on lies / And slander evenhandedly with truth." Virgil, *Aeneid* 4.178–191. *The Aeneid*, trans. Robert Fitzgerald (New York: Random House, 1983), 102.

93 "In the centre of the world, situated between earth and sky and sea, at the point where the three realms of the universe meet, is a place from which everything the world over can be seen, however far away, and to its listening ears comes every sound. There Rumour lives, in a home she has chosen for herself on a hilltop. Night and day the house lies open, for she has given it a thousand apertures and countless entrances, with never a door to barricade the thresholds. The whole structure is of echoing brass, and is full of noises, repeating words and giving back the sound it hears." Ovid, *Metamorphoses* 12.40–61. *The Metamorphoses of Ovid*, trans. Mary Innes (London: Penguin, 1955), 269.

94 Drawing on some of the same words from the *Aeneid*, Cesare Ripa in his *Iconologia* describes the good Fame (Fama Buona) as a woman holding a trumpet in her right hand, signifying the universal shouts or applause that can be spread to the ears of all men: "Donna con una tromba nella mano dritta . . . La tromba significa il grido universale sparso per gl'orecchi de gl'huomini." The first *Iconologia* was published in Rome in 1593 without illustrations. The following reference is based on the first illustrated edition which appeared in 1603 and was reprinted in 1611 by P. P. Tozzi, Padua, see *Iconologia, Padua, 1611* (New York: Garland, 1976), 154–155.

95 "Tutta cinta di Penne/Della mia Tromba al suono/Io che la Fama sono/Vuò riportare a Garamanti, a gl'Indi/Sì felice Natale;/Ecco già scuoto l'ale,/E con volo giocondo/Io voglio empir del nato Infante il Mondo." [I, who am Fame all adorned with feathers, want to report to the Africans and the Asians such a happy birth with the sound of my trumpet. Behold, I already shake my wings, and with joyful flight I want to fill the world (with the news) of the newborn infant.] Fame's first recitative in *La contesa d'onore*.

96 The presence of trumpets in serenatas was not unheard of in this period, though their use was still distinctive. Spitzer and Zaslaw explain that through the end of the seventeenth century, winds in general in most serenatas were typically scarce. The serenata ensemble was mainly an orchestra of bowed strings, and trumpet parts were arranged on an ad hoc basis when needed for special effect, but most often for opening *sinfonie*. See *The Birth of the Orchestra*, 125–126. For further analysis on the rhetoric of trumpet arias in seventeenth-century opera, also see Edward H. Tarr and Thomas Walker, "'Bellici carmi, festivo fragor': die Verwendung der Trompete in der italienischen Oper des 17. Jahrhunderts," *Hamburger Jahrbuch für Musikwissenschaft* 3 (1978): 143–203.

97 "Ma di tromba guerriera/Qual armonico suono à noi s'appressa!/Giunge quella Gran Dea, a cui concessa/Anno gl'Astri la sorte/D'eternar l'Uomo ad onta ancor di morte." [But what a harmonious sound of the war trumpet approaches us! That great goddess comes, to whom the stars have given the chance to make man eternal even in spite of death.]

98 "Oh magnanimo Rege! Udite come/Risuona in sì bel giorno/Di belle glorie adorno/Festoso, e grande di LUIGI il nome?"

99 "Hidden Antiquity, you ancient Rumors, show me the Kings I must remember, for my task is to give length to lives." Statius, *Thebaid*, 4.32–34. Statius P. Papinius (Publius Papinius), *Thebaid; Seven against Thebes*, trans. Charles Stanley Ross (Baltimore: The Johns Hopkins University Press, 1994), 83.

100 "Sì che resisterà/Al tempo ingrato, e rio/La sua grand'Alma./La tromba mia saprà/Ognor del cieco oblio/Portar la palma." [Yes, his great soul will resist against ungrateful and cruel Time. My trumpet will always carry the palm of victory over blind Oblivion.]

101 "Con cento trombe/Pronta, e giuliva/Di riva in riva/Io spiego il Vol./Lieto, e giocondo/ Festeggi il Mondo,/Ch'ai rai s'illustra/Del nuovo Sol." [Quick and joyous I unfold my flight with a hundred trumpets from shore to shore. May the world – which glorifies itself in the rays of the new Sun – celebrate happily and joyfully.]

102 Joel Fineman explains that allegory's linearity was a topic of contention among classical rhetoricians. He notes that Quintilian found this aspect of allegory a defect, an excess of metaphor that led to obtuse allusion (*Institutio Oratoria* 8.6. 14–15). For his comments on Quintilian, and extended discussion of allegory's temporal and spatial dimension, see "The Structure of Allegorical Desire," in *Allegory and Representation. Selected Papers from the English Institute, 1979– 80*, ed. Stephen J. Greenblatt (Baltimore: The Johns Hopkins University Press, 1981), 26–60.

103 *The Naked Man*, 673–674. In a larger sense, Lévi-Strauss frames his discussion of ritual as a contrast to mythic thought, which he claims divides up the same continuum into large distinctive units, but separates them by differential gaps.

104 Ibid., 674.

105 Quoting George Puttenham (*The Arte of English Poesie*, 1589), Fineman writes: "This is why allegory is 'the courtly figure,' as Puttenham called it, an inherently political and therefore religious trope, not because it flatters tactfully, but because in deferring to structure it insinuates the power of structure, giving off what we can call the structural effect." "The Structure of Allegorical Desire," 33.

106 Edward Muir, *Ritual in Early Modern Europe* (Cambridge University Press, 1997), 4–5.

107 "Ora formar conviene/Liete voci d'applausi/Per così illustre Femina Regale/E far la rima al suo gran merto eguale./Voi del nostro voler genij seguaci/Ad Armonie soavi/Or frettolosi, or gravi/Movete i plettri, e non vi spiaccia

intanto/Col vostro suono accompagnarne il canto." Excerpt from the Moon's recitative, "Eccone al fine su le romane arene," from *La notte festiva*. The copy of the libretto cited here is preserved in I-Rc, Vol. Misc. 1645.

108 For a discussion of ritual as imagined enactments of group cohesion, see David Kertzer, "The Power of Rites," in *Ritual, Politics, and Power* (New Haven: Yale University Press, 1988), 1–14.

109 Muir, *Ritual in Early Modern Europe*, 4–5. Using this last phrase about a "labyrinth of dissonance," Muir borrows from Don Handelman's concept of "public events," see *Models and Mirrors*, 9.

110 In any discussion of "public" and "private" it is important to recognize the multiple and ambiguous character of that opposition. For example, political theorist Jeff Weintraub notes that public/private distinctions rarely constitute a single paired opposition but, instead, comprise a complex family of often-related juxtapositions. See Weintraub's "The Theory and Politics of the Public/Private Distinction," in *Public and Private in Thought and Practice: Perspective on a Grand Dichotomy*, ed. Jeff Weintraub and Krishan Kumar (University of Chicago Press, 1997), 1–42, especially 2–3, and also see the volume's preface, xi–xvii.

4 The cantata, the pastoral, and the ideology of nostalgia

1 "[I]bo ed Chalcidico quae sunt mihi condita uersu / carmina pastoris Siculi modulabor auena. / certum est in siluis inter spelaea ferarum / malle pati tenerisque meos incidere amores / arboribus: crescent illae, crescetis, amores." Virgil, *The Eclogues of Virgil*, trans. David Ferry (New York: Farrar, Straus, Giroux, 1999), 83.

2 Lorenzo Bianconi, *Music in the Seventeenth Century*, trans. David Bryant (Cambridge University Press, 1987), 204.

3 Other scholars have considered the influence of opera on the cantata, though mostly during earlier periods of the cantata's development in the Italian context. As representative examples, see Gloria Rose, "The Italian Cantata of the Baroque Period," in *Gattungen der Musik in Einzeldarstellungen: Gedenkschrift Leo Schrade*, ed. Wulf Arlt, Ernst Lichtenhahn, and Hans Oesch (Berne: Francke, 1973), 655–677; Margaret Murata, "The Recitative Soliloquy," *Journal of the American Musicological Society* 32, no. 1 (1979): 45–73; her "Further Remarks on Pasqualini and the Music of *MAP*," *Analecta Musicologica* 19 (1979): 125–145; Lorenzo Bianconi and Thomas Walker, "Production, Consumption and Political Function of Seventeenth-Century Opera," *Early Music History* 4 (1984): 256–257; Robert Holzer, "Music and Poetry in Seventeenth-Century Rome: Settings of the Canzonetta and Cantata Texts of Francesco Balducci, Domenico Benigni, Francesco Melosio, and Antonio Abati" (Ph.D. diss., University of Pennsylvania, 1990); John Walter Hill, *Roman Monody, Cantata, and Opera from the Circles around Cardinal Montalto*, 2 vols. (Oxford University

Press, 1997). Of the more recent studies, some have considered the relationship between genres more broadly, as in Murata's "Image and Eloquence: Secular Song," in *The Cambridge History of Seventeenth-Century Music*, ed. Tim Carter and John Butt (Cambridge University Press, 2005), 378–425. Other examples address this issue by looking at a particular composer's approach, such as Colin Timms, "The Dramatic in Vivaldi's Cantatas," in *Antonio Vivaldi. Teatro musicale, cultura e società*, ed. Lorenzo Bianconi and Giovanni Morelli (Florence: L. S. Olschki, 1982), 64–72; and Michael Talbot, "How Recitatives End and Arias Begin in the Solo Cantatas of Antonio Vivaldi," *Journal of the Royal Musical Association* 126 (2001): 169–192. Also see the recent edited volume of essays, *Aspects of the Secular Cantata in Late Baroque Italy*, ed. Michael Talbot (Burlington, VT: Ashgate, 2009), for similar focused studies, though of particular mention for the question of genre interaction within the Italian context is the essay by Hendrik Schulze, "Narration, Mimesis and the Question of Genre: Dramatic Approaches in Giovanni Legrenzi's Solo Cantatas, Opp. 12 and 14," 55–78. Though useful and informative, most of these studies have not offered a more detailed and complicated viewpoint that interrogates the influence and relationship between the cantata and opera within the Arcadian milieu.

4 For a sampling of scholars who have studied the role and status of singers in the Roman chamber context see Giovanni Morelli, "Una celebre 'cantarina' romana del Seicento: la Giorgina," *Studi Secenteschi* 16 (1975): 157–180; Bianca Maria Antolini, "Cantanti e letterati a Roma nella prima metà del Seicento: alcune osservazioni," in *In cantu et in sermone: For Nino Pirrotta on his 80th Birthday*, ed. Fabrizio della Sella and Franco Piperno (Florence: L. S. Olschki, 1989), 347–363; Margaret Murata, "Singing about Singing," in *In cantu et in sermone*, 363–382; also her "Roman Cantata Scores as Traces of Musical Culture and Signs of its Place in Society," in *Atti del XIV congresso della Società internazionale di musicologia, Bologna, 1987: trasmissione e recezione delle forme di cultura musicale*, Vol. I (Turin: Edizioni di Torino, 1990), 272–284; Giancarlo Rostirolla, "Alcune note sulla professione di cantore e di cantante nella Roma del Sei e Settecento," *Roma Moderna e Contemporanea: Rivista Interdisciplinare di Storia* 4 (1996): 37–74; Arnaldo Morelli, "Una cantante del Seicento e le sue carte di musica: il 'Libro della Signora Cecilia,'" in *"Vanitatis, fuga, aeternitatis amor." Wolfgang Witzenmann zum 65. Geburtstag*, ed. Sabine Ehrmann-Herfort, Markus Engelhardt, and Wolfgang Witzenmann (Laaber: Laaber Verlag, 2005), 307–327. More recently, Roger Freitas, *Portrait of a Castrato: Politics, Patronage, and Music in the Life of Atto Melani* (Cambridge University Press, 2009).

5 For a thoughtful treatment of the Neoplatonic origins and rise of early opera, see Gary Tomlinson, *Metaphysical Song: An Essay on Opera* (Princeton University Press, 1999), specifically chapters 1–2, "Voices of the Invisible" and "Late Renaissance Opera," 3–27. On the revival of humanist ideals of good taste within the more Enlightenment context of Arcadian Rome, see Vernon Hyde Minor's study of the rise of *buon gusto* in *The Death of the Baroque and the Rhetoric of*

Good Taste (Cambridge University Press, 2006), esp. chapter 2, "*Buon Gusto,*" 26–60.

6 Holzer recognizes the important mutual influence exerted between the cantata and opera, especially in the cantata's early development, citing the examples of Ottavio Tronsarelli's musical poetry as evidence for chamber vocal music's aspirations to dramatic or semi-dramatic presentation. See "Music and Poetry in Seventeenth-Century Rome," 263–266.

7 Freitas, "Singing and Playing: The Italian Cantata and the Rage for Wit," *Music and Letters* 82, no. 4 (2001): 509–542, see especially 514–520.

8 There are very few critical or polemical sources of two period that regard the cantata in any detail. Among the primary sources that address the cantata is Giovanni Mario Crescimbeni's *Commentari del Canonico Gio. Mario Crescimbeni custode d'Arcadia intorno alla sua Istoria della volgar poesia*, Vol. I (Rome: de'Rossi, 1702), in which he includes a short discussion of the cantata in chapter XII, 236–241 (see chapter 3 for further discussion of this document). In his careful charting of the rise of the term "cantata," Robert Holzer notes that cantata texts never received the attention that poetic theorists had given the canzonetta, at least not until Crescimbeni's time. See his chapter "The Cantata I – Terminology and Traditions," in "Music and Poetry in Seventeenth-Century Rome," 262. I will also consider a brief and somewhat fantastical description of the cantata in Book VII of Crescimbeni's *L'Arcadia del Canonico Gio. Mario Crescimbeni* later in this chapter. Other early eighteenth-century sources on the cantata include Johann Mattheson, *Das neu-eröffnete Orchestre* (Hamburg: Schiller, 1713), 177–178, and his *Der vollkommene Capellmeister* (Hamburg: 1739), 214–216; Francesco S. Quadrio, *Della storia e della ragione d'ogni poesia*, Vol. II (Milan: Agnelli, 1741), 334–338; and Johann Adolph Scheibe, *Critische Musikus* (Hildesheim, NY: G. Olms; Wiesbaden: Breitkopf & Härtel, 1970 [1745]), 380–492, 503–543.

9 It is well known that literary sources of pastoral imagery are often traced back to the pastoral poetic model of Theocritus's *Idylls*, a model that in Italy was better known through Virgil's *Eclogues*, which was frequently translated and imitated in the vernacular throughout the fifteenth and sixteenth centuries. See Giuseppe Gerbino's recent study, *Music and the Myth of Arcadia in Renaissance Italy* (Cambridge University Press, 2009), especially Part I, "Music in Arcadia: An Unsettled Tradition," for exploration of the humanist tradition that inspired these Renaissance poetic developments that affected musical composition.

10 For many imitators and followers of the classical pastoral, the retreat from worldliness was a stance necessary to embrace the contemplative life required for poetry to thrive. As Boccaccio in his *Genealogia deorum gentilium libri* wrote "[Poetry] never seeks a habitation in the towering palaces of kings or the easy abodes of the luxurious; rather she visits caves on steep mountainsides, or shady groves, or argent springs, where are the retreats of the studious." *Boccaccio on Poetry; Being the Preface and Fourteenth and Fifteenth Books of Boccaccio's*

Genealogia deorum gentilium libri *in an English Version with Introductory Essay and Commentary by Charles G. Osgood* (Princeton University Press, 1930), 24. Susan M. Dixon reminds us that during the Renaissance (and later among the Arcadians) the classical tradition of using nature or a garden setting was a critical backdrop for intellectual and poetic pursuits. And even the tradition of writing on trees was a recurring theme in eighteenth-century Arcadian literature, a revived ancient and Renaissance trope in which trees were inscribed with verses to express love, or as mournful reminders of a beloved deceased Arcadian. See Dixon, *Between the Real and the Ideal: The Accademia degli Arcadi and its Garden in Eighteenth-Century Rome* (Newark, DE: University of Delaware Press, 2006), 54, 82.

11 Danielle Lecoq and Roland Schaer note that as long ago as the first century BCE the term "Golden Age" began to appear as a term conferring a chronological dimension to what was merely a structural classification, thus shifting from myth to history. See "Ancient, Biblical, and Medieval Traditions," in *Utopia: The Search for the Ideal Society in the Western World*, ed. Roland Schaer, Gregory Claeys, and Lyman Tower Sargent (New York: The New York Public Library/Oxford University Press, 2000), 35.

12 Holzer notes that the pastoral enjoyed a burst of popularity at the beginning of the seventeenth century with Giambattista Marino's *Sampogna*, a collection of "idilli favolosi" and "idilli pastorali," which helped to popularize the thematics of the pastoral and love in the early part of the century; see "Music and Poetry in Seventeenth-Century Rome," 275. Margaret Murata observes that songs of love had become so common by the 1660s that they developed their own catalogue of clichés; see "Singing about Singing," 364.

13 Ellen Harris, *Handel and the Pastoral Tradition* (Oxford University Press, 1980), 18.

14 In *Handel and the Pastoral Tradition*, Harris briefly explores the extent to which the pastoral cantata better, more easily, and more regularly embraced the same tenets of reform outlined for operatic dramaturgy. In Harris's estimation the differences between pastoral opera and cantatas were only a matter of degree, see 56–57.

15 Several of Crescimbeni's publications describe the Academy's Olympic Games (see especially *I giuochi olimpici celebrati dagli Arcadi nell'Olimpiade DCXX* [Rome: Monaldi, 1701]); however, his description in the section "Notizie d'Arcadia," appended to the conclusion of *La bellezza della volgar poesia* (Rome: Buagni, 1700), 217–230, is among his first and most succinct accounts of these rituals. See *La bellezza della volgar poesia*, 221.

16 In *Between the Real and the Ideal*, Dixon reviews the diversity of literary forms required in "competitions" in the *Giuochi Olimpici*, and discusses in detail the organization and performances of these games, see 29. It is important that we treat this notion of *singing* poetry in the Arcadians' Olympic contests carefully. Though the word or phrase "cantare" or "cantare nel Bosco Parrasio" comes

up frequently in both archival and published Arcadian documents, it is unclear the extent to which this really refers to the act of singing musically, rather than merely to recitation. My own analysis of Crescimbeni's writings and of documents in the Arcadian archive, held at Rome's Biblioteca Angelica (I-Ra) suggests variability in the use of this word. At times "cantare" may be used for poetic and even prose recitation. Occasionally there are hints that actual music plays some kind of accompanying role. For instance, in Crescimbeni's *L'Arcadia*, he describes an elegy recited by an Arcadian nymph as accompanied by the sound of a beautiful flute. See *Elegia d'Elettra* from Prosa VIII "Delle Corone, che adoperano gli Arcadi ne' Giuochi Olimpici," *L'Arcadia*, 48. There is also a suggestion from the poetry collected in the archive that some items termed "cantata" were likely meant to be instrumental, such as a "Cantata per Tromba, della S.ra Contessa Prudenza Gabrielli Capizucchi, detta fra gli Arcadi Elettra Citeria" (I-Ra, *Archivio Arcadia*, ms. 5.132, cc.188r–188v); however, the extent to which these texts were imagined or actually performed as music is difficult to determine.

17 Ralph Nash cites such a moment in chapter 11 of Sannazaro's *Arcadia* for which such demanding expertise is described: "even if by reason of the covert language [his song] was little understood by us, nevertheless it did not follow that it was not heard by each man with the closest attention." See Nash, *Arcadia & Piscatorial Eclogues* (Detroit: Wayne State University Press, 1966), 118.

18 The shepherd reference was also religiously rooted. The academy adopted the Infant Jesus as its protector since it was simple shepherds of Bethlehem who were the first to be told of the birth of Christ, who in His own right would be celebrated as the Good Shepherd. For further background, see Riccardo Merolla, "Lo stato dell chiesa," in *Letteratura italiana: storia e geografia*, Vol. II: *L'età moderna* (Turin: Giulio Einaudi, 1988), 1019–1109. Dixon adds to this explanation by noting that the adoption of the Christ child – a popular trope in eighteenth-century Italy – was also symbolic of the Arcadians' desire to resist individualized favors from one powerful earthly patron so that free discourse could be mainted, see *Between the Real and the Ideal*, 74.

19 This very duality (complexity/simplicity) as a reactionary stance to opera was even recognized by Bononcini who later in his career noted that cantatas represent "a labor much greater than that required to compose an opera, because such works permit no 'stuffing' – and that is the truth. They are written so as to satisfy not only listeners, but also those who possess a complete understanding of the art" [*una fattica assai maggiore che di fare un'Opera, perché non si permette in tali Composizioni fare alcuna empitura, e tanto basti. Elle sono fatte acciò possano satisfare non solo gl'ascoltanti, ma ancora a chi possiede una intelligenza intera dell'Arte*]. From a quoted letter from Bononcini to the diplomat Giovanni Zamboni, preserved in the Bodleian Library, GB-Ob (MS Rawl. letters 130), fols. 148–149v, see Lowell Lindgren's "Introduction," in Giovanni Bononcini,

Cantatas, Vol. X of *The Italian Cantata in the Seventeenth Century* (New York: Garland, 1985), x–xiii.

20 A term used by Mauro Calcagno in "Signifying Nothing: On the Aesthetics of Pure Voice in Early Venetian Opera," *The Journal of Musicology* 20, no. 4 (2003): 461–497. Calcagno sets up his article by beginning with these eighteenth-century reflections to indicate the profound and yet belated reactions to what emerged in Venice within the Incogniti circles and the institution of public theater. See his opening quote from Gian Vincenzo Gravina's "Della tragedia" (1715) in which the former member of the Arcadians laments the point to which culture and music drama had descended: "The philosopher remains confined to schools, the poet to academies; and for the people what is left in the theaters is only pure voice, stripped of any poetic eloquence and of any philosophical feeling" (461).

21 Much of this has been determined by our past scholarly approaches and priorities, which leaned heavily towards composers already canonized, such as Handel, and to a lesser extent Alessandro Scarlatti. There has been some focused scholarship on the cantatas of Gasparini and Caldara, but far less on local composers such as Lanciani, Amadei, and Cesarini.

22 Alessandro Scarlatti (1660–1725) anchored much of his Roman career on the composition of chamber cantatas, as well as other secular and sacred vocal music. There have been numerous scholarly studies on Scarlatti's cantata output and compositional approach. Among those that were most relevant for this study are Edwin Hanley's indispensable resource, "Alessandro Scarlatti's *cantate da camera*: A Bibliographic Study" (Ph.D. diss., Yale University, 1963); as well as Malcolm Boyd's research on the topic in "Form and Style in Scarlatti's Chamber Cantatas," *Music Review* 25 (1964): 17–26; along with his introduction to the edition *Cantatas by Alessandro Scarlatti*, Vol. XIII: *The Italian Cantata in the Seventeenth Century* (New York: Garland, 1986); the essays by Maria Caraci, "Le cantate romane di Alessandro Scarlatti nel fondo Noseda," and Reinhard Strohm, "Scarlattiana at Yale," in *Händel e gli Scarlatti a Roma*, ed. Nino Pirrotta and Agostino Ziino (Florence: L. S. Olschki, 1987), 93–112 and 113–152 respectively; Laura Damuth, "Alessandro Scarlatti's Cantatas for Soprano and Basso Continuo, 1693–1705" (Ph.D. diss., Columbia University, 1993). Among the most recent work, see Norbert Dubowy, "'Al tavolino medesimo del Compositor della Musica': Notes on Text and Context in Alessandro Scarlatti's *cantate da camera*," in Talbot, *Aspects of the Secular Cantata in Late Baroque Italy*, 111–134, which was published after this present monograph was completed.

23 *Commentari*, 241.

24 Edwin Hanley notes in his appendix that different parts of this disclaimer appear in different manuscript versions. See "Alessandro Scarlatti's *cantate da camera*," 112–114.

25 In a well-known portrait of Scarlatti, the title page and first recitative of this very cantata are displayed to the left of the composer. The portrait dates from the first years of the eighteenth century, and today is displayed at the Civico Museo Bibliografico Musicale in Bologna (a reproduction of the portrait is printed in

Roberto Pagano and Lino Bianchi, eds., *Alessandro Scarlatti* [Turin: Edizioni Rai, 1972], 304). Hanley's index lists thirty-one sources for *Al fin m'ucciderete*, see his Index I, no. 21, in "Alessandro Scarlatti's *cantate da camera*," 92.

26 In Dubowy's recent essay "Notes on Text and Context in Alessandro Scarlatti's *cantata da camera*," the author presents a convincing interpretation of the overall narrative scope of this cantata, one that is much more complex and varied, but that also justifies the distinctly different arias of the RARA formal scheme. See his discussion and analysis, as well as his references for possible sources of borrowings from a previous Scarlatti cantata, *Io morirei contento* (H 340), 131–134.

27 In his article, Calcagno references Ellen Rosand's "Barbara Strozzi, *virtuosissima cantatrice*: The Composer's Voice," *Journal of the American Musicological Society* 31 (1978): 241–281, to make the point that the imbalances between word and voice and sound and meaning not only were explored in the first Venetian operas, but also could be found in other genres, like the cantata. See "Signifying Nothing," 462.

28 Using several mid-century cantata examples as evidence, Freitas contextualizes the specific desire to privilege unexpected rhetorical turns as part of a larger intellectual and cultural trend in which style of rhetorical delivery (in conversation, in rhetorical competitions, or in cantatas) was what constituted substance, rather than subject matter itself. See "Singing and Playing: The Italian Cantata and the Rage for Wit"; for quotation above see 524; and for examples examined see esp. 526–541.

29 The repudiation of and distancing from seventeenth-century literary and theatrical models is more complicated than is usually rendered. We often characterize critics of the late seventeenth century, like the Arcadians, as being anti-Marinist, which was largely true. However, as Dixon rightly points out, Crescimbeni didn't condemn Marino directly; in fact, Marino is included and lauded as one of several exemplary poets in the 1698 *Istoria della volgar poesia*. Marino himself is not criticized, but the profusion of Marino-like imitations we know as *marinismo* is. See *Between the Real and the Ideal*, 28.

30 Melania Bucciarelli explores the compositional and rhetorical strategies of the early eighteenth-century Dresden composer Johann David Heinichen, in order to survey how a text's rhetorical framework could influence the compositional process, even by allowing a growing independence of musical discourse in relation to verbal discourse. She describes how in Heinichen's discussion of Italian operatic style, he examines the musical means to imitate emotions and elicit them in listeners: "he pays attention to musical *inventio* – rather than *decoratio* – and provides extensive examples of how poetry can guide the composer in finding ideas for the setting of an aria even when poetry fails to provide any." *Italian Opera and European Theatre, 1680–1720* (Turnhout: Brepols, 2000), 26. In this comment Bucciarelli notes the contemporary techniques developed by composers who were frequently faced with the task of setting uninspiring poetry, both in opera and certainly in cantata compositions.

31 Lowell Lindgren writes that Roman audiences not only preferred Scarlatti's academic style, but in general preferred music or operas that were "sostanziosi." See "Il dramma musicale a Roma durante la carriera di Alessandro Scarlatti (1660–1725)," in *Le muse galanti: la musica a Roma nel Settecento*, ed. Bruno Cagli (Rome: Istituto dell' Enciclopedia Italiana, 1985), 35–57, especially 41–45.

32 Lindgren also cites passages from Ferdinando's letters to Scarlatti, among which is included the prince's recommendation: "uno stile più tosto ameno ed arioso, che studiato"; "una musica più tosto facile" and "più tosto allegra." Ibid., 40. For details of Ferdinando and Scarlatti's correspondence, see Mario Fabbri, *Alessandro Scarlatti e il principe Ferdinando de' Medici* (Florence: L. S. Olschki, 1961), quotes are from letters dated August 9, 1704, 55; April 8, 1706, 69.

33 For a full quote of Zambeccari's letter (dated April 16, 1709), see Lodovico Frati, "Un impresario teatrale del Settecento e la sua biblioteca," *Rivista Musicale Italiana* 18 (1911): 69. Excerpts of this letter are also cited in Lindgren's "Il dramma musicale," 41.

34 For Crescimbeni's mention of Bononcini, see *Commentari*, 241.

35 Comparing Scarlatti with Bononcini, John Ernest Galliard recorded in 1716 that: "Of later year, *Aless. Scarlatti* and *Bononcini* have brought *cantata's* to what they are at present; *Bononcini* by his agreable and easie style, and those fine inventions in his *basses* (to which he was led by an Instrument upon which he excels); and *Scarlatti* by his noble and masterly turns." "To the Lovers of Musick," a two-page address included in Galliard, *Six English Cantatas after the Italian Manner Compos'ed by M Galliard* (London: J. Walsh and J. Hare, 1716).

36 For in-depth consideration of Bononcini's range of compositional styles (including elements that were clearly not just elegant and graceful), as well as a review of Bononcini's cantata reception by his contemporaries, his professional colleagues, and French critics, see Lowell Lindgren, "Bononcini's 'agreable and easie style, and those fine inventions in his *basses* (to which he was led by an instrument upon which he excels),'" in Talbot, ed., *Aspects of the Secular Cantata in Late Baroque Italy*, 135–175, which was published after this present monograph was completed.

37 Giovanni Bononcini (1670–1747) achieved fame within Rome and across Europe as a consummate composer of both cantatas and opera. For biographical background regarding Giovanni Bononcini and his dramatic works, see Lowell Lindgren, "A Bibliographic Scrutiny of Dramatic Works Set by Giovanni and his Brother Antonio Maria Bononcini" (Ph.D. diss., Harvard University, 1972). In the introduction to the Bononcini cantata volume, Lindgren notes that the widespread circulation of manuscript copies of Bononcini's early Roman cantatas, along with his first six serenatas and the acclaimed *Il trionfo di Camilla*, was significant in helping to spread Bononcini's reputation beyond the Italian peninsula. See Lindgren, "Introduction," in Bononcini, *Cantatas*, x.

38 See Lindgren's discussion of this work and its comparison with the composer's other cantatas in "Bononcini's 'agreable and easie style,'" 154–162.

39 The remainder of the cantata text makes it clear that the protagonist of the story is the Arcadian shepherdess Lidia.

40 In the Garland facsimile no indication of tempo change is indicated, though Lindgren documents that in GB-Lbl, Add 14,184, the 3/8 section is marked *Presto assai*, and similarly in other manuscripts of this cantata. See "Bononcini's 'agreable and easie style,'" 154.

41 As graceful as parts of this cantata's opening may be, the rest of the cantata takes on a number of more drastic modulations and text expression, especially in the two subsequent recitative sections, as discussed in further detail in ibid., 158. What is critical to recognize is the variety of compositional approaches not just from cantata to cantata, but even within a single cantata composition.

42 For a thorough treatment of opera's polemics which frequently addressed the controversial issue of the genre's need to entertain versus its duty to ennoble, see Renato Di Benedetto, "Poetics and Polemics," in *The History of Italian Opera*, Vol. VI: *Opera in Theory and Practice, Image and Myth*, ed. Lorenzo Bianconi and Giorgio Pestelli, trans. Kenneth Chalmers and Mary Whittall (University of Chicago Press, 2003; originally published as *Teorie e techniche, immagini e fantasmi*, Vol. VI of *Storia dell'opera italiana*, Turin: Edizioni di Torino, 1988), 1–71, especially 1–27.

43 Of the critical voices during this period, Pier Jacopo Martello is most vociferous in his argument for the centrality of delight in vocal dramatic music, and the ineffectiveness and acknowledged rejection by audiences of a more serious style. See *Della tragedia antica e moderna* (Rome: F. Gonzaga, 1715), translated in Enrico Fubini, *Music and Culture in Eighteenth-Century Europe: A Source Book*, ed. Bonnie J. Blackburn, trans. Wolfgang Freis, Lisa Gasbarrone, and Michael Louis Leone (University of Chicago Press, 1994), 56–57; the complete Fifth Session has been translated by Piero Weiss in "Pier Jacopo Martello on Opera (1715): An Annotated Translation," *Musical Quarterly* 66 (1980): 378–403.

44 In his introduction to *L'Arcadia*, Crescimbeni argues that these histories were especially important for an academy that departed from the norms, activities, and governance of other conventional intellectual societies. See *L'Arcadia*'s frontispiece, "L'autore a chi legge."

45 In this same introduction ("L'autore a chi legge"), the author specifies that his rendition of "Arcadia" is based on the history and documentation of the society's activities until 1706. In *La bellezza della volgar poesia*, 217–230, Crescimbeni appends a final section called "Notizie d'Arcadia," which serves as a short description of the academy's history and dealings to date but with an approach and tone quite different from *L'Arcadia*. Minor reads *L'Arcadia* as participating in a rhetorical tradition used by earlier pastoral writers, such as one of the first practitioners, Theocritus, and later in the pastoral writings of Sannazaro. He sees Crescimbeni adopting a similar approach in which descriptions of things

that actually exist contrast with things treated with poetic license and fantasy. See "Crescimbeni's Words," in *The Death of the Baroque*, 85–86. We might also come to understand Crescimbeni's literary departure and conceptual approach to *L'Arcadia* as linked to other contemporary Arcadian criticism, such as that espoused by Gioseffo Orsi, Ludovico Antonio Muratori, and Gian Vincenzo Gravina who defined the importance of verisimilitude as a quality of reality filtered through the poetic imagination, allowing for alternations in historical facts and/or anachronisms. See Dixon's discussion of this in *Between the Real and the Ideal*, 30.

46 Other secondary sources offer their own paraphrases of Prosa IV, V from Libro Settimo of Crescimbeni's *L'Arcadia*; see Ralph Kirkpatrick, *Domenico Scarlatti* (Princeton University Press, 1953), 44; Edward J. Dent, *Alessandro Scarlatti: His Life and Works* (1905; repr. London: Edward Arnold, 1960); and Pagano and Bianchi, *Alessandro Scarlatti*, 179–181. For a more complete transcription of the document, see Mario Rinaldi, *Arcangelo Corelli* (Milan: Curci, 1953), 270–273.

47 In *L'Arcadia*, Crescimbeni notes that at the Fifth Olympic Games of the Arcadians (Quinta Stagione, Ragunanza Seconda Generale nel Bosco Parrasio, Domenica 12 Giugno 1695) the society allowed female shepherds to participate for the first time. Dixon examines the portrayal of the female protagonists in *L'Arcadia*. Though referred to as nymphs, Dixon argues that they are also shepherdesses, the kind of noble women who were seen to be as competent to participate in the same Arcadian "games" as their fellow shepherds or "pastori." They also are characterized as nymphs: beautiful and charming, but seeking new knowledge and thus conveying the sense of "keen, but impressionable students," as Dixon explains. In this latter sense, the nymphs in *L'Arcadia* underscored their difference to men, but likewise signified metaphorically what "Arcadia" represented: beauty, sweetness, grace, simplicity, and naiveté. For more on female Arcadians and their role in the society, see "Women in Arcadia," *Eighteenth-Century Studies* 32, no. 3 (1999): 371–375.

48 *L'Arcadia*, 287.

49 Corelli, Scarlatti, and Pasquini were admitted to the Academy of Arcadians on April 26, 1706. See Fabrizio Della Seta's appendix for reproduction of documentary evidence in "La musica in Arcadia al tempo di Corelli," in *Nuovissimi studi corelliani. Atti del terzo congresso internazionale (Fusignano, 4–7 settembre 1980)*, ed. Sergio Durante and Pierluigi Petrobelli (Florence: L. S. Olschki, 1982), 141.

50 Corelli was an employee of Ottoboni from 1690 to 1712 and regularly provided *sinfonie* and *concerti* for the cardinal's weekly gatherings and more celebratory sponsored occasions. See Hans Joachim Marx, "Die Musik am Hofe Pietro Kardinal Ottobonis unter Arcangelo Corelli," *Analecta Musicologica* 5 (1968): 104–177.

51 Giambattista Felice Zappi (1667–1719) was an early founder and luminary of the Accademia degli Arcadi. Trained as a lawyer in Bologna, he moved to Rome

in 1687 and worked for the Curia, but found his real passion in poetry and frequented the city's illustrious literary circles. He was regarded as one of the most talented poets of the first generation of Arcadian writers. For background on Zappi's biography see *Rime dell'avvocato Giovambattista Felice Zappi, e di Faustina Maritti sua consorte* (Venice: Francesco Storti, 1757).

52 *L'Arcadia*, 289.

53 Zappi describes such experimental exchanges as happening in the "delicious Partenope," what Crescimbeni footnotes as Naples, where the lawyer Zappi worked with Scarlatti on several occasions while the composer was in the service of the viceroy, the Count of San Stefano, ibid.

54 The first piece, "Cantata da Tirsi," *Dunque, o vaga mia diva*, is reproduced textually by Crescimbeni as a brief recitative followed by a strophic aria; the second, "Altra Cantata del medesimo Tirsi, Daliso, e Silvia," *Vorrei un zeffiretto* appears as a dialogue, opening with a short aria by Daliso and a narrated recitative, followed by Silvia's response first as a recitative, then aria, ending with a duet of resolution between the two lovers. Both cantata excerpts are "Arcadian" in poetic style and content.

55 *L'Arcadia*, 292.

56 "Restava intanto ognuno sopraffatto in vedere, come mai gareggiassero que' due sì eccellenti Maestri, l'uno di Poesia, l'altro di Musica; ed i loro gareggiamento giunse a tal segno, che appena ebbe l'uno terminato di replicare l'ultimo verso della novella Aria, che l'altro chiuse l'ultima riga della sua Musica. Ora questa nuova maniera di fare all'improvviso Musicale Accademia piacque tanto alla Brigata, che con essa vollero chiudere la conversazione." Ibid., 293.

57 In his extensive study of Scarlatti's chamber cantatas, Edwin Hanley pointed out that no settings of texts by Zappi had been identified among Scarlatti's cantatas. Hanley, "Alessandro Scarlatti's *cantate da camera*," 7, and to my knowledge, we have not yet found other cantatas that set these texts. See Dubowy, "Notes on Text and Context in Alessandro Scarlatti's *cantate da camera*," 123–127 for further speculation on Zappi and Scarlatti's relationship. We know from Crescimbeni's collected *Vite degli Arcadi illustri*, Vol. IV, that Zappi was particularly praised for his skills at improvising poetry, citing the very example of this musical *accademia* as evidence. See Francesco Maria Mancurti's entry for Zappi in the *Vite*, 143–181, esp. 161. The description of this improvised moment is uncannily similar to the famous description penned by Charles de Brosses in his *Lettre familière* of the well-known Arcadian poetic improviser, Bernardino Perfetti: "At first these followed each other slowly enough. Then, little by little, the poet's animation increased, and as he warmed to his task the harpsichordist played more loudly. Toward the end the poet was declaiming like a man inspired, poet and accompanist going on together with an amazing rapidity." Translated quote from Ernest Hatch Wilkins, *A History of Italian Literature*, revised by Thomas G. Bergin (Cambridge, MA: Harvard University Press, 1974), 328.

58 Here I draw in particular on the brief comments made by Pagano, Kirkpatrick, and Dent, see n46.

59 Della Seta, "La musica in Arcadia al tempo di Corelli," 123–148.

60 Ibid., 125–126. Della Seta notes in the transcription of Crescimbeni's document (141) that in point #10 it says it is obligatory for the musicians to leave a copy of their music in the Arcadian archive, as would be requested from any other shepherd. He qualifies that no music existed among the documents he surveyed in the archive (which at that time was partially under repair, thus limiting total access). My own survey of the archive also produced no evidence of actual scores.

61 *L'Arcadia*'s "L'autore a chi legge."

62 Ralph Nash, "Introduction" to *Arcadia & Piscatorial Eclogues*, 23. Nash also writes that Sannazaro's process of imitation in *Arcadia* is "dynamic, and it is focused on combining and blending features common to several different modes of prose and poetry . . . [he] arrives at a sense of literary tradition, almost a literary history" (23).

63 *L'Arcadia*'s "L'autore a chi legge."

64 Dixon's recent book, *Between the Real and the Ideal* and Minor's *The Death of the Baroque* are, to some extent, exceptions.

65 In her article, "Women in Arcadia," (n2), Dixon notes those who see the Academy of Arcadians and their activities as essentially frivolous, including Vernon Lee (Violet Page), *Studies of the Eighteenth Century in Italy*, 2nd edn (London, 1907), 7–64; and Cesare d'Onofrio, *Roma val bene un'abiura: storie romane tra Cristina di Svezia, Piazza del Popolo e l'Accademia dell'Arcadia* (Rome: Fratelli Palombi, 1976), 263–290. Those who praise the society for its progressiveness include Walter Binni, "La letteratura nell'epoca arcadica razionali," in *Storia della letteratura italiana*, Vol. VI: *Il Settecento*, ed. E. Cecchi and N. Spegno (Milan: Garzanti, 1968), 326–460; and to some extent Hanns Gross, *Rome in the Age of Enlightenment: The Post-Tridentine Syndrome and the Ancien Régime* (Cambridge University Press, 1990). More recent treatments that evaluate the importance of Arcadia include Christopher M. S. Johns, *Papal Art and Cultural Politics: Rome in the Age of Clement XI* (Cambridge University Press, 1993); Francesca Santovetti, "Arcadia a Roma Anno Domini 1690: accademia e vizi di forma," *Modern Language Notes* 112, no. 1 (1997): 21–37; C. Leri, "The 300th Anniversary of the Accademia dell'Arcadia. Conference Papers," *Lettere Italiane* 50, no. 1 (1998): 140–145; along with Dixon, *Between the Real and the Ideal*, and Minor, *The Death of the Baroque.*

66 See Gerbino's *Music and the Myth of Arcadia in Renaissance Italy* for a historically comparative treatment of Arcadia in the Renaissance context as opposed to this later, early Enlightenment revival, in which strong opposition to a recent past – that is, Italian poetry and drama of the seventeenth century – highly influenced the symbolic adoption of Arcadia and the pastoral as an ideal.

67 See chapter 1 for further discussion.

68 Several of Muratori's writings address these strong feelings; however, a useful starting point is his *Opere del proposto Lodovico Antonio Muratori*, Vol. VIII (Arezzo: Belloti, 1768), 1–35. In this context of placing his version and arguments of reform in opposition to the Arcadians, see Vincenzo Ferrone, *The Intellectual Roots of the Italian Enlightenment*, trans. Sue Brotherton (Atlantic Highlands, NJ: Humanities Press, 1995), 99–105.

69 As noted in chapter 1, the schism of 1711 would be an irreversible mark on the development and future of Arcadia. Thanks to Gravina's organization and mobilization of dissenters, Arcadia would never fully regain the intellectual integrity it evoked in the late seventeenth century and first years of the eighteenth. For further analysis of Gravina's ideological stance and argument with Arcadia, see Amedeo Quondam, *Cultura e ideologia di Gianvincenzo Gravina* (Milan: U. Morsia, 1968), as well as Domenico Consoli, *Realtà e fantasia nel classicismo di Gian Vincenzo Gravina* (Milan: Casa Editrice Bietti, 1970).

70 Minor, *Death of the Baroque*, 43. For the quote derived from Muratori, see *Della perfetta poesia italiana* (Modena: Soliani, 1706), repr. and ed. by Ada Ruschioni (Milan: Marzorati Editore, 1972), book I, chapter 14, 167–193.

71 Della Seta, "La musica in Arcadia al tempo di Corelli," 132.

72 Quondam, "L'istituzione Arcadia: sociologia e ideologia di un'accademia," *Quaderni Storici* 23 (1973): 389–438.

73 Ibid., 394. Quondam cites Muratori's proposal to form an Italian republic of letters, a proposal seen within the Arcadian "machine" as encroaching on its own territory and thus attacked by one of the Arcadians' most renowned thinkers and ideologues, the cleric and canon Francesco Bianchini.

74 Johns, *Papal Art and Cultural Politics*.

75 As Johns notes, given her dramatic conversion to Catholicism and her abdication of her throne, it is not surprising that Christina's Catholicism left a decided impression on her circle. Ibid., 216 n5.

76 Recall that this range of interests is carefully elucidated in *L'Arcadia*'s survey of the shepherds' many activities and specialties.

77 Johns stipulates that Clement XI's reinvigoration of sacred traditions and history was not merely to re-esteem the Catholic faith and its institutions in a post-Counter-Reformation age, but to do so at a time when the political privileges of the church had been under siege or denied by more powerful absolutist Catholic monarchies. *Papal Art and Cultural Politics*, 22.

78 Ibid., 38. In this same chapter, Johns argues that although these attitudes (papal conservatism and fervor for secular reform) were not new, they coalesced to new effectiveness. The writings of Crescimbeni (which bear a similarity to other works of the Clementine Roman period with encyclopedic tendencies) are most striking in their juxtaposition of Arcadian and Paleochristian attitudes prevalent in early *settecento* Roman intellectual life (25).

79 Touraine, "Society as Utopia," in *Utopia: The Search for the Ideal Society in the Western World*, ed. Schaer *et al.*, 20.

80 In her critical analysis of nostalgia, Svetlana Boym stresses that "nostalgia is not 'antimodern'; it is not necessarily opposed to modernity but coeval with it. Nostalgia and progress are like Jekyll and Hyde: doubles and mirror images of one another." Her point helps to illuminate how the Arcadians' redemptive and utopian impulses, even if self-absorbed in the past, were still acutely linked to the emerging sense of "progress" that permeated the early eighteenth century. See "Nostalgia and Discontents," *The Hedgehog Review* 9, no. 2 (2007): 7–18.

81 *La bellezza della volgar poesia* (1700), "Notizie d'Arcadia," 221–222.

82 *Le vite degli Arcadi illustri. Scritte da diversi autori, e pubblicate d'ordine della Generale Adunanza da Giovanni Mario Crescimbeni, canonico di S. Maria in Cosmedin, e custode d'Arcadia* (Vol. I, 1708; II, 1710; III, 1714; IV, 1727; V, 1751), and *Notizie istoriche degli Arcadi morti* (Vol. I, 1720–1721; II, 1720–1721; III, 1721), both series published by de' Rossi in Rome. For the series *Vite*, Crescimbeni commissioned other Arcadian writers to document the lives of the most illustrious members of the society, noting their achievements, their particular area of expertise, and any mark of rank, or professional position. Each *vita* was voted upon by a committee of evaluators, referred to as *deputati*. The *Vite*, along with the *Notizie storiche*, are often overlooked as sources; they document information concerning the lives of seminal figures for music history, including patrons, cultural critics, librettists, and composers.

83 In his landmark study, *How Societies Remember*, sociologist Paul Connerton argues that conceptions and *re*-collected knowledge of the past (real or fictionalized) are best conveyed and sustained by ritual performances. In these commemorative acts, Connerton identifies a "rhetoric of re-enactment," in which three distinguishable modes are typically articulated: calendrical, verbal, and gestural. Evidence may be difficult to obtain for the Arcadians' verbal or gestural re-enactments, but surely we can identify their effective deployment of calendrical re-enactment in the *Giuochi* and *Annoverazione*, which contained "special points at which the activity of recapitulation [became] the special focus of communal attention." See Connerton's theorizing on commemorative ceremonies in *How Societies Remember* (Cambridge University Press, 1989), 65–71.

84 As historian David Lowenthal suggests, the effort to preserve the past is often an effect of no longer being intimate enough with that legacy to rework it creatively. See *The Past is a Foreign Country* (Cambridge University Press, 1985), xxiv.

85 In a note to his readers, "A chi legge," Crescimbeni suggests that the academy saw fit to write such tributes to past lives (of those whose generous support and accomplishments made the group what it is today) since they have currently spent time writing about illustrious members who are still alive and active. *Notizie istoriche degli Arcadi morti*, Vol. I, 17.

86 The presence of death in Arcadia was a long-standing trope in literature (from the classical to the early modern period) and, of course, in painting, made famous in Poussin's *Et in Arcadia ego*, *c.*1638–1640. In his masterful study, "*Et in Arcadia ego*: Poussin and the Elegiac Tradition," in *Meaning in the Visual*

Arts (University of Chicago Press, 1955), 295–320, Erwin Panofsky stresses the Arcadians' elegiac treatment of death as a vehicle for remembrance, and thus revival. A similar interpretation of the act of memorializing is offered by Dixon who argues that the acknowledgment of death for the Arcadians may have been a way to mourn the deceased, but also could have been a way to encourage members to aspire to their model and fame after their own deaths. See *Between the Real and the Ideal*, 70.

87 The notion of a "lapide di memoria" is described by Crescimbeni in *Le vite degli Arcadi illustri*, Vol. I. Earlier in *La bellezza della volgar poesia*, Crescimbeni instructs that all deceased members should be memorialized on paper to note the sad day of their deaths; if famous, their memory would be made eternal in a marble statue of their likeness. *La bellezza della volgar poesia* (1700), "Notizie d'Arcadia," 221–222. Dixon's research and study of the Arcadian conception of *Bosco Parrasio* helps to clarify some details. She notes that the *lapide* were mostly in the form of small plaques, and were usually hung or displayed somewhere, eventually on the walls of the Arcadian amphitheater, or inside the *serbatoio*, the archival room, that flanked the amphitheater once the Arcadians founded and built a permanent garden location. She adds that it is likely no statues or real portraits existed. See *Between the Real and the Ideal*, 70–74, 82. Minor hypothesizes how these epitaphs "address[ed] the passerby to ponder the life of the one so described and thus to ponder on his or her own life. These plaques, which still exist, were, perhaps, the objects of threnodies, and remain brief forms of the pastoral elegy as commemorations and celebrations of the poetic abilities of past Arcadians." *Death of the Baroque*, 146.

88 *The Past is a Foreign Country*, 321.

89 Muratori, for example, strongly urged his fellow countrymen (who for him were mostly men of letters) to address the problems of the day, an issue he felt had been ignored or overlooked by Italy's many academies, including the Arcadians. See *Opere* VIII, 1–35. Gravina similarly looked at his present world as a place that needed moral renewal. He saw danger in the Arcadians' absorption with pastoral poetry and utopian fantasies, which could lead to idleness and delusion. Rather, promoting "classicism" (through drama, poetry, rhetoric) was a function for restoring in youth a sense of moral rectitude, teaching good judgment and rationality. Many of Gravina's ideas about the usefulness of classicism are found in *Della division d'Arcadia, lettera ad un'amico*, published anonymously in Naples, 1711, reprinted in Gravina, *Scritti critici e teorici*, ed. Amedeo Quondam (Rome: G. Laterza, 1973), 469–478; also see Quondam's *Cultura e ideologia di Gianvincenzo Gravina*.

90 Cf. n65 for a list of scholars who focus on evaluating Arcadia. I have found the two recent art historical studies by Dixon and Minor to offer some of the more insightful readings of Arcadia's cultural impact. In *Death of the Baroque*, Minor thoughtfully explores the foundations of "pastoralism" as a way to complicate the Arcadians' cultural posture, efficacy, and impact on European Enlightenment.

Minor reads the Arcadians' pastoralism as both intellectually and culturally motivated as well as politically directed. He wants to promote a theory of the pastoral that underscores a sense of "polysemy" and "doubleness," a recognition of dualistic qualities at the core of the Arcadians' behavior and ideology. However, it also appears that he is willing to give the Arcadians a deeper sense of self-awareness in their ability (via the pastoral) to create a "fictive world that has an intimate relation to the real world." In essence, it does not seem that this author finds the contradictory dualities embedded in the Arcadians' cultural landscape as particularly ineffectual. For examples of these points, see 139–141, 165–169. Dixon's stance in *Between the Real and the Ideal* is somewhat different. Unlike Minor, she does not see the Arcadians as so able to fluidly negotiate the boundaries between republican or monarchical systems, the past and present, the ideal and real. Their failure, as she reads it, results from a destabilizing dependence on a monarchical court system (the Curia), the traditional patronage and elite values of which infiltrated the academy, despite their idealistic experimentation with republicanism. The Arcadians' idealized self-representation, Dixon argues, did not seem to match the more mundane (and less utopian) achievements the academy actually realized. For examples of these points, see 15–16.

91 See chapter 1 for details.

92 Crescimbeni's sketch is held at Rome's Biblioteca Angelica (I-Ra, Arcadia ms. 35, fols. 3v–4r). The sketch at very least captures a similar large gated entrance, the terraced staircases, interrupted at various levels by a series of statues and obelisks, with the large amphitheater placed at the very top, surrounded by a decorated rotunda.

93 As art historians, both Dixon and Minor focus their studies on analyzing the architectural and artistic details of the garden. See Dixon, *Between the Real and the Ideal*, chapter 3, "The Ideal Bosco Parrasio," 54–82, and Minor, *Death of the Baroque*, chapter 6, "The Parrhasian Grove," 127–169. Also see the brief description by John Pinto, "Architecture and Urbanism," in *Art in Rome in the Eighteenth Century*, ed. Edgar Peters Bowron and Joseph J. Rishel (Philadelphia: Merrell in association with Philadelphia Museum of Art, 2000), 125–126.

94 Dixon, *Between the Real and the Ideal*, 82.

95 For a discussion of the antinomies inherent to all Arcadias, see Françoise Choay, "Utopia and the Philosophical Status of Constructed Space," in *Utopia: The Search*, ed. Schaer *et al.*, 346–353, especially 347.

96 Daniel Chua, *Absolute Music and the Construction of Meaning* (Cambridge University Press, 1999), 42–43.

97 Di Benedetto, "Poetics and Polemics," 3.

98 See his "Introduction" to *Music and Culture in Eighteenth-Century Europe: A Source Book*, 1–34; quote on 2.

99 See chapter 1 for further background on the debates and polemics directed at seventeenth-century opera.

100 For an in-depth study of the effects of spoken dramaturgical reform on the writing and conception of opera, see chapter 4, "Italian Tragedy and *dramma per musica*," in Bucciarelli, *Italian Opera and European Theatre*, 81–104; along with her own study, the author cites the important contributions on this subject made by Piero Weiss and Reinhard Strohm.

101 In fact, it was Crescimbeni, as the official guardian of the academy and protector of Italian culture, who was the first to formulate such an accusation in *La bellezza della volgar poesia*, along with similar remarks made in later years by Charles Burney, who wrote of Italian drama, "The passion for dramas in music has ruined true tragedy, as well as comedy in this country." For both quotes see Di Benedetto, "Poetics and Polemics," 17–18.

102 Important to this context was the librettist Count Girolamo Frigimelica Roberti, and the decade following included influential works by Domenico David and Apostolo Zeno. See Harris Saunders for the connection of these literati to the acclaimed Accademia Animosi, an extension of Arcadia, in "The Repertoire of a Venetian Opera House (1678–1714): The Teatro Grimani di San Giovanni Gristosomo" (Ph.D. diss., Harvard University, 1985), 28–54.

103 Bucciarelli, *Italian Opera and European Theatre*, xix.

104 ". . . tali non oserei quasi chiamarle, non si convenendo loro, anzi abborrendosi da loro (se pure han da essere perfette) la Musica, quale a' nostri giorni s'usa." *Della perfetta poesia italiana*, 572.

105 As Fubini notes, Le Cerf realized that the complete elimination of music from drama contradicted the basic aspiration of French (as well as Italian) classicism, which was that ancient drama was set and performed musically. See *Music and Culture in Eighteenth-Century Europe*, 5. Jean-Laurent Le Cerf de la Viéville's main criticisms appear in *Comparaison de la musique italienne et de la musique française* (Brussels: François Foppens, 1705; repr. Geneva: Minkoff, 1972). For excerpts translated into English see Oliver Strunk, *Source Readings in Music History*, rev. and ed. Leo Treitler (New York: Norton Press, 1998), 489–507; and Fubini, *Music and Culture in Eighteenth-Century Europe*, 73–78. Saint-Évremond's essay *Sur les opéras* first appeared in 1684; it appears in English in *The Works of St. Évremond Made English from the French Original*, 2nd edn (J. J. Knapton, 1728).

106 *Della perfetta poesia italiana*, 577.

107 Piero Weiss carefully traces the various steps and attempts at revitalization taken by literary critics and reformers at the turn of the eighteenth century. See "Teorie drammatiche e 'infranciosamento': motivi della 'riforma' melodrammatica nel primo Settecento," in *Antonio Vivaldi. Teatro musicale, cultura e società*, Vol. II, ed. Lorenzo Bianconi and Giovanni Morelli (Florence: L. S. Olschki, 1982), 273–296.

108 *La bellezza della volgar poesia*, 141.

109 *Commentari del Canonico Gio. Mario Crescimbeni*, 235.

110 Robert Freeman, *Opera Without Drama: Currents of Change in Italian Opera 1675–1625*. Studies in Musicology 14 (Ann Arbor, MI: UMI, 1981 [1967]), 21–22.

111 Weiss, "Pier Jacopo Martello on Opera (1715): An Annotated Translation," 383.

112 Ellen Harris argues that the dramatic pastoral was essentially a modern form, born in sixteenth-century Italy through the writings of de' Beccari, and more importantly, through Giambattista Guarini's *Il pastor fido*, and was recognized as such a hundred years later in Crescimbeni's literary histories. See "The Pastoral in Italy," in *Handel and the Pastoral Tradition*, 16–17.

113 See Chua's *Absolute Music and the Construction of Meaning*. Chua describes pastoral drama as the paradigmatic product of modernity: "Modern in form, ancient in content, the pastoral embodies the split which modernity makes to measure itself against the past." He also notes that in opera it is music that serves as the central mechanism to bring "the reality of the pastoral's past into present experience," 29–30.

114 Fubini, *Music and Culture in Eighteenth-Century Europe*, 19.

115 See chapter 1 for brief details on Gravina and the enacted schism within the Academy of Arcadians.

116 The first *Della division d'Arcadia, lettera ad un amico* (Naples, 1711) was later published posthumously in Verona, 1726.

117 *Della divisione d'Arcadia* (1726), see *Scritti critici e teorici*, ed. Quondam, 483.

118 *Della tragedia* (Naples: Nicolò Naso, 1715), in *Scritti critici e teorici*, ed. Quondam, 503–592.

119 *Della tragedia* covers these very issues in several sections throughout Libro Uno (see *Scritti critici e teorici*, ed. Quondam). For example, in section I, "Fine della poesia," Gravina writes: "Therefore, tragedy, when it realizes its true ideal, has the ability to render to the people the fruits of philosophy and of eloquence, in order to correct customs and speech: those in our own theater, are further corrupted rather than reformed," 508; or in section XX, "Contro i moderni tragici," Gravina contends: "But the current theater only teaches the people to talk pompously and rave acutely, exercising their madness through such childish advice," 532. Also see Minor, "A Short History of the Academy of Arcadians," in *Death of the Baroque*, 121–126, for a useful discussion of Gravina's training as jurist and moralist, as well as his views on religious and moral reform.

120 Freeman, *Opera without Drama*, 32. Along these same lines, Freeman points out a lack of consistency in this document, e.g., Gravina demonstrates unevenness in his interpretations of Aristotle's *Poetics*; at times he is conservative while at others he is liberal; see the author's summary, 34.

121 *Della tragedia, Libro uno*, in *Scritti critici e teorici*, ed. Quondam, 559.

122 Ibid., 560.

123 Ibid., 555–556.

124 Ibid., 556.

125 See chapters XXXV, "Distinzione della melodia e dell'armonia" and XXXVI, "Dell'antica rappresentazione" of Gravina's *Della tragedia*, in *Scritti critici e teorici*, ed. Quondam, 560–568; the same points have been summarized by Freeman in *Opera without Drama*, 34.

126 Della Seta reports that there are at least three sonnets collected in the Arcadian manuscripts held at the Biblioteca Angelica, Rome; see mss. 11–12 as catalogued by Barbara Tellini Santoni, *Inventario dei manoscritti (1–41)* (Rome: La Meridiana, 1991). In one of these documents, Della Seta also reveals how Scarlatti attacks the "schismatics" who had been headed by Gravina. The author sees this poem potentially as a response by Scarlatti to the insinuation that he colluded with these rebels. See "La musica in Arcadia," 127–128.

127 In this regard, we might compare Handel's dramatic cantatas and his solo and duet cantatas with instruments as more extreme versions of cantatas that veered towards the quasi-operatic in style. For an introduction and background to these works, see Hans Joachim Marx, ed., *Kantaten mit Instrumenten*, I–III, *Hallische Händel-Ausgabe*, series 5, Vols. III–V (Kassel: Bärenreiter, 1994, 1995, 1999); and for an interpretive discussion of these cantatas' function and aesthetic milieu, see Ellen Harris, "Women's Voice/Men's Voices," in Harris, *Handel as Orpheus: Voice and Desire in the Chamber Cantatas* (Cambridge, MA: Harvard University Press, 2001), 49–84.

128 See chapter 1 for further discussion of the dramaturgical limitations and waning popularity of pastoral opera.

129 As Minor makes clear, pastoral poetry often uses *parataxis*, the absence of syntactic connections or conjunctions, and avoidance of linking between phrases and clauses, to create a sense of speed, briskness, piling up, condensation, and isolation of certain stylistic elements. See *Death of the Baroque*, 159.

5 Epilogue

1 Crescimbeni heaped singular scorn on *Giasone* for its mixing of genres, poetic debasement, and lack of verisimilitude through its use of arias, even though it was not the only opera of this period in this style. This discussion was printed in *La bellezza della volgar poesia* (Rome: Buagni, 1700), 106–107.

2 We see this concern registered in print most famously in Giovanni Domenico Ottonelli's *Della christiana moderatione del theatro. Libro detto l'Ammonitioni a' recitanti per avvisare ogni christiano a moderarsi da gli eccessi nel recitare* (Florence: Gio. Antonio Bonardi, 1652).

3 On the question of enchantment in opera's early history, see Daniel Chua, *Absolute Music and the Construction of Meaning* (Cambridge University Press, 1999), 29–40.

4 For a critical look at opera's pastoral beginnings, see Gary Tomlinson, "Pastoral and Musical Magic in the Birth of Opera," in *Opera and the Enlightenment*, ed.

Thomas Bauman and Marita Petzoldt McClymonds (Cambridge University Press, 1995), 7–20.

5 Enrico Fubini, *Music and Culture in Eighteenth-Century Europe: A Source Book*, ed. Bonnie J. Blackburn, trans. Wolfgang Freis, Lisa Gasbarrone, and Michael Louis Leone (University of Chicago Press, 1994), 5.

6 Downing Thomas, *Aesthetics of Opera in the Ancien Régime, 1647–1785* (Cambridge University Press, 2002), 6.

7 Reinhard Strohm, *Dramma per musica: Italian Opera Seria of the Eighteenth Century* (New Haven: Yale University Press, 1997), 13.

8 See Martha Feldman's *Opera and Sovereignty: Transforming Myths in Eighteenth-Century Italy* (University of Chicago Press, 2007), for a recent and seminal representative of this kind of analysis.

Bibliography

Ademollo, Alessandro. *I teatri di Roma nel secolo decimosettimo*. Bologna: Forni Editore, 1969. (Originally published Rome: Pasqualucci, 1888.)

Ago, Renata. *Carriere e clientele nella Roma barocca*. Rome: Laterza, 1990.

"Hegemony over the Social Scene and Zealous Popes (1676–1700)." In *Court and Politics in Papal Rome, 1492–1700*. Edited by Gianvittorio Signorotto and Maria Antonietta Visceglia. Cambridge University Press, 2002. 229–246.

Allsop, Peter. *Arcangelo Corelli: New Orpheus of our Times*. Oxford University Press, 1999.

"Problems of Ascription in the Roman Sinfonia of the Late Seventeenth Century: Colista and Lonati." *Music Review* 50, no. 1 (1989): 34–44.

Altman, Rick. *Film/Genre*. London: BFI Publishing, 1999.

Antolini, Bianca Maria. "Cantanti e letterati a Roma nella prima metà del Seicento: alcune osservazioni." In *In cantu et in sermone: For Nino Pirrotta on his 80th Birthday*. Edited by Fabrizio Della Seta and Franco Piperno. Florence: L. S. Olschki, 1989. 347–363.

Arkayin, Asir. "The Second Siege of Vienna and its Consequences." *Revue Internationale d'Histoire Militaire* 46 (1980): 107–117.

Bakhtin, Mikhail. *The Dialogic Imagination: Four Essays*. Edited by Michael Holquist. Translated by Caryl Emerson and Michael Holquist. Austin: University of Texas Press, 1981.

Speech Genres and Other Late Essays. Edited by Caryl Emerson and Michael Holquist. Translated by Vern W. McGee. Austin: University of Texas Press, 1986.

Barazzi, Antonella. "Una cultura per gli ordini religiosi." *Quaderni Storici* 40, no. 2 (2005): 485–517.

Battistini, Andrea. *Il barocco: cultura, miti, immagini*. Rome: Salerno Editrice, 2000.

Benjamin, Walter. *The Origin of German Tragic Drama*. Translated by John Osborne. New York: Verso, 1998. (Originally published as *Ursprung des deutschen Trauerspiels*, 1928.)

Besutti, Paola. "Oratori in corte a Mantova: tra Bologna, Modena e Venezia." In *L'oratorio musicale italiano e i suoi contesti (secc. XVII–XVIII). Atti del convegno internazionale, Perugia, Sagra musicale umbra, 18–20 settembre 1997*. Edited by Paola Besutti. Florence: L. S. Olschki, 2002. 406–420.

Besutti, Paola, ed. *L'oratorio musicale italiano e i suoi contesti (secc. XVII–XVIII). Atti del convegno internazionale, Perugia, Sagra musicale umbra, 18–20 settembre*

1997. In *Quaderni della Rivista Italiana di Musicologia* 35. Florence: L. S. Olschki, 2002.

Bianchi, Lino. *Carissimi, Stradella, Scarlatti e l'oratorio musicale.* Rome: De Santis, 1969.

"Dall'oratorio di Alessandro Scarlatti all'oratorio di Handel." In *Händel e gli Scarlatti a Roma.* Edited by Nino Pirrotta and Agostino Ziino. Florence: L. S. Olschki, 1987. 79–92.

Bianconi, Lorenzo. *Music in the Seventeenth Century.* Translated by David Bryant. Cambridge University Press, 1987. (Originally published as *Il Seicento.* Turin: Edizioni di Torino, 1982.)

Bianconi, Lorenzo and Thomas Walker. "Production, Consumption and Political Function of Seventeenth-Century Opera." *Early Music History* 4 (1984): 209–296.

Binni, Walter. "La letteratura nell'epoca arcadica razionali." In *Storia della letteratura italiana.* Vol. VI. Edited by Emilio Cecchi and Natalino Spegno. Milan: Garzanti, 1968. 326–460.

Bissel, Ward. *Artemisia Gentileschi and the Authority of Art.* University Park, PA: Pennsylvania State University Press, 1999.

Boccaccio, Giovanni. *Boccaccio on Poetry; Being the Preface and Fourteenth and Fifteenth Books of Boccaccio's* Genealogia deorum gentilium libri *in an English Version with Introductory Essay and Commentary by Charles G. Osgood.* Princeton University Press, 1930.

Boiteux, Martine. "Fêtes et traditions espagnoles à Rome au XVIIe siècle." In *Barocco romano e barocco italiano: il teatro, l'effimero, l'allegoria.* Edited by Marcello Fagiolo and Maria Luisa Madonna. Rome: Gangemi, 1985. 117–134.

Bononcini, Giovanni. *Cantatas by Giovanni Bononcini.* Edited by Lowell Lindgren. The Italian Cantata in the Seventeenth Century 10. New York: Garland, 1985.

Boscarino, Salvatore. *Juvarra architetto.* Rome: Officina, 1973.

Bossa, Renata. "Corelli e il cardinal Benedetto Pamphilij. Alcune notizie." In *Nuovissimi studi corelliani. Atti del terzo congresso internazionale (Fusignano 4–7 settembre 1980).* Edited by Sergio Durante and Pierluigi Petrobelli. Florence: L. S. Olschki, 1982. 218–222.

Boyd, Malcolm. *Cantatas by Alessandro Scarlatti.* The Italian Cantata in the Seventeenth Century 13. New York: Garland, 1986.

"Form and Style in Scarlatti's Chamber Cantatas." *Music Review* 25 (1964): 17–26.

"The Italian Serenata and Related Genres in Britain and Germany: Some Observations." In *Giacomo Francesco Milano e il ruolo dell'aristocrazia nel patrocinio delle attività musicali nel secolo XVIII.* Edited by Gaetano Pitarresi. Reggio Calabria: Laruffa Editore, 2001. 515–527.

"Rome: The Power of Patronage." In *The Late Baroque Era: From the 1680s to 1740.* Edited by George J. Buelow. Englewood Cliffs, NJ: Prentice Hall, 1986. 39–65.

Boym, Svetlana. "Nostalgia and Discontents," *The Hedgehog Review* 9, no. 2 (2007): 7–18.

Braudel, Fernand. *Civilisation matérielle et capitalisme (XVe–XVIIIe siècle)*. 3 vols. Paris: Armand Colin, 1979.

Broom, William A. "Political Allegory in Alessandro Melani's Oratorio *Golia abbattuto.*" *Journal of Musicological Research* 3 (1981): 383–397.

Bucciarelli, Melania. *Italian Opera and European Theatre, 1680–1720: Plots, Performers, Dramaturgies*. Turnhout: Brepols, 2000.

Buono, Luciano. "Forme oratoriali in Sicilia nel secondo Seicento: il dialogo." In *L'oratorio musicale italiano e i suoi contesti (secc. XVII–XVIII). Atti del convegno internazionale, Perugia, Sagra musicale umbra, 18–20 settembre 1997*. Edited by Paola Besutti. Florence: L. S. Olschki, 2002. 115–139.

Burke, Peter. *Popular Culture in Early Modern Europe*. New York: Harper and Row, 1978.

Cagli, Bruno. "Produzione musicale e governo pontificio." In *Le muse galanti: la musica a Roma nel Settecento*. Edited by Bruno Cagli. Rome: Istituto dell' Enciclopedia Italiana, 1985. 11–21.

Calcagno, Mauro. "Signifying Nothing: On the Aesthetics of Pure Voice in Early Venetian Opera." *The Journal of Musicology* 20, no. 4 (2003): 461–497.

Cametti, Alberto. *Cristina di Svezia, l'arte musicale e gli spettacoli teatrali in Roma. Bernardo Pasquini–Arcangelo Corelli–Alessandro Scarlatti*. Rome: Tipografia Romano Mezzetti, 1931.

Il Teatro Tordinona poi di Apollo. 2 vols. Tivoli: Aldo Chicca, 1938.

Cannizzo, Luigia. "Vent'anni di storia di un teatro romano: il Capranica (1678–1698)." In *Il libro di teatro. Annali del Dipartimento musica e spettacolo dell'Università di Roma 1990*. Edited by Roberto Ciancarelli. Rome: Bulzoni Editore, 1991. 31–46.

Caraci, Maria. "Le cantate romane di Alessandro Scarlatti nel fondo Noseda." In *Händel e gli Scarlatti a Roma*. Edited by Nino Pirrotta and Agostino Ziino. Florence: L. S. Olschki, 1987. 93–112.

Carboni, Fabio, Theresa M. Gialdroni, and Agostino Ziino. "Cantate ed arie romane del tardo Seicento nel Fondo Caetani della Biblioteca Corsiniana: repertorio, forme, strutture." *Studi Musicali* 18 (1989): 49–192.

Carpanetto, Dino and Giuseppe Ricuperati. *Italy in the Age of Reason*. London: Longman, 1987.

Carter, Tim. "Italian Opera after 1637." In *The Cambridge History of Seventeenth-Century Music*. Edited by Tim Carter and John Butt. Cambridge University Press, 2005. 270–277.

Chartier, Roger. *Cultural History: Between Practices and Representations*. Translated by Lydia G. Cochrane. Ithaca: Cornell University Press, 1988.

Chirico, Teresa. "L'inedita serenata alla regina Maria Casimira di Polonia: Pietro Ottoboni committente di cantate e serenate (1689–1708)." In *La serenata tra Seicento e Settecento: musica, poesia, scenotecnica. Atti del convegno internazionale di studi (Reggio Calabria, 16–17 maggio 2003).* Vol. II. Edited by Nicolò Maccavino. Reggio Calabria: Laruffa Editore, 2007. 397–450.

Chua, Daniel. *Absolute Music and the Construction of Meaning.* Cambridge University Press, 1999.

Cohen, Ralph. "History and Genre." *New Literary History* 17, no. 2 (1986): 203–218.

Collins, Jeffrey Laird. *Papacy and Politics in 18th-Century Rome: Pius VI and the Arts.* Cambridge University Press, 2004.

Colonna, Prospero. *I Colonna dalle origini all'inizio del secolo XIX.* Rome: Serono, 1927.

Connerton, Paul. *How Societies Remember.* Cambridge University Press, 1989.

Connors, Joseph. "Alliance and Enmity in Roman Baroque Urbanism." *Römisches Jahrbuch der Bibliotheca Hertziana* 25 (1989): 207–294.

Consoli, Domenico. *Realtà e fantasia nel classicismo di Gian Vincenzo Gravina.* Milan: Casa Editrice Bietti, 1970.

Coulanges, Philippe Emmanuel, marquis de. *Mémoires de M. de Coulanges, suivis de lettres inédites de M.me de Sévigné, de son fils, de l'abbé de Coulanges [. . .] publiés par M. de Monmerqué.* Paris: Imprimerie de P. Didot, 1820.

Crescimbeni, Giovanni Maria. *L'Arcadia del Canonico Gio. Mario Crescimbeni.* Rome: de'Rossi, 1708.

    La bellezza della volgar poesia. Rome: Buagni, 1700.

    Commentari del Canonico Gio. Mario Crescimbeni custode d'Arcadia intorno alla sua Istoria della volgar poesia. Vol. I. Rome: de'Rossi, 1702.

    I giuochi olimpici celebrati dagli Arcadi nell'Olimpiade DCXX. Rome: Monaldi, 1701.

    L'istoria della volgar poesia. Rome: Chracas, 1698.

    Notizie istoriche degli Arcadi morti. 3 vols. Rome: de'Rossi, 1720–1721.

    Le vite degli Arcadi illustri. Scritte da diversi autori, e pubblicate d'ordine della generale adunanza da Giovanni Mario Crescimbeni, canonico di S. Maria in Cosmedin, e custode d'Arcadia. 5 vols. Rome: de'Rossi, 1708–1751.

Croce, Benedetto. *Estetica come scienza dell'espressione e linguistica generale: teoria e storia.* Bari: G. Laterza, 1902.

Croce, Franco. *Tre momenti del barocco letterario italiano.* Florence: Sansoni, 1966.

Crowther, Victor. *The Oratorio in Bologna (1650–1730).* Oxford University Press, 1999.

    The Oratorio in Modena. Oxford: Clarendon Press, 1992.

D'Accone, Frank. *The History of a Baroque Opera: Alessandro Scarlatti's Gli equivoci nel sembiante.* Monographs in Musicology 3. New York: Pendragon Press, 1985.

Dahlhaus, Carl. *Schoenberg and New Music.* Translated by Derrick Puffet and Alfred Clayton. Cambridge University Press, 1988.

Damuth, Laura. "Alessandro Scarlatti's Cantatas for Soprano and Basso Continuo, 1693–1705." Ph.D. diss., Columbia University, 1993.

Dandelet, Thomas. "Setting the Noble Stage in Baroque Rome: Roman Palaces, Political Contest, and Social Theater, 1600–1700." In *Life and the Arts in the Baroque Palaces of Rome: Ambiente Barocco.* Edited by Stefanie Walker and Frederick Hammond. New Haven: Yale University Press for the Bard Graduate Center for Studies in the Decorative Arts, 1999. 39–51.

Spanish Rome 1500–1700. New Haven: Yale University Press, 2001.

Darnton, Robert. *The Great Cat Massacre and Other Episodes in French Cultural History.* New York: Vintage Books, 1985.

Deleuze, Gilles. *The Fold: Leibniz and the Baroque.* Translated by Tom Conley. Minneapolis: University of Minnesota Press, 1993. (Originally published as *Le pli: Leibniz et le Baroque,* 1988.)

Della Seta, Fabrizio. Appendix to "La musica in Arcadia al tempo di Corelli." In *Nuovissimi studi corelliani. Atti del terzo congresso internazionale (Fusignano, 4–7 settembre 1980).* Edited by Sergio Durante and Pierluigi Petrobelli. Florence: L. S. Olschki, 1982. 141.

De Lucca, Valeria. "'Dalle sponde del Tebro alle rive dell'Adria': Maria Mancini and Lorenzo Onofrio Colonna's Patronage of Music and Theater between Rome and Venice (1659–1689)." Ph.D. diss., Princeton University, 2009.

Dent, Edward J. *Alessandro Scarlatti: His Life and Works.* London: Edward Arnold, 1960 (first published 1905).

Derrida, Jacques. "The Law of Genre." In "On Narrative," special issue of *Critical Inquiry* 7, no. 1 (1980): 55–81. (Also appears in *Glyph* 7 [1980]: 176–232.)

De Sanctis, Domenico. *Columnensium procerum imagines, et memorias nonnullas.* Rome: A. Bernabò, 1675.

Di Benedetto, Renato. "Poetics and Polemics." In *The History of Italian Opera,* Vol. VI: *Opera in Theory and Practice, Image and Myth.* Edited by Lorenzo Bianconi and Giorgio Pestelli. Translated by Kenneth Chalmers and Mary Whittall. University of Chicago Press, 2003. (Originally published as *Teorie e techniche, immagini e fantasmi,* Vol. VI of *Storia dell'opera Italiana.* Turin: Edizioni di Torino, 1988. 1–71.)

Dixon, Susan M. *Between the Real and the Ideal: The Accademia degli Arcadi and its Garden in Eighteenth-Century Rome.* Newark, DE: University of Delaware Press, 2006.

"Women in Arcadia." *Eighteenth-Century Studies* 32, no. 3 (1999): 371–375.

D'Onofrio, Cesare. *Roma val bene un'abiura: storie romane tra Cristina di Svezia, Piazza del Popolo e l'Accademia dell'Arcadia.* Rome: Fratelli Palombi, 1976.

Dooley, Brendon, ed. and trans. *Italy in the Baroque: Selected Readings.* New York: Garland, 1995.

Dreyfus, Lawrence. *Bach and the Patterns of Invention.* Cambridge, MA: Harvard University Press, 1996.

Dubowy, Norbert. "Le due *Giuditte* di Alessandro Scarlatti: due diverse concezioni dell'oratorio." In *L'oratorio musicale italiano e i suoi contesti (secc. XVII–XVIII).*

Atti del convegno internazionale, Perugia, Sagra musicale umbra, 18–20 settembre 1997. Edited by Paola Besutti. Florence: L. S. Olschki, 2002. 259–288.

"Ernst August, Giannettini und die Serenata in Venedig (1685–86)." *Analecta Musicologica. Veröffentlichungen der musikgeschichtlichen Abteilung des Deutschen Historischen Instituts in Rom* 30, nos. 1–2 (1998): 167–235.

"'Al tavolino medesimo del Compositor della Musica': Notes on Text and Context in Alessandro Scarlatti's *cantate da camera*." In *Aspects of the Secular Cantata in Late Baroque Italy*. Edited by Michael Talbot. Burlington, VT: Ashgate, 2009. 111–134.

Duff, David. "Introduction." In *Modern Genre Theory*. Harlow: Pearson Education, 2000. 1–24.

Dyck, Heinrich. "Islam at Vienna's Gates." *Military Heritage* 4 (2002): 34–43.

Erlich, Victor. *Russian Formalism: History-Doctrine*. 3rd edn. New Haven: Yale University Press, 1981.

Fabbri, Franco. "A Theory of Musical Genres: Two Applications." In *Popular Music Perspectives*. Edited by David Horn and Philip Tagg. Exeter: International Association for the Study of Popular Music, 1982. 52–81.

Fabbri, Mario. *Alessandro Scarlatti e il principe Ferdinando de' Medici*. Florence: L. S. Olschki, 1961.

Fabbri, Paolo. *Il secolo cantante*. Bologna: Il Mulino, 1990.

Fagiolo dell'Arco, Maurizio. *La festa barocca. Corpus delle feste a Roma*. Vol. I. Rome: De Luca, 1997.

Fagiolo dell'Arco, Maurizio and Silvia Carandini. *L'effimero barocco: strutture della festa nella Roma del '600*. Rome: Bulzoni Editore, 1977.

Farmer, David. *The Oxford History of Saints*. 5th edn. Oxford University Press, 2003.

Feldman, Martha. "Magic Mirrors and the Seria Stage: Thoughts towards a Ritual View." *Journal of the American Musicological Society* 48, no. 3 (1995): 423–484.

Opera and Sovereignty: Transforming Myths in Eighteenth-Century Italy (University of Chicago Press, 2007).

Fenlon, Iain. "Music and Festival." In *Europa Triumphans: Court and Civic Festivals in Early Modern Europe*. Vol. I. Edited by J. R. Mulryne, Helen Watanabe-O'Kelly, and Margaret Shewring. Burlington, VT: Ashgate, 2004. 47–55.

Ferrone, Vincenzo. *The Intellectual Roots of the Italian Enlightenment*. Translated by Sue Brotherton. Atlantic Highlands, NJ: Humanities Press, 1995.

Findlen, Paula. *Possessing Nature: Museums, Collecting, and Scientific Culture in Early Modern Italy*. Berkeley: University of California Press, 1994.

Fineman, Joel. "The Structure of Allegorical Desire." In *Allegory and Representation: Selected Papers from the English Institute, 1979–80*. Edited by Stephen J. Greenblatt. Baltimore: The Johns Hopkins University Press, 1981. 26–60.

Franchi, Saverio. *Drammaturgia romana: repertorio bibliografico cronologico dei testi drammatici pubblicati a Roma e nel Lazio*, Vol. I: *1600–1700*; Vol. II: *1701–1750*. Sussidi Eruditi 42 and 45. Rome: Edizioni di Storia e Letteratura, 1988–1997.

"Il principe Livio Odescalchi e l'oratorio 'politico.'" In *L'oratorio musicale italiano e i suoi contesti (secc. XVII–XVIII). Atti del convegno internazionale, Perugia, Sagra musicale umbra, 18–20 settembre 1997*. Edited by Paola Besutti. Florence: L. S. Olschki, 2002. 141–258.

Franchi, Saverio, ed. *Percorsi dell'oratorio romano. Da "historia sacra" a melodramma spirituale. Atti della giornata di studi (Viterbo 11 settembre 1999)*. In *Colloquia* 1. Rome: Istituto di Bibliografia Musicale, 2002.

Frati, Lodovico. "Un impressario teatrale del Settecento e la sua biblioteca." *Rivista Musicale Italiana* 18 (1911): 64–84.

Freeman, Robert. *Opera without Drama: Currents of Change in Italian Opera 1675–1725*. Studies in Musicology 14. Ann Arbor, MI: UMI, 1981. (Originally presented as the author's dissertation thesis, Princeton, 1967.)

Freitas, Roger. *Portrait of a Castrato: Politics, Patronage, and Music in the Life of Atto Melani*. Cambridge University Press, 2009.

"Singing and Playing: The Italian Cantata and the Rage for Wit." *Music and Letters* 82, no. 4 (2001): 509–542.

Fubini, Enrico. *Music and Culture in Eighteenth-Century Europe: A Source Book*. Edited by Bonnie J. Blackburn. Translated by Wolfgang Freis, Lisa Gasbarrone, and Michael Louis Leone. University of Chicago Press, 1994.

Galliard, John Ernest. *Six English Cantatas after the Italian Manner Compos'ed by M Galliard*. London: J. Walsh and J. Hare, 1716.

Garrard, Mary D. *Artemesia Gentileschi: The Image of the Female Hero in Italian Baroque Art*. Princeton University Press, 1989.

Gaye, Vera. *L'opera critica e storiografica del Crescimbeni*. Parma: Guanda, 1970.

Gerbino, Giuseppe. *Music and the Myth of Arcadia in Renaissance Italy*. Cambridge University Press, 2009.

Gianturco, Carolyn. "The Cantata: A Textual Approach." *The Well Enchanting Skill. Music, Poetry, and Drama in the Culture of the Renaissance: Essays in Honour of F. W. Sternfeld*. Edited by John Caldwell, Edward Olleson, and Susan Wollenberg. Oxford University Press, 1989. 41–51.

"Cristina di Svezia scenarista per Alessandro Stradella." In *Cristina di Svezia e la musica. Convegno internazionale: Roma, 5–6 dicembre 1996*. Rome: Accademia Nazionale dei Lincei, 1998. 45–70.

"The 'Staging' of Genres Other than Opera in Baroque Italy." In *Music in the Theater, Church, and Villa: Essays in Honor of Robert Lamar Weaver and Norma Wright Weaver*. Edited by Susan Parisi. Warren, MI: Harmonie Park Press, 2000. 113–129.

Goldmann, Lucien. *The Hidden God: A Study of the Tragic Vision in the Pensées of Pascal and the Tragedies of Racine*. Translated by Philip Thody. New York: The Humanities Press, 1964.

Gravina, Gian Vincenzo. The following works by Gravina are collected in *Scritti critici e teorici*, ed. Quondam.

Della divisione d' Arcadia: lettera ad un'amico. Naples, 1711.

Della divisione d'Arcadia. Verona, 1726.

Della ragion poetica, Libro I. Rome, 1708.

Della tragedia, Libro I. Naples, 1715.

Discorso sopra l'Endimione. Rome, 1692.

Scritti critici e teorici. Edited by Amedeo Quondam. Bari: Laterza, 1973.

Griffin, Thomas. "Alessandro Scarlatti e la serenata a Roma e Napoli." In *La musica a Napoli durante il seicento. Atti del convegno internazionale di studi (Napoli, 11–14 aprile 1985).* Edited by Domenico Antonio D'Alessandro and Agostino Ziino. Rome: Torre d'Orfeo, 1987. 351–368.

"The Late Baroque Serenata in Rome and Naples: A Documentary Study with Emphasis on Alessandro Scarlatti." Ph.D. diss., University of California, Los Angeles, 1983.

Gross, Hanns. *Rome in the Age of Enlightenment: The Post-Tridentine Syndrome and the Ancien Régime.* Cambridge University Press, 1990.

Habermas, Juergen. *The Structural Transformation of the Public Sphere: An Inquiry into the Category of Bourgeois Society.* Translated by Thomas Burger, with assistance from Frederick Lawrence. Cambridge, MA: The MIT Press, 1989.

Hammond, Frederick. *Music and Spectacle in Baroque Rome: Barberini Patronage under Urban VIII.* New Haven: Yale University Press, 1994.

Handelman, Don. *Models and Mirrors: Towards an Anthropology of Public Events.* Cambridge University Press, 1990.

Hanley, Edwin. "Alessandro Scarlatti's *cantate da camera*: A Bibliographic Study." Ph.D. diss., Yale University, 1963.

Hansell, Sven Hostrup. "Orchestral Practice and the Court of Cardinal Pietro Ottoboni." *Journal of the American Musicological Society* 19, no. 3 (1966): 398–403.

Harris, Ellen. *Handel and the Pastoral Tradition.* Oxford University Press, 1980.

Handel as Orpheus: Voice and Desire in the Chamber Cantatas. Cambridge, MA: Harvard University Press, 2001.

Heller, Wendy. *Emblems of Eloquence: Opera and Women's Voices in Seventeenth-Century Venice.* Berkeley: University of California Press, 2003.

"The Queen as King: Refashioning Semiramide for *Seicento* Venice," *Cambridge Opera Journal* 5, no. 2 (1993): 93–114.

Herczog, Johann. "Introduction." In *Oratorii, overo Melodrammi sacri,* by Arcangelo Spagna. Lucca: Libreria Musicale Italiana, 1993. ix–xxviii.

Heyink, Rainer. "Pietro Paolo Bencini, 'uno de' più scelti maestri della corte di Roma.'" *Händel-Jahrbuch* 46 (2000): 101–124.

Hill, John Walter. *Roman Monody, Cantata, and Opera from the Circles around Cardinal Montalto.* 2 vols. Oxford University Press, 1997.

Holmes, William. *La Statira by Pietro Ottoboni and Alessandro Scarlatti: The Textual Sources.* New York: Pendragon Press, 1983.

Holt, Fabian. *Genre in Popular Music.* University of Chicago Press, 2007.

Holzer, Robert. "Music and Poetry in Seventeenth-Century Rome: Settings of the Canzonetta and Cantata Texts of Francesco Balducci, Domenico Benigni, Francesco Melosio, and Antonio Abati." Ph.D. diss., University of Pennsylvania, 1990.

Hough, Graham. *A Preface to* The Faerie Queene. London: G. Duckworth, 1962.

Israel, Jonathan I. *Radical Enlightenment: Philosophy and the Making of Modernity, 1650–1750.* Oxford University Press, 2001.

Johns, Christopher M. S. *Papal Art and Cultural Politics: Rome in the Age of Clement XI.* Cambridge University Press, 1993.

Johnson, Eugene. "Jacopo Sansovino, Giacomo Torelli, and the Theatricality of the Piazzetta in Venice." *Journal of the Society of Architectural Historians* 59 (2000): 436–453.

Johnson, Joyce L. and Howard E. Smither, eds. *The Italian Oratorio 1650–1800: Works in a Central Baroque and Classic Tradition.* 31 vols. New York: Garland, 1986–1987.

Johnson, Victoria, Jane Fulcher, and Thomas Ertman. *Opera and Society in Italy and France from Monteverdi to Bourdieu.* Cambridge University Press, 2007.

Kallberg, Jeffrey. *Chopin at the Boundaries: Sex, History, and Musical Genre.* Cambridge, MA: Harvard University Press, 1996.

"The Rhetoric of Genre: Chopin's Nocturne in G Minor." *Nineteenth Century Music* 11, no. 3 (1987): 238–261.

Kendrick, Robert. "Devotion, Piety and Commemoration: Sacred Songs and Oratorios." In *The Cambridge History of Seventeenth-Century Music.* Edited by Tim Carter and John Butt. Cambridge University Press, 2005. 324–377.

"Intertextuality in Scarlatti's Cambridge *Giuditta*." Paper presented at a symposium on the oratorio at Northwestern University, Evanston, IL, 2000.

"What's So Sacred about 'Sacred' Opera?: Reflections on the Fate of a (Sub)genre." *Journal of Seventeenth-Century Music* 9, no. 1 (2003). Available at http://sscm-jscm.press.uiuc.edu/jscm/v9no1.html.

Kertzer, David. *Ritual, Politics, and Power.* New Haven: Yale University Press, 1988.

Kirkpatrick, Ralph. *Domenico Scarlatti.* Princeton University Press, 1953.

Krims, Adam. *Rap Music and the Poetics of Identity.* Cambridge University Press, 2000.

Kristeva, Julia. "Word, Dialogue, and Novel." In *Desire in Language: A Semiotic Approach to Literature and Art.* Edited by Leon S. Roudiez. Translated by Thomas Gora, Alice Jardine, and Leon S. Roudiez. New York: Columbia University Press, 1980. 64–91.

Lanfranchi, Ariella and Enrico Careri. "Le cantate per la Natività della B.V. Un secolo di musiche al Collegio Nazareno di Roma (1681–1784)." In *Händel e gli Scarlatti a Roma.* Edited by Nino Pirrotta and Agostino Ziino. Florence: L. S. Olschki, 1987. 304–305.

Lanham, Richard. *Handlist of Rhetorical Terms.* 2nd edn. Berkeley: University of California Press, 1991.

Lavagnino, Emilio. *Il Palazzo della Cancelleria e la chiesa di S. Lorenzo in Damaso*. I palazzi e le case di Roma 1. Rome: Casa Editrice "Roma," 1924.

La Via, Stefano. "Il Cardinale Ottoboni e la musica: nuovi documenti (1700–1740), nuove lettere e ipotesi." In *Intorno a Locatelli: studi in occasione del tricentenario della nascita di Pietro Antonio Locatelli – 1695–1764*. Vol. I. Edited by Albert Dunning. Lucca: Libreria Editrice Musicale, 1995. 319–526.

Le Cerf de la Viéville, Jean-Laurent, sieur de Freneuse. *Comparaison de la musique italienne et de la musique française*. 2nd edn. 3 books in 1 vol. Brussels: François Foppens, 1705. (Reprinted Geneva: Minkoff, 1972.)

Lecoq, Danielle and Roland Schaer. "Ancient, Biblical, and Medieval Traditions." In *Utopia: The Search for the Ideal Society in the Western World*. Edited by Roland Schaer, Gregory Claeys, and Lyman Tower Sargent. New York: The New York Public Library/Oxford University Press, 2000. 35–82.

Lee, Vernon (Violet Page). *Studies of the Eighteenth Century in Italy*. 2nd edn. London, 1907.

Leri, C. "The 300th Anniversary of the Accademia dell'Arcadia. Conference Papers." *Lettere Italiane* 50, no. 1 (1998): 140–145.

Lévi-Strauss, Claude. *The Naked Man*. Translated by John and Doreen Weightman as Vol. IV of *Introduction to a Science of Mythology*. New York: Harper and Row, 1981. (Originally published as *L'Homme nu* [Paris: Plan, 1971].)

Levy, Evonne. *Propaganda and the Jesuit Baroque*. Berkeley: University of California Press, 2004.

Lindgren, Lowell. "A Bibliographic Scrutiny of Dramatic Works Set by Giovanni and his Brother Antonio Maria Bononcini." Ph.D. diss., Harvard University, 1972.

"Bononcini's 'agreable and easie style, and those fine inventions in his basses (to which he was led by an instrument upon which he excels).'" In *Aspects of the Secular Cantata in Late Baroque Italy*. Edited by Michael Talbot. Burlington, VT: Ashgate, 2009. 135–175.

"Il dramma musicale a Roma durante la carriera di Alessandro Scarlatti (1660–1725)." In *Le muse galanti. La musica a Roma nel Settecento*. Edited by Bruno Cagli. Rome: Istituto dell' Enciclopedia Italiana, 1985. 35–57.

"Introduction." In Giovanni Bononcini, *Cantatas*. Edited and selected by Lowell Lindgren. Vol. X of *The Italian Cantata in the Seventeenth Century*. New York: Garland, 1985.

"Le opere drammatiche 'romane' di Francesco Gasparini, 1689–1699." In *Francesco Gasparini (1661–1727). Atti del primo convegno internazionale (Camaiore, 19 settembre–1 ottobre 1978)*. Edited by Fabrizio Della Seta and Franco Piperno. Florence: L. S. Olschki, 1981. 174–175.

Lionnet, Jean. "Introduction." In *La Cappella Giulia*, Vol. I: *I vespri nel XVIII secolo*. Edited by Jean Lionnet. Lucca: Libreria Musicale Italiana, 1995. xxvi–xxix.

"La musique à Saint-Louis des français de Rome au XVIIe siècle." *Note d'Archivio per la Storia Musicale*, n.s., Anno III, 1985, Supplemento, première partie; Anno

IV, 1986, Supplemento, deuxième partie: les documents (Venice: Fondazione Levi).

Lowenthal, David. *The Past is a Foreign Country*. Cambridge University Press, 1985.

Lyons, John D. "Unseen Space and Theatrical Narrative: The 'Récit de Cinna.'" *Yale French Studies* 80, *Baroque Topographies: Literature/History/Philosophy* (1991): 70–90.

Macartney, Carlie A., ed. *The Habsburg and Hohenzollern Dynasties in the Seventeenth and Eighteenth Centuries*. New York: Harper and Row, 1970.

Maccavino, Nicolò. "La serenata a Filli *Tacete aure tacete* e altre serenate datate 1706 di Alessandro Scarlatti." In *La serenata tra Seicento e Settecento: musica, poesia, scenotecnica. Atti del convegno internazionale di studi (Reggio Calabria, 16–17 maggio 2003)*. Vol. II. Edited by Nicolò Maccavino. Reggio Calabria: Laruffa Editore, 2007. 451–522.

McClary, Susan. "Turtles All the Way Down (On the 'Purely Musical')." In McClary, *Conventional Wisdom: The Content of Musical Form*. Berkeley: University of California Press, 2000. 1–21.

Maffei, Scipione. *Teatro italiano, o sia scelta di tragedie per uso della scena*. Verona: J. Vallarsi, 1723–1725.

Mangini, Giorgio. "Betulia liberata e *La morte dell'Oloferne*: momenti di drammaturgia musicale nella tradizione dei 'trionfi di Giuditta.'" In *Mozart, Padova e la Betulia liberata: committenza, interpretazione, e fortuna delle azioni sacre metastasiane nel '700. Atti del convegno internazionale di studi 28–30 settembre 1989*. Edited by Paolo Pinamonti. Florence: L. S. Olschki, 1991. 145–172.

Maravall, José Antonio. *Culture of the Baroque: Analysis of a Historical Structure*. Translated by Terry Cochran. Minneapolis: University of Minnesota Press, 1986. (Originally published as *La Cultura del Barroco: análisis de una estructura histórica*. Esplugues de Llobregat: Ariel, 1975.)

Martello, Pier Jacopo. *Della tragedia antica e moderna*. Rome, 1715.

Marx, Hans Joachim. "Bemerkungen zu szenischen Aufführungen barocker Oratorien und Serenaten." *Basler Jahrbuch für historische Musikpraxis* 23 "Barockoper: Buhne – Szene – Inszenierung" (1999): 133–150.

"Die Musik am Hofe Pietro Kardinal Ottobonis unter Arcangelo Corelli." *Analecta Musicologica* 5 (1968): 104–177.

"Unveröffentlichte Kompositionen Arcangelo Corellis." In *Studi corelliani. Atti del primo congresso internazionale (Fusignano, 5–8 settembre 1968)*. Edited by Adriano Cavicchi, Oscar Mischiati, and Pierluigi Petrobelli. Florence: L. S. Olschki Editore, 1972. 53–61.

Marx, Hans Joachim, ed. *Kantaten mit Instrumenten*, I–III, *Hallische Händel-Ausgabe*, series 5, Vols. III–V. Kassel: Bärenreiter, 1994, 1995, and 1999.

Matitti, Flavia. "Il Cardinale Pietro Ottoboni mecenate delle arti: cronache e documenti (1689–1740)." *Storia dell'Arte* 84 (1995): 156–243.

Mattheson, Johann. *Das neu-eröffnete Orchestre*. Hamburg: Schiller, 1713.

Der vollkommene Capellmeister. Hamburg: C. Herold, 1739.

Maylender, Michele. *Storia delle accademie d'Italia*, Vol. I. Bologna: Capelli, 1926. (Repr. Bologna: Arnaldo Forni, 1976.)

Ménestrier, Claude. *Traité des turnois, iuostes, carrousels, et autre spectacle publics.* Lyon, 1669.

Menzini, Benedetto. *L'Arcadia restituita all'Arcadia.* Rome: Gio. Battista Molo, 1692.

Merolla, Riccardo. "Lo stato dell chiesa." In *Letteratura italiana: storia e geografia,* Vol. II: *L'età moderna.* Turin: Giulio Einaudi, 1988. 1019–1109.

Metzger, Bruce M. and Roland E. Murphy, eds. *The New Oxford Annotated Bible with Apocryphal/Deuterocanonical Books.* Oxford University Press, 1991.

Miller, Peter. *Peiresc's Europe: Learning and Virtue in the Seventeenth Century.* New Haven: Yale University Press, 2000.

Milton, Henry. *Filippo Juvarra, Drawings from the Roman Period, 1704–1714.* 2 vols. Rome: Edizioni dell'Elefante, 1984.

Minor, Vernon Hyde. *The Death of the Baroque and the Rhetoric of Good Taste.* Cambridge University Press, 2006.

"Ideology and Interpretation in Rome's Parrhasian Grove: The Arcadian Garden and Taste." *Memoirs of the American Academy in Rome* 46 (2001 [2002]): 183–228.

Mischiati, Oscar. "La cantata secondo Erdmann Neumeister e l'oratorio secondo Arcangelo Spagna: una possibile analogia?" In *Percorsi dell'oratorio romano. Da "historia sacra" a melodramma spirituale. Atti della giornata di studi (Viterbo 11 settembre 1999).* Edited by Saverio Franchi. Rome: Istituto di Bibliografia Musicale, 2002. 95–98.

Momigliano, Arnaldo. *The Classical Foundations of Modern Historiography.* Berkeley: University of California Press, 1990.

Moore, Allen. "Categorizing Conventions in Music Discourses: Style and Genre." *Music and Letters* 82, no. 3 (2001): 432–442.

Morei, Michel Giovanni. *Memorie istoriche dell'adunanze degli Arcadi.* Rome: de' Rossi, 1761.

Morelli, Arnaldo. "Alessandro Scarlatti maestro di cappella in Roma ed alcuni suoi oratorio: nuovi documenti." *Note d'Archivio per la Storia Musicale,* n.s., 2 (1984): 117–144.

"'Un bell'oratorio all'uso di Roma': Patronage and Secular Context of the Oratorio in Baroque Rome." In *Music Observed. Studies in Memory of William C. Holmes.* Edited by Colleen Reardon and Susan Parisi. Warren, MI: Harmonie Park Press, 2004. 333–351.

"Una cantante del Seicento e le sue carte di musica: il 'Libro della Signora Cecilia.'" In *"Vanitatis, fuga, aeternitatis amor." Wolfgang Witzenmann zum 65. Geburtstag.* Edited by Sabine Ehrmann-Herfort, Markus Engelhardt, and Wolfgang Witzenmann. Laaber: Laaber Verlag, 2005. 307–327.

"La circolazione dell'oratorio italiano." *Studi Musicali* 1 (1997): 105–186.

"Mecenatismo musicale nella Roma barocca: il caso di Cristina di Svezia." *Quaderni Storici* 22, no. 95 (1997): 387–408.

"'Il muovere e non il far maravigliare.' Relationships between Artistic and Musical Patronage in the Roman Oratory." *Italian History and Culture* 5 (1999): 13–28.

"La musica a Roma nella seconda metà del Seicento attraverso l'Archivio Cartari-Febei." In *La musica a Roma attraverso le fonti d'archivio. Atti di convegno internazionale (Roma 4–7 giugno, 1992).* Edited by Arnaldo Morelli, Bianca Maria Antolini, and Vera Vita Spagnuolo. Lucca: Libreria Musicale Italiana Editrice, 1994. 107–136.

"Gli oratori di Bernardo Pasquini: problemi di datazione e di committenza." In *Percorsi dell'oratorio romano: da "historia sacra" a melodramma spirituale.* Edited by Saverio Franchi. Rome: Istituto di Bibliografia Musicale, 2002. 67–94.

"Oratorii ovvero sacre musicale tragedie?" In *Mozart, Padova e la Betulia liberata: committenza, interpretazione, e fortuna delle azioni sacre metastasiane nel '700.* Edited by Paolo Pinamonti. Florence: L. S. Olschki, 1991. 275–287.

Il tempio armonico: musica nell'Oratorio dei Filippini in Roma (1575–1705). Analecta Musicologica 27. Laaber: Laaber Verlag, 1991.

Morelli, Giovanni. "Una celebre 'cantarina' romana del Seicento: la Giorgina." *Studi Secenteschi* 16 (1975): 157–180.

Morson, Gary Saul. "Bakhtin, Genres, and Temporality." *New Literary History* 22, no. 4 (1991): 1071–1092.

Mugnos, Filadelfo. *Istoria della augustissima famiglia Colonna.* Venice: Turrini, 1658.

Muir, Edward. *Ritual in Early Modern Europe.* Cambridge University Press, 1997.

Murata, Margaret. "Further Remarks on Pasqualini and the Music of *MAP*." *Analecta Musicologica* 19 (1979): 125–145.

"Image and Eloquence: Secular Song." In *The Cambridge History of Seventeenth-Century Music.* Edited by Tim Carter and John Butt. Cambridge University Press, 2005. 378–425.

Operas for the Papal Court, 1621–1668. Ann Arbor, MI: UMI, 1981.

"The Recitative Soliloquy." *Journal of the American Musicological Society* 32, no. 1 (1979): 45–73.

Review of *L'oratorio musicale italiano e i suoi contesti (secc. XVII–XVIII),* edited by Paola Besutti, and *Percorsi dell'oratorio romano da "historia sacra" a melodramma spirituale,* edited by Saverio Franchi. *Journal of Seventeenth-Century Music* 11, no. 1 (2006): par 2.3. Available at www.sscm-jscm.org/jscm/v11/no1/murata/html.

"Roman Cantata Scores as Traces of Musical Culture and Signs of its Place in Society." In *Atti del XIV congresso della Società internazionale di musicologia, Bologna, 1987. Trasmissione e recezione delle forme di cultura musicale.* Vol. I. Turin: Edizioni di Torino, 1990. 272–284.

"Singing about Singing." In *In cantu et in sermone: For Nino Pirrotta on his 80th Birthday.* Edited by Fabrizio Della Seta and Franco Piperno. Florence: L. S. Olschki, 1989. 363–382.

"*Theatrum intra Theatrum* or, The Church and Stage in 17th-Century Rome." In *Sleuthing the Muse: Festschrift for William F. Prizer*. Edited by Kristine K. Forney and Jeremy L. Smith. Hillsdale, NY: Pendragon Press, forthcoming.

Muratori, Lodovico Antonio. *Opere del proposto Lodovico Antonio Muratori*. Vol. VIII. Arezzo: Belloti, 1768.

   Della perfetta poesia italiana. Vol. II. Edited by Ada Ruschioni. Milan: Marzorati Editore, 1972. (Originally published Modena: Soliani, 1706.)

   Della regolata divozione de' Cristiani. Venice: Girolamo Albrizzi, 1752.

Nash, Ralph. *Arcadia & Piscatorial Eclogues*. Detroit: Wayne State University Press, 1966.

Neale, Stephen. *Genre*. London: British Film Institute-Film Availability Services, 1980.

Neveu, Bruno. "L'esprit de reforme à Rome sous Innocent XI (1676–89)." *Dix-Septième Siècle* 50, no. 2 (1998): 203–218.

   "Politique ecclésiastique et controverses doctrinales en Rome 1683 à 1705." *Bulletin de la Société d'Histoire Moderne* 74, no. 10 (1975): 11–18.

Nicastro, Guido. *Metastasio e il teatro del primo Settecento*. Letteratura Italiana Laterza 33. Bari: Laterza, 1973.

Nussdorfer, Laurie. *Civic Politics in the Rome of Urban VIII*. Princeton University Press, 1992.

   "The Politics of Space in Early Modern Rome." *Memoirs of the American Academy in Rome* 42 (1997): 161–186.

Olszewski, Edward J. "Decorating the Palace: Cardinal Pietro Ottoboni (1667–1740) in the Cancelleria." In *Life and the Arts in the Baroque Palaces of Rome: Ambiente Barocco*. Edited by Stefanie Walker and Frederick Hammond. New Haven: Yale University Press, for The Bard Graduate Center for Studies in the Decorative Arts, 1999. 93–111.

   "The Enlightened Patronage of Cardinal Pietro Ottoboni (1667–1740)." *Artibus et Historiae* 23, no. 45 (2002): 139–165.

   "The Painters in Cardinal Pietro Ottoboni's Court of the Cancelleria, 1689–1740." *Römisches Jahrbuch der Bibliotheca Hertziana* 31 (1998): 119–212.

   "The Tapestry Collection of Cardinal Pietro Ottoboni." *Apollo* 116 (1982): 103–111.

Opacki, Ireneusz. "Royal Genres." Translated by David Malcolm. In *Modern Genre Theory*. Edited by David Duff. New York: Longman Press, 2000. 118–126.

Ottonelli, Giovanni Domenico. *Della christiana moderatione del theatro. Libro detto l'Ammonitioni a' recitanti per avvisare ogni Christiano a moderarsi da gli eccessi nel recitare*. Florence: Gio. Antonio Bonardi, 1652.

Ovid. *The Metamorphoses of Ovid*. Translated by Mary Innes. London: Penguin, 1955.

Pagano, Roberto and Lino Bianchi, eds. *Alessandro Scarlatti: catalogo generale delle opera a cura di Giancarlo Rostirolla*. Turin: Edizioni Rai, 1972.

Panofsky, Erwin. "*Et in Arcadia ego*: Poussin and the Elegaic Tradition." *Meaning in the Visual Arts: Papers in and on Art History*. University of Chicago Press, 1955. 295–320.

Pastor, Ludwig von. *The History of the Popes*. Vols. XXXII and XXXIII. London: Routledge and Kegan Paul, 1957.

Pastura, Maria Grazia. "Legislazione pontificia sui teatri e spettacoli musicali a Roma." In *La musica a Roma attraverso le fonti d'archivio. Atti del convegno internazionale (Roma 4–7 giugno, 1992)*. Edited by Arnaldo Morelli, Bianca Maria Antolini, and Vera Vita Spagnuolo. Lucca: Libreria Musicale Italiana, 1994. 167–176.

Penna, Andrea. "Il primo teatro pubblico di Roma. Le vicende del Teatro Tordinona nel XVII secolo." *Studi Romani* 46 (1998): 227–268.

Pinto, John. "Architecture and Urbanism." In *Art in Rome in the Eighteenth Century*. Edited by Edgar Peters Bowron and Joseph J. Rishel. Philadelphia: Merrell in association with Philadelphia Museum of Art, 2000. 125–126.

Piperno, Franco. "'Anfione in Campidoglio': presenza corelliana alle feste per i concorsi dell'Accademia del Disegno di San Luca." In *Nuovissimi studi corelliani. Atti del terzo congresso internazionale*. Edited by Sergio Durante and Pierluigi Petrobelli. Florence: L. S. Olschki, 1982. 151–208.

"Musica e musicisti per l'Accademia del Disegno di San Luca (1716–1860)." In *La musica a Roma attraverso le fonti d'archivio. Atti del convegno internazionale (Roma 4–7 giugno, 1992)*. Edited by Arnaldo Morelli, Bianca Maria Antolini, and Vera Vita Spagnuolo. Lucca: Libreria Musicale Italiana, 1994. 553–563.

"Le orchestre di Arcangelo Corelli." In *L'invenzione del gusto: Corelli and Vivaldi*. Edited by Giovanni Morelli. Milan: Ricordi, 1982. 42–48.

"La sinfonia strumentale del primo Seicento," *Studi Musicali* 4 (1975): Part 1, 145–168; 5 (1976): Part 2, 95–141.

"Su le sponde del Tebro: eventi, mecenati e istituzioni musicali a Roma negli anni di Locatelli. Saggio di cronologia." In *Intorno a Locatelli: studi in occasione del tricentenario della nascita di Pietro Antonio Locatelli – 1695–1764*. Vol. I. Lucca: Libreria Editrice Musicale, 1995. 793–877.

Platania, Gaetano and Joëlle Fontaine. "Innocent XI Odescalchi et l'esprit de 'Croisade.'" *Dix-Septième Siècle* 50, no. 2 (1998): 247–276.

Poultney, David. "Scarlatti and the Transformation of the Oratorio." *Musical Quarterly* 59 (1973): 584–601.

Powers, Harold. "Il Serse trasformato." *Musical Quarterly* 47 (1961): 481–492.

Puttenham, George. *The Arte of English Poesie*. 1589.

Quadrio, Francesco S. *Della storia e della ragione d'ogni poesia*. Vol. II. Milan: Agnelli, 1741.

Quondam, Amedeo. *Cultura e ideologia di Gianvincenzo Gravina*. Milan: U. Morsia, 1968.

"L'istituzione Arcadia: sociologia e ideologia di un'accademia." *Quaderni Storici* 23 (1973): 389–438.

Rak, Michele. "Le macchine comiche: il sistema del teatro meccanico nel Settecento italiano e alcuni documenti romani di fine secolo." In *Il teatro a Roma nel Settecento*, Vol. 1. Rome: Istituto dell' Enciclopedia Italiana, 1989. 259–319.

Rava, Arnaldo. *Il teatro Ottoboni nel palazzo della Cancelleria*. Rome: Reale Istituto di Studi Romani, 1942.

Redfield, Robert. *Peasant Society and Culture*. University of Chicago Press, 1956.

Rinaldi, Mario. *Arcangelo Corelli*. Milan: Curci, 1953.

Ripa, Cesare. *Iconologia, Padua, 1611*. New York: Garland, 1976.

Rosand, Ellen. "Barbara Strozzi, *virtuosissima cantatrice*: The Composer's Voice." *Journal of the American Musicological Society* 31 (1978): 241–281.

"Handel Paints the Resurrection." In *Festa Musicologica: Essays in Honor of George T. Buelow*. Edited by Thomas J. Mathiesen and Benito V. Rivera. Stuyvesant, NY: Pendragon Press, 1995. 7–52.

Opera in Seventeenth-Century Venice: The Creation of a Genre. Berkeley: University of California Press, 1991.

Rose, Gloria. "The Italian Cantata of the Baroque Period." In *Gattungen der Musik in Einzeldarstellungen: Gedenkschrift Leo Schrade*. Edited by Wulf Arlt, Ernst Lichtenhahn, and Hans Oesch. Berne: Francke, 1973. 655–677.

Rostirolla, Giancarlo. "Alcune note sulla professione di cantore e di cantante nella Roma del Sei e Settecento." *Roma Moderna e Contemporanea: Rivista Interdisciplinare di Storia* 4 (1996): 37–74.

Ruf, Wolfgang. "Dramatik und Lyrik in den Oratorien und Serenaten Handels." *Göttinger Händel-Beiträge* 9 (2002): 21–36.

Sadie, Stanley, ed. *New Grove Dictionary of Music and Musicians*. 2nd edn. London: MacMillan, 2001.

Saint-Évremond, Charles de Marguetel de Saint-Denis, seigneur de. *The Works of Monsieur de St. Évremond, made English from the French original; with the life of the author*. 2nd edn. London: J. J. Knapton, 1728.

Salerno, Luigi. *Piazza di Spagna*. Naples: Di Mauro, 1967.

Santoni, Barbara Tellini. *Inventario dei manoscritti (1–41)*. Accademia Letteraria Italiana-Arcadia. Rome: La Meridiana, 1991.

Santovetti, Francesca. "Arcadia a Roma Anno Domini 1690: accademia e vizi di forma." *Modern Language Notes* 112, no. 1 (1997): 21–37.

Sarnelli, Mauro. "Percorsi dell'oratorio per musica come genere letterario." In *Percorsi dell'oratorio romano. Da "historia sacra" a melodramma spirituale. Atti della giornata di studi (Viterbo 11 settembre 1999)*. Edited by Saverio Franchi. Rome: Istituto di Bibliografia Musicale, 2002. 137–197.

Sartori, Claudio. *I libretti italiani a stampa dalle origini al 1800*. Cuneo: Bertola & Locatelli, *c.*1990–1994.

Sartori, Orietta. "Notizie di interesse musicale in un antico periodico a stampa: il *Foglio di Foligno*." *Esercizi Musica e Spettacolo* 16–17 (1997–1998): 87–119.

Saunders, Harris. "The Repertoire of a Venetian Opera House (1678–1714): The Teatro Grimani di San Giovanni Gristosomo." Ph.D. diss., Harvard University, 1985.

Saussure, Ferdinand de. *Course in General Linguistics*. Edited by Charles Bally, Albert Sechehage, and Albert Riedlinger. Translated by Roy Harris. LaSalle, IL: Open Court, 1986 [1916].

Scarlatti, Alessandro. *Cantatas by Alessandro Scarlatti*. Edited by Malcolm Boyd. The Italian Cantata in the Seventeenth Century 13. New York: Garland, 1986.

    La Giuditta. In *Gli oratorii di Alessandro Scarlatti*. Edited by Lino Bianchi. Rome: De Santis, 1964.

    La Giuditta di "Cambridge." In *Gli oratorii di Alessandro Scarlatti*. Edited by Lino Bianchi. Rome: De Santis, 1966.

    La Statira. Edited by William C. Holmes. Vol. IX of *The Operas of Alessandro Scarlatti*. Cambridge, MA: Harvard University Press, 1985.

Scheibe, Johann Adolph. *Critische Musikus*. Leipzig: Breitkopf, 1745. (Repr. Hildesheim: G. Olms; Wiesbaden: Breitkopf & Härtel, 1970.)

Schiavo, Armando. *Il Palazzo della Cancelleria*. Rome: Staderini, 1964.

    "Il teatro e altre opere del cardinale Ottoboni." *Strenna dei Romanisti* 33 (1972): 344–352.

Schmalzriedt, Siegfried, ed. *Aci, Galatea e Polifemo in Ausdrucksformen der Musik des Barock: Passionsoratorium, Serenata, Rezitativ*. Veröffentlichungen der Internationalen Händel-Akademie. Laaber: Laaber Verlag, 2002.

Schulze, Hendrik. "Narration, Mimesis and the Question of Genre: Dramatic Approaches in Giovanni Legrenzi's Solo Cantatas, Opp. 12 and 14." In *Aspects of the Secular Cantata in Late Baroque Italy*. Edited by Michael Talbot. Burlington, VT: Ashgate, 2009. 55–78.

Selden, Margery Stomne. "Alessandro Scarlatti's Oratorio *La Giuditta*: A Communication." *Journal of the American Musicological Society* 22 (1969): 304–305.

Selfridge-Field, Eleanor. "Juditha in Historical Perspective. Scarlatti, Gasparini, Marcello, and Vivaldi." In *Vivaldi veneziano europeo*. Edited by Francesco Degrada. Florence: L. S. Olschki, 1980. 135–153.

Signorotto, Gianvittorio and Maria Antonietta Visceglia, eds. *Court and Politics in Papal Rome, 1492–1700*. Cambridge University Press, 2002.

Smith, Ayana. "The Mock Heroic, an Intruder in Arcadia: Girolamo Gigli, Antonio Caldara and *L'Anagilda* (Rome, 1711)." *Eighteenth-Century Music* 7, no. 1 (2010): 35–64.

Smither, Howard. *A History of the Oratorio*, Vol. I: *The Oratorio in the Baroque Era: Italy, Vienna, Paris*. Chapel Hill: University of North Carolina Press, 1977.

    "Oratorio and Sacred Opera, 1700–1825: Terminology and Genre Distinction." *Proceedings of the Royal Musical Association* 106 (1980): 88–104.

Snyder, Jon R. *L'estetica del barocco*. Bologna: Il Mulino, 2005.

Spagna, Arcangelo. "Discorso intorno a gl'oratorii." In *Oratorii, overo Melodrammi sacri*. Vol. I. Rome: Gio. Francesco Buagni, 1706. (Reprinted and edited by Johann Herczog in *Musurgiana* 25. Lucca: Libreria Musicale Italiana, 1993.)

    Fasti sacri. Rome, 1720.

    Melodrammi scenici. Rome, 1709.

Spagnoletti, Angelantonio. *Prìncipi italiani e Spagna nell'età barocca*. Milan: Mondadori, 1996.

Sparling, Heather. "Categorically Speaking: Towards a Theory of (Musical) Genre in Cape Breton Culture." *Ethnomusicology* 52 (2008): 401–425.

Specchi, Alessandro. *Il nuovo teatro delli palazzi di Roma*. Rome, 1699.

Spitzer, John and Neal Zaslaw. *The Birth of the Orchestra: History of an Institution, 1650–1815*. Oxford University Press, 2004.

Staffieri, Gloria. "Arcangelo Corelli compositore di 'sinfonie.' Nuovi documenti." In *Studi corelliani IV. Atti del quarto congresso internazionale (Fusignano, 4–7 settembre 1986)*. Edited by Pierluigi Petrobelli and Gloria Staffieri. Florence: L. S. Olschki, 1990. 335–357.

Colligite fragmenta: la vita musicale romana negli "Avvisi Marescotti" (1683–1707). Lucca: Libreria Musicale Italiana Editrice, 1990.

Standen, Edith. "Tapestries for a Cardinal-Nephew: A Roman Set Illustrating Tasso's *Gerusalemme liberata*." *Metropolitan Museum of Art Journal* 16 (1982): 147–164.

Statius (Publius Papinius). *Thebaid; Seven Against Thebes*. Translated by Charles Stanley Ross. Baltimore: The Johns Hopkins University Press, 1994.

Stefani, Gino. *Musica barocca: poetica e ideologia*. Milan: Bompiani, 1974.

Stein, Louise. "'Una música de noche, que llaman aquí serenata': A Spanish Patron and the Serenata in Rome and Naples." *La serenata tra Seicento e Settecento: musica, poesia, scenotecnica. Atti del convegno internazionale di studi (Reggio Calabria, 16–17 maggio 2003)*. Vol. II. Edited by Nicolò Maccavino. Reggio Calabria: Laruffa Editore, 2007. 333–372.

Stephen, Ruth. "A Note on Christina and her Academies." In *Queen Christina of Sweden: Documents and Studies*. Edited by M. von Platen. Stockholm: P. A. Norstedt & Söner, 1966. 365–371.

Stocker, Margarita. *Judith: Sexual Warrior: Women and Power in Western Culture*. New Haven: Yale University Press, 1998.

Striedter, Jurij. *Literary Structure, Evolution and Value: Russian Formalism and Czech Structuralism Reconsidered*. Cambridge, MA: Harvard University Press, 1989.

Strohm, Reinhard. *Dramma per musica: Italian Opera Seria of the Eighteenth Century*. New Haven: Yale University Press, 1997.

"Scarlattiana at Yale." In *Händel e gli Scarlatti a Roma*. Edited by Nino Pirrotta and Agostino Ziino. Florence: L. S. Olschki, 1987. 113–152.

Strunk, Oliver. *Source Readings in Music History*. Edited and revised by Leo Treitler. New York: Norton Press, 1998.

Swale, David. "The 'Judith' Oratorios of Alessandro Scarlatti." *Miscellanea Musicologica* 9 (1977): 145–155.

Tabacchi, Stefano. "Le riforme giudiziarie nella Roma di fine Seicento." *Roma Moderna e Contemporanea* 5, no. 1 (1997): 155–174.

Talbot, Michael. "How Recitatives End and Arias Begin in the Solo Cantatas of Antonio Vivaldi." *Journal of the Royal Musical Association* 126 (2001): 169–192.

"'Loving without Falling in Love': Pietro Paolo Bencini's Serenata *Li due volubili*." *La serenata tra Seicento e Settecento: musica, poesia, scenotecnica. Atti del convegno internazionale di studi (Reggio Calabria, 16–17 maggio 2003)*. Vol. II. Edited by Nicolò Maccavino. Reggio Calabria: Laruffa Editore, 2007. 373–396.

"The Serenata in Eighteenth-Century Venice." *Royal Musical Association Research Chronicle* 18 (1982): 1–50.

"Vivaldi's Serenatas: Long Cantatas or Short Operas?" In *Venetian Music in the Age of Vivaldi*. Edited by Michael Talbot. Burlington, VT: Ashgate, 1999. 67–96.

Talbot, Michael, ed. *Aspects of the Secular Cantata in Late Baroque Italy*. Burlington, VT: Ashgate, 2009.

Talbot, Michael and Colin Timms. "Music and the Poetry of Antonio Ottoboni (1646–1720)." In *Händel e gli Scarlatti a Roma*. Edited by Nino Pirrotta and Agostino Ziino. Florence: L. S. Olschki, 1987. 367–438.

Tamburini, Elena. *Due teatri per il principe: studi sulla committenza teatrale di Lorenzo Onofrio Colonna (1659–1689)*. Rome: Bulzoni Editore, 1997.

"Luoghi teatrali per la serenata nella Roma del Seicento. Il falso convito di Gian Lorenzo Bernini." *La serenata tra Seicento e Settecento: musica, poesia, scenotecnica. Atti del convegno internazionale di studi (Reggio Calabria, 16–17 maggio 2003)*. Vol. II. Edited by Nicolò Maccavino. Reggio Calabria: Laruffa Editore, 2007. 523–546.

Tarr, Edward H. and Thomas Walker. "'Bellici carmi, festivo fragor': die Verwendung der Trompete in der italienischen Oper des 17. Jahrhunderts." *Hamburger Jahrbuch für Musikwissenschaft* 3 (1978): 143–203.

Tateo, Francesco. "Arcadia e Petrarchismo." *Atti e memorie dell'Accademia degli Arcadi* 9, nos. 2–4 (1991–1994): 19–33.

Taviani, Ferdinando. *La commedia dell'arte e la società barocca. La fascinazione del teatro*. Rome: Bulzoni Editore, 1970.

Tcharos, Stefanie. "Beyond the Boundaries of Opera: Conceptions of Musical Drama in Rome, 1676–1710." Ph.D. diss., Princeton University, 2002.

"The Serenata in Early 18th-Century Rome: Sight, Sound, Ritual, and the Signification of Meaning." *Journal of Musicology* 23, no. 4 (2006): 528–568.

"The Serenata in the Eighteenth Century." In *The Cambridge History of Eighteenth-Century Music*. Edited by Simon Keefe. Cambridge University Press, 2009. 492–512.

Thomas, Downing. *Aesthetics of Opera in the Ancien Régime, 1647–1785*. Cambridge University Press, 2002.

Timms, Colin. "The Dramatic in Vivaldi's Cantatas." *Antonio Vivaldi. Teatro musicale, cultura e società*. Edited by Lorenzo Bianconi and Giovanni Morelli. Florence: L. S. Olschki, 1982. 64–72.

Todorov, Tzvetan. *Genres in Discourse*. Translated by Catherine Potter. Cambridge University Press, 1990.

Tomlinson, Gary. *Metaphysical Song: An Essay on Opera*. Princeton University Press, 1999.

"Pastoral and Musical Magic in the Birth of Opera." In *Opera and the Enlightenment*. Edited by Thomas Bauman and Marita Petzoldt McClymonds. Cambridge University Press, 1995. 7–20.

Touraine, Alain. "Society as Utopia." In *Utopia: The Search for the Ideal Society in the Western World*. Edited by Roland Schaer, Gregory Claeys, and Lyman Tower Sargent. New York: The New York Public Library and Oxford University Press, 2000. 18–31.

Trowell, Brian. "*Acis, Galatea and Polyphemus*: A 'serenata a tre voci'?" In *Music and Theatre: Essays in Honour of Winton Dean*. Edited by Nigel Fortune. Cambridge University Press, 1987. 31–94.

Valesio, Francesco. *Diario di Roma 1700–1742*. Edited by Gaetana Scano in collaboration with Giuseppe Graglia. 6 vols. 1700–1707. (Reprinted Milan: Longanesi, 1977–1979.)

Viale Ferrero, Mercedes. *Filippo Juvarra, scenografo e architetto teatrale*. Turin: Edizioni d'Arte Fratelli Pozzo, 1970.

"Stage and Set." In *Opera on Stage*. Edited by Lorenzo Bianconi and Giorgio Pestelli. Translated by Kate Singleton. University of Chicago Press, 2002. 60–65.

Villari, Rosario, ed. *L'uomo barocco*. Bari: Laterza, 1991.

Virgil. *The Aeneid*. Translated by Robert Fitzgerald. New York: Random House, 1983.

The Eclogues of Virgil. Translated by David Ferry. New York: Farrar, Straus, Giroux, 1999.

Vitali, Carlo. "Italy – Political, Religious and Musical Contexts." In *The Cambridge Companion to Handel*. Edited by Donald Burrows. Cambridge University Press, 1997. 24–44.

Volpicelli, Maria Letizia. "Il teatro del Cardinale Offoboni al Palazzo della Cancelleria." In *Il teatro a Roma nel Settecento*. Vol. II. Rome: Istituto dell' Enciclopedia Italiana, 1989. 681–763.

Waddy, Patricia. "Inside the Palace: People and Furnishings." In *Life and Arts in the Baroque Palaces of Rome: Ambiente Barocco*. Edited by Stefanie Walker and Frederick Hammond. New Haven: Yale University Press, for the Bard Graduate Center for Studies in the Decorative Arts, 1999. 21–37.

Seventeenth-Century Roman Palaces: Use and Art of the Plan. Cambridge, MA: The Architectural Foundation, MIT Press, 1990.

Walker, Stefanie and Frederick Hammond, eds. *Life and Arts in the Baroque Palaces of Rome: Ambiente Barocco*. New Haven: Yale University Press, for The Bard Graduate Center for Studies in the Decorative Arts, 1999.

Wallerstein, Immanuel. *The Modern World-System: Capitalist Agriculture and the Origins of the European World-Economy in the Sixteenth Century*. 3 vols. New York: Academic Press, 1974.

Walser, Robert. *Running with the Devil: Power, Gender, and Madness in Heavy Metal Music*. Hanover, NH: University Press of New England, 1993.

Warwick, Genevieve, ed. *Caravaggio: Realism, Rebellion, Reception*. Newark, DE: University of Delware Press, 2006.

Weintraub, Jeff. "The Theory and Politics of the Public/Private Distinction." In *Public and Private in Thought and Practice: Perspective on a Grand Dichotomy*. Edited by Jeff Weintraub and Krishan Kumar. University of Chicago Press, 1997. 1–42.

Weiss, Piero. "Opera and the Two Verisimilitudes." In *Music and Civilization: Essays in Honor of Paul Henry Lang*. Edited by Edmond Strainchamps, Maria Rika Maniates, and Christopher Hatch. New York: Norton, 1984. 117–126.

"Pier Jacopo Martello on Opera (1715): An Annotated Translation." *Musical Quarterly* 66 (1980): 378–403.

"Teorie drammatiche e 'infranciosamento:' motivi della 'riforma' melodrammatica nel primo Settecento." In *Antonio Vivaldi. Teatro musicale, cultura e società*. Vol. II. Edited by Lorenzo Bianconi and Giovanni Morelli. Florence: L. S. Olschki, 1982. 273–296.

Wilkins, Ernest Hatch. *A History of Italian Literature*. Revised by Thomas G. Bergin. Cambridge, MA: Harvard University Press, 1974 [1954].

Williams, Raymond. *Marxism and Literature*. Oxford University Press, 1977.

The Sociology of Culture. New York: Schocken Books, 1982.

Zappi, Giovan Battista. *Rime dell'avvocato Giovambattista Felice Zappi, e di Faustina Maritti sua consorte*. Venice: Presso Francesco Storti, 1757.

Zeno, Apostolo. *Poesie sacre drammatiche*. Venice: C. Zane, 1735.

Zizek, Slavoj. "'I Hear You with My Eyes' or The Invisible Master." In *Gaze and Voice as Love Objects*. Edited by Renata Salecl and Slavoj Zizek. Durham, NC: Duke University Press, 1996. 93–94.

Index